Sabrina Ellebrecht
Mediated Bordering

Political Science | Volume 77

This open access publication has been enabled by the support of POLLUX (Fachinformationsdienst Politikwissenschaft)

and a collaborative network of academic libraries for the promotion of the Open Access transformation in the Social Sciences and Humanities (transcript Open Library Politikwissenschaft 2020)

This publication is compliant with the "Recommendations on quality standards for the open access provision of books", Nationaler Open Access Kontaktpunkt 2018 (https://pub.uni-bielefeld.de/record/2932189)

Karl-Franzens-Universität **Graz** | Universität **Wien** Bibliotheks- und Archivwesen | Bergische Universität **Wuppertal** | Carl von Ossietzky-Universität (University of **Oldenburg**) | Freie Universität **Berlin** (FU) (Free University of Berlin) | Georg-August-Universität **Göttingen** | Goethe-Universität-**Frankfurt/M** (University of Frankfurt am Main) | Gottfried Wilhelm Leibniz Bibliothek – Niedersächsische Landesbibliothek | Gottfried Wilhelm Leibniz Universität **Hannover** | Humboldt-Universität zu **Berlin** | Justus-Liebig-Universität **Gießen** (University of Giessen) | Ludwig-Maximilians-Universität **München** (LMU) | Martin-Luther-Universität **Halle-Wittenberg** | Max Planck Digital Library | Ruhr-Universität **Bochum** (RUB) | Sächsische Landesbibliothek Staats- und Universitätsbibliothek **Dresden** (SLUB) | Staatsbibliothek zu **Berlin** (Berlin State Library) | ULB **Darmstadt** | Universität **Bayreuth** | Universität **Duisburg-Essen** | Universität **Hamburg** (UHH) | Universität **Potsdam** (University of Potsdam) | Universität **Vechta** | Universität zu **Köln**| Universitäts- und Landesbibliothek **Düsseldorf** (University and State Library Düsseldorf) | Universitäts- und Landesbibliothek **Münster** (University of Munster) | Universitätsbibliothek **Bielefeld** (University of Bielefeld) | Universitätsbibliothek der Bauhaus-Universität **Weimar** (University of Weimar) | Universitätsbibliothek **Erlangen-Nürnberg** (FAU University Erlangen-Nürnberg) | Universitätsbibliothek **Hagen** (Fernuni Hagen) (University of Hagen) | Universitätsbibliothek **Kassel** | Universitätsbibliothek **Koblenz-Landau** | Universitätsbibliothek **Konstanz** (University of Konstanz) | Universitätsbibliothek **Leipzig** (University of Leipzig) | Universitätsbibliothek **Mainz** (University of Mainz) | Universitätsbibliothek **Marburg** | Universitätsbibliothek **Osnabrück** (University of Osnabrück) | Universitätsbibliothek **Passau** | Universitätsbibliothek **Siegen** | Universitätsbibliothek **Würzburg** | Zentral- und Hochschulbibliothek **Luzern** (ZHB) (Central and University Library of Lucerne) | Zentralbibliothek **Zürich** (Central Library of Zurich) | Bundesministerium der Verteidigung | Landesbibliothek **Oldenburg** (State Library of Oldenburg) | Leibniz-Institut für Europäische Geschichte | Stiftung Wissenschaft und Politik

Sabrina Ellebrecht is a Senior Researcher in Sociology at the Centre for Security and Society at the University of Freiburg, Germany, where she currently leads the Mercator Foundation research group "The Police In An Open Society." Her research interests lie in the fields of border and migration studies, political sociology, critical security studies, and police research. She was previously a visiting fellow at the DFG-Research Training Group "Topology of Technology" at the Technische Universität Darmstadt, and a visiting researcher the University of KwaZulu Natal in Durban, South Africa and the Jawaharlal Nehru University in New Delhi, India.

SABRINA ELLEBRECHT
Mediated Bordering
Eurosur, the Refugee Boat, and the Construction
of an External EU Border

[transcript]

Doctoral Dissertation in Sociology at the Albert Ludwig University of Freiburg, submitted in 2017, defended in 2018.

Bibliographic information published by the Deutsche Nationalbibliothek
The Deutsche Nationalbibliothek lists this publication in the Deutsche Nationalbibliografie; detailed bibliographic data are available in the Internet at http://dnb.d-nb.de

This work is licensed under the Creative Commons Attribution-NonCommercial-NoDerivatives 4.0 (BY-NC-ND) which means that the text may be used for non-commercial purposes, provided credit is given to the author. For details go to
http://creativecommons.org/licenses/by-nc-nd/4.0/
To create an adaptation, translation, or derivative of the original work and for commercial use, further permission is required and can be obtained by contacting rights@transcript-verlag.de
Creative Commons license terms for re-use do not apply to any content (such as graphs, figures, photos, excerpts, etc.) not original to the Open Access publication and further permission may be required from the rights holder. The obligation to research and clear permission lies solely with the party re-using the material.

© 2020 transcript Verlag, Bielefeld

All rights reserved. No part of this book may be reprinted or reproduced or utilized in any form or by any electronic, mechanical, or other means, now known or hereafter invented, including photocopying and recording, or in any information storage or retrieval system, without permission in writing from the publisher.

Cover layout: Maria Arndt, Bielefeld
Printed by Majuskel Medienproduktion GmbH, Wetzlar
Print-ISBN 978-3-8376-4753-2
PDF-ISBN 978-3-8394-4753-6
https://doi.org/10.14361/9783839447536

Table of content

Foreword | 7

1 Introduction | 9
1.1 Your Hunter and Helper: Surveil and Assist | 9
1.2 Mediated Bordering: The Objectives,
 Premises and Structure of the Study | 12
1.3 Acknowledgements | 19

PART I: MEDIATED BORDERING.
THINKING AND RESEARCHING POLITICAL BORDERS

2 European Spaces – Schengen Borders? | 23
2.1 Shifting Borders | 23
2.2 Europe as Borderland with Polysemic,
 Heterogeneous, and Overdetermined Borders | 39
2.3 Europe as Empire with Medieval,
 Cosmopolitan or Postnational Borders | 47
2.4 Network Europe and Networked (Non-)Borders | 57
2.5 Europe's Border(s): Novel Policies,
 New Perspectives, Challenged Methodologies | 60

3 Thinking and Researching Political Borders | 63
3.1 The Spectral Character of Any Border | 63
3.2 Mediated Bordering and
 the Territorial Border as Intermediary | 69
3.3 Researching Political Borders: *In Situ* or *In Actu*? | 73

PART II: EUROSUR – THE EUROPEAN
BORDER SURVEILLANCE SYSTEM

4 "EUROSUR on the Screen" | 85
4.1 EUROSUR's Graphical User Interface:
 Communication Device, Format, Network | 87
4.2 The European Situational Picture | 112
4.3 The Common Pre-Frontier Intelligence Picture (CPIP) | 117
4.4 EUROSUR on the Screen:
 The Depiction of an External EU Border? | 124

5 EUROSUR on Paper – in the Official Journal of the EU | 127
5.1 Schengen as a Postnational Laboratory
and Framework for Negotiations (1985-1997) | 129
5.2 In Search for New, Supranational Heads (1997-2003) | 133
5.3 Coordinated Cooperation along
the Virtual Border (2003-2008) | 143
5.4 From the EUROSUR Roadmap to its Draft Regulation
(2008-2011): National Infrastructures,
Supranational Incentives | 150
5.5 "This is A Beautiful Situation Here" – EUROSUR's
Drafting Procedures and the Pilot Phase (2011-2012) | 172
5.6 EUROSUR as an Item of Law:
the Final Regulation of 22 October 2013 | 178

6 EUROSUR: IT's Mediation | 183

PART III: THE REFUGEE BOAT – VEHICLE, MOVING TARGET, INTEGRATING FIGURE OF EU BORDERING

7 Site Inspection: On Boats and Ships,
their Appropriation for Flight and Migration | 193
7.1 What Characterizes Boats and Ships as Vehicles? | 193
7.2 Appropriation of Boats and Ships
for Flight and Unauthorized Migration | 199
7.3 What Difference Does the Boat Make? | 209

8 Seaborne Migration: Europe's Boat-Migrants
and their Refugee Vessels | 211
8.1 Boats and Border Enforcement in the Mediterranean | 212
8.2 "When You See the Boat, the Boat Tells the Story" | 234
8.3 What Story Does the Boat Tell? | 254

9 Seaborne Bordering: Legal Negotiations on Boats
and Boat-Migrants in EU Border Policies | 257
9.1 Maritime Spaces and Territorial Border Enforcement | 259
9.2 Legitimizing Maritime Interception
as a Border Enforcement Practice | 263
9.3 The Refugee Boat: Virtually (at) the Border | 279

10 The Emergence of Viapolitics | 283

Bibliography | 291

Foreword

The cover of this book shows the drawing of a boat. Without any contextual information, the drawing inspires different interpretations about what the vessel represents: without cargo, passengers or equipment on board, its connotation remains unclear. When transcript proposed the cover to me, and when I discussed it with colleagues, one ventured that the drawing seems like a patrol boat meant to detect something suspect. Due to this notion of enforcement that she sensed, she advised not to use it. Others took the drawing for a refugee boat and thus found it well-suited to the title of this book. The ambiguity that the drawing of an empty vessel of a certain shape and size is able to evoke led me to decide on it.

The actual vessel, on which the drawing has been modeled, came to be publicly known when it fell victim to an arson attack: on the night of November 9, 2018 it was set on fire and virtually destroyed at its location in Wittenberg, Germany. To this day, the police presume it to be a politically motivated act of violence based on both the historical date and that they found Germanic runes from the right-nationalist network Reconquista Germanica inscribed on the boat.

The vessel had come to Wittenberg as an exhibit during the Reformation anniversary in 2017. A student group from Salzburg and their anthropology professor had organized a shipwreck from Sicily and installed it in Wittenberg as the "antithesis" to the exhibition's topic "gates of freedom." Wittenberg's mayor described the vessel's role and function for Wittenberg as inspiring public discourse on the treatment of migrants and refugees in Europe. Following the arson attack, reports emphasized that the boat had brought its passengers – 244 women, men and children from Eritrea – unscathed from Libya to Sicily.

The watercraft: a monument or even memorial, a shipwreck, an object of art, a hero, an innocent carrier of refugees and a target of a politically motivated act of violence. The cover drawing shall evoke the ambiguities, the flexible meaning and oscillating reference of the visual and verbal metaphor of a small boat.

In order to analytically understand a phenomenon, the question cannot be limited to the nature of what we see but also has to analyze the nature of how we do our seeing. I thank the preview editors' team at transcript for the cover proposal and for thereby bringing the occurrences in Wittenberg to my attention.

Freiburg, August 2019

1 Introduction

1.1 YOUR HUNTER AND HELPER: SURVEIL AND ASSIST

In the early hours of October 3, 2013, one week before the European Parliament was to vote on the operating rules of the European Border Surveillance System (EUROSUR), a 20-meter trawler capsized off the Italian island of Lampedusa. On board the vessel were over 500 migrants, reportedly from Ghana, Somalia and primarily from Eritrea. The vessel had sailed from Misrata, Libya, for almost 48 hours and was about 600 meters off the coast of Lampedusa when it faced a distressing situation: the vessel had begun to take on water, and, in order to attract attention, a passenger set fire to a blanket. Unfortunately, petrol that had spilled on the deck ignited and the vessel caught fire. Some passengers jumped in the water to avoid the flames and others moved to one side, causing the boat to capsize. The vessel started sinking with the majority of passengers in its hull; those passengers who managed to escape the trawler fought to stay afloat, some for more than three hours, clinging onto empty water bottles or the corpses of fellow passengers.

Fishermen were the first to reach the scene. They managed to take 47 migrants on board and alerted the Italian Coast Guard, who set out for the emergency response. In total, 155 persons were rescued from the scene. The salvage work went on for ten days. By October 12, divers had retrieved a total of 359 dead bodies from the vessel, which had sunk 47 meters below the water's surface. Pictures of body bags lined up in the port of Lampedusa and of numbered coffins in the island's hangar replaced the usual images of an overcrowded boat, stuffed with African migrants, which commonly accompanies Western news on maritime migration to Europe.

The Lampedusa shipwreck of October 2013 marks a caesura: firstly, it had been the accident with the highest death toll involving Europe-bound migrants aboard a boat until that date; secondly, it changed the public debate on European Union border policies as it directed the claim for European search and rescue operations toward border enforcement agencies. However, can your hunter be your helper? And where is the border at which the distinguishing decision is taken, where is it decided whether you are being hunted or assisted? During that night of October 3, 2013, the hunter had not surveilled well enough. A vessel jam-packed with more than 500 migrants had almost reached Lampedusa without being detected. Thus, the friend was sent out for rescue and condolences. Italian Prime Minister Enrico Letta declared the victims Italian citizens post-mortem and announced a state funeral. Meanwhile the hunter did what he had to do: the public prosecutors in Agrigento launched investigations into the infringement of the applicable migration law against each of the 155 survivors.[1]

In parallel, the European Parliament (EP) held plenary sessions in Strasbourg (from October 7 to 10, 2013) and voted on the regulation establishing the European Border Surveillance System (EUROSUR). EUROSUR stood both for intensified surveillance practices and an increased surveillance apparatus, along with the (visual) integration of national surveillance information into a common situational picture. Both the EUROSUR network, which facilitates the exchange of information and is used to generate situational pictures, and the legislation concerning its operating rules have been gradually developed between 2008 and 2013. Both network and regulation put forward the rules for the exchange of border-related information. They establish the "communication formats" (Ericson/Haggerty 1997: 33) of border surveillance and control and thus "provide the means through which the police think, act, and justify their actions" (ibid). They program EU border policing.

The Lampedusa tragedy directed unexpected attention to the EUROSUR Regulation. The question of whether surveillance served the hunter or the helper

---

[1] The details of the event as summarized and described here are based on a selection of various accounts in the press (Yardly/Povoledo 2013; Braun 2013; Davies 2013; Messia/Wedeman/Schmith-Spark 2013; Rühle 2013; ANSAmed (N.N.) 2013; Associated Press (N.N.) 2013). Details concerning the number of people, their nationality, the point of departure, the duration of the journey as well as details on the distress situation and the emergency response are not always consistently reported. Accounts of survivors which have been in the news one year after the tragedy (Nelson 2014; Mittelstaedt/Popp 2014) shed light on the actual distress situation and the struggle to stay afloat; they particularly render the situational assessment by Deputy Prime Minister Angelino Alfano somewhat irritating in which he claimed that "it happened close to shore [...]. Had they been able to swim, they would have been safe" (quoted in Yardly/Povoledo 2013).

occupied public attention.[2] The EP Greens, who had attempted in vain to integrate a rescue obligation into the EUROSUR Regulation, strove for its renegotiation. It was hoped that the high number of fatalities would pressure legislators toward not passing a regulation for more surveillance without an explicit obligation of rescue. Yet, on October 9, 2013, the European Parliament passed the operating rules of EUROSUR without an explicit obligation of rescue. The Council of the European Union (EU) adopted the regulation on October 22, 2013, and since December 1, 2013, EUROSUR is operational. Surveil and – if necessary – rescue remained the lowest common denominator.

It was a coincidence that the disaster of Lampedusa preceded the parliamentary vote. For EUROSUR, however, this resulted in a spin of its legitimizing narrative. Thus far, EUROSUR was framed as merely a "technical framework" or "tool." In fact, it had been difficult for its critics to attract public attention to its political ingredients and repercussions. Moreover, during negotiations between the European Council, the EP and the European Commission (EC), member states had been reluctant to accept any mention of "saving lives at sea" as part of new provisions.

Now, under the impression of the 365 migrant fatalities, EUROSUR emphasized the prospect of contributing to saving migrants' lives at sea. EUROSUR "will make an important contribution in protecting our external borders and help in saving lives of those who put themselves in danger to reach Europe's shores" declares Cecilia Malmström, then Commissioner for Justice and Home Affairs, on the occasion of the EP's vote.[3] Better surveillance paired with interagency cooperation was framed as the all-in-one solution: By detecting migrant vessels, both illegal immigration and migrant fatalities were to be prevented. Thereby, the potential amicable gesture of the hunter's tool supports its necessity.

However, distinguishing between illegal immigrants and shipwrecked persons, and thus the decision to be a hunter or helper, occurs situationally. Yet,

---

2 A commentary which strongly pointed out this ambivalence has been published by Deutsche Welle (Berger 2013). Its German heading "Eurosur – Dein Feind und Helfer" (Engl.: *Eurosur – your friend and assistant*) inspired the title of this section.

3 At the occasion of the EP's vote, Malmström explicitly established a link between the tragedy of Lampedusa and the objectives and potentials of EUROSUR. The commissioner advances a formulation that hints at the controversies between member states concerning immigration policies: "The EU and its Member States need to work hard to take decisive measures and show solidarity both with migrants and with countries that are experiencing increasing migratory flows" (Malmström 2013).

surveillance as an allegedly non-invasive measure as well as the multi-purpose aim of detecting small boats are framed as being detached from the political process of sorting vessels' passengers. Situational awareness provides an overview. Surveillance is, in fact, thought of as a way to direct operations and resources. Effectively, "you are not going to collect information, if you are not going to act."[4] Hence the question whether surveillance mechanisms are programed toward preventing illegal immigration or toward saving lives at sea surfaces once again. What do law enforcement officers want to do once they spot the boats? One means, conflicting ends, and the vessel as a mobile target.

The migrant vessel and the European Border Surveillance System, the small boat and the big system of systems: these two sites are not only opponents in the cat and mouse of border surveillance and control. The boat can also be interpreted as the 'humanitarian subtext' and proof of EUROSUR's necessity. The two empirical chapters of this study examine the EUROSUR and the migrant vessel as sites of EU bordering. Both sites are institutive for the emergence of an external border to the EU. They are mediators to the emergence of a supranational EU border, in the sense that they catalyze and craft a level of Europeanization which hitherto and otherwise had been impossible. Examining this level of supranationality through two of its mediators, this study is about the emergence of an external border to the EU.

1.2 MEDIATED BORDERING: THE OBJECTIVES, PREMISES AND STRUCTURE OF THE STUDY

Tackling an object of inquiry which itself is under construction challenges the methodology of a study. How to approach an object of inquiry which itself does not exist? ... But wait a minute: doesn't it seem as if there *is* an external EU border?

Referring to the notion of a territorial state border, an EU border does not exist. The EU neither has a territory, nor is it clearly delineated where Europe ends geographically. However, the absence of a geopolitical border cannot only be attributed to potential difficulties in routing it. The notion of the territorial border has not only been challenged at the empirical level; it has been deessentialized in

---

4   EUROSUR Project Manager at Frontex, personal interview (May 15, 2012).

(political) geography (van Houtum 2005; Elden 2010a, 2010b, 2011), international relations (Agnew 1994, 2008; Scott/van Houtum 2009), sociology (Walters 2002, 2006; Wimmer/Glick Schiller 2002) and by studies from cultural anthropology (Anzaldúa 1987; Sahlins 1989; Paasi 1996; Pries 2008).[5] Political borders cease to be conceptualized as lines, as the "natural" confinement of nation-states. Subsequently, a study which examined the EU border by comparing it to the territorial state border and which was in search of the edges of EU territory, of lines, maps and their defining peace treaties, could no longer be carried out empirically (Walters 2002: 563-565). Theoretically and methodologically, such a border would appear obsolete. And still, even without a delineated EU territory, the operative effect of an EU border seems to be existent. How can this kind of political border be characterized and investigated?

The possibility of conceiving of political borders in terms of a post-territorial, post-modern, post-national or post-Westphalian constellation presupposes that political borders exist beyond the modern understanding of political control, and of authority as territorial sovereignty. "This is not self-evident," argues Georg Vobruba (2010: 434), pointing to an understanding of borders and territory that sees them as mutually constitutive. In fact, the figure of the territorial border has condensed the modern principles to an extent that hinders concepts of territory and border which are *not* mutually constitutive (Elden 2011; Allies 1980: 9). The attribute territorial is taken to qualify as political.

This epistemological challenge finds inspiration in the empirical example of the external border(s) of the EU. Moreover, one can observe how the empirical example of the external borders of the EU has altered the epistemological and methodological premises of border studies (Scott 2011). Just as the EU has been thought of as "nothing less than the emergence of the first truly postmodern international political form" (Ruggie 1993: 140), its border constellation provides an empirical example of how political borders can be thought beyond the territorial state.

Correspondingly, the search for an adequate methodology goes on: How do you study a border without knowing *where* to go for research and *what* to study? Do I have to travel to Gibraltar or Lampedusa to research the emergence of an EU border? Or rather to the Evros, the Greek-Turkish border crossing and contact zone? Or rather should I travel to Brussels, or visit the Frontex Headquarters

---

5   The disciplinary assignment should not be read too rigidly, as contemporary border studies understand themselves as interdisciplinary (cf. Newman 2006a).

in Warsaw. Who should be my interview partner, i.e. who do I consider most relevant as an actor of bordering? Who is bordering? Apparently: there is no geographical answer to the question of the strategic research object in border studies and the corresponding field of research.

The methodological uncertainty is further complicated by the spectral character of any border. Not only does the EU have no clear territorial border, borders are generally characterized by their phenomenal indeterminacy and fuzziness, which is to say that there is no phenomenon of a border as such (Cremers 1989: 38; Vasilache 2007: 38-47). Andreas Vasilache notes that the odd and at the same time particular character of any border is "that it unfolds its effects through its presence and materiality, but consistently loses this presence whenever it becomes the subject of contemplation itself" (Vasilache 2007: 40). Accordingly, a border only "becomes always tangible only as a proxy" (ibid) or through representations. The border appears *as* something (Cremers 1989: 38). Yet, which things maintain an indexical relationship to a given political border? *As what* does the respective border appear, and *as what* should it thus be researched? Are there strategic, that is, preferable objects of inquiry when analyzing a political border?

During the last three decades, the emergence and effectiveness of an EU border has predominantly been studied either *as* institutional integration or *as* practices of exclusion and subversion.

Conceptualizing a political border as a contract and methodologically taking it for its *institutional integration* entails analyzing a contract and investigating its level of integration and institutionalization. Consequently, one has to examine further agreements and amendments, and consider to what degree EU regulations and directives have been absorbed into national legal settings. Correspondingly, research on the external borders of the EU has focused on the 1990 Schengen Agreement, its Convention, amendments and its integration into the EU body of law. These analyses are underpinned by an understanding of border *as* institutional integration. But are political borders contractually established institutions that exist beyond their *in actu* operationalization? Is a border socially effective by elite decision?

Rather than the mere document of the contract, or the map, I am interested in the production of these things, as they mediate a given political border: this is to say that they stabilize a network of references and tasks, align obligations, and thereby establish the power that is necessary for a political entity to enforce borders. The development of the EUROSUR network, which will be analyzed below, provides a valuable example of a map that is not only produced by a "new" technology (GIS-generated digital map), but which also "maps" the operational area of a postnational border. Its development and its map will not be analyzed *as* representations of the border. The emergence of the EU border will rather be analyzed *via* the EUROSUR development phase.

The second proxy used to study borders is spatial practices and interactions. In the course of the spatial turn, and its emphasis on spatial practices and bordering practices, borders, too, have been analyzed *in actu*. By this I refer to a focus on practices of exclusion, discrimination and segregation for a deduction of border characteristics. From this perspective, borders are "dispersed a little everywhere" (Balibar 2002b: 71) and no longer where they used to be, that is at the border-line. This perspective is underpinned by an understanding of borders *as* interaction between border police and border crossers. These studies have predominantly been ethnographic. As apt as the description might be from the perspective of experiencing bordering, do borders exist as spatial practices? Are they constituted by their violations and control, and thus the cat and mouse between border police and border crosser? Would they not exist without these practices?

I take issue with this praxeological approach of analyzing borders with a focus on practices of exclusion, discrimination and segregation. This isn't to say that these practices do not occur in the context of border management and border policing. However, borders are neither produced nor reproduced "bottom-up" on a daily basis; it is not border guards who produce the border through their patrolling routines, nor is it border violations which shape its constitution. Also, political borders are not as volatile as an emphasis on bordering practices might suggest. Therefore, neither the production of borders nor its reconfigurations should be analyzed *from the perspective* of spatial practices. Without intending to solve the chicken-or-the-egg question, I nonetheless argue that in the case of borders it makes sense to actually *start* the analyses with the *things* that mediate them, with the interobjective presence of political borders. Even if political borders are manmade, it is through technical mediation, and not through situational interaction that they unfold social effectiveness to a permanent, that is, relatively stable and durable extent.

This study is informed by the two aforementioned perspectives and by various analyses conducted under their premises. Yet, it proposes a somewhat different approach. As outlined above, the construction of an external EU border will be analyzed from the perspective of two of its mediators: the EUROSUR and the small boat. The methodology thus draws on Bruno Latour's distinction between intermediaries and mediators (see particularly Latour 1993: 79-82, 2005: 37-42, 106-120). It takes on board the premise that selected research objects (in this case the EUROSUR and the small boat) do not merely "represent," "manifest" or "reflect" the object of investigation (in this case an external EU border), but substantially bring it about, engineer and tune its quality and form.

According to Latour, an intermediary "transports meaning or force" without transforming it, while mediators "transform, translate, distort, and modify the meaning or the elements they are supposed to carry" (Latour 2005: 39). This distinction particularly changes how a researcher looks at an object of inquiry. Taking the difference between silk and nylon as intermediary – the example is Latour's (ibid: 40) – a researcher sees this difference as "transporting faithfully" (ibid) the social meaning that silk was for high-brow and nylon for low-brow. Silk and nylon are looked at as indicative or reflective of a particular status. Taken as intermediary, the shine, fabric, touch and feel of silk in contrast to that of nylon renders the social difference tangible; while the piece of cloth remains "wholly indifferent to its composition" (ibid). Taken as mediator, by contrast, the composition is what the researcher focusses on. He or she then examines how the chemical and manufacturing differences between silk and nylon fabricate and establish that which is socially effective as a tangible class difference in the first place.

If borders are thought of as intermediaries, this entails that their tools, guards, fences, institutions or practices are thought of as manifestations, representations or illustrations of the border as such. Meanwhile, understanding a border as a construction of mediators, its guards, institutions, contracts, surveillance gadgetry, and control practices are analyzed with regard to their crafting, stabilizing and assembling of that which is socially effective as the political border in question. Analyzing a given border as intermediary would only allow describing the two identities which are marked and separated by it. Its political performance could not be explicated. Analyzing mediators, by contrast, allows studying and explaining the fabric and the quality of a political border. In order to enquire about a border's program, its sorting mechanisms and decisions, its markers and tools need to be considered, deciphered, and unpacked with regard to their constitution. As a methodological perspective to border studies, this allows for attention to be paid to the rules, morals, fantasies, cohesions, institutional corridors, political compromises and technical fixes that become part of a border's fabric, as they are inscribed in the political construction of the border and its "tools." From the many mediators that are currently constructing an external EU border, I have selected two, which craft the border to a salient extent.

In sum, a border does not exist, bordering is mediated. Therefore, I attempt not to study the emergence of an EU border *as*, but rather *via* its tools, markers, enforcers, contesters. Taken as mediators, the migrant vessel and the EUROSUR will be analyzed with regard to their contribution in the construction of a political EU border. It shall be examined in how far they transform, distort, and shape supranational border policies. Framing these sites as mediators, it is argued that they transform and reconfigure the EU border in a unique way. In other words, it is assumed that without EUROSUR there would not be this level of supranationality, and that without the migrants' boat, there would not be this kind of supranational mandate. It is a kind of journey that is mediated by the boat, and certain kinds of policies which are composed and delegated by the EUROSUR. These things are in the mix when the decision between hunter and helper is made.

This study examines the construction and crafting of a supranational border from the perspective of two of its mediators: the European Border Surveillance System (EUROSUR) and the migrant vessel. The leading question of this study for the emergence of an external EU border is thus translated into the study of two empirical sites understood as its central mediators. Thus, the objective of this study is twofold: firstly, the emerging supranational, external EU border is analyzed as an example of a post-Westphalian, post-modern, post-national political border. This epistemological objective is a contribution to thinking about political borders beyond the modern state. Secondly, the external EU border is considered an intermediary imagination. Its already operative level of supranationality is mobilized, relocated, furthered, and legitimized by means of its mediators. Examining their design, this study unfolds how the kind and quality of the political border, which the EU shows, is crafted, shaped, produced and eventually stabilized.

1.2.1 Structure of the Study

This book is divided into three parts. Following the introduction, Part I discusses concepts, theories and methodological challenges to the study of borders in general and the study of the construction of a supranational EU border in particular. Chapter 2 examines in how far the Schengen Convention constitutes an empirical novelty and whether it has (already) triggered a supranational EU border. I will then review selected analytical assessments of the Schengen Process, which draw on the example of Europe's borders while describing the reconfiguration of political borders in general. Critically engaging with these analyses, chapter 3 offers a general discussion of the distinctive conceptual characteristics of political borders, by analyzing the relation between thinking and researching borders.

The following six chapters constitute the empirical parts of the study at hand. Part II (chapters 4 to 6) examines the making of the European Border Surveillance System, EUROSUR, as a result of two parallel processes: the ICT-based network and the legislation concerning its operating rules. Both products gradually developed between 2008 and 2013. The EUROSUR development phase is equally the period of investigation. Chapter 4 dissects the graphical user interface (GUI) of the system and thereby describes the setup of the EUROSUR IT-network; chapter 5 retraces the political negotiations which led to the EUROSUR Regulation. Chapter 6 discusses in what respect the technical network mediated the political process. I will discuss in how far the mere development phase of the EUROSUR has enabled the mobilization of the limits to border policing, and has increased competences on the side of the Frontex agency. Furthermore, the analysis will assess how the composition of an external border is mobilized and tuned by the denomination of a space called "pre-frontier" area.

Part III (chapters 7 to 9) follows the vehicle of the small boat both through the trends of Europe-bound flight and migration and through images, perceptions and surveillance efforts on the site of the European spectator. Chapter 7 gauges the particularities of boats and ships as means of transport and technology of movement taking into account their peculiar relationship to the medium of the sea. Analyzing the earliest empirical case of the appropriation, reception, and perception of boats and ships in the context of flight and migration, namely the case of the Vietnamese boat-people, the chapter extracts the political significance of the vehicular facilitator. Chapter 8 starts by describing the trends in Europe-bound migration by sea since the 1990s, including the numbers of deaths at sea. Section 8.2 then provides a detailed analysis of the verbal and visual reference to the "refugee boat" as unseaworthy, small and overcrowded, while section 8.3 takes issue with this seemingly self-explanatory image and summarizes the different narratives, fantasies, and judgements projected to the hybrid of the refugee boat. Chapter 9 probes the vessel's role in distinguishing the migrants' legal status. The analysis focuses on those legal arguments which revolve around the vessel itself: the vessel as stateless, as in distress, as suspicious, and thus as a target of surveillance activities. This allows testing the hypothesis that a prioritization of the vehicle in legal and operational reasoning – while at the same time bypassing or postponing addressing the human cargo – allows for operational practices which otherwise would have been difficult, if not impossible, to justify. Overall, I consider how far the hybrid of refugee boat acts as an integrating, if not mandating, figure in the construction of a supranational EU border. The refugee boat, in this arrangement, no longer crosses or subverts the border; it virtually *is* (at) the border.

The study concludes with chapter 10, which summarizes the findings and works out the characteristics and qualities of the external EU border. In concluding, the chapter finally shows the specific, if not constitutive, ambivalent features of EU border policies, and explores the emergence of viapolitics.

1.3 ACKNOWLEDGEMENTS

Since the premise of this work is that a given process mediates the character and quality of its product, I shall put forward the many mediators that contributed to this study, made it possible, and transformed its design and content to the point of a book publication. In doing so, I express my heartfelt thanks to those things, circumstances, persons, colleagues, friends, and family members that supported and enabled the "drawing-together" of this work.

This work would not have been possible without a scholarship of the International Graduate Academy (IGA) Freiburg, which also provided for a parental year and allowed me to conduct the research for this book. A guest scholarship at the German Research Foundation's graduate college "Topography of Technology" in 2013 offered the time and environment for a profound analysis of the material of the EUROSUR. The academic exchange and personal support of that time were decisive to the realization and analytical direction of the entire study. I thank Prof. Helmut Berking, Prof. Martina Löw, Paul Gebelein, Florian Stoll, and Christiane Habeck.

My research and writing have profited from discussions with colleagues at the Institute of Sociology and the Center for Security and Society at the University of Freiburg. For their critical commenting on different parts of the manuscript, I am grateful to Cornelia Schendzielorz, Sabine Blum, Gernot Saalmann, Simone Rufer, Sebastian Weydner-Volkmann, Matthias Eichenlaub and Elisa Orrú.

I particularly thank my supervisor Stefan Kaufmann for his support, trust in my work, and his constructive advices throughout. Ari Sitas, as my second supervisor, encouraged me to think more in terms of border qualities rather than functionalities. Hermann Schwengel supervised this work in its early stages. His good humor and respect for diversity of opinions have been and will always be exemplary to me.

I thank Kathleen Heil for a first copyediting of the manuscript, and Jacob Reilley, Alexander Craig, Nicholas Eschenbruch and particularly Michelle Miles and Graeme Currie for their thorough proofreading of different parts. Marius Hägele assisted me with the formatting of this book. All mistakes remain my own.

Finally, mediation does not occur without motivation: I thank my friend and colleague Ilka Sommer whose confidence and pragmatism pushed me to submit the dissertation in February 2017. My husband, Nils Ellebrecht, supported me throughout this work both emotionally, and practically by exchanging ideas, reading and discussing parts of the manuscript and helping me out with the design of figures. He has been a critical and constant source of support and encouragement. Thanks for surviving the "rush-hour" together. My heartfelt appreciation goes to our sons, who cheered me up when the writing wouldn't flow. I owe you time. I am grateful to my parents, Heiner and Bernadette Große-Kettler, to my siblings, and my godmother, Ursula Huster.

The detached mediators to this study have been my interview partners. I thank my interview partners at Frontex, the European Commission and European Parliament for their time and their opinions, insights and expertise that they were willing to share with me. I thank the journalist Wolfgang Bauer for sharing background on his investigative boat crossing, and Prof. Sonja Buckel for an exchange on the case of the *Marine I*. Not all (background) conversations and interviews can be cited. This applies in particular to discussions with officials during the EUROSUR development phase, but also with NGO staff and lawyers in Gran Canaria and Sicily. Quotations from interviews are cited from non-verbatim transcriptions, particular individual emphases in the intonation are marked in italics. In instances where English translations of German texts were not available, I've translated quotations of those works myself.

Mediated Bordering. Thinking and Researching Political Borders

2 European Spaces – Schengen Borders?

2.1 SHIFTING BORDERS

When speaking about borders in and around Europe, one often refers to the 1985 Schengen Agreement along with its 1990 Implementing Convention, its amendments, and development within the EU legal framework.[1] Schengen is the epitome of border policies in Europe.

The term Schengen stirs up associations of both the abolition and the proliferation of borders. This peculiar ambivalence, however, has been built into the Schengen Process from its beginning. When the "Agreement [...] on the gradual

---

[1] The Agreement between the Governments of the States of the Benelux Economic Union, the Federal Republic of Germany and the French Republic on the gradual abolition of checks at their common borders [hereafter cited as Schengen Agreement] was signed by representatives of the Benelux countries, France and West Germany on June 14, 1985. The Convention Implementing the Schengen Agreement [hereafter cited as Schengen Implementing Convention (SIC) or Schengen Convention] was signed on June 19, 1990. On September 1, 1993, it entered into force. The SIC only took practical effect on March 26, 1995 after different technical and legal prerequisites were in place. The Schengen Agreement and Convention are international agreements. Both were transferred into EU law in the form of Protocols to the Treaty of Amsterdam, i.e., the Treaty of the European Union [hereafter cited as TEU], which entered into force on May 1, 1999. Since then, the Schengen Agreement and Convention are published in the Official Journal of the EU (OJ L 239/1, September 22, 2000, p. 11-18 and 19-62). Elspeth Guild argues that it is however still justified to continue to refer to "Schengen rules" due to "the continuity of the acquis although technically it has been subsumed into the legal bases" of the EU (Guild 2001: 2, original emphasis). This corresponds to the general usage of the term "Schengen rules" or just "Schengen" which is also adopted in this work.

abolition of checks at their common borders" was signed by representatives of the Netherlands, Belgium, Luxembourg, France and West Germany on June 14, 1985, it was first and foremost thought of as a step toward peace, stability, and freedom in Europe. The five signatory states individually went ahead toward fulfilling Article 8 of the 1957 Treaty of Rome, which requested European states to work toward a common market.² The latter would essentially be based on four freedoms of movement: of goods, of capital, of services, and of persons. As the founding treaty of the European Economic Community (EEC) envisioned, Europe – as a peace project – would concretize along the practical, economic freedoms of market integration. In fact, while in the 18th and 19th century, territorial borders essentially and literally grounded the European construction (Febvre 1988; Branch 2011), Schengen (initially) proposed the reverse: it constructed Europe on de-bordering.

For such a border treaty to even be possible, something had to have changed fundamentally in the meaning and functioning of political borders. This change in the perception of political borders started evolving after the end of the Second World War. After 1945, reconciliation was no longer achieved by separating two countries, but by integrating their economies. This has been promoted by the 1948 Marshall plan, taken up by the Schuman Declaration, and institutionalized via the 1951 foundation of the European Coal and Steal Community (ECSC) (Kreis 2010: 90-93). Economic interdependency between European states was thought to peacefully integrate previously bellicose states; as such it was the functionalist answer to two World Wars. Borders related to the European construction were understood as an economic issue and problematized as barriers to the peaceful integration of states into a common market. The historian Georg Kreis commented that, in post-1945 Europe, "national borders are something negative and overcoming borders is something positive" (ibid: 86). In this "functionalist philosophy of peace" (Burgess 2009: 136) the free movement of individuals was of major importance to the European construction.

Even though the area constituted was termed "Schengen area" rather than "Europe," passport-free travel translated a sense of freedom to the everyday life of the people of Europe. Likewise, the European Commission stressed in May

---

2   The Treaty of Rome, officially called the Treaty Establishing the European Economic Community (TEEC), is the founding act of the European Economic Community (EEC). It was signed on March 25, 1957 and came into force on January 1, 1958. Art. 8 (1) TEEC states that "the common market shall be progressively established during a transitional period of twelve years."

1992 that the free movement of individuals was essential to the idea of a people's Europe by rhetorically asking:

"What purpose would Article 8a serve if individuals were still to be subject to one or other of the current controls or formalities? How would they perceive the change if it were limited to the legal environment of firms?"[3]

In fact, freedom of movement of individuals was perceived as *the* citizen-friendly element in the European integration process. Similar to the later introduction of the Euro as a common currency, Schengen brought about changes which were directly visible (demolition of stationary border posts) and experienceable in everyday life (and during holidays) of European citizens (Siebold 2013: 12).[4] That way, freedom of movement translated into a benchmark of a peaceful Europe. At the same time, the abolition of borders, the "Europe without frontiers," took shape as the "new mythology" (Raffestin 1992: 158).

2.1.1 The Twin Imperative of Freedom and Security

The abolition of borders and the principle of free movement came, however, with the "twin imperative of Schengen" (Walters 2004: 683): that of greater security. Yet, this imperative did not so much act as a constitutive principle *per se*, but rather as *conditio sine qua non* to the realization of free movement. Concerns over the free movement of individuals had effectively impeded the goal of the common market among EEC member states. This is illustrated, for instance, by an inquiry conducted by the UK's House of Lords Select Committee on the Eu-

---

3 Abolition of border controls, Communication from the Commission to the Council and the European Parliament. SEC(92) 877 final (May 8, 1992), [hereafter cited as Abolition of border controls, SEC(92) 877 final].

4 Angela Siebold's impressive study of the history of the Schengen process and its reception in French, Polish and German print media demonstrates the spirit of Schengen on the basis of comprehensive materials. Siebold provides a detailed insight into the political tensions as well as public expectations and fears that accompanied the Agreement. She examines the impact, which the fall of the Iron Curtain in 1989 had on the Schengen process, and its reception in the three countries. Her study is particularly valuable in tracing how, post-1989, external borders were increasingly charged as a security issue (Siebold 2013: 115-139) and in how migration became to be conceived of as "border crime" (ibid: 279-327).

ropean Communities into the completion of the internal market.[5] Elspeth Guild summarizes the Committee's report in the following way:

"It [the Committee] received evidence from various officials who made it clear that an internal market without frontiers was fully possible for goods, services and capital. The mechanism of the frontier for goods: customs controls were capable of abolition and replacement by random checks. However, border controls on persons could not safely be abolished. The reason: this would give rise to an increased security risk." (Guild 2001: 9)

While random checks on goods and services appeared feasible and without side-effects,[6] an easing of controls on persons provoked uncertainties together with the somewhat vague fear of relinquishing control over what is going on "inside" one's national territory. The citizen-friendly element was thus the most uncomfortable and worrying aspect for public administrations and security agencies. Moreover, in the light of vague risks, different national security authorities ranging from police to border guards to military were uncertain about their job description, their mandates and competences in the new context. Security agencies' concerns thus stemmed from reconfigurations of both the subject and the object of security. In other words: both threat conceptions and competences were readjusted. On the one side, the threat of migration as a *transnational* crime shaped up; on the other site, the fear of losing competences and control gained strength.

After signing the Schengen Agreement, signatory states took five years to ratify it in their national parliaments, and to formulate the 1990 Implementing Convention. The latter only took practical effect after another five years. On March 26, 1995, national borders fell to the five signatory states and the two new contractors, Italy and Spain. Passport control at the borders between those countries was no longer a standard procedure. Even though Schengen continued to function as a pan-European narrative of freedom and rapprochement after the 1989 fall of the Berlin Wall and the successive collapse of the Soviet Union, un-

---

5 House of Lords Select Committee on the European Communities (1992): Border Controls on Persons, 22nd Report of Session 1989-1989 (HL paper 90), London: HMSO.

6 Checks on the movement of goods and services had successively been abandoned among EEC member states, custom policies were already harmonized in July 1968 (Hobbing 2006: 170). This is to say that in terms of customs regulations, EU countries share, in fact, a common external border. However, the fact that this does not foster the image of a common border stresses the dominance of person's mobility for the political integration of border policies in Europe.

certainties and notions of threat intensified with the construction of Europe no longer being reduced to its part west of the Iron Curtain. In French and German print media, the fear of an increase in criminal activities and an influx of "thieves and illegals" was initially portrayed as coming almost exclusively from the East (Siebold 2013: 273-275). However, in the course of the first ten years of the Schengen Process, the scenario of raids and incursions of criminal gangs from the East became discursively conflated with the theme of migration. In this course, the principle of free movement was related to the act of crossing external Schengen borders; at the same time, migratory endeavors of all kinds to Schengen states, including the search for asylum, were often summarized as "border crime" (ibid: 279). Different commentators witnessed a securitization of migration, that is, a political and societal framing of migration as a security issue.[7] Jef Huysmans, for instance, pinpointed that public debates were dominated by the projection of possible side effects: "one expected that the market would not only improve free movement of law-abiding agents, but would also facilitate illegal and criminal activities by terrorists, international criminal organizations, asylum-seekers and immigrants" (Huysmans 2000: 760).

In fact, while mobility became part of the self-conception on the part of Union citizens, the free movement of non-Europeans across Schengen borders – classified as Third Country Nationals since the 1990 Schengen Convention – was greeted with the suspicion of illegality. Moreover, the term "migration," encompassing the doubt about its legality, was increasingly reserved for movement across Schengen external borders, while European citizens' movement was framed as "mobility" and an expression of freedom (Benedikt 2004: 12). At the same time, Schengen border crossings were conceived of as a transnational phenomenon, "which is neither attributable to a classical military threat from the

---

7 The diagnosis of a securitization of migration is "largely uncontested" (Ger.: *weitestgehend unbestritten*) in the literature on EU migration policies (Ratfisch/Scheel 2010: 90). However, the concept of securitization is not always applied and referred to in the social constructivist sense of the Copenhagen School, which focusses on speech acts (Buzan/Waever/Wilde 1998), but more frequently developed from a Foucaultian analysis of governmentality which has been developed in critical distinction by the so called Paris School around Didier Bigo (1996, 2002), Jef Huysmans (2000, 2008), and Thierry Balzacq (2005; 2008). Paradigmatic studies on the securitization of migration have been provided by Ceyhan/Tsoukala (2002); Aradau (2004); Şemşil (2008), Bourbeau (2011), and Basaran (2011). For a discussion on the concept of securitization cf. Roe (2012) and Balzacq et al. (2015).

outside, nor to domestic crime" (Kaufmann 2006: 38). The new transnational risks were embodied by different figures: the masses of illegal immigrants, criminals, the mafia, and terrorists. What unites them is the attestation of being transnationally organized, of operating in international networks, and of being difficult to locate or interdicted in their movements or purposes. Being transnational renders them "the central issue of internal security" (ibid). As a consequence, the completion of the common internal market brought along the operational field of internal security, which Didier Bigo has described and criticized as being based on a security continuum:

"[T]he issue was no longer, on the one hand, terrorism, drugs, crime, and on the other, rights of asylum and clandestine immigration, but they came to be treated together in the attempt to gain an overall view of the interrelation between these problems and the free movement of persons within Europe." (Bigo 1994: 164)

Bigo's central thesis is that the reconfiguration of the security field is not to be interpreted as a response to new threats, but as something that emerged from within the security field itself (Bigo 1996). He further claims that the securitization of migration is not the reason but the effect of a proliferation of control policies and technological infrastructure (Bigo 2002: 73). Bigo's thesis is supported by a 1988 Commission's report on the progress made with regard to Article 8 of the EEC treaty. The Commission reported a situation in which traditional border checks had lost their functional purpose between EEC member states and in which a common denominator for different policy fields and administrations was sought. Meanwhile, the free movement of persons was described as a crosscutting theme touching upon different policy fields:

"For several years now, because of the complex nature of the issues involved, the many and varied aspects of the problems involved have been discussed in a number of different fora (the Schengen Group, the Trevi Group, the Immigration Group, Political Cooperation meetings, the Council of the Ministers and the Council of Europe). This review of the work being done in these somewhat disconnected bodies is intended both to clarify the rather confused picture and to refocus the strategy so as to keep the overall programme, and each individual part of it, on target."[8]

---

8   European Commission (1988): Communication of the Commission on the abolition of controls of persons at intra-community borders, COM(88) 640 final (December 7, 1988), [hereafter cited as Abolition of controls of persons at intra-community borders,

The above passage shows that the national authorities and administrations behind these "somewhat disconnected bodies" which were used to operate *in parallel* at the same border, were now supposed to operate "elsewhere."

In the territorial frame, the border is considered the locus of legitimate intervention by law enforcement authorities – intervention taking place in fields as diverse as immigration, transportation, and commodity exchange. At the border, these regulations occur in parallel and in combination. As the common locus of intervention is rescinded, a common program among the different authorities and administrations was felt necessary. That which was previously united geographically would now be merged by a common vision, an "overall programme."[9]

In consequence, the gradual abolition of common borders among Schengen signatory states prompts the fear of suffering a loss of legitimate possibilities to intervene and to regulate access to one's territory and welfare state. This sovereign anxiety prevailed even though present frontier controls were described as "largely ineffective" by the Commission.

"What we are looking for are better controls and we believe they exist. […] the Commission has never said that frontier zones should be 'no go' areas for the enforcement agen-

---

COM(88) 640 final]. For a contemporary legal opinion on the Schengen Agreement, cf. Erhard Stobbe (1989).

9   The "overall programme," which was still in development in 1988, took shape in the creation of the Area of Freedom, Security and Justice (AFSJ) in the Treaty of Amsterdam 1999 and concretized in measurements in the Tampere (1999-2004), the Hague (2004-2009) and the Stockholm Programme (2009-2014). The format of detailed, multi-annual programs with concrete objectives has been abandoned after 2014. With the 2009 Treaty of Lisbon evening the pillar system, and thus the distinction between intergovernmental arrangements and communitarian policies, Justice and Home Affaires now subsume the "somewhat disconnected bodies" under the heading of internal security. In the Post-Stockholm Process the general (now European!) principles in Justice and Home Affairs are at issue. The Commission presented its strategic vision in its Communication "An open and secure Europe: making it happen" (COM(2014) 154 final). For documentation and analysis of this process, see particularly Jörg Monar's annual analysis of Justice and Home Affairs, first published in 1999 in the *Journal of Common Market Studies*. In addition, Christian Kaunert and colleagues (2012) have discussed whether "European Homeland Security" offers a unifying program.

cies. If evidence or reasonable suspicion exists, of course an individual can be stopped or apprehended. But what must go is the routine, mindless interference with the great mass of ordinary innocent travellers going about their legitimate business."[10]

On the one side, "innocent travellers carrying on their legitimate businesses" should not be molested by control procedures; at the same time "better controls" turn into a prerequisite to the seamless travel of "the great mass of ordinary innocent travellers". In this logic, the seamless travel of *bona fide* passengers rests fundamentally on the effectiveness of migration and border control as well as the urgent prerequisite to sort out the *male fide* passenger.

To balance the loss of systematic control along national borders, compensatory measurements were established beyond the geographically mediated transformation of control. These compensatory control measures consisted of police cooperation, cooperation in dealing with criminal matters, judicial assistance, common visa procedures, and the establishment of the Schengen Information System (SIS)[11], among other provisions. Further compensations, or rather redistribution of control and responsibilities, were fixed in the 1990 Dublin Convention and its subsequent amendments of 2003 and 2013.[12]

---

10 European Commission (1988): "Halfway to 1992: The Commission takes stock," press release from November 9, 1988.

11 For an analysis of the development process of SIS (and SIS II), the implementation of the SIS in France, Germany and the Netherlands, and a discussion about the remedies for third country national, see Evelien Brouwer (2008). For a critical discussion on the SIS II, see the Statewatch analysis by Ben Hayes (2005).

12 At the center of the Dublin system is the rule that asylum applications have to be processed by the EU member state in which the applicant first entered. From its beginning, the system has been criticized for unduly burdening countries at the outer limits of the union and "protecting" landlocked member states. Member states that are inland such as Germany and France receive a disproportionate number of applications. The system has been convicted of exacerbating the principle of non-refoulement (German Federal Constitutional Court, Order of the Second Senate of January 25, 2011 - 2 BvR 2015/09 -, para. 1-3) and continues to provoke a discussion about whether a fleeing person should be allowed to choose the country for his or her asylum application. For a thorough discussion of the latter argument, see Stephen Legomsky (2005). For a pointed critique of the Dublin system and a discussion of different cases against it, see Sílvia Morgades-Gil (2015). Since the summer of migration in 2015, controversies

As Ruben Zaiotti notes the compensatory measures acted as "litmus test" (Zaiotti 2011: 144) to the regime of free movement. In consequence, a repressive European migration and border control regime is sketched out as a prerequisite to the waiving of checks at internal borders. In sum, from its beginning, security concerns dominated the operationalization of the Schengen cooperation to an extent that commentators clearly saw "ministries of Interior, border guard, police and customs agencies in the driving seat" (Jeandesboz 2009).[13] Albeit successful as a Pan-European narrative of freedom and rapprochement, "Schengen" effectively became associated with a proliferation of control, with restrictive asylum and migration laws across Europe, and in parts also with a fortification of the European Union. For the first 15 years of the Schengen acquis, Mechthild Baumann even sees a paradigm shift from freedom to security in the operationalization of the Schengen Process and comments that "that which began as the thought of a Europe without border controls resulted in a highly institutionalized security union" (Baumann 2008: 29). Of the twin principles of Schengen, security turned out to be the parasitic twin. The parasitic twin affected the becoming and institutionalization of Europe's borders as it *charged* the imaginary of the external border and its need for controls with the suggestion of a migration-induced security deficit.

2.1.2 If Not a Border, What Do the Schengen Rules Constitute?

From the beginning, the notion of "external borders" evoked both twins: freedom *and* security. Even though the Schengen rules did not change the classic concept of statehood or the concept of frontiers in international public law (Müller-Graff 1998: 15), they did, however, contribute to the blurring of the classic distinction between internal and external security. The distinction between "internal frontier" and "external borders" introduced by the Schengen Implementing Convention modified the meaning and functioning as well as the quality and dimension of political borders in Europe.

---

over the Dublin regulations, the distribution of refugees and migration within the EU have increased among EU member states.
13 Earlier accounts of this development include Monica den Boer and Laura Corrado's (1999) analysis of the incorporation of the Schengen rules into the EU legal framework and Virginie Guiraudon's (2003) account of the securitization of immigration policies in Europe.

According to the Schengen Implementing Convention (hereafter cited in the text) "internal borders" are "the common land borders of the [Schengen states], their airports for internal flights and their ports for regular ferry connections exclusively to and from other ports within the territories of the [Schengen states] and not calling at any ports outside these territories". Complementing this, "external borders" were defined negatively as Schengen states' "land and sea borders and their airports and sea ports, provided that they are not internal borders". However, the attribute "external" was not meant to indicate the new locus of common (Schengen) control. As border controls were supposed to be waived between Schengen states, controls were meant to happen "elsewhere." The introduction of a reference called "external border" was evasive rather than restructuring. Initially, the classification "external borders" was presented as rather formal and neutral, as it meant to "avoid the sensitive issue of who should be legally responsible for their management" (Zaiotti 2011: 71). In the context of the ECC, by contrast, "external borders" have been evoked as "community borders" and been offered as "symbols of a new collective European identity" (ibid: 81).[14]

Nonetheless, in the Schengen context, the reference to "external borders" turned into a problematization of "security deficits" caused by the abolition of internal controls. The two questions of *Who would be in charge?* and *On what legal basis?* remained both sensitive and unresolved issues – and continue to be today. With regard to the question of "which actions should be taken at Community level and which should be left to intergovernmental cooperation," the Commission recommended that "attention should be focused on practical effectiveness rather than on matters of legal doctrine."[15] The legal document that wanted to dissolve and reorganize the borders in Europe led to a proliferation of security *practices* while putting on hold the common legal ground.

---

14 The 1985 Adonnino Reports are considered historical evidence of the vision of "A People's Europe." The report of June 1985 contains a proposal for a Europe which would be more experienceable and visible to its citizens in everyday life. Many of its proposals, such as the European flag and anthem, European passport and driving license were taken up. The Committee for a People's Europe was set up by the European Council meeting in Fontainebleau in June 1984. The reports were named after the committee's chair Pietro Adonnino a former Italian Christian Democrat Member of the European Parliament (cf. Teasdale 2012).

15 Abolition of controls of persons at intra-community borders, COM(88) 640 final, para. 14.

Figure 1: The Schengen Area in July 2019

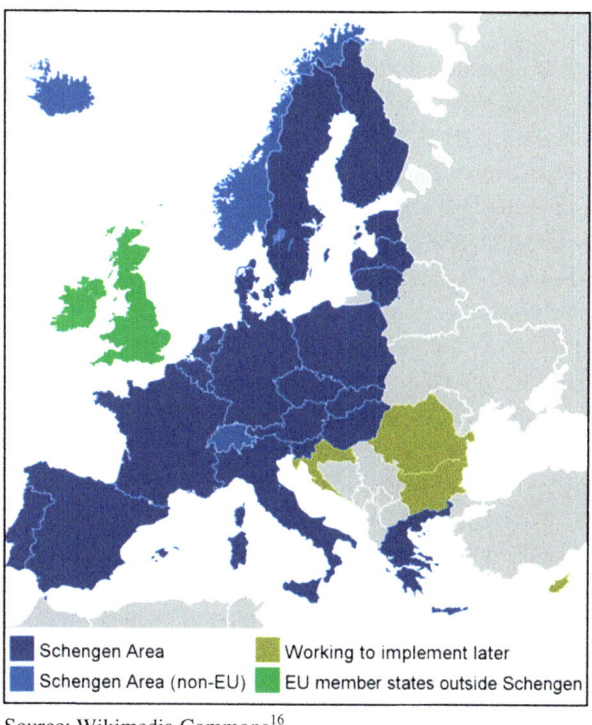

Source: Wikimedia Commons[16]

Even though it is cartographically representable, Schengen does not constitute a political entity *within* territorial frontiers; nor does it lay out a Europe *without* frontiers. The Schengen area is not even congruent with Europe, neither in its geographical nor institutional scope.

Geographically the Schengen area (not territory!) is constituted by its member states. Yet, EU membership and the application of the Schengen rules and privileges do not routinely correspond with each other, even though the Schengen acquis was transferred into EU Law with the 1997 Treaty of Amsterdam. Instead, different spaces of affiliation and cooperation exist within Europe. The application of the Schengen acquis and EU membership are still different

---

16 Wikimedia Commons, at: https://commons.wikimedia.org/wiki/File:Schengen_Area_Labelled_Map.svg (accessed July 15, 2019). The work has been released into the public domain by its author, CrazyPhunk.

frameworks for cooperation. In July 2019, the Schengen area consists of 22 of the 28 EU member states, and is encircled by 7,721 km of land borders and 42,673 km of sea border.

The 1985 club of five has thus gradually expanded; Spain, Portugal and Italy already joined the Schengen states when the Schengen Implementing Convention was brought into force in 1993. They were thus among the first countries to implement the Schengen acquis. Even though Greece signed the acquis in 1992, its full application, and thus the removal of border controls with EU member states, was not realized until 2000.[17] In 1996, the Schengen acquis was to be applied in Sweden, Denmark, Finland, Norway and Iceland.[18] Sweden, Denmark and Finland abolished border controls in 2001. Norway and Iceland are not EU members, but are part of the Nordic Passport Union and have been officially classified as associates with the Schengen area and activities since 1999.[19] The other two non-EU countries to have negotiated their associative status, Switzerland and Liechtenstein in 2008[20] and in 2011[21] respectively, together with Norway and Iceland, are part of the European Free Trade Association (EFTA). Two EU member states, the UK and Ireland, have negotiated opt-outs from the Schengen acquis when the intergovernmental agreement was transferred into EU law with the Treaty of Amsterdam.[22] As a result, for every regulation concerning Justice and Home Affairs, individual negotiations need to be held with the UK

---

17 Council Decision of December 13, 1999 on the full application of the Schengen acquis in Greece, in: OJ L 327 (December 9, 2000), p. 58.

18 Decision of the Executive Committee of 22 December 1994 on bringing into force the Convention implementing the Schengen Agreement of 19 June 1990, in OJ L 239, December 22, 1994, p. 130-132.

19 Agreement concluded by the Council of the European Union and the Republic of Iceland and the Kingdom of Norway concerning the latter's association with the implementation, application and development of the Schengen acquis, in: OJ L 176, July 10, 1999, p. 36.

20 Council Decision of November 27, 2008 on the full application of the provisions of the Schengen acquis in the Swiss Confederation, in: OJ L 327, December 5, 2008, p. 15.

21 Council Decision of December 13, 2011 on the full application of the provisions of the Schengen acquis in the Principality of Liechtenstein, in: OJ L 334, December 5, 2011, p. 37.

22 Council Decision of February 28, 2002 concerning Ireland's request to take part in some of the provisions of the Schengen acquis, in: OJ L 64, March 7, 2002, p. 20.

and Ireland.[23] For newcomers to the EU, opt-outs are not possible. Instead, EU membership obliges to work toward the fulfillment of the Schengen acquis. Today, EU membership thus precedes the opportunity of free movement which is related to Schengen and the fulfillment of its requirements.

The first enlargement round in 2004 encompassed ten countries, namely Estonia, Latvia, Lithuania, Malta, Poland, Slovakia, Slovenia, Czech Republic, Hungary and Cyprus. In 2007, Bulgaria and Rumania joined in the so-called second round of eastern enlargement. The latest accession was Croatia in 2013. Bulgaria, Rumania, Cyprus and Croatia do not fully implement the Schengen acquis; internal borders with the EU are still controlled. Finally, the micro-states Monaco, San Marino and Vatican City do not participate in Schengen activities. However, they are *de facto* part of the Schengen area as free movement is possible with a Schengen visa. Schengen's geography is this mediated by a complex set of rules and affiliations.

On the institutional level, the external borders represent two political entities: the national member state of the EU, and the supranational European Union. They are thus justifiably characterized as "double encoded" (Ger.: *doppelcodiert*)[24]. The political meaning of double encoded borders translates to a situation where shared responsibilities multiply and centralized competences are reduced. Exemplary of this new take – and also of the early confusion about it – is Friedrich Heckmann's 1996 circumscription of the new European policies he saw triggered by the Schengen rules:

---

23 The negotiations on the "Brexit," i.e., the terms and conditions of how the UK will leave the EU, are not controversial with regard to the control of persons. As both the UK and Ireland do not implement the Schengen acquis, a Brexit would not change the arrangement of identity checks along the border between the UK and Ireland. It would, however, require customs control.

24 The term "double encoded" (Ger.: *doppelcodiert*) has been termed by Andreas Müller in his doctoral thesis, which is quoted by Georg Vobruba (2012: 97, 99, 136). Maurizio Bach describes the border constellation as "institutional supercoding" which is characterized by "processes of superposition and asymmetrization" Bach (2010: 165-171). Stéphane Rosiere recognizes a three-leveled sovereignty between the regional, the national, and the community level, which is characterized "by a post-modern graduality, more than by classical isonomy" (Rosiere 2002: 52).

"Every state has *less* borders in the previous sense of the term. At the same time, however, each state has become co-responsible for *more* borders and must, for the sake of its own security [...], take an interest in the *different* borders [that are now relevant, S.E.]: the Oder-Neisse line has also become France's new eastern border, Germany has to take interest in what happens of the Strait of Gibraltar, everyone is interested in Italy's borders with the Schengen area, and also in what is going on between Italy and Albania." (Heckmann 1996: 12, emphasis added)

Less borders within Europe means more common concerns. Cooperation in border enforcement is considered to be "in the interest of one's own security" (Heckmann 1996: 12). This reciprocal understanding and arrangement of security is at the center of the Schengen acquis. Correspondingly, the Head of Research and Development at Frontex considers this proliferation of responsibility for external border security to be the "consequences of having Schengen":

"It is not about how good you are at your part of the Schengen external border. The idea should be that we create a similar level of control and awareness at *all* parts of the border because only then it works. I mean, if you're in Germany you have a very high standard, you check everything you have everything under control, but what does it mean if in France they don't do it? Your backdoor is open."[25]

To close the backdoor, Schengen rules are established as rules of cooperation among member states. The need for an increase in cooperation, however, is not caused by an increase in cross-border crime. It is implied in the agreement to leave the task of control to any member state at the outer edge of the Schengen area. Hence, Schengen creates, conceals and anchors the "stringent necessity to cooperate with regard to securing the common EU external border" (Vobruba 2012: 135). Or as Boldizsár Nagy puts it, Schengen "compelled [member states] to harmonize" (Nagy 2006: 105). Consequently, the Schengen rules – the *acquis communautaire* – do not fix an external border to the European Union. Rather, its external borders (note the plural) "mark the scope of the application of the European law as well as the extent of the European space of institutionalized intergovernmental cooperation" (Bach 2010: 171). Effectively, the Schengen rules do not constitute an EU border *per se*, but a "cascading interdependence" (Zielonka 2006: 3) which demands cooperation in different policy fields. More-

---

25 Head of Research and Development at Frontex, personal interview (May 27, 2011).

over, an external EU border is not erected as a result of land surveying or demarcation, but rather from the required cooperation of institutions.

In sum, the transfer of control from internal to external borders clearly is more than a geographic shift. It triggered institutional transformation with regard to the meaning and functioning of borders in the EU, as it meant conducting a common mandate while being under national legislation and budget. But how does this work in practice? Would the mandate of border guards remain national while at the same time their 'job description' was communitarian? In fact, the Schengen constellation is constantly concerned with the tension between the national and the European level. This is a tension which became manifest, for instance, at the occasion of the Lampedusa tragedy of October 2013 described in the introduction to this study. Italy's Deputy Prime minister Angelino Alfano stated that "the toll is unfortunately a tragic one" and declared the shipwreck "a European tragedy, not just an Italian one" (quoted in *The Telegraph* (N.N.) 2013). Declaring it a European tragedy calls for sharing the burden and for European solidarity. At the same time, it diverts responsibility as Lampedusa acts as the gate to Europe and not Italy alone. If, however, Lampedusa were officially considered a European and not an Italian island, this would not only affect any proclaimed responsibility but also budget, logistics and the distribution of arriving migrants and refugees.

What did and what do the Schengen rules thus constitute? The Schengen Agreement and Convention neither redraw any boundaries, nor do they fix a territory. The two legal papers, the Schengen Agreement and its Implementing Convention, did not bring about a legal authority for an external EU border and it did not create common border policies. What Schengen constitutes is the need for cooperation in border, migration and asylum policies. Unlike Latour's description of a process of inscription, in which "paper always appears at the end" (Latour 1986: 17), these two papers thus mark the beginning (and not the concealment) of displacements and mobilizations of competences in security policies in the EU. John Torpey has worked out that the Weberian state which monopolizes the legitimate means of violence is being amplified by the monopoly of the legitimate means of movement (Torpey 1998, 2000: 5). Schengen set this dual monopoly at disposal. It requested that decision over the movement of people be mutually recognized between Schengen signatories.

The apparent geographic shift detached the competence to restrict the liberties of person without a reasonable suspicion from the locus of the geographic-administrative border. To a certain extent, the exceptional competence of the border was displaced to an "elsewhere" and mobilized to relativize the monopoly on the legitimate means of movement the purpose of mutual recognition in this area. This demonopolization was expressed in two ways. First, national borders at the outer edge of the constituted area were no longer merely a subject of national, but of European concern. The mutual recognition of decisions at the external borders resulted in an urge to standardize migration, asylum and border control policies. Second, the legal borders of individual rights "as regards the position and crossing of borders now derives not only from the national law but also from European community law" (Guild 2001: 3). Both rights and competences are no longer commonly united on a territory and separated vis-à-vis other territories by a border. The incongruity between rights and competences is the central feature of postnational borders in Europe.

The discordance on which border control is based by way of the Schengen Agreement has been aptly described by Tugba Basaran's distinction between the geography of territory as a basis of political mapping and the geography of law and the space of government (Basaran 2008: 341, 2011: 1-8, 44-48): the legal borders of rights are still territorial, as obligations vis-à-vis third country nationals are limited within a territory. The legal borders of policing, however, are mobilized in so far as competences no longer stop at the geographical border line as rights do. As the territorial congruence between the legal borders of rights and the legal borders of policing has been diffused by way of the Schengen arrangement, different forms of operational cooperation and practical assistance were mobilized without a new European institution or a common legal authority.

Effectively, the Schengen Process results from a transformed understanding of the meaning and functions of political borders and has in turn contributed to the reconfiguration and redefinition of how borders are understood and operationalized in Europe. This has further changed the way borders are theorized, imagined, experienced, and researched. It is hence no coincidence that the empirical example of Europe's borders has left its mark on the epistemological and methodological premises in border studies. In the following, I will discuss prominent interpretations of Europe's borders and the Schengen Process with regard to their contribution to the epistemological and methodological change they brought to the study of political borders in general. Étienne Balibar and Jan Zielonka provide early examples for a transformed understanding of borders, which triggered a shift in how and as what borders have become to be researched since the 1990s. As Georg Vobruba systematizes Zielonka's take on borders, I also review his interpretation as a relatively recent analysis of the "postnational border constellation". Although Giorgio Agamben's work does not deal with a border conception, his *homo-sacer triology* has influenced both academic and activist takes on the effects of the EU's border on refugees and their rights and thus offers an ancillary analysis of its qualities. Last but not least, I examine the network analogy with regard to its contributions to border studies, particularly as it is advanced in the early studies of Didier Bigo. I have selected these authors because their contributions are classic examples of a transformed understanding of borders and, in consequence, have pioneered a transformed research design.

2.2 EUROPE AS BORDERLAND WITH POLYSEMIC, HETEROGENEOUS, AND OVERDETERMINED BORDERS

Étienne Balibar's analysis of Europe's borders has been particularly influential. His descriptions of the vacillating nature of borders have acquired a classic status (Balibar 1998). Moreover, his way of theorizing borders has altered the contemporary understanding of borders in general: borders are now studied as practices of control, exclusion, selection and subversion; they are studied "wherever the movement of information, people, and things is happening and is controlled" (Balibar 2002b: 71). Even though Balibar's work has been more influential among continental scholars than Anglophone scholars, Chris Rumford sees him as the "leading theorist of Europe's borders" (Rumford 2011: 37). In fact, the works of the French philosopher have affected contemporary understandings of borders beyond academia. The notion of ubiquitous borders (Balibar 2002b: 71) has been picked up by non-governmental organizations and activists alike to critique practices of social marginalization, racism and xenophobia – all matters of concern to Balibar – as daily occurrences in EU border policies.

Balibar's conceptualization of the vacillating nature of borders has provoked a reassessment of the relation between borders and space. According to Balibar, borders can be considered the point of crystallization with regard to the constitution of political space. Subsequently, analyzing them has allowed Balibar to discuss the state of democracy, as well as the concepts of citizenship and identity in relation to Europe. Throughout Balibar's works, the border appears as a "meta-institution," which conditions all other institutions in a democracy and thus encompasses its antinomies (Celikates 2010: 70). Although Balibar's thoughts on borders are part of his wider philosophical discussions of democracy, violence, universalism and citizenship, the following review restricts itself to those texts that explicitly deal with the borders of Europe. I will work closely with his texts in order to detail Balibar's conception of borders beyond the mainstream reading of borders being "dispersed a little everywhere" (Balibar 2002b: 71).

Balibar's first piece on borders was a book contribution in 1998 entitled "The Borders of Europe". Therein Balibar elaborated on the vacillation of borders, explicitly breaking with the European consciousness of a single real identity and the border as "a supersensible 'thing' that should be or not be – here or there, a bit beyond (*jenseits*) and just short of (*diesseits*) its ideal 'position,' but always somewhere" (Balibar 1998: 216-217, original emphasis) With this contribution, Balibar clearly challenges the need to localize borders. In the lectures and texts that followed – the essay "World Borders, Political Borders" (Balibar 2002b)[26] and the monograph *Politics and the Other Scene* (Balibar 2002a)[27], Balibar continuously reflects upon borders in relation to citizenship, identity, and democracy in Europe. His characterization of a border as overdetermined, polysemic, and heterogeneous (he uses the latter term as a synonym for vacillating) offers a systematic take toward a transformed understanding of borders, which diffuses notions of the geographic border-line.

The overall interest and political impetus of Balibar's oeuvre is the concept and the possibility of transnational citizenship and the attempt to "civilize the notion of cultural identity" (Balibar 2009: 202). He analyzes the functioning and enforcement of political borders with regard to these concepts. In its reception, his threefold characterization of political borders as overdetermined, polysemic, and heterogeneous, has seen a systematic bias for the latter two features. I shall thus deal with them in a first step, and then turn to the characteristic of overdetermination. Reviewing Balibar's characterization, I intend to trace why the two characteristics of polysemy and heterogeneity resonated more with EU border studies than the characteristic of overdetermination, which has been rather neglected.

2.2.1 Polysemy and Heterogeneity of Borders

The polysemic character of borders captures the plain fact that borders are experienced differently by different people. Likewise, the crossing of borders requires different means from different people. While the latter notion points to the dif-

---

26 The essay is a translation of a lecture which Balibar delivered in French on October 4, 1999 during his invitation to the "Institut Français de Thessalonique" and to the Department of Philosophy at the Aristotle University of Thessaloniki.
27 The monograph includes two chapters on borders ("What is a border" and "The Borders of Europe"), which have been reviewed broadly but seldom been contextualized into the frame of his political philosophy on political space and citizenship.

ferentiation of legal titles, the first aspect alludes to its phenomenological virtue. A person from a rich country not only benefits from citizenship in a welfare state, but is also by means of nationality allowed a "surplus of rights – in particular, a world right to circulate unhindered" (Balibar 2002a: 82). The experience is one of seamless travel, of freedom from inconveniences. For a poor person from a poor (Muslim) country, by contrast, traveling is a hassle, starting from the visa procedures and the guarantee to be documented, to the checks, looks and suspicions during movement. Pointing to the difference "between those who 'circulate capital' and those 'whom capital circulates,'" Balibar sees borders as operators "of an international class differentiation" and as "instruments of discrimination and triage" (ibid). This is to say that social inequalities are not only reproduced and stabilized by means of borders, but that border policies function to privilege some while cutting off others (right to move). According to Balibar, this bears a "world *apartheid*, or a dual regime for the circulation of individuals" (ibid, original emphasis), as the privileged have the ability to not only travel but also have a monopolized definition of the legitimate means of movement.

Balibar sees the polysemic nature of borders resting on a fundamental ambivalence of the role of the border vis-à-vis the state. The differentiation executed by border personnel at the border supports "the notion of national citizen and, through that notion, a certain primacy of the public authority over social antagonisms" (Balibar 2002a: 82). Border guards thus not only enforce privileges, they represent them. Yet, with an increase in transnational traffic, public authority (generally, the state) is caught in the "contradictory position of having to both relativize *and* to reinforce the notion of identity and national belonging" (ibid, original emphasis). This double-bind illustrates that border work is a decision on whether movement is allowed or restricted. According to Balibar, the selection criteria converge not least with social inequality and racism. The differentiation or selection that borders operationalize has also been circumscribed by others. In fact, most authors identify political borders with the function of selection and the regulation of membership. Ulf Hedetoft, for instance, introduces the metaphor of the "asymmetric membrane" in order to evoke the image of borders being identified by their essential function "to protect against unwanted entrance [...] from the other side" (Hedetoft 2003: 152). In a more technical tone, different German sociologists have circumscribed political borders as "sorting machines" (Mau 2010) and "selection machines" (Kaufmann/Bröckling/Horn 2002: 7).

Effectively, border policies present themselves differently to different people, which results in a scattered application of rights. Furthermore, border policies play out their functions differently, not only to different people but also to "'things' and 'people' – not to mention what is *neither thing nor person*: viruses, information, ideas" (Balibar 2002a: 91, original emphasis). Balibar formulates the "empirico-transcendental question of *luggage*," which asks "whether people transport, send, and receive things, or whether things transport, send, and receive people" (ibid, original emphasis).

The figurative question of luggage is indeed an inspiring concept to differentiate power while at the same time sticking to the ambitions of symmetric anthropology: who moves – the airplane or the passenger?, who is moved – the migrant or the refugee?, who carries/is carried?, what carries/is carried – in the case of a boat: the water or the vehicle?, and what about carrier sanctions and the arrangement of luggage during return flights? I by no means intend to adopt a disrespectful tone when taking human beings for "luggage". Rather, I attempt to gauge a systematic concept by which the power dynamics around the legitimate means of movement and the rules of transportation can be explored further. For it is not only about the allowance to move – as was the case for Torpey's example of the passport – but also about the resources, capacities and vehicles to do so and to be transported *en route*. Determining whether politics are applied and rights guaranteed for the carrier or the luggage is an important distinction to characterize the mode of politics at work on this age of migration and mobility.

Let us go back to Balibar's characterization of political borders and his second characteristic: the heterogeneity of borders describes the changing nature of borders as a transformation from a localizable phenomenon to a vacillating one. According to Balibar, borders "are no longer localizable in an unequivocal fashion" (Balibar 2002a: 91). Without a localizable anchor to control practices, the term border "is profoundly changing in meaning" (Balibar 2002b: 71). Yet, counter to notions of a borderless word, Balibar opposes that rather than disappearing, "borders are being both multiplied and reduced in their localization and their function; they are being thinned out and doubled, becoming border zones, regions, or countries where one can reside and live" (Balibar 2002a: 92). This diagnosis of a vacillating appearance or apparition of borders as areas, points, or situations offers a conceptual departure from the borderline as the only imaginable spatial form of political borders. In this context, the following quotation has acquired an almost archetypal status.

"The borders of new politico-economic entities, in which an attempt is being made to preserve the functions of the sovereignty of the state, are no longer at all situated at the outer limit of territories: they are dispersed a little everywhere, wherever the movement of information, people, and things is happening and is controlled." (Balibar 2002b: 71)

The resulting proliferation of borders has been accepted and reproduced widely among border scholars. To a certain extent, Balibar has given an answer to Georg Kreis's (2010: 86) question of "what remains of borders once they have been suspended." What remains is practices of control, the sovereign competence to restrict the liberties of others. The difference is that the asymmetric power of policing which had been restricted before to the locus of the administrative border line is now extended to situations which are defined as border crossings. Balibar illustrates this "heterogeneity" or "vacillation" of borders by deploying spatial metaphors, some of which describe the new spatiality of borders by simply negating its "old" territorial state, but maintaining the need to localize them. Borders "are no longer at the border" (Balibar 1998: 217). At the same time, the heterogeneity of borders stems from a corresponding proliferation of control competences. Securing borders is equal to securing sovereignty – that is, borders are not marginal or peripheral "to the constitution of a public sphere but rather are at the center" (Balibar 2002b: 72). In terms of political space as public sphere, borders are a central institution. In terms of their locus and the locus of practices of inclusion and exclusion, borders are "dispersed a little everywhere, wherever the movement of information, people, and thing is happening and is controlled" (ibid: 71). Studying borders means researching control practices and the struggles they provoke. The focus is on encounters between enforcement authorities and deviants.

Additionally, the concept of the vacillating border does not localize the Other as a foe on the other side of the border. With his elaborations on "the other scene," Balibar remains consistent with his conceptualization of borders as well as in his construction of the alterity projected by vacillating borders. Drawing on the Freudian notion of the "other scene" as "the representation of the *essential heterogeneity* of psychic processes," Balibar (2002a: xii, original emphasis) evokes "the no less essential heterogeneity of political processes".

"[T]he *other scene of politics* is also *the scene of the other*, where the visible-incomprehensible victims and enemies are located at the level of fantasy. Secrecy, counter-information, and fantasmatic otherness must have some common root; at least they produce conjoint effects." (Balibar 2002a: xiii, original emphasis)

The primacy of imagination applies here as well. The other appears in imagining him or her, and not through contact or encounters.

Overall, the reception of Balibar's analysis has been dominated by dissolving the geographical-physical connotation of political borders and shifting it to an understanding of borders as social practices. The new ubiquity of borders has inspired new research agendas. Effectively, the characteristic of heterogeneity has been read and researched as practices of social and racial discrimination. However, with an increasing number of practices being studied as border, it has been "obscured" (Johnson et al. 2011: 61) what a border actually is. Even though I share this critique, I doubt that it can at all be determined what a border actually is. This is due to the spectral character of any border, which will be further elaborated in section 3.1.

2.2.2 Overdetermination and the World-Configuring Function of Borders

With the characteristic of overdetermination, Balibar emphasizes more than the mere acknowledgement of borders being cultural and historical products – a description he considers "commonplace of history textbooks" (Balibar 2002a: 79). Any border is overdetermined in so far as it is never "the mere boundary between two states" (ibid). A border incorporates an interrelation to an imagination of global order. Each individual border sanctions, reduplicates or relativizes the world ordering ideology, or "super-border" (Balibar 2009: 195).

Any given political border is legitimized and stabilized by echoing the super-border. As a consequence, it incorporates a *"double meaning*, local and global" (Balibar 2009: 201, original emphasis). The "'partition' or 'distribution' of the World space" enacted by means of operationalizing a border "reflects the regime of meaning and power under which the World is represented as a 'unity' of different 'parts'" (ibid). For example, as a synecdoche for the separation of the world into East and West during the Cold War period, the Berlin Wall illustrates the idea of overdetermination almost as an ideal type. The confrontation between capitalism and socialism is the super-border for the individual borders between camps, blocs, and states. Balibar also mentions the example of the European colonial empires, which overdetermined political decompositions between the 1494 Treaty of Tordesillas and the Cold War period.[28] According to him, the durability of borders largely stems from their world-configuring function, and thus from the rationale and the imagination of order that is dominant in world politics. "Without the *world-configuring* function they perform, there would be no borders – or no lasting borders" (Balibar 2002a: 79, original emphasis). Accordingly, what stabilizes political borders is not to be found their material robustness or terrestrial grounding. They are stable rather because they have become internal-

---

28 Carl Schmitt (2003 [1950]: 86-100) identified the modern overdetermination as global linear thinking.

ized as an "essential reference of [...] collective, communal sense" (ibid: 78) and are thus thought of as natural, good, necessary, or even existential.

Moreover, the philosopher emphasizes that a border's overdetermination – that is, the fact that a border "is always *over*determined, and in that sense sanctioned, reduplicated and relativized by other geopolitical divisions [...] is by no means incidental or contingent; it is intrinsic" (Balibar 2002a: 79, original emphasis). Without a particular worldview, no border of this particular kind would emerge. The kind of border narrowly depends on political ideology and imagination of the world, which is intrinsic to border policies. According to Balibar, what happens at Europe's external borders says more about how we look at the world than about what is happening in the world. He underlines the relation between an imaginary pattern of political space (worldview), and the concrete reality of border policies and the practices of border control.

While I have discussed Schengen borders from the perspective of negotiating the national and the European frame of border policies, the characteristic of overdetermination adds the question about distinguishing a rationality of order on a global scale. In the context of an emerging border to the EU, the question of world-configuration understood as the search for the super-border and an ideology that bestows the practical division of the globe with a sense of legitimate order is left indeterminate and un-ascertained. Balibar, however, sees competition with regard to bestowing rationality to the bordering process in Europe: competing frames formulate the super-border. In the Alexander von Humboldt lecture titled "Europe as borderland," which Balibar gave at Nijmegen University in November 2004, he presented an analysis of different schemes of the spatial-political projections which are at work in the political organization of space and borders in Europe.[29] Balibar sees "four different (and conflicting) *schemes of projection* of the figure of Europe within the global world" (Balibar 2009: 190, original emphasis): the clash-of-civilizations pattern; the global network pattern; the center–periphery pattern; and the crossover pattern. These *"four conflicting patterns* of 'political spaces'" (ibid: 194, original emphasis) differ both in their construction of Europe and their representation of borders. According to Balibar, different patterns are "associated with *opposite policies* concerning nationality and citizenship, residence and mobility, activity and security: in short, they are

---

29 The lecture was published as an equally titled essay in *Environment and Planning D* in 2009. Quotations have been taken from the 2009 article rather than from the 2004 lecture.

opposite ways of 'constituting' Europe (or, possibly, resisting its constitution)" (ibid, original emphasis). The figure of the border is turned into the hallmark with regard to the concretization and manifestation of that concept. He argues that each pattern:

> "is not only a way to figure a 'political space,' involving a different idea of the intrinsic relationship between politics and spatiality, it is also a different way to understand what a 'border' exactly means, how it works and how it is reproduced" (Balibar 2009: 201).

The first pattern of differentiation is *the clash-of-civilizations pattern* (Balibar 2009: 194-196). Operating on a civilizational super-border, this pattern deploys notions of Samuel Huntington's "clash of civilizations" and Carl Schmitt's "Grossräume," and differentiates along an essentialist understanding of religion, culture, and belonging. The figure of the border might be phenomenologically fuzzy and dispersed, but its legal and political operationalization is sharp. The political border appears as guarantor of law and order and requires terrestrial grounding as a clear line of demarcation. Imagining political space and political border in terms of the second, *the global network pattern* means thinking politics in terms of connections, flows, and processes of circulation. As a result, the projection of the global network "embodies the idea of a limit of traditional representations of political spaces, the reaching of a point where the political space becomes hardly representable" (Balibar 2009: 196). Projecting *the center-periphery pattern* to the political space of Europe means sketching interdependencies and strategic alliances. In accordance with world system theory, the center-periphery pattern evokes the EU with border areas, zones, or marches arranged as concentric circles. Balibar sees these images being productive when EU enlargement and integration is discussed. This pattern also underpins the analysis of the European Neighborhood Policy (EPN). In this projection, political borders are instruments and institutions of political diplomacy and bargaining and express the reach of European integration. Fourth, *the crossover pattern* corresponds to Balibar's vision of "Europe as a borderland". Albeit critical about the state of Europe, the philosopher evokes the potential of Europe as a borderland, a "land" which constructively lives on the in-between status and radical democracy; with the heterogeneity of issues, religions, people and cultures of its place. A "land" of liminality which thus goes for radical democracy, rather than exceptional decisions. As a borderland, the construction of Europe has an integrative and civilizing potential. Because it offers a meeting point for the many, Europe is always becoming. In Balibar's vision, the heterogeneity and differences of people, cultures, and religions in Europe will neither clash nor integrate, but demand an "unending process of translation" (Balibar 2009: 209).

"'Borderland' is the name of the place where the opposites flow into one another, where 'strangers' can be at the same time stigmatized and indiscernible from 'ourselves,' where the notion of citizenship, involving at the same time community and universality, once again confronts its intrinsic antinomies." (Balibar 2009: 210)

Balibar's own conception of "Europe as a borderland" – a notion he formulated as a vision and a conceptual basis for radical critique – resonates with the political will of an open Europe despite all odds.

In sum, a central aspect of Balibar's border conception is his diagnosis that the authority to enforce borders is no longer located and thereby restricted to the territorial border as a geographically defined administrative place. Sovereignty has split, both with regards to its "targets" and with regard to its function, and allows for ubiquitous (border) control practices. This leads to a proliferation of control practices in kind and in location. Balibar thereby directs attention to those forms of sovereign control that "prevail" despite the Schengen induced abolishment of internal borders within Europe, and despite the announcement of a borderless world. With his emphasis on the vacillation and ubiquity of borders, Balibar stresses that borders are not abolished nor dissolved, but rather transformed and multiplied. However, the reception of ubiquitous and vacillating borders, as well as the diagnosed proliferation of borders has obscured what their political character actually is. The vague conflation (and sometimes suggestive inversion) of geography and polity, geographic-juridical borders and practices of security personnel (be it border guards, police, or civilians), led to a translation of spatial metaphors into the realm of political constitutionalism. Balibar approaches borders as practices of segregation, of subversion and control, of violent inequality. In doing so, he could show that bordering not only occurs along territorial lines. In addition, dissolving them doesn't dissolve discrimination and violence. Yet, in turn, this wide understanding contributes to a conceptual uncertainty with regard to the political border, its field and object of research.

2.3 EUROPE AS EMPIRE WITH MEDIEVAL, COSMOPOLITAN OR POSTNATIONAL BORDERS

Conceiving of Europe as an empire deviates strongly from Balibar's notion of borderland, particularly with regard to the envisioned role of a political Europe in the world. While the notion of borderland embodies a sort of low threshold dealing with alterity, the concept of empire works "to maintain the fiction of a 'high point'" (Rumford 2011: 90). In a borderland, borders are the point in time and space where things can turn into their radical opposites. They demand radical democracy yet elicit a global apartheid. Under these premises, thinking and researching political borders means examining the struggles of daily practices of border enforcement and subversion. It can also mean encountering radical exclusion and discrimination; these "findings" are in turn related to the constitution of the border. By contrast, borders in an empire are fuzzy and soft. They are negotiated and negotiable *arrangements*, which can be examined by looking at institutional decision-making, legislation, and processes of regional integration.

The description of Europe as an empire has been deployed most influentially in two quite different works: first, in Jan Zielonka's (2006) *Europe as Empire: The Nature of the Enlarged EU* and second in Ulrich Beck's and Edgar Grande's (2007) *Cosmopolitan Europe*. The deployment of the term empire is justified on opposite premises. In the case of Zielonka, it was a critique on the tone in EU enlargement policy in the case. In the case of Beck and Grande, it was as invocation of the "last politically effective utopia" (Beck/Grande 2007: 2).[30] While Zielonka describes the EU as neo-medieval empire with a scattered public sphere and scattered legal zones, Beck and Grande envision the EU as a cosmopolitan empire, which bears the potential of universal integration, but lacks its construction from below. Whereas Zielonka uses the term with the impetus of "a polemic response to the mainstream literature on European integration" (Zielonka 2006: 2), Beck and Grande affirmatively use the term to call for a cosmopolitan Europe.

According to Beck and Grande, statehood and sovereignty (Ger: *Herrschaft*) can be reconceptualized with regard to the political form of Europe, namely "through a new conception of empire freed from imperialistic and nationalistic connotations, one which must be opened up in a cosmopolitan fashion and reoriented toward consensus and law" (Beck/Grande 2007: 94). Zielonka, by contrast, deploys the term to precisely criticize the imperialistic behavior of the EU in its neighborhood policies (even more pronounced in Zielonka 2008, 2013a, 2013b). The efforts of the EU in its neighborhood are "truly imperial in the sense that the EU tries to impose domestic constraints on other actors through various forms of

---

30 A thorough discussion comparing the two works and their different notions of empire has been provided by Chris Rumford. He concludes that "empire (in any formulation) is not a satisfactory framework within which to understand European transformations" as it cannot get rid of the hybris of the high point (Rumford 2011: 90-109, here 90).

economic and political domination" (Zielonka 2008: 471). The metaphor of the empire – once deployed to criticize and envision – is used to depart from the Westphalian model of state as the ideal of polity and as *the* analytical frame for the study of the political, cultural, economic, and legal transformations of an 'ever closer' Europe.

2.3.1 Thinking Beyond the Westphalian Model: Neo-Medieval or Cosmopolitan Polity?

Despite their opposite inclinations, both perspectives depart from a perceived inadequacy of the Weberian state as a model to analyze contemporary EU polity. The role of borders comes into play when the empire defines its shape and limits, as well as in its relation to the environment. Zielonka presents the neo-medieval alternative while Beck and Grande's advocated alternative is cosmopolitan. How do these different analyses of the construction of Europe relate first to the notion of Europe's borders and second to the Schengen rules?

Generally, the works of Zielonka are less concerned with the nature of Europe's borders as such. The appearance of borders is rather taken as symptom of EU polity, which Zielonka examines with regard to the Union's enlargement process and its neighborhood policy in the East and the Mediterranean. As a consequence of the enlargement process, but also as general implication of the EU's neighborhood policy, clear lines of demarcation are given up and the notion of "soft borders in flux" (Zielonka 2006: 2, 167) is adopted. Enlargement not only constantly sets European borders and thus the notion of a defined and stable political entity at disposal. Moreover, according to Zielonka, "enlargement renders the rise of the European state impossible" (ibid: 9).

Zielonka draws the conclusion that European polity should not be analyzed by superimposing a comparison with the Westphalian model of polity. He suggests the 'neo-medieval empire' as an alternative lens. By applying the medieval paradigm, three aspects gain visibility. First, a divergence in the different functions of borders from one geographical (territorial) border line to the overlap of different authorities. Second, a polycentric system of authority and multiple loyalties. And third, the imperial and "evangelizing" character of EU relations in its neighborhood (Zielonka 2013b: 5-6). By describing Europe's borders in resemblance to a "medieval" setting, the taken for granted geographical or territorial connotation of borders is opened up for a way of thinking political borders beyond the Westphalian state.

"One of the advantages of the medieval paradigm is that it represents a perfect contrast to the dominant Westphalian paradigm. The Westphalian paradigm is about the concentration of power, sovereignty and distinct identities, while the medieval one is about overlapping authorities, divided sovereignty and multiple identities. The Westphalian paradigm is about fixed and relatively hard borderlines, while the medieval one is about soft border zones that undergo regular adjustments. The Westphalian paradigm is about military impositions and containment, while the medieval one is about the export of laws and modes of governance." (Zielonka 2013b: 6)

In this perspective, borders are not part of foreign relations. They are part of neighborhood policy, for without the Westphalian state; there can be no such international system. Similarly, Beck and Grande strongly emphasize the need to strip off the "conceptual straightjacket of methodological nationalism" (Beck/Grande 2007: xii). And still, according to Beck and Grande, Europe as cosmopolitan empire[31] inevitably comes with five dilemmas: the universalistic dilemma, the integration dilemma, the insecurity dilemma, the boundary dilemma, and the peace dilemma. Embracing the notion of cosmopolitan borders would then mean to accept Europe's "boundary dilemma," that is, the dialectic "of opening and closing of borders" (ibid: 261-262) and of overcoming *and* preserving the national. It would mean accepting "shared uncertainties and shared dilemmas" (ibid: 263).

This identity-generating dedication and transfiguration to dilemmas, that is, to concepts and situations offering two options – none of which brings a satisfying result – is essential to Beck's and Grande's construction of Europe. This resilient dealing with antagonisms also underpins the notion of "borderland" put forward by Balibar. Balibar (2002a: 82), however, differentiates between the potential of a vision of European policies and the (what he terms) "double-bind" of contemporary EU border policies.

While Balibar cautions the anti-democratic condition of the border itself, independent of the political entity which operates it, Beck and Grande problema-

---

31 Beck and Grande (2007: 60-71) identify ten features fundamental to the European Empire: 1) asymmetrical political order, 2) open and variable spatial structure with flexible and mobile borders, 3) multinational societal structure, 4) integration through law, consensus and cooperation, 5) welfare versus security, 6) horizontal and vertical institutional integration, 7) network power, 8) cosmopolitan sovereignty, 9) ambivalence of delimitation and delineation, and 10) emancipatory versus repressive cosmopolitanism.

tize whether a society "whose key features is the political variability of its geographical boundaries" still counts as one society (Beck/Grande 2007: 94).

Both Zielonka's as well as Beck and Grande's elaborations on Europe's borders address the idea of the Union's borders. Meanwhile, the Schengen Agreement and its rules for the operationalization of border control are put aside, either as an example of geographic differentiation in the case of Beck and Grande (2007: 247), or as an envisaged "hard border regime" of which "a growing body of evidence suggests that the system is unduly harsh, impractical, and at odds with the Union's main foreign policy objectives" (Zielonka 2006: 3). In 2013, Zielonka repeated that "[i]n contemporary Europe borders are also remarkably fuzzy despite the Schengen system" (Zielonka 2013b: 5). In both conceptions, Schengen borders thus differ from the borders of the European Union. This is demonstrated when contextualizing the standard quotation used when referring to Zielonka's portrayal of Europe's border: "[i]n due time, [...] will probably be less territorial, less physical, and less visible" (Zielonka 2006: 4). However, this characterization is preceded by a discrimination between the idea of the European Union and the Schengen Process – "indeed, the Union is likely to end up with soft border zones in flux rather than with hard and fixed external borderlines as envisaged by Schengen" (ibid). While his assessment of Europe's polity takes up the non-finality of the Union, and while the "soft borders in flux" stand for the possibility to negotiate and design foreign policies, Schengen, in Zielonka's view, stands for the reverse impetus, that is, the search for clear and fixed external borderlines and for the notion of a fortress Europe. In his view, not a

"'fortress Europe,' but a 'maze Europe' is likely to emerge [...]. In such a 'maze Europe' different legal, economic, security, and cultural spaces are likely to be bound separately, cross-border multiple cooperation will flourish, and the inside/outside divide will be blurred. In due time, the EU's borders will probably be less territorial, less physical, and less visible. They will not look like fortified lines on the ground, but like zones where people and their identities mingle. In this sense, they will resemble the borders of a neo-medieval Europe rather than the borders of a Westphalian Europe." (Zielonka 2006: 4)

The construction of Europe and the Schengen system work on conflicting premises with regard to their respective constructions of Europe. Focusing on the Union's polity under the condition of Eastern enlargement, Zielonka analyzes the institutional forms of a construction of Europe.

2.3.2 Europe and its Postnational (Border) Constellation

Georg Vobruba, whose research aims to sharpen the conception of political borders beyond the territorial and Westphalian frame (Vobruba 2010: 434-435), abstracts a large number of Zielonka's observations to formulate the conception of "the postnational border constellation."[32] Drawing on the works of Maurizio Bach and Rainer Lepsius, the sociologist advances an analysis of Europe's borders as object of negotiations in the process of European institutional integration.

From this perspective, borders are conceptualized as institutions. Vobruba gauges the characteristics of the postnational constellation by analysis of the transformation of political sovereignty and of political borders. In his exposition, the term "postnational" points to a political setup in which different spatial frames compete.[33] Thus, in the postnational constellation, this competition underpins and reconfigures the functioning and meaning of political sovereignty and political borders (Vobruba 2012: 5). In the case of the European postnational constellation, Vobruba notes that institutional integration is increasingly European, while social integration remains national in outlook. The institutional integration is thus further advanced than the integration of the people. The tension between the national frame and the European frame is amplified by two factors: First, Europe's integration-elite and the common European man or woman are not aligned by the direct representation of interests. It comes to a situation in which the elites are trying to convince the people that European integration would be beneficial to them. These attempts, however, elicit skepticism rather than trust, for their perception is that national sacrifices are requested for a common Europe. Second, the national elites refer to the European frame in a manner that helps them score in the national frame. According to Vobruba "political spaces are constituted by the mutual interrelation of institution building and social relations" (ibid: 3). The (political) space between an institutionally ever integrating Europe and the number of national actors reluctant to European social integration is full of tension.

---

32 The postnational constellation has been described by Jürgen Habermas in an essay collection (2001 [1998]). At the center of Habermas's concern is the democratic organization of political representation and control following the congruent form of the nation-state. Vobruba does not take Habermas' normative stance; he is rather interested in the observation of institutional change by 'the people' (Ger.: *die Leute*).

33 In 1993 Hermann Schwengel already formulated that the competition of spatial frames will be central to European politics (Schwengel 1993).

"The sociology of Europe incorporates the different perspectives on these tensions in a differentiation between the national and European levels, and relates them to institution-building." (Vobruba 2008: 34-35)

The tension between the national and the European level is thus an endogenous factor to the emergence of the EU's external border as institution. Therefore, Vobruba argues that Europe's borders are best analyzed from the perspective of a European sociology, which focusses on the competition between the national and the European policy level as a spatial frame for the fulfillment of needs. According to Vobruba, European sociology should be developed from the starting point of this tension – that is, from the "difference national/European" (Vobruba 2008: 34). The described tension can be seen more clearly under the premises of a transformed concept of political sovereignty, which Vobruba presents as "legitimized by output" (Vobruba 2012: 58). In brief, postnational sovereignty is based on the evaluation of the performance of governance. The national and the European political 'caterer' compete for acceptance and the public *attribution* of sovereignty.

Against this methodological background Vobruba (2010, 2012) presents a threefold characterization of the postnational border constellation: First, under the condition of the postnational border constellation, political borders no longer condense all functions of social closure, but are rather characterized by their dissociation. He argues that "processes of functional differentiation across space" alters the functioning of segmentary, political borders (Vobruba 2012: 111). Second, under the condition of a postnational border constellation, the operation of border is subject to negotiation. Borders are thus subject to and dependent on negotiations (Ger.: *verhandlungsabhängig*). Third, in the postnational constellation, the permeability of political borders is operated hand in hand with selectivity. In other words: Borders are characterized by a selective permeability. In 2010 Vobruba described the dissociation of different functions of social closure – once condensed in the political border of the nation-state – with reference to Maurizio Bach (2010: 159), who draws on Max Weber's remarks on open and closed social relations (Weber 1972: 23-35). Vobruba sees that the

"functions of borders to define economic, cultural, linguistic and political spaces – and where applicable to close them – are no longer merged. It is rather the case that a complex pattern of overlapping, yet not coinciding, spaces is developing." (Vobruba 2010: 443)

In certain respects, the dissociation of the different functions of social closure is not only a characteristic of the postnational border constellation, but brings it about. The first is both impetus to the latter as well as its characteristic. In consequence, individuals and groups negotiate their access to privileges or rights, to economic relations or political participation, along different boundaries and affiliations. In the case of Europe's borders, this dissociation is partly triggered by the constituting four freedoms of the European Communities: the free movement of goods, persons, services and capital. These four freedoms have not only inspired the dissociation of labor and capital from national economies (Vobruba 2010: 439), they also render the responsibilities and competences of social and legal systems ambiguous, unclear and diffuse.

The description of overlapping spaces, which are also to be found to a certain degree in Balibar, Zielonka, Beck and Grande, describes *the new* neither in terms of form nor content but rather in terms of overlaps and simultaneity; according to Vobruba, however, this remains unsatisfactory.

He first observed that the functions of closure are no longer coinciding at borders, portraying the phenomenon, following Bach, as a characteristic of the postnational border constellation in 2010. He then spelled out this process in 2012 with the help of the theory of functional differentiation, asking for the requirements and qualitative changes that functional differentiation pose on segmentary, political borders. Vobruba suggests that "processes of functional differentiation spanning manifold spaces" (Vobruba 2012: 111) change the functioning of segmentary, political borders (that is, nation-state borders). For, as different institutions and actors observe functional differentiation and thus think in those terms, this kind of differentiation occurs in addition to the traditional differentiation whenever political borders are enforced. In the course of time, nation-state borders are not only reconsidered, but also given a new mandate.

The second attribute of the postnational border constellation consists in the empirical observation that border policies depend on negotiations and that their permeability is subject to bargaining agreements. Even though borders have always been subject to political bargaining, the issue concerns the routing and the geographic course of borders, which was seen as resistant to negotiation. The dependence on negotiations in the case of the postnational constellation is different: the negotiations do not revolve around the course of a given border which would require the acceptance of the two parties on both sides; they rather concern the *quality* and the *functions of social closure* (Vobruba 2012: 102, emphasis added). In this frame, the conditions attached to mobility across a given border are far more cumbersome and contested than the course of that border. Moreover, these conditions are part of political negotiations on development aid, trade agreements, readmission agreements, and the like. The right to move has turned into a traded resource that is particularly at stake in the EU neighborhood policies. According to Vobruba, the essentially new characteristic in this constellation is that a core object of statist sovereignty has turned into a matter for negotiations and transnational cooperation (ibid: 102). At the same time, this also means that the monopoly on the legitimate means of movement (Torpey 1998) is challenged, in the sense that it is not only transferred to the European level but subject to international diplomacy.

The third attribute concerns the permeability of borders. Even though it is common ground that borders cannot be hermetically closed, their permeability both justifies border control and proves it inefficient. However, the characteristic of selective permeability (Ger.: s*elektive Durchlässigkeit*) does not merely stress that access is regulated by the sovereign authority, access and mobility rights are rather negotiated between governments or administrations and their counterpart, in the sense of the second characteristic. In the postnational border constellation, the permeability of political borders thus entails an active selectivity. In the case of Europe's postnational border constellation, the question of who is allowed to move and cross Europe's borders is negotiated between European governments and their counterpart in third countries. The modern understanding of sovereignty is thereby contested, as the selection at the border is no longer undertaken by a state. The selection and its criteria are rather themselves negotiated between the parties on both sides of a border (Vobruba 2012: 106). As a result, the permeability of Europe's borders is exposed to political and diplomatic negotiations. In this context, the *Other* turns into a strategic partner.

Finally, institution building in European border policies is described as a process of "deficient institutionalization" (Ger.: *defizitäre Institutionalisierung*), a compromise based on the lowest common denominator. Deficits in the process of integration must constantly be fixed, thus spurring further integration. This incrementalism can either be evaluated as a muddling through or as a quite pragmatic approach to get things done.

Methodologically these different analyses entail that borders are analyzed as negotiated and negotiable *institutions*. To the researcher both the bargaining processes as well as the policy results are of concern when studying the development of the EU external border *as* institution. Under this methodological premise the focus departs from a given border being identified with the specific functions it fulfills, such as migration control, customs control or the protection of a community from foreign threats, and falls back on the border as an institutionalized process (rule) to legitimately claim authority (cf. Müller 2013).

2.3.3 Sovereign Europe, the Border as Exceptional Institution, and Bordering as Exceptional Practices

Taking an approach that is in some ways diametrically opposed, the Italian philosopher Giorgio Agamben developed his argument not in terms of the reach of institutionalized common EU rules, but rather with regard to exceptions to the rule of law, and the observation that the exception is becoming the rule.

Agamben (1998, 2000, 2005) initiated an analysis of Europe's borders that foregrounds legal structures and sheds light on the relation between individual and power, which, he, in his *Homo-Sacer-series*, explores as the interrelation between sovereign power and bare life. His conceptions of "bare life," "homo sacer," "exception," "the camp," and "sovereign power" attracted explosive attention. Moreover, in this reading of Agamben's work, the refugee began to appear as the constitutive figure of the border itself, while, at the same time, the concept of the *homo sacer* offered to theorize what was empirically contested along Europe's borders. Through the lenses of Agamben's work, the border or rather its constitutive practices of selection are conceived of and analyzed *as* exception. In this way, the border is analyzed both *as* institution – when its exceptional power is spotted and *as* practices of subversion, struggle, and contestation – when rights are claimed in vain.

Elspeth Guild already argued in 2001 that "[t]he individual with rights accruing from the different levels is the catalyst for the redefinition of European borders" (Guild 2001: 3). Agamben successfully proposed concepts for studying these reconfigurations. Agamben's generalized exception has been reframed as the generalized biopolitical border by Nick Vaughan-Williams (2012) who locates the border "where exceptional measures, practices and characteristics formerly associated with borders between states in the conventional sense become routinised and dispersed throughout global juridical-political space." (ibid: 108) Although this has been widely debated (cf. Rajaram/Grundy-Warr 2004; Darling 2009), Agamben himself did not propose Europe-bound refugees or migrants as an example of homines sacri. He did, however, take on board Hannah Arendt's observation of rights being only applicable to those individuals who are still integrated in society and in the state-system: the citizens. Agamben argues that "the paradox is that precisely the figure that should have embodied human rights more than any other – namely the refugee – marked instead the radical crisis of the concept" (Agamben 2000: 18). Recently, however, his priviledged position in EU border and migration studies has been subject to greater critical scrutiny (cf. Schindel 2017; Whitley 2017; Owens 2009).

2.4 NETWORK EUROPE AND NETWORKED (NON-)BORDERS

When it comes to unbundling the spatial imagination of the territorial container, and with it the notion of the Westphalian state, the metaphor of the network and the description of the network society have provided a widely accepted alternative. In fact, imaginations of networks "dissolve the classic images of the state as a machine, as an organism or as a territorial body" (Kaufmann 2007: 7). The graphical model by which the notion of network represents the ordering of political and social relations is "a flatly hierarchized, modularly arranged, and communicative tightly coupled matrix" (ibid). In the imagination, relations are based on communication, on flow, are themselves flow. Electronic communication technology unhitches the terrestrial ground as the basis and medium of sociation. While territorial spaces are characterized by the quality of being exclusive (Simmel), networks are non-exclusive, as individuals and groups can be part of different networks at the same time. The network metaphor is thus also deployed to evoke notions of individual freedom and of emancipation (not only from the local). It stresses possibilities and choices, rather than circumstances and exclusivity. Networks are essentially detached from territory or terrestrial obligations or restrictions. However, if political relations, if the state's body is imagined as network, what happens to its borders? Where are the limits in the assignment and ordering of modules and communication hubs? Is there a place which political borders hold, in the fluid world of network?

In 1993, John Ruggie already described a "space of flow" as the "nonterritorial global economic region" which is "premised on [...] the 'sovereign importance of movement,' not of place" (Ruggie 1993: 172-173, quoting Lattimore). This space of flow, which according to Castells (2008: 42) is the material basis of the network society, is "operating in real time, [and] [...] exists alongside the spaces-of-places that we call national economies" (Ruggie 1993: 172). When Ruggie and also Castells selected the term to describe a relation of flux and movement, their examples did not primarily refer to individuals and the free movement of persons, but were concerned with industrial production and the peculiar characteristics of global chains of production. Networks initially were thought to supersede national economies. Kenichi Ohmae's (1990) borderless world is an interlinked global market; the political function of borders is obsolete in this scenario. What Ruggie, Castells but also other globalization theorists haunted during the 1990s, was the question whether global was an obstinate phenomenon, a space of its own, beyond territory or, as some framed it, deterritorialized. Worldwide economic interconnectivity seemed to suggest just that. Ruggie observes

"a remarkable growth in transnational microeconomic links over the past thirty years or so, comprising markets and production facilities that are designated by the awkward term 'offshore' – *as though they existed in some ethereal space* waiting to be reconceived by an economic equivalent of relativity theory. In this offshore area, sourcing, production, and marketing are organized within 'global factories,' in some instances 'global offices,' and most recently the 'global lab' – real-time transnational information flows being the raw material of all three." (Ruggie 1993: 141, emphasis added)

To some extent, global in this formulation as offshore meant "elsewhere." Elsewhere, where the tax system is more convenient, and where workers' rights are less demanding for the employer. Elsewhere is beyond local or national obligations. Elsewhere is beyond the control of the public sphere. Global as nonterritorial appears as the space without restrictions, neither of terrestrial gravity nor of national bureaucracies or legal systems.

With regard to the network's applicability to political spatial forms, Balibar notes that "the global network also embodies the idea of a limit of traditional representations of political spaces, the reaching of a point where the political space becomes hardly representable" (Balibar 2009: 196). However, this is not the case for political relations which can be imagined as networked or imagined to function in a network-centric way. This is at the bottom of Bigo's analysis of Europe and its borders. In 1996 Bigo saw that the practices of control and surveillance that the police enacted with individuals in Europe were reconfigured toward networked policing and remote control (Bigo 1996: 13). This transformation is based on and expressed by multiple changes: changes with regard to the objectives of surveillance and control, with regard to technology, with regard to the legitimate location of surveillance and control, and with regard to the conception of security. In his analysis, Bigo relates the rise of the new field of internal security, which he traced in the Schengen Agreement, the Trevi Group and the Europol, to the organizational reconfiguration of security agencies in Europe. His central question has been, whether the 'new' network centric approach can be interpreted as a response to the emergence of transnational criminal networks and the perceived necessity of prosecution across borders, or second, as an effect of increasing Europeanization or third, whether the reasons are to be found within the security domain itself (ibid: 15). His answer: the restructuring of police work across Europe does not respond to new threats, but endogenously invents a new field of operation. This field is sketched as transnational, erratic and itself unpoliced, and thus requires new forms of policing. Both the notion of internal security and of transnational risks mutually strain each other. Bigo describes this scenario which is at the bottom of the security field as a security continuum. Bigo's central argument which he continues to develop until today, is the increasing self-sufficiency of the security field as a (transnational) network (see particularly Bigo 1996, 2000, 2006, 2014).

The image as well as the functioning of a political border change in this perspective: "Rather than the edge or the wall, the border becomes a strategic node within a transnational network of control" (Walters 2004: 682). Walters describes Bigo's border conception as "the rise of the networked (non)border [...] in which networks of control come to substitute for the functions that were previously physically concentrated at the border" (ibid: 679-680). According to Walters, Bigo sketches a "networked (non)border" which is constituted by "a joint responsibility and the locus of a new practice of police cooperation" (ibid: 682) rather than a dividing line. Stefan Kaufmann, who also draws on Bigo's concept of securitization when analyzing the reconfiguration of EU borders, emphasizes, in addition to changes in organization and justification, consequences for the topography of political borders. Unlike others who saw control practices de-territorializing, Kaufmann (2006) identifies three characteristics of the new border regime which follow from the *locus* of specific control practices: first, a forward displacement (Ger.: *Vorverlagerung*) of the border which is realized by policies and military forces who exceed and redefine their area of author and field of operation; second, a tightening (Ger.: *Verdichtung*): of the border, in which border control "has been transformed from the control of border crossing points to a permanent surveillance of the entire line" (ibid: 37) and third, an infolding (Ger.: *Einstülpung)* of the border: control and surveillance, formerly executed by the border police, is appearing within the public sphere, albeit strategically dislocated. Facilitated by technological and information networks, which could be operated privately or by police forces, border control penetrates the inside of a nation-state. Balibar's ubiquity of borders is 'tamed' by this border topography.

The border is either organized as a network or it is overcome by networks. Doris Schweitzer's analysis of Manuel Castells's concept of a network-society shows that the topography of a networked society allows for a radicalization of bordering processes. In the context of border studies, the term "assemblages" (Ong/Collier 2005; Marcus/Saka 2006) refers to the distribution of bordering practices and institutions across geographical space, on different political scales, and through technologies. Ultimately, the term network is as dazzling as it is omnipresent. The thing that shall be described by the term network seems however, "imprecise, contradictory and indefinite" (Kaufmann 2007: 8). In this regard, the net appears, similar to the sea, as opposite of the land (Schweitzer 2011: 57). As part of a network, even law enforcement might occur elsewhere. And elsewhere implies beyond the line.

With regard to the European construction, the network metaphor also goes beyond the notion of a homogenous space. European is rather an attribute to the cities and hubs within a global connection. However, with regard to the invocation of threats and risks, the notion of network has provided the basis for a reconfigured notion of security and, in turn, different legitimate locations to the authority and competences of border polices.

2.5 EUROPE'S BORDER(S): NOVEL POLICIES, NEW PERSPECTIVES, CHALLENGED METHODOLOGIES

In modern politics, the concept of political borders is inextricably linked to the figure of the line on the one hand, and to the concept of territory on the other. A line of demarcation – be it as cartographic abstraction or military installation – indicates the scope and reach of sovereign power. Political borders thus define a spatial mandate and mark the limits of a particular order. It is this mandate that distinguishes them from other markers of social stratification and functional differentiation. And it is this mandate which prevails, while modern concepts of political organization and political space are deconstructed, reassessed and reconfigured both in the social sciences and in politics.

From the 1970s onwards, the notion of a border being grounded or located, has drained away from its compression in the symbolic and graphical form of a territorial border-line. And since the 1990s, analyzing borders does not work without at least verbally departing from the model of the Westphalian state in its Weberian description. Often this is succeeded by evoking a transformed spatiality of political borders and by describing a detachment of 'the border' from 'territory.' Now, that borders are no longer where there used to be, researchers are requested to *relocate the research field*. Where to conduct research on the external border of the EU? And what to choose as object of investigation? Is a political border – if not territorial – a disembodied research object?

Throughout the analyses reviewed in the above sections 2.2 to 2.5, the way in which spatial metaphors and imaginaries serve to unbundle the notion of the territorial border and the ideal of the Weberian state have been examined. However, the examinations have also shown that the locus of the physical border is not of central concern to the different authors they are concerned with the state of democracy (Balibar) the quality of Europe's internal polity (Zielonka, Beck/Grande), or the general tension between the European and the national level (Vobruba). Other analyses have focussed on the discrepancy between the vision of Europe as a lawful project and the discriminatory access to individual rights (Agamben). Moreover, the network metaphor has proven to be concerned with the self-sufficiency of the network itself which does not provide a vision of Europe.

Overall, the works reviewed above have proceeded to analyze political borders *as* something: *as* institution, *as* practices of selection and exclusion, *as* exception to the rule of law, *as* organized network or apparatus. They all come with the impetus to deessentialize and denaturalize political border, thereby ultimately describing what substitutes the territorial border. Schengen provoked the opportunity and the necessity to conceptualize borders without territory in breaking with the equation of geographical borders marking political authority. With regard to the novelty the Schengen rules mark, "the new" can be identified by two parallel reconfigurations:

- The authority over the legitimate means of violence is no longer monopolized, but organized in a polycentric fashion, which is to say that enforcement personnel, surveillance tools and patrolling strategies are no longer allocated in or at the expanses of a national territory (code: geography), but according to communitarian needs (code: occurrences or migratory pressure). This demonopolization results in an incongruity, if not discrepancy, between the border police mandate – that is, legal border of policing, and the legal borders of individual rights.
- At the same time, another monopoly manifests itself: the authority over the legitimate means of movement appears with the institutional necessity (that of Schengen) to pool the resources at the supranational level. Thereby an emphasis on migration and mobility policies accumulates. However, the authority over the legitimate means of movement – the latter being framed and expressed as rights of the individual(!) – is highly contested both with regard to its application, distribution and enforcement practices.
- Analyzing the interplay of these monopolies is gauging a new mode of politics, which goes beyond territorial and bio-political characteristics. The emergence of viapolitics has been sketched by William Walters (2011, 2014, 2015), and will be further assessed in the two empirical chapters of this work.

In so doing, this study of the emergence of an external EU border does not look for a substitute of the territorial border; nor will I trace its novel spatial distributedness but rather explore two construction sites of the EU external border. I will not analyze the history of these sites as breaking with the border itself; instead, I will analyze how these sites mediate that which is socially effective as the EU external border. For every site crafts the kind and quality of the border in a particular way. Empirically speaking, how does this new EU border under construction acquire acceptance, stability and validity? Methodologically speaking: how is it possible to get a graspe of political borders? Setting forth the argument that the spectral character of any border requires a methodology that focuses on the processes and results of mediation, the following chapter expounds the methodological premise of this work.

3 Thinking and Researching Political Borders

In the introduction to this study, I have already noted that the methodological uncertainty that one encounters when researching an external EU border is further complicated by the spectral character of any border. This spectral character refers to the phenomenological indeterminacy and fuzziness of borders in general. This is to say that there is no phenomenon of a border *as such*. Consequently, borders are only tangible and experienceable by their proxy or representation (cf. Cremers 1989: 38; Vasilache 2007: 38-47). The methodological uncertainty of the concrete case – the EU external border – is thus further complicated by an epistemological uncertainty concerning the study of political borders in general. In the following, I will explicate what I term 'the spectral character of a border' and ask, in a second step, about the methodological consequences of researching the EU external border(s). This section thus explores the relation between thinking and researching political borders.

3.1 THE SPECTRAL CHARACTER OF ANY BORDER

Spectral is an attribute attested to phenomena which cannot quite be grasped, the presence of which could be contested or doubted due to constant volatilization. A ghost is present as one or many apparitions, rather than as a reality. To a certain extent, the thought of it is more powerful than its materiality.

Can this attribute aptly be applied to political borders? Political borders concretize in walls, fences, surveillance gadgetry, border guards or lines of demarcation. These appearances are quite manifest, immovable, adamant, obtrusive, and sometimes hardly surmountable. Their legal-administrative decisiveness, their constructional strength and robustness bestow a concreteness, objectivity, and durability – and, in parts, also irreducibility – to political borders. At first glance this may contradict the notion of spectrality. Borders are not wafts of mist or phantasmagoric shadows through which one could pass or march through. They are rather accurately measured, clear-cut, and brutally real. And yet, we do not encounter the border *per se*, but the official enforcing it; we do not touch the border *per se*, but a wall of bricks or barbed-wire fence; neither do we cross the border itself, but the line of demarcation or the physical installation of the border-post. That which appears to us as political border is but its abstraction, representation, or appresentation (Husserl): while the cartographic border-line *abstracts* and thereby epitomizes the course and the grounding of borders,[1] the border guard *represents* what Dimitris Papadopoulos and colleagues have described as "double-R axiom," namely the simultaneous definition of "positive rights and representation within the national territory, and the non-existence of rights and symbolic presence *beyond* the nation's borders" (2008: 6, original emphasis). Finally, different material border installations – fences, flags, gates or chicken feathers attached to a bar (the examples are Cremers's 1989: 36) – appresent and thereby make visible, define and mark territories so that they become socially perceivable and effective (Cremers 1989: 29-37).

Like a specter, which *"appears* to be present itself during a visitation" (Derrida 2006: 126, original emphasis), the border appears to be present itself during the encounter between border guard and border crosser, during the study of a map, or during the contemplation of the Israeli West Bank barrier. And yet, if a researcher joins or observes these situations, contemplates the wall, or studies mapmaking, she does not study the border itself, but its apparitions, its proxies, its phantom objects. Whatever the substance of the border, it is socially available and effective via its proxies. In turn, the expectation, imagination, and belief that there is *more* – that there is, in fact, *something substantial, a valid system* behind or beyond these appearances, contributes to the relative stability and validity of a given political border. The thought of a border indeed seems more powerful than its materiality. How is this real (and by no means ephemeral) power of the border constituted? What is the substance or fabric of the border, if not its measurement, ground; the guards, or the brick in the wall?

---

1 Only few authors have analyzed the processes and epistemological premises that go into the drawing and interpreting of a line. Two notable exceptions are first, the Swedish geographer Gunnar Olsson (1991), who distinguished between three concepts of the line: the equal sign (=), the slash (/) and the dash (–) which he takes as representations of three different epistemologies, namely realism, dialectic, and signification (cf. Pickles 2004), and second, Angus Cameron (2011), who in his essay publication "Ground zero – the semiotics of the boundary line," provided a comprehensive discussion on the graphic figure of the boundary line.

Drawing on the first sociological definition of border by Georg Simmel, the substance of the border itself is not to be found in its materiality or location, but based on social relations and their interactions (Ger.: *Wechselwirkungen*)[2]. Socio-political relations as well as the collective psyche coagulate and objectify in the border. Using the example of the line of demarcation, Simmel illustrates "the incomparable firmness and clarity which the social processes of demarcation receive from being spatialized" (1997 [1908]: 144). He writes:

"Every boundary is a psychological, more precisely, a sociological event; but through its investment in a line in space, the relationship of reciprocity attains a clarity and security in both its positive and negatives sides – indeed often a certain rigidity – that tends to be denied the boundary so long as the meeting and separating of forces and rights has not yet been projected into a sensory formation, and thus as it were always remains in a status nascens." (Simmel 1997 [1908]: 144)

As "psychological" (Ger.: *seelische*) or as Simmel emphasizes "sociological events," borders result from interactions and imaginations. However, these social processes of demarcation remain events during which rights and forces compete and are negotiated, until they are "projected into a sensory formation"; until they are invested "in a line in space" or stabilized via materialization. The "relationship of reciprocity" only turns into a sociological fact when it appears as border. Drawing on Simmel, Natalià Cantó Milà underlines that "the projection of demarcation onto space strengthens the border and perpetuates it" (Milà 2006: 192). Here the emphasis lies on an aspect which has mostly been neglected in the reception of the Simmelian border definition: the coagulation, or hardening (Ger.: *Gerinnung*) of the social processes to a thing which itself becomes part of interactions.

In the course of the spatial turn, Simmel's border definition regained prevalence. His dictum that the border "is not a spatial fact with sociological effects, but a sociological fact that forms itself in space" (Simmel 1997 [1908]: 144) was often quoted to deessentialize and denaturalize the concept of the territorial border. This has corresponded to a general trend in border studies since the 1970s: borders are no longer described and analyzed in terms of geomorphological pat-

---

2 A central concept throughout Simmel's work is that of interaction. The German term "Wechselwirkungen" denotes reciprocity, reciprocal interrelations, reciprocal effects, mutual influence, without causal explanations. The English translation "interaction" does not satisfyingly transport these conceptual implications.

terns, but as social processes, practices, and imaginations. The central research interest in border studies has thus shifted from the *Where?* of borders to the *How?* of bordering (van Houtum/van Naerssen 2002; Newman 2006a, 2006b; Rumford 2006).

As a result, border studies are no longer dominated by geographers, but have become an interdisciplinary research field, in which Simmel's relational thinking has turned into an epistemological consensus. Furthermore, Simmel's definition was considered empirically bidden. Lena Laube, for instance, sees that Simmel's 1908 definition "has never had greater validity, than under the conditions of globalization" (Laube 2013: 292). In the reception of the Simmelian border definition, what can be traced in different fields since the spatial turn is the deessentializing impetus stressed by the relational character of phenomena. This has occurred to an extent so that the concept of boundedness has been awkwardly avoided, as Jeff Malpas (2012) has criticized and countered. Just as the spatial turn has fostered a proliferation, if not diffusion, of what counts as spatial, relational thinking in border studies, it has diffused what constitutes a border (Johnson et al. 2011: 61). Likewise, globalization is quoted as the empirical condition to an epistemological premise, an argument which confuses epistemological perspective and empirical finding. But this allegation cannot duly be advanced toward the Simmelian border conception. Even though Simmel did stress the socially produced character of borders, his relational thinking also acknowledged the "physical force" and the "living energy" of material products. Simmel acknowledges the material, the built environment as part of the interactions.

"once it has become a spatial and sensory object that we inscribe into nature independently of its sociological and practical sense, then this produces strong repercussions on the consciousness of the relationship of the parties. Whereas this line only marks the diversity in the two relationships, […] it becomes a living energy that forces the former together and will not allow them to escape their unity and pushes between them both like a physical force that emits outward repulsions in all directions" (Simmel 1997 [1908]: 143).

It is at this point that it becomes spooky, that the border reveals its spectrality. Not only because borders are based on social relations, which, as grounding reasons are neither tangible nor visible but rely on objectified proxies. Even more, the objectified border, the proxies, come to life and are, as borders, endowed with a "physical force," a "living energy," and a certain amount of actorness or agency. Simmel, who gave particular attention to the small things from the handle of a cup to the ruins of a castle, attested a living energy and social quality to them. As objects these things are inscribed into the environment and act independently from the sociological and practical processes that brought them about.

In a modification of the Marxian wooden table as commodity that is more than wood, one could say the following about the objectified apparitions of political borders: once a fence, the Rhine or the Mediterranean acts the part of a political border (Ger.: *tritt auf als*) "it changes into a thing which transcends sensuousness" (Marx 1976: 163). As a commodity, the table is no longer merely made out of wood, but it is product and perpetuator of the societal relations of production. Borders, fences, gates, rivers and information systems are no longer merely made of barbed wire, bricks, water, and information, but are products and perpetuators of the selection and prioritization of societal relations.

These interrelations are constantly fixed – in the sense of being repaired, maintained, and iterated – by all of the border's proxies. Similarly, the social relations that are regulated and expressed via passports, databases, migrant vessels, fences, visa or asylum applications synthesize into the space of a legitimate border, which is valid *qua* itself. That which is socially produced comes into life as a border – as a thing. Not only does it structure the relations between individuals, but the products also relate among each other.

Thus, the spectral character of a border does not stem from its liminality. It is rather the "living energy" and "physical force" of a border's proxies which renders the political border an odd thing. Proxies are endowed with a quality that Marx (1976 [1867]: 128) termed "ghostly/phantom objectivity" (Ger.: *gespenstische Gegenständlichkeit*). The living relations and interaction that produced it – in Marx's case the commodity; in the case of this study, the border – are dead. Its constituting forces and its reasons are atrophied and obliterated. What remains is the border, with the insistence to be maintained and its claim to be vital to sociation (Ger.: *Vergesellschaftung*). In other words, what remains is the material presence of the border's proxies, their objectivity, which claims to be vital on its own. This isn't to say that its existence was independent from human production; however, it is stressed that its existence continues without the iteration of the process of production. The border continues being, remains there, physically bearing a lively energy.

The spectral character of any border implies that border objects and their proxies are of a ghostly objectivity. *Qua* the border object, a quality of the relations between people and a mode of interaction turns into an imperative that drives their relations. Once objectified, the thing requires to be purchased, obtained or protected; social interactions are redirected toward that purpose. Subsequently, the malleable character of societal relations disappears from view. This phenomenon that "a relation between people takes on the character of a thing and thus acquires a 'phantom objectivity,' an autonomy that seems so strictly rational and all-embracing as to conceal every trace of its fundamental nature: the relation between people," has been described as reification by Georg Lukács (1976 [1923]: 83). Just as the commodity has been interpreted as the ideological statue (Ger.: *ideologisches Standbild*) of the societal relations of production (Marchart 2013: 84), the border can be interpreted as the ideological statue of the societal relations of inclusion and exclusion.

The interrelations with the proxy turn into primary interaction. The border is protected and subverted; it is torn down, climbed and defended. The social relations that crystallize in and at the border are hardly straightforward. Relations are mediated by the manifold proxies that make up a given border. Ultimately, the spectral character of borders encompasses two aspects. First is the paradox intrinsic to reification, and second is the manifoldness of possible material manifestations and symbolic representations in apparitions. Reification is based on the paradox that "a relational social structure is objectified" (Ger.: *verdinglicht*), and that thereby "its processual character is quiesced and shut down" (Marchart 2013: 84). This is traceable for the case of the territorial border that has been reified and indeed naturalized to the extent that its relational and processual character is hidden from view.

Methodologically, the paradox intrinsic to reification prompts the question whether it is more strategic to research process or product, machine or performance, relations or object. The second aspect of the spectral character of a border lays in its manifold apparitions. Jacques Derrida has described this spectral contextual reference in interpretation of the Marxian analysis of commodity fetishism in the following way: "One represents it [the specter] to oneself, but it is not present, itself, in flesh and blood" (Derrida 2006: 126). Proxies, that is, the representations (of the border) that one presents to oneself, are an expression of how a political border is "presumed, reconstructed, [and] fantasized" (ibid: 24).

A border, therefore, does not exist. It is never "present, itself, in flesh and blood," but finds expression in how we construct its proxies. The border thus appears in a variety of material and symbolic forms. It assumes concrete appearance, it falls into place as proxy. In its etymological proximity to spectrum, 'spectral' also refers to the arbitrariness of the form through which the societal processes of demarcation manifest themselves. This has also been expressed by Balibar's characterization of borders as heterogeneous or vacillating, which always appear here and there in different forms. Here it is again clear that Balibar didn't describe the new geographical locations or positions of borders, but rather new apparitions. These new apparitions, however, couldn't emerge without the specification of a place. "Appearance requires an openness that allows emergence, but appearance, as it is always the appearance of some thing, is always a *taking place*, which is to say that it is always the establishing of a certain *there"* (Malpas 2012: 237, original emphasis).

The manifoldness in appearances in possible representations of the border demands that the selection of the object of investigation (the one object that is researched out of many) may be justified with regard to the objectives of a study. Calling on the spectral character of any border effectively means readjusting the researcher's spotlight: the border is not socially produced, but its proxies are. In other words, if a border only appears as *some* thing, if it is only available and experienceable via its proxies, this has consequences for the research process. Proxies are the concrete and material manifestation of that which is imagined and believed to be the reason, the ground, the ought-to-be of the specter. It is the production and construction that is available to research. Hence we must ask, what status do the different proxies have in the research process? What weight should be attributed to selected border objects when researching the empirical example of the EU external border? And which research objects and research sites should be selected in the first place? The following sections address these methodological questions. I will argue that the Latourian distinction between intermediary and mediator allows for a research perspective that works through the paradox of reification.

3.2 MEDIATED BORDERING AND THE TERRITORIAL BORDER AS INTERMEDIARY

Realizing that the political border of interest is only available in the form of proxies, a researcher readjusts the spotlight shedding full light on a border's proxy. What does she see? Well, a proxy; in the case of this study, it could be a gate, a wall, a situation, a practice, a database, an administrative line of demarcation, a refugee camp. Yet, the central question at this point is less: *What does one see?* but rather: *How does one look at it?* How does one interpret the *relation* between a given proxy, for example the database of the Schengen Information System and the object of investigation – that is, the EU external border? Acknowledging the spectral character of any border, a researcher cannot tackle the proxy as a representation or abstraction of societal demarcation, but might realize that what she is looking at is a construction site through which a social thing is mediated. The proxy mediates a certain aspect and quality of the object of inquiry.

What has been described as proxy so far, has been termed "mediator" in the works of Bruno Latour (cf. particularly Latour 1993: 79-82, 2005: 37-42, 106-120). According to the French philosopher, mediators "transform, translate, distort and modify the meaning or the elements they are supposed to carry" (Latour 2005: 39). That which is carried, the social thing, the actor-network, or in the case of this study the border, is garnered by many mediators which each contribute their fabric and functioning to the apparition and social effectiveness of an EU external border. The mobilization, relation and interplay of many mediators allow the border to appear, and stabilize the demarcation iterated via the manifold mediators. At the same time, each mediator has its own mode of being produced and being appropriated. The durability of social relations – and a border is a cardinal example for a relation being perceived as durable (robust, natural and lasting) – is yielded by material artifacts, technologies, maps or legal items which condense interactions and resolve conflicts among humans. In fact, "whenever we discover a stable social relation, it is the introduction of some non-humans that accounts for this relative durability" (Callon/Latour 1994: 359). These non-humans are the proxies, the items, the representations, sites or mediators available to research. Now, how to go about these proxies; how to turn them into research sites?

When investigating political borders, the researcher deals with a phenomenon that is often perceived to be quasi natural or primordial. According to Latour these phenomena are thought of as intermediaries, that is, as things that are 'out there,' ready-made. Intermediaries do not appear to be socially produced, but rather does it seem as if they have, in fact, produced, shaped, and constituted society. These intermediaries appear to be at the bottom of things. Moreover, certain phenomena are not only *thought of* as intermediaries, but indeed *behave* as such, as a "black box counting for one" (Latour 2005: 39). These intermediaries are extremely autonomous. They are not in the mix, but set the terms. These intermediaries "transport meaning or force without transformation" (ibid); they define, without being defined.

The modern territorial border can duly be regarded as an intermediary. It claims irreversibility for itself and the state it demarcates. Moreover, borders and territory seem only to be definable in mutual reference to one another. In modern politics, the French legal theorist Paul Alliès critically notes that "territory always seems linked to possible definitions of the state; it gives it a physical basis which seems to render it inevitable and eternal" (Allies 1980: 9). In fact, the territorial border is the type of political border that is reified and naturalized to the extent that despite contemporary globalization theories and the proliferation of flows it is often perceived as the last landmark, and an almost cardinal point of orientation. Despite being engaged by discussion on globalization theories and spatially sensitive sciences as well as their traps and turns, and despite vehement countering of substantialistic take on borders, the territorial border maintains an explanatory status. In fact, it seems that the territorial border even trips the spatial turn and globalization theories. By providing data on cross-border movement, for instance, territorial borders paradoxically function as an indicator and a place of measurement for the space of flows. Concepts of exclusion, fixity, and the topographical imagination of surface, which have been critically assessed in the works of the spatial turn, are reinserted into border studies through the type "territorial border" (Elden 2010a: 801; Painter 2010).

Moreover, together with the spatial turn and its deessentializing and denaturalizing impetus, there is a general unease among social scientists when taking the borders grounding or material presence into account. At times, researchers appear afraid of buying into a substantialistic take on borders. For instance, the Italian scholar Paolo Cuttitta, rejects the distinction between territorial and social borders, argued for by David Miller and Sohail Hashmi (Miller/Hashmi 2001) stating that their distinction was misleading, since it would suggest that territorial borders were not socially produced. However, what Cuttitta rejects is neither the concept of territorial border nor of social borders. He finds fault with the allegedly misleading contrasting juxtaposition, as he apprehends a conclusion by analogy between territory and an essentialist conception of borders. In his own works, however, Cuttitta finds that the strength of territoriality from which the border profited as a means to define and secure a socio-political entity, is now penetrating social, political and legal practices globally (Cuttitta 2006: 38, 2007). What strength does he have in mind, which does not stem from physical terrain or material installation? And did this strength then change materiality?

When dealing with an object of inquiry that behaves as intermediary, deconstructing it as social product counters essentialism, however, it does not explain the strength, quality and effectiveness of a political border. This is why in the aforementioned example territory maintains its somewhat ghostly strength despite being denounced as socially produced. Moreover, with emphasis on social construction borders are by implications evoked as volatile and up to change by (subversive) practices.

The methodological consequence of this perspective is to study the border as practices. However, borders are neither produced nor reproduced 'bottom-up' on a daily basis; it is not border guards who produce the border through their patrolling routines, nor is it border violations which shape its constitution. Also, political borders are not as volatile as an emphasis on bordering practices might suggest. In the case of this "rare exception," Latour notes, in which a phenomenon behaves as intermediary, it "has to be accounted for by some extra work – usually by the mobilization of even more mediators" (Latour 2005: 40). This quotation elucidates why things that behave as intermediaries are so powerful, even to the effect of naturalization or sacralization: due to many, many mediators; no phantom strength or mystical force, but countless material mediators, each contributing to the stability of a social relation while at the same time leaving its individual qualitative mark. As

"most of the features of what we mean by social order – scale, asymmetry, durability, power, hierarchy, the distribution of roles [and also the international state system with its political borders] – are impossible even to define without recruiting socialized nonhumans. Yes, *society is constructed, but not socially constructed.*" (Latour 1999: 198, original emphasis)

Therefore, neither the production of borders nor its reconfigurations should be analyzed from the perspective of social practices. For the case of borders, and other intermediaries that behave as such, it makes sense to actually start the analysis with the sites, proxies, items that mediate them, and explore how it does what it does, and how this doing came about.

In sum, territorial mediation has been so successful for the case of the political border that the territorial border behaves as intermediary and provides an intermediary imagination of the international system. Acknowledging the spectral character of a border does not imply that the political border in question was not real only because it is constructed via proxies. It rather implies that something as durable as a political border is mediated. In fact, it even has to be mediated in order to acquire durability. Nevertheless, albeit from the ethnographic perspective, things and apparitions can be effective as intermediaries, the researcher should neither consider his object of investigation readymade nor counter it as a fetish. He is rather asked to decipher the many mediators that support the intermediary imagination. The spectral character of any border reminds the researcher that her object of inquiry is only available to her in terms of proxies. These proxies can be *observed* to behave *either* as mediators *or* as intermediaries. However, when *analyzing* them, the researcher must take them as mediators. "At the level of observation, intermediaries are an integral part of the empirical phenomenon and must therefore be taken into consideration; as prefaces of the observer, however, they are theoretical artifacts which must be avoided as far as possible" (Schulz-Schaeffer 2008: 149).

3.3 RESEARCHING POLITICAL BORDERS: *IN SITU* OR *IN ACTU*?

When researching any given political border the question thus is: How can a researcher avoid getting trapped by an intermediary? How to get around the fact that one does take the observation for the border? Before laying out the notion of "mediated bordering" – which provided the title of this book – I shall illustrate further the difference between mediator and intermediary with reference to three works of site-specific art. All three projects engage with the question of what constitutes, expresses or produces art, while at the same time problematizing and irritating the relation between the 'being art' and the process of 'producing art'; its being made, its being staged and its taking place. These works may bestow a sensibility to the challenge of analyzing mediation, but also to the analytic gaze that the focus on mediation opens up. The following examples are presented as snapshots and serve to play with perspectives, challenging the idea of art, the border appearing *as* something.

3.3.1 Site Specificity

In 1991, a thirty-year-old man got permission to collect species and plants in the rainforest of Venezuela. He spent three weeks in the Orinoco River basin outside Caracas. Once a week, a boat would reach him to pick up transparent boxes containing the pieces of tropical nature, he had collected.

This time it was not an anthropologist who dwelled in the tropics, but the artist Mark Dion, who was working on his exhibition *On Tropical Nature*. Contrary to a scientist's expectation, these boxes were not transferred to a laboratory, where the "various plants and insects as well as feathers, mushrooms, nests and stones" (Kwon 2002: 28) could have been microscopically studied. Instead they were taken to 'Sala Mendoza,' an art institution in Caracas. There, "[i]n the gallery space of the Sala, the specimens [...] were uncrated and displayed like works of art in themselves" (ibid). *On Tropical Nature* not only displayed these pieces of nature. The installation also included those artifacts and instruments that allowed Dion to collect, study and display tropical nature. Likewise, a photograph displaying Dion with a butterfly net in the middle of 'nature' turned the artist into an explorer as much as it defined the 'being out there exploring' as a performance of art.[3]

---

3 The photograph, taken by Bob Braine, has been reproduced in Dion (2003).

The issues raised by Dion's art project *On Tropical Nature* not only concerns the nature of (tropical) nature, thus challenging concepts such as authenticity and originality. Dion also contributes to the debate on cultural interventions and representations with regard to nature. Moreover, *On Tropical Nature* broaches the question of what constitutes a *site*, a prevalent issue in art since the late 1960s. Where is the place, the *site* of things?

Where does one have to go in order to encounter, experience, or study *tropical nature* or, in the case of this study, the *EU external border*? Is it into the jungle or into a museum (for the case of Dion); is it to Lampedusa, the Balkan route or the Frontex headquarters in Warsaw (for the case of the EU external border)? Applied to political borders, generally one could ask further: which piece, which segment of the Cold War does one look at when holding a piece of the Berlin Wall in one's hands? A piece of a political border or a museal artifact? Does radar, does the SIS database or the barbed wire fence in Ceuta reveal the EU's external border? What exactly are we looking for in the search for "tropical nature" or the "EU external border" respectively? Ultimately, Dion's work touches upon ontological questions while, at the same time, pushing the need for a localizable origin and the grounding of essence. In *On Tropical Nature* he dissolved these demands praxeographically – as has been done in border studies when gauging the nature of the border. Does the praxeographic, deconstructivist approach obscure or reveal the nature of nature. Does it obscure or reveal the nature of a given political border?

Richard Serra's *Tilted Arc* of 1981 (figure 2), by contrast, emphasizes notions of original and fixed location. Serra responded to the United States Arts-in-Architecture program with a massive curved wall (of 3.65 meter height, 36.58 meter width and 6,5 centimeter depth) built out of corten steel in the middle of the Federal Plaza in New York.

By means of the *Tilted Arc*, Serra put emphasis on the uniqueness of a work and its particular relation to its location. As such, he argued that it was non-transferable to another location. Reactions to the *Tilted Arc*, however, were mixed. The ones who worked in the adjoining offices facing the Federal Plaza found it inconvenient to walk around the massive wall at lunchtime or when rushing to the office in the morning. According to city officials, the arc attracted rats, garbage, and crime. Yet, attempts to have *Tilted Arc* removed were fiercely countered by Serra himself, as he considered his work of art in relation to its site, and not a random artifact independent of its environment.

Figure 2: Richard Serra, "Tilted Arc," Federal Place NY, (destroyed)

Source: http://art-nerd.com/newyork/site-of-richard-serras-tilted-arch/
© VG Bild-Kunst, Bonn 2020

"To remove is to destroy" was thus his answer to the different attempts to have his work shifted elsewhere. "As I pointed out," Serra elaborated,

"Tilted Arc was conceived from the start as a site-specific sculpture and was not meant to be 'site-adjusted' or […] 'relocated.' Site-specific works deal with the environmental components of given places. The scale, size and location of site-specific works are determined by the topography of the site, whether it be urban or landscape or architectural enclosure. The works become part of the site and restructure both conceptually and perceptually the organization of the site." (quoted in Kwon 2002: 12)

In 1989, the *Tilted Arc* was deinstalled and destroyed. In 1989 the Iron Curtain also fell. In the case of political borders, deinstallation is more complicated. This isn't to say that Serra's *Tilted Arc* was no political issue. Still, when border posts were deinstalled as a consequence of the Schengen Agreement, this did not mean that the national borders between France and Germany, for instance, no longer existed. There seems to be a certain 'rest.'

Figure 3: Daniel Buren, "Within and Beyond the Frame," 1973

Source: Souvenir photo, at: https://blogs.uoregon.edu/danielburen/posts/
© VG Bild-Kunst, Bonn 2020

A third impetus in site-specific art can be interpreted as a critical engagement with institutional frames of art practices and valuation. For example, with *Within and Beyond the Frame* of 1973, Daniel Buren literally crossed boundaries by hanging one half of his installation out of the museum's window (figure 3).

The museum was the conventional frame where art is supposed to be found, and which bestows a sense of art to the things it frames, maybe by means of a spotlight, a signpost, and the very fact that it is placed in an art institution. In a refined manner, Daniel Buren asks for the appropriate place of art, and puts the focus on irritating this meaning: are the rags, which are hanging 'outside' on the clothesline no longer art, as they left the frame of a museum? Is the attribution applied to things dependent on their location? For the purposes of this study: does it make a difference whether a migrant arrives at the airport, is found on a truck, or on a boat off the coast of Lampedusa? In Buren's installation, a decoding and recoding of conventions, a window of emancipation is opened by irritation. Applied again to political borders, our gaze is turned to the institutional set-up – to the border *as institution*.

That which might irritate in art not only irritates but confounds political borders. When representatives of a nation's border move beyond their frame – that is, beyond the territorial borders of the nation deploying and mandating said borders, their presence irritates and requires a situational mandate. In application of the distinction between mediator and intermediary, these projects can be described as sites of interventions (where art is mediated), as opposed to the site of effects (where art behaves as intermediary, or rather where things behave as art). These engagements with site-specific art bring to the fore a methodological finesse that boils down to difference between researching borders *in actu* or *in situ*.

3.3.2 In Situ or In Actu?

When Stefan Kaufmann, Ulrich Bröckling and Eva Horn write in the introduction to their anthology on border violators (Ger.: *Grenzverletzter*) that borders "only exist *in actu*, as technical devices and social arrangements of inclusion and exclusion as well as of opening" (Kaufmann/Bröckling/Horn 2002: 7, original emphasis), their statement entails a similar tension as described above. Are borders constituted via performance or via machines? Where is the load in this socio-technical hybrid of "technical devices and social arrangements" (ibid)? Should a given border be studied as process or product? While negating the existence of a border as such, the authors deploy a praxeological concept of borders, in which humans not only perform bordering, but also devices and arrangements. They continue:

"No matter how narrow or wide meshed the bordering forces set the filter between inside and outside, they always distinguish between lawful and unlawful crossings, between legal and illegal border crossers. [...] The border regime may change, what remains is the principle of selection." (Kaufmann/Bröckling/Horn 2002: 7)

The border is identified by its filtering function and observed in the devices and arrangements that *perform* this function. It is this performance that is analyzed when gauging the existence of a border *in actu*.

With a somewhat different impetus, although with a focus on bordering practices, too, Sabine Hess and Vassilis Tsianos propose to analyze borders *in situ*, "in the sense of a *doing borders* as a dynamic field of conflict and negotiation between different local, regional, national and transnational actors" (Hess/Tsianos 2010: 248, original emphasis). Their idea is to study the border as it is taking place and more important so, as it is contested, crossed, and violated. They argue for an "inductive praxeographical method" which is able to reveal "the conflicting genesis and implementation of the border regime from the perspective of the many actors involved" (ibid: 256). In this perspective, a given border can only be analyzed in the local or rather situational contexts, where "an enormous gap between theory, 'paper' and practice is revealed" (ibid).

The tension between these two praxeographic approaches reflects the fact that a site of intervention (where the object of investigation is mediated) can be approached from very different points of departure. (1) First, the site can be analyzed in terms of tools and apparatuses. This would center attention on the appropriation of the object of investigation and the translations and mediations inscribed into it. (2) Second, the object of investigation, the site, could be studied by a sort of mini-genealogy, which would investigate how it has been produced, as well as what kind of decisions, beliefs, consensus, rules and beliefs are built into it and have become part of the site (3) Third, a given site can be analyzed in terms of contestations and struggles. All three trajectories are part of a praxeological or rather praxeographic turn; they shed light on different aspects of construction.

The notion of "mediated bordering" is part of that turn and takes on board a specific methodology. Rather than focusing on the performance, on "doing border," the impetus of "mediated bordering" centers attention on the generalizable principle that is stabilized by the iteration and institutionalization of ideas, practices, and obligations. Mediators – as the sites of these iterations and institutionalizations – are studied to understand how stabilization is brought about and made possible. Moreover, they are examined in order to trace and understand the quality of the (larger) thing that is mediated. The distinction between site of effects and site of intervention helps to pinpoint this. The site of effects – in the case of this study: the external EU border – can be examined by assessing the sites of intervention: in this case, different sites where bordering is mediated and thus researchable. According to Knut Ebeling, this (site-specific) methodology reflects the premises that "each site gives away a different visibility or different sight and therefore a different theory of history" (Ebeling 2007: 321). As a methodological approach to border studies, this allows us to pay special attention to the performances, practices and struggles, the artifacts, things, and material installations as well as the frames, rules and institutions that become part of a border's fabric. This kind of approach underlines the notion of site-specificity in the sense that selected research objects, practices, interactions, or sites do not merely 'represent,' 'manifest' or 'reflect' the object of investigation (in this case an external EU border) but rather substantively bring it about. While the border remains spectral, its mediators can be studied, for bordering is mediated.

EUROSUR – The European Border Surveillance System

Part II: EUROSUR – The European Border Surveillance System

Since December 2, 2013, the European Border Surveillance System, EUROSUR, has been operational. This is to say that, since that day, most EU member states share "border related information" via a designated electronic network, the EUROSUR network.

The immediate purpose of EUROSUR is the generation of a situational picture, the so-called European Situational Picture (ESP). For this purpose, information is exchanged between EU member states and the Frontex agency. Apart from the information sent by participating member states, Frontex receives and processes information in agreement with third parties and uses surveillance information from different apparatuses such as radar, satellite, or drones. The visualization of the information is executed by means of a geographic information system (GIS). The ESP is then circulated among EUROSUR participants. The integration of information in the ESP is thought to increase "situational awareness" and the "reaction capability" along the external borders of the EU.[1]

Yet, after more than five years of being operational, it is still unclear whose "reaction capability" it is meant to increase: will the hunter be able to fence off migrants earlier, in a spatiotemporal sense, before they can claim rights or asylum in the EU? Or will the friend be fast enough to save migrants' lives at sea?

So far, EUROSUR's intrinsic ambivalence has not been resolved in favor of one side. While its success is attributed to knowledge items such as trend or risk analysis anticipating "migratory pressure" and the course of migrants' routes,

---

1   Regulation (EU) No 1052/2013 of the European Parliament and of the Council of October 22, 2013 establishing the European Border Surveillance System (Eurosur), in: OJ L 295/11-26, November 6, 2013, [hereafter cited as EUROSUR Regulation (EU) No 1052/2013], Art. 1.

this respective knowledge is apparently not used for coordinating rescue operations: The documented number of migrants drowning in the Mediterranean Sea has increased fivefold since EUROSUR became operational, from 600 deaths at sea in 2013 to 3,538 in 2014; 3,771 in 2015; 5,096 in 2016; 3,139 in 2017 and 2,277 in 2018. Estimates for 2019: 820 by July 31, 2019.[2]

This part of the book will not, however, focus on the operational performance and consequences of the European Border Surveillance System. Rather, it will reconstruct the development phase of EUROSUR. This focus on the development phase is based on the premise that certain aspects of EUROSUR can only be made sense of when reconstructing the negotiations, the work involved, and the resolution of controversies that preceded the system. The focus lays on the political objectives and normative will that went into the making of the system. During the process of establishing a network, however, many tools, talents and tactics are needed that might not be part of the final product, not even its maintenance. In other words: the politics of the development process cannot necessarily be fully reconstructed from the final product. Temporary concessions sometimes become invisible once the system is up and running. Consequently, the following examination of EUROSUR's formation deals with the period of its political, legal and technical development as well as the respective test phases and negotiations involved.[3] The development phase – from the commissioning of the EUROSUR Roadmap in February 2008 to when the EUROSUR Regulation took effect in December 2013 – will thus be the period of investigation.

The development phase comprised two parallel processes: on the one hand, the politically and legally sustainable drafting of a generally acceptable regula-

---

2   Numbers according to UNHCR statistics, at: http://data.unhcr.org/mediterranean/regional.php (accessed July 31, 2019), and according to UNHCR news of January 24, 2014, at: https://www.unhcr.org/news/latest/2014/7/53d0e2d26/unhcr-calls-urgent-european-action-end-refugee-migrant-deaths-sea.html (accessed July 31, 2019). For a discussion on the availability of data concerning the deaths of migrants at sea as well as the different sources and methods of data collection, and the politics of these numbers, see section 8.1.3.

3   Sometimes development and planning phases are even the subject of a monograph without yielding an actual result. For a famous example, see Latour's analysis of the technological vision of a personal rapid transit system in Paris called Aramis (Latour 2002 [1993]).

tion; and, on the other, the development of an IT application to make the EUROSUR network technically feasible.

This process yielded two products: the EUROSUR Regulation of 22 October 2013 and the electronic EUROSUR network – in other words, the IT application. Both products, the software and the regulation, are the products of a complex process of institutional negotiations between different officials of the European Commission (EC), the member states, Frontex and (not least) software engineers. Both products have also ultimately stabilized a political compromise that had been reached during the development phase, and which is – in Latour's (1986) fullest sense – *inscribed* into the system. By studying the development phase, I unpack this inscription process and inspect it for signs of controversies, crossroads, important incentives, decisive agreements and constant reservations.

This second part of the book is structured in a way that underlines my intention to separately investigate the development of these two products while also relating their mutual intertwining alternately from the perspective of each respective result. Chapter 4 starts by inspecting "EUROSUR on the screen," it traces the development of the IT application by outlining selected elements of EUROSUR's graphical user interface and by exploring the way these technical fixtures emerged and gained acceptance during the development phase. Chapter 5 explores the process of EUROSUR's legal establishment, thereby illustrating to what extent EUROSUR by its Regulation accomplishes the next step in the EU's Integrated Border Management (IBM). Finally, chapter 6 discusses the effect of the parallel development of software and regulation, outlining in how EUROSUR's dual development not only facilitates the exchange of information, but also *mediates* the outline of an external EU border.

4 "EUROSUR on the Screen"

> When I first saw the EUROSUR on the screen,
> I finally realized what it was all about.
> *BG Major Świąteka[1]*

Today, EUROSUR is perceived and identified through the cartographic image of the European situational picture (ESP). The ESP, which is generated by a geographic information system (GIS) and visualized as a map with border-related information, emblematically stands for the exchange of information between EU member states and the Frontex agency. This "EUROSUR on the screen" is the object that is shown when the EUROSUR project is presented in public. For instance, when Erik Berglund, then Director of Capacity Building at Frontex, spoke about EUROSUR during a workshop at the European Parliament in 2012, he provided a screenshot of the map, commenting that this was what EUROSUR looked like.[2]

---

1   Border Guard Major Aleksandra Świąteka (Director of the International Relations Office, Polish Border Guard, Warsaw): "The Commission's proposal for EUROSUR," presentation during the conference "Keeping the EU's External Borders Secure. Frontex and the Use of New Technologies" at the Academy of European Law (ERA) in Trier on May 15 and 16, 2012 [hereafter cited as BG Major Świąteka: EUROSUR Presentation (May 16, 2012)]. The statement quoted is from a bilateral conversation following her presentation.
2   Erik Berglund (Head of Capacity Building at Frontex): "European Border Surveillance System (EUROSUR): Objectives and State of Play," presentation during the workshop "An Emerging e-Fortress-Europe? Border Surveillance, Frontex and Migration Control" at the European Parliament in Brussels on June 26, 2012, at: http://www.gruene-europa.de/an-emerging-e-fortress-europe-7509.html (accessed June 26, 2012).

This statement particularly and only gains relevance when considering that, during the first four years of the development phase – and thus also during the first years of my research – there was neither a map nor an image connected to the EUROSUR system. It was a vision that was lacking visualization. "How will it look" was thus an incredibly pressing question, particularly since the different elements that were supposed to be integrated by EUROSUR are quite heterogeneous: the 2008 EUROSUR Roadmap[3] mentions different authorities and existing surveillance systems, a vast amount of discontinuously generated information, such as occurrence reports by member states, Frontex's risk analysis, police and intelligence information from Europol, geodetic and meteorological data, daily news, close to real-time surveillance data sent by surveillance gadgetry such as radar or satellite, as well as information from the "pre-frontier area" provided, for instance, by Immigration Liaison Officers (ILO). In being able to "show" EUROSUR, Berglund allegedly demonstrated what the system amounted to, and that it all fit into one picture.

"How will it look?" was, however, more than a question of curiosity, which I as a researcher shared. The availability of a desktop IT application was also a critical element in the development phase, as the quotation heading this section illustrates. "When I first saw the EUROSUR on the screen, I finally realized what it was all about," Border Guard Major Aleksandra Świąteka, Director of the International Cooperation Bureau of the Border Guard Headquarters in Warsaw, reported of the pilot phase. Ostensibly, the electronic map – the "EUROSUR on the screen" – is where 'things' come together. According to Świąteka, seeing the electronic map helps to understand and justify the practical efforts and institutional restructuring that the European Commission has required of member state authorities in the development phase of the EUROSUR since 2008. It is on the screen where efforts come together.

This chapter inspects the "EUROSUR on the screen" in order to explore the drawing together and the concentration of efforts that went into the EUROSUR. The site-inspection explores the communication format that is offered and required by the application's graphical user interface (GUI). I start by describing the graphical features of the GUI, such as menu items and design. I then trace their development by looking into controversies and variations that preceded the technical implementation onscreen. Finally, the digital 'objects' and their devel-

---

[3] European Commission (2008): Examining the Creation of a European Border Surveillance System (EUROSUR), COM(2008) 68 final (February 13, 2008), [hereafter cited as EUROSUR Roadmap, COM(2008) 68 final].

opments are correlated to their textual fixation in the EUROSUR Regulation. The chapter thus looks into the question of how political compromises are translated and operationalized into IT classifications, which in turn amount to binding rules in a regulation. Furthermore, the particularities of the European situational picture (ESP) and the Common Pre-frontier Intelligence Picture (CPIP) which also (e)merge "on screen" are discussed. The chapter ends with a discussion on visualization as the most powerful form of meditation in the EUROSUR network. The ESP lends the supranational EU border the necessary image and the necessary appreciation, thereby accomplishing a level of integration and Europeanization that hitherto and otherwise would have been impossible.

4.1 EUROSUR'S GRAPHICAL USER INTERFACE: COMMUNICATION DEVICE, FORMAT, NETWORK

Using the EUROSUR network means accessing a password-protected graphical user interface (GUI) on a personal computer. Once logged in, the user has access to an electronic map portraying the situation along the external borders of the EU in the form of a geo-tagged depiction of "border-related" information. The center of the GUI consists of a representation of the European continent in white on a light blue background. This acts as a kind of pinboard to which border-related information on a given geographical location can be added in the form of tags that include various expandable data fields. The interface has interactive features that allow the user to both read and input information.

The electronic map of the EUROSUR network and its graphical user interface were presented to me in the context of a "briefing"[4] with the responsible project manager for the EUROSUR network at Frontex in May 2012. The project manager has been in charge of the development, modeling and programming of the EUROSUR network and its graphical user interface since November 2009,

---

4 The "briefing" was offered to me instead of a participant observation in the Frontex Situational Center (FSC) that I initially asked for. This seemingly insignificant change of terms underlines how Frontex maintains the prerogative of interpretation. Neither the agency nor its services remain passive while under observation; rather, it is the agency who informs those "outside the border guard community" by means of a briefing. My object of investigation thus turned itself into the subject of explanation.

88 | Mediated Borders

Figure 4: EUROSUR on the screen

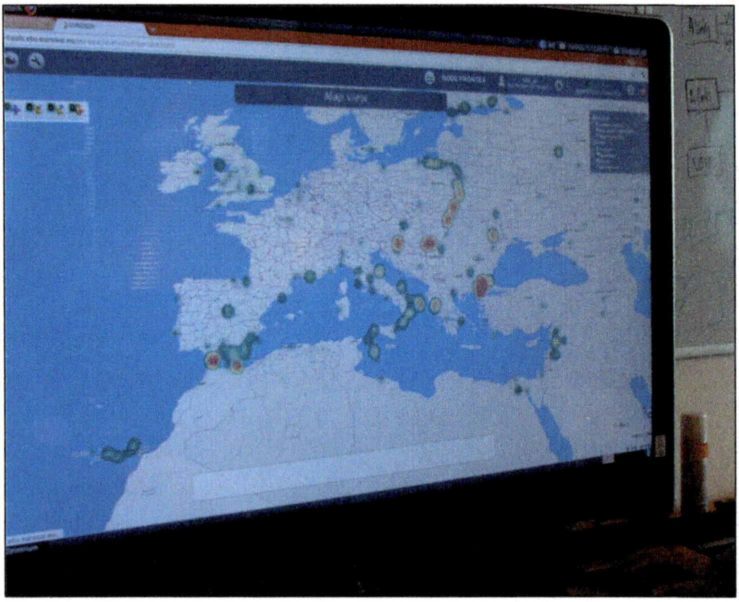

Source: own photograph, taken in May 2012

and he has been discussing and negotiating the system's features with the participating member states since March 2010. During our conversation[5] he appeared to highly identify with the computer-generated network, which culminated in the sentence "I am the network." To him, his being the network not only consists of his expertise in software engineering, but also his bringing together member states and convincing them to routinely share information.

---

5   Both the "briefing" with the project manager [hereafter cited as EUROSUR Project Manager at Frontex, personal interview (May 15, 2012)] and the follow-up telephone conversation [hereafter cited as EUROSUR Project Manager at Frontex, telephone interview (June 26, 2012)] required authorization by the Head of the Research and Development Unit at Frontex. Further communication via email also required authorization. Regarding several responses, concerning, for example, the usage of data and screenshots, authorization by the European Commission or the Head of Research and Development Unit at Frontex was required. Not all requests were granted.

"I have a long experience in international relations [...]. And I know where the difficulties are. So instead of doing a big bang technical solution, because it is not technical, what I did when I arrived here – they asked me: 'You should work in the EUROSUR network.' And I say, 'Okay, I know how to do it.' I call the member states, and got them – three, four meetings – asking them: 'What information do you manage today that you *may* be willing to share with others?' And that is the starting point. And then I will give you the minimum technology to support that exchange, the minimum!"[6]

This statement can be quite surprising in that the system developer, and thus the main figure in terms of technical feasibility and implementation, states that "it is not technical." Moreover, despite political rhetoric's emphasis of EUROSUR as a "technical framework"[7] and the "system of systems,"[8] and despite being characterized as surveillance behemoth by critical commentators,[9] EUROSUR is presented as minimalistic in terms of its technological setup. Hence, a new question arises: What kinds of difficulties are located beyond technicality?

Judging by the objectives of EUROSUR – namely, increasing the interoperability of existing surveillance systems, information exchange, and situational awareness among border agencies in the EU – and taking seriously that these are not technical issues, the focus falls on the willingness, acceptance and compliance of EU member states to share information with each other and possibly with an institution at the supranational level of the EU. Subsequently, the legal discrepancies in terms of information policies turn out to be important. Regarding already existing formats of information exchange and data sharing between law enforcement agencies in the EU, such as the Schengen Information System (SIS), European Dactyloscopy (EURODAC), and the Visa Information System (VIS), Leon Hempel and colleagues note that "interactions become even more complicated at the transnational level of the EU: the cultural, social, organiza-

---

6 EUROSUR Project Manager at Frontex, personal interview (May 15, 2012).
7 EUROSUR Roadmap, COM(2008) 68 final.
8 Ibid.
9 Initial reactions to the Commission's envisioning of EUROSUR focused on the type and amount of surveillance technology that could be connected to the system. Particularly the involvement of the arms industry and the number of FP7 projects mentioning EUROSUR as a possible "end user" initiated criticism. Often the amount of money spent in research and development has been taken as an indication of its being "big and bad." In this context, the term 'drones' was deployed as a controversial stimulus and a platform of critique (cf. Kasparek 2008; Tsianos 2009, Monroy 2011).

tional and legal differences between the data exchanging law enforcement authorities increase to a maximum of complexity" (Hempel/Carius/Ilten 2009: 5-6). In practical terms, this means that the exchange of information is hampered more by disharmony and a lack of trust between organizations (Balzacq/Hadfield 2012; Aden 2014) than by the incompatibility of the technical systems used by administrations. Generally, the exchange of information between law enforcement agencies – particularly the exchange of operational information – is a sensitive issue. A NATO press officer mentioned to me that European member states routinely refrain from sharing information rather than the other way around. Anecdotally, he noted that even the brand of toilet paper provided in ministries was treated as classified information. The general secrecy and non-disclosure claimed by administrations can be deployed as a means to keep control over one's own information and avoid being monitored from the outside.

Hempel et al. see the reluctance of some member states to exchange information as a "symbolic answer to the overall EU strategy of integrating national security policies at EU level, thereby consuming essential parts of national sovereignty" (Hempel/Carius/Ilten 2009: 10). In fact, a centralized technical system could allow unwanted control and comparability both between member states and between the states and the European Commission. Effectively, information exchange means that internal procedures become visible and hence subject to evaluation, comparison and, ultimately, control. Maintaining authority over one's own national information can be considered a strategic element against Europeanization. Moreover, exchanging information also requires compliance to a reporting format that might differ from national routines and thus cause extra work.

In order to eventually persuade member states to share information via the EUROSUR network, a bottom-up approach dominated the development phase during which all steps and propositions were carefully considered. This incrementalism is alluded to in the passage quoted above: "I call the member states, and got them, three, four meetings, asking them […]. And this is the starting point."[10] It becomes clear that convincing member states to listen to the proposal is hard work already. Creating the conditions for a starting point required "three, four meetings"[11] to mitigate skepticism and to make initial inquiries into the national status quo in terms of the availability of information and data.

---

10 EUROSUR Project Manager at Frontex, personal interview (May 15, 2012).
11 Ibid.

Thus, the starting point has been to create a general inventory of the kind of information national border authorities collect in their institutions. The tentative phrasing of "information [...] that you may be willing to share with others"[12] requires for principle willingness. Political, administrative and legal details – such as who will be entitled to request information, who will receive it, how much administrative effort or even restructuring will be needed, and how the information will be used – are set aside for the moment. By taking stock of the kind of information national authorities manage today, a list is made that assembles border-related information, which will then be further addressed.

4.1.1 Europeanization by Design: Defining and Designing "Border-Related Incidents"

As soon as a list is available, its content can be sorted, organized and categorized. Thus, according to the preliminary schema of the pilot phase, border-related incidents were to be grouped as either "illegal immigration," "crime," "crisis" or "other." The responsible project manager at Frontex (P.M.) described the genesis of the classificatory schema as follows:

P. M.: The first thing I created was a schema with four types of information and this schema is a tree that can be expanded or cut.

S.E.: And what kind of information is that?

P.M.: They [that is, the member states] say that they want to share information on illegal immigration, crime, crisis and other. [...] I am using the information of the member states here. They say: "Crisis for us is: if there was a fire in the forest and we have to abandon the [border] crossing point, this is a crisis for us, or we are using a border guard helicopter to evacuate people from a boat. This is not illegal immigration and this is not crime, so crisis." So this is the starting point: "What do you want to share?" And I facilitate that in a system which is extensible, stretchable.

My interviewee describes a situation here in which representatives from member states have exemplified their operations and difficulties related to border policing, which they were asked to group and evaluate. At face value this can be un-

---

12 EUROSUR Project Manager at Frontex, personal interview (May 15, 2012).

derstood as striving for a common heuristic ("this is crisis for us"[13]). Information-sharing has two requirements: it requires a principle willingness *and* a format that is understood and accepted by all participants. "You need to have common definitions," the Head of the Research and Development Unit at Frontex stressed, "because otherwise it is going to be a big mess." He explained:

"If somebody is considering this coming under this heading and somebody else considers this as being under another heading, and then the whole structure gets completely lost. So you have to have these common definitions before you can start developing any system like this."[14]

To achieve these two requirements, a classificatory schema needs to resonate both with the local (that is, individual) conditions of different national border authorities and with the global view of the European Commission. How things are named must thus be vague enough for all authorities to locate their issues while creating the impression of that they are represented correctly. They must also make sense in the context of a common task. The elements of such a classification must bridge and translate between the local and the global level, between national concern and European outlook. The classificatory schema for sorting border-related information that the project manager proposed to the representatives of the member states thus had to function as a "boundary object" (Star/Griesemer 1989) – that is, it had to be "both plastic enough to adapt to local needs [...], yet robust enough to maintain a common identity across sites" (ibid: 393).[15] In the case of EUROSUR's classificatory schema, the challenge was that it had to first create (rather than maintain) this common identity, which member states were reluctant.

---

13 EUROSUR Project Manager at Frontex, personal interview (May 15, 2012).
14 Head of Research and Development at Frontex, telephone interview (October 28, 2011).
15 Susan Star and James Griesemer identify four types of boundary objects: repositories, ideal types, coincident boundaries, and standardized forms. The characterization of coincident boundaries almost reads like a description of EUROSUR's functional raison d'être. They are "common objects which have the same boundaries but different internal contents. They arise in the presence of different means of aggregating data and when work is distributed over a large-scale geographic area" (Star/Griesemer 1989: 410-411).

Ultimately, the question of how to reach an agreement regarding adequate titles is centrally related to the communication of local events under a common European heading. Apart from streamlining understanding, it also concerns prioritizing issues according to relevance for the shared responsibility of Schengen borders. This is because discussing the meaning of different types of border-related information inevitably triggers a discussion on the critical point when a local phenomenon becomes an issue that should be considered a problem for the entire Schengen area. Thereby, claims and complaints by individual member states are put into comparison and hence into (a European) perspective.

The search for common definitions prepares and, if successful, also supports the formalization of information exchange. However, there is more at stake than formalization. In their study on the creation of information infrastructures and the role of categories therein, Geoffrey Bowker and Susan Star stress that "[s]eemingly purely technical issues like how to name things [...] in fact constitute much of human interaction and much of what we come to know as natural" (Bowker/Star 2000: 326). In this sense, the EUROSUR on the screen and the menu bar of its graphical user interface provide a new way of looking at the border, while also proposing a mode of naturally recognizing the external border of the EU as emerging from events, issues and trends of concern. In order to reify and naturalize EUROSUR's classificatory schema, its defined types of border-related incidents are reformulated as: (a) *technical* – which in this case means as *digital* menu items, (b) *iconographic* – they are represented as icons, and (c) *legal* – they are fleshed out in the regulation as a sub-layer of events and are partially furnished with examples. Consequently, border-related incidents appear as menu items and graphical icons on the graphical user interface (GUI) and as sub-layers of the events layer as in the software architecture of the GIS and in the legislation. In this way, the common definition of types of border-related information is successively stabilized.

Technical Framework: Border-Related Incidents as Menu Items

When the test-application was shown to me in May 2012, the schema was already part of the menu bar. By transforming the schema of four types of information into menu items, it became the first element in the infrastructure of the EUROSUR network. The schema was thus transformed from a loose question of "Under which heading would you communicate your event?" to an IT item that is materially available, selectable and clickable. Moreover, different types of border-related incidents were identified and proposed by the national coordination centers (NCCs) of member states participating in the test phase.

This resulted in a series of items in the menu bar and the so-called "incident catalogue," an inventory of all incidents relevant for the common enforcement of the external EU borders.[16]

Figure 5: Catalogue of "border-related" incidents" in the test application

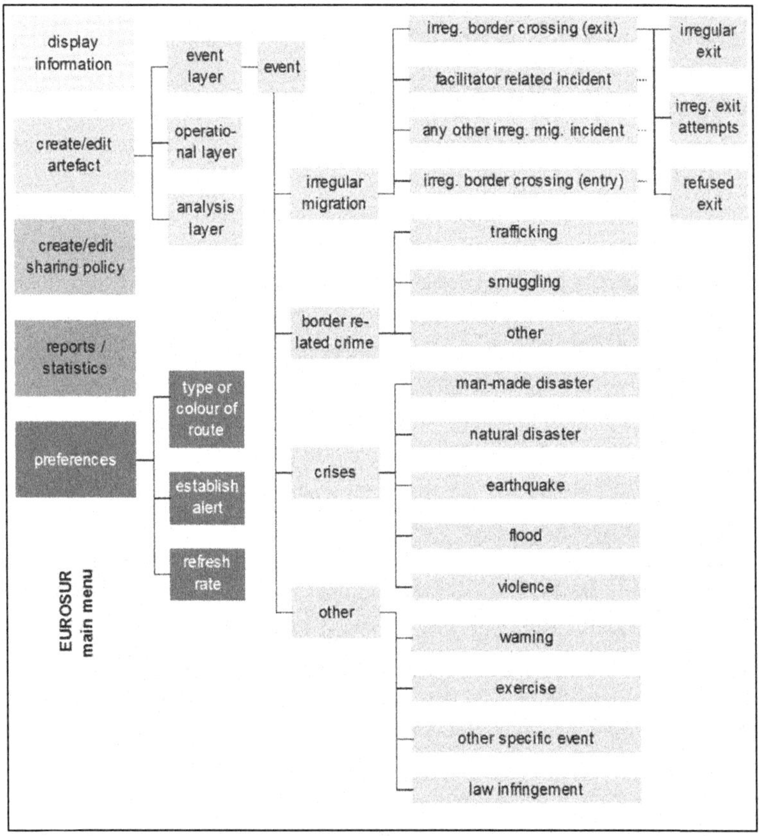

Source: own reconstruction, designed by Nils Ellebrecht

---

16 Up to today, the incident catalogue is subject to constant adjustment, and is not officially in the public domain. As these incidents sort out events relevant to border control, the process of defining them illustrates a European consensus about what is regarded border criminality, despite of the absence of a common EU immigration and asylum law.

During the pilot phase, participating member states could assess whether the schema was working in practice and how it could be amended and differentiated. As a result, two capabilities were tested in the pilot phase: fitting the classificatory schema with the views, needs and interests of the participating member states, and the usability of the IT application. For participants, testing the application included getting used to a certain way of looking at the border and of perceiving information as border-relevant.

This customization is supported by the interactive features of the platform that allows the user to both enter and retrieve information. The user can also filter the information by navigating the menu items to select certain types of incidents. They will then receive a map on, for instance, cross-border crime. Similarly, when a user intends to input information into the system, they are asked to select from the different types of border-related incidents and to classify the information according to this agreed schema. In the meantime, both the application and the schema remained flexible; the system is "extensible, stretchable"[17] and can also be reduced. This certainly evokes an atmosphere of "playing around" with the EUROSUR network in a non-binding way. Thus, rather than participating in new intergovernmental or communitarian obligations, the personnel at the NCCs became used to interacting in an electronic network. Rather than discussing common policy objectives or programs, member state representatives discussed menu items.

Iconographic Framework: Border-Related Incidents as Icons

All border-related incidents are rendered commensurable by way of icons. This has effects on both cartography and organization. Each type of incident has an assigned icon (cp. figure 6).[18] The fact that the different icons have been designed to imitate traffic signs[19] – and hence appear mainly in red and yellow with a round or triangular shape – alludes to a self-image of border policing as the regulation of movement and traffic. The protection of borders has thus been transformed into the control of routes and entry points.

---

17 EUROSUR Project Manager at Frontex, personal interview (May 15, 2012).

18 As an anecdote, it is interesting to mention that, when I was at the network office, the icon for a stolen car had just been developed after the Eastern authorities requested it be a border-related crime. In addition, the ability to delete messages was added during the pilot phase, when there was also a monthly update of the application.

19 Head of Research and Development at Frontex, telephone interview (October 28, 2011).

Figure 6: EUROSUR Icon Examples

Source: "EUROSUR: The Pilot," presentation slide[20]

The translation of the type of incident into an icon visually condenses the information, thus reducing the material for the part of the electronic map in question. The icons are placed according to where the incident has occurred. If a series of events are reported in a single area, the red icon is surrounded by blue circles, which is meant to attract the operator's attention. In addition, the current number of incidents at a particular spot is indicated in bold numbers on top of the incident icon. The operator can drag the cursor over the icon to display the individual events and to select the respective incident report. In practical terms of information exchange between border agencies in the EU, the icons bridge existing language gaps: While the EUROSUR network is set up in English, it is not the working language in most national offices.

The common iconographic language may therefore be able to compensate for potential communication difficulties. Apart from these language barriers, icons are also able to bridge diverging interpretations of issues and even work when common definitions have not yet been fully achieved. They even out incongruences and national divergences. They approximate understanding without consensus by offering the flexibility to apply individual perspectives and fill a common icon with individual examples. They embody the quality of boundary objects.

The semantic interoperability offered by icons suggests a common understanding, even when its content is still contested. The icons thus facilitate usability, and they visually offer and anticipate a consensus even before it has been reached. Moreover, the symbolism of traffic signs suggests that there are set rules for movement in Europe. Finally, by way of accumulating events, the necessity to act seems obvious when looking at the map.

---

20 Gregorio Ameyugo Catalán (Frontex): "EUROSUR. The Pilot," presentation during the European Day for Border Guards at the Frontex Headquarter on May 24, 2010 in Warsaw, Poland, at: http://www.ed4bg.eu/files/files/ Ameyugo_FRONTEX.pdf (accessed September 28, 2011), here slide 10. (Repository S. Ellebrecht)

Figure 7: Mapping border-related events

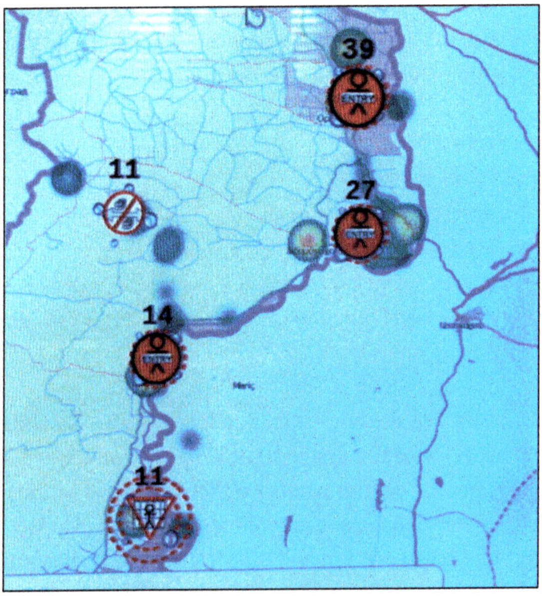

Source: own photograph, taken in May 2012, revised in color

Legal Framework:
Border-Related Incidents as "Sub-Layers" of the "Event Layer"

The consensus on the kind of information to be shared and on how to sort it has been addressed in the EUROSUR legislative proposal of December 12, 2011[21] and fixed in the EUROSUR Regulation of October 22, 2013.

In the latter, the different types of information are circumscribed as "sub-layers" of the "events layer." Article 9 (3a-d) of the EUROSUR Regulation states:

---

21 European Commission (2011): Proposal for a regulation of the European Parliament and of the Council – Establishing the European Border Surveillance system (EUROSUR), COM(2011) 873 final (December 12, 2011) [hereafter cited as "EUROSUR draft regulation" or "EUROSUR legislative proposal" COM(2011) 873].

"The events layer of the national situational picture shall consist of the following sub-layers:
- (a) a sub-layer on unauthorised border crossings, including information available to the national coordination centre on incidents relating to a risk to the lives of migrants;
- (b) a sub-layer on cross-border crime;
- (c) a sub-layer on crisis situations;
- (d) a sub-layer on other events, which contains information on unidentified and suspect vehicles, vessels and other craft and persons present at, along or in the proximity of, the external borders of the Member State concerned, as well as any other event which may have a significant impact on the control of the external borders."

At this point, it becomes clear that the regulation largely describes the software architecture of a geographic information system (GIS). It is, however, remarkable that the regulation does not list the full number of border-related incidents to be communicated – that is, that is does not provide an incident catalogue. The technical option of selecting items from a menu translates in the regulation into an information request and hence as "the national situational picture *shall* consist"[22] of these types of information. At this point, playing around with a test application becomes an obligation to communicate certain things in a certain way under defined headings. Thus, the inventory of border-related information has been transformed from a list into a classificatory schema of four types, a selection option in a menu bar, and finally a request for a particular kind of information.

Bowker and Star aptly emphasized that classifications "are powerful technologies. Embedded in working infrastructures they become relatively invisible without losing any of that power" (Bowker/Star 2000: 255). Indeed, the EUROSUR network offers a new working infrastructure, which in turn produces a new perspective on the task of border management. The process of establishing a working infrastructure for the exchange of information that is acquired and integrated into the relations between border authorities seems to weigh more than the content of the information itself.

---

22 EUROSUR Regulation (EU) No 1052/2013, Art. 9 (3a-d), emphasis added.

P.M.: I used to use this anecdote, this metaphor: this system is the train system, the station, the train, the trucks, but the cargo and the passengers is an issue for you, the users. So, I provide you with a secure train system; cargo and passengers are up to you.

S.E.: It is a huge system.

P.M.: In fact, it is small. Look at this; this will sound philosophical, but look, this network that I have created is using the minimum technology because I know that technology is not the issue. And the application may change, the security of the network may change, the network itself may change, it could be a dedicated network in the future; but what should be permanent is the community of people that are getting used to sharing information; that part should be permanent, and how they do it. We have a super solution now that may evolve and may change.[23]

The border-related incidents (whether as menu items, icons or sub-layers) are offered as a new convenient way of judging and sorting what is happening at the border. They are proposed as *wagons* of the "secure train system" to transport information. However, even though presented as intermediary, the classificatory schema of border-related incidents does not simply *transport* information. It mediates a new way of perceiving the external border of the EU. It is therefore worth stressing that the entire process successfully continued without defining "border-related." The monopoly of interpretation lies in the act of visualizing information on the EUROSUR electronic map. What makes it onto the map becomes relevant for common border policies.

4.1.2 Sorting, Reporting and Evaluating Information

Having developed a classificatory schema to sort border-related information, member states were asked to report events using the different headings available on the GUI. Generally, occurrence reports are an essential part of police work; internally, they fulfill the function of documentation and accountability. Furthermore, they can be used as pieces of information to be forwarded to other institutions. When information is forwarded among several institutions, as in the EUROSUR network, further agreements are required, concerning:

---

23 EUROSUR Project Manager at Frontex, personal interview (May 15, 2012).

- the format of the report,
- the degree of automatization of sending information,
- the selection of information based on one's own preferences for or against sharing,
- the selection of information based on its relevance to the common border.

During the test phase, participating member states used the preliminary format of an incident report. The decisions regarding the degree of automatization and the selection of information to be forwarded in the network were left to the individual member states, whose representatives could "play" with the system. It is important to stress that the incident report as displayed in the photograph in figure 8 shows the version that was available in May 2012, which has most likely since been updated. It shows the format in the test phase that provided several features that are no longer part of the application description in the EUROSUR Regulation. The value of presenting and discussing the format anyway lies in the fact that significant aspects that fostered the compliance of member states with the EUROSUR network can be demonstrated in this test version. It shows that different material development steps are not merely incomplete stages of the end product; they are seminal mediators that provide of the potential for further acceptance and development. Accordingly, they resemble those "fragments of the story" which Michel de Certeau recognized in the sailing ship painted on the sea, indicating "the maritime expedition that made it possible to represent the coastlines" (Certeau 2013 [1984]: 121). Although the sailing ships become invisible through the transformation of the depiction of coastlines into maps, they represent and call to mind the operations from which the map resulted.

Incident Reports

In the frame of the EUROSUR network, incident reports can be considered the basic format of information exchange between member states. Border-related incidents are entered into the system by clicking on the pencil icon, which is called the "artifact editor." In the language of EUROSUR users, the occurrence is then transformed into an "artifact." A so-called "new artifact" consists of the following nine details, which the artifact editor requests in an input mask: type, creator, owner, impact, state, layer, location, updated, and description. To enter an incident report, these boxes must be filled in.

Figure 8: Reporting incidents from the border

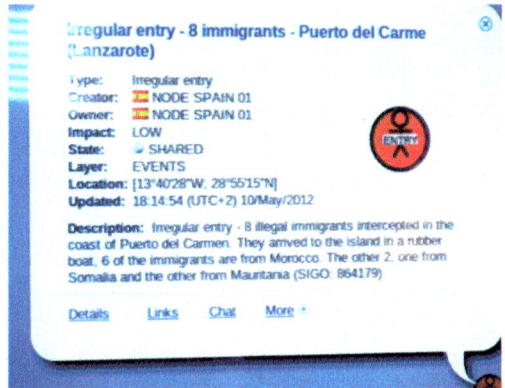

Source: own photograph, taken in May 2012, revised in color

These reports on events can be published on the national situational pictures (NSP) of the reporting member state, meaning they remain with that member state, or they can be forwarded to selected partners and also appear on their maps. When published on the electronic map; incident reports are represented by different icons, as described above. If we click on an icon, a file card pops up in the shape of a speech bubble, displaying the information that has been filled in the boxes (see figure 8). Given the fact that the communication format of the incident report structures both the reporting and the reception of the information on "border-related" events, it is worth discussing its different elements.

In the "artifact editor," the author selects a "type" of "border-related incident" from the menu. The classification of the incident also appears in text format in the first line of the file card as "type." Figure 8 provides an example of an incident report for an "irregular entry." The respective icon, placed on the top right side of the file card, repeats the type. This again underlines the importance of the iconographic translation of the classification: The graphical image, the "traffic sign," supports the standardization of common definitions, as it translates particular events into icons of common concern. Moreover, the last box at the bottom of the speech bubble asks for a "description" to accompany the information on the reported event.

This means that the sorting is illustrated, and the classification is performed and customized. Moreover, other participants are able to see whether a respective heading has been chosen appropriately. These three boxes – type (selected from the menu bar), icon (which visualizes the incident accordingly) and description – support the customization of incidents to the classificatory schema through paraphrasing.

The next five boxes negotiate the issues of ownership and authority over information and data. The first two boxes distinguish the "creator" from the "owner" of information. With regard to the information provided by member states, the owner of the information is identical with the creator of an incident report. However, the "owner" of information could also be a source or party who is not part of the EUROSUR network, but who provides information on agreement. Information regarding vessel traffic, for instance, might be provided and owned by EMSA. In this case, the creator of the information in the EUROSUR network would, however, be Frontex. Likewise, Frontex might be the "creator of information" during Joint Operations (JOs), while the "owner of the information" would be the host country. According to the terms of use, any participating national coordination center (NCC) – or in the language of EUROSUR, every users or node – could be the creator of information. Frontex is also a node, yet it lacks the mandate of an investigative authority. However, in the interactive setup of the IT application, the entry of information is not bound to the rights of that information or data. In the case of the EUROSUR network, it could thus happen that Frontex, although not allotted an investigative mandate, can create information relevant to the operationalization of border policies. The standard in information security, according to which an institution which creates and stores information is the initial owner of that information,[24] is thus made flexible. Moreover, the distinction between owner and creator might become increasingly sensitive when it comes to operational information: will a Maltese border guard be allowed to report something he sees in the Italian waters to Frontex and vice versa? Does reporting imply operational obligations? Who creates information during a joint operation? And is reporting different from being responsible?

The labeling of a participant as the "owner" of information demonstrates a signaling effect toward member states, in the sense that their sovereignty is documented by being named the owner of the information in the reporting system, but the legal framework of informational sovereignty is unsettled by the very distinction between the creator and the owner of information. As a node, Frontex can create information without having the rights to generate surveillance information itself. The lack of sovereign competence is compensated for by referring to the "owner."

---

24 Information Security Glossary, sub voce "Information Owner," at: http://www.your window.to/information-security/gl_informationowner.htm (accessed August 7, 2019).

The next three boxes – "impact," "state" and "layer" – further interfere with the setup of the ownership of information by relating the assessment of information to the way it should be treated and shared in the network.

The "impact" refers to the assignment of an "indicative impact level," which ranges from "high" to "medium" to "low." During the test phase, only those incident reports were requested to be sent to Frontex that had been assigned a medium or high impact level, while low impact reports were kept at the NCCs. This offered them the possibility to use the system without exchanging all of the information all of the time. Additionally, the box "state" indicates whether the information in the incident report is to be kept "closed" (that is, with the NCC) or whether it is to be "shared" with other network participants. During the test phase only, it was possible for member states to decide what information they wanted to share with what other participants.

The box "layer" sorts different kinds of information and offers the following options: "events layer," "analysis layer" and "operational layer." All three layers reveal and negotiate the tension between local issues and the assessment of their relevance for common European border policies. Considering member states' strong reluctance to exchange information on national procedures and events, and thereby disclose it to a European view, the processes during the test phase were intended to demonstrate that local events are part of a bigger picture (materialized in the ESP) and that there was therefore a "responsibility to share."[25] However, while filling in information, operators did not necessarily apply a European perspective, but were also selective and influenced by national interests. For instance, local occurrences that have been dramatized and assigned a high impact level may suggest (that is, create evidence for) a desire for more funding. Conversely, controversial or low-standard operational practices could be hidden in the system by assigning them a low impact status (or simply by not reporting them at all). The following two sections will describe these temporary conces-

---

25 Jargon among officials at the European Commission and Frontex responsible for the EUROSUR development phase (December 2012). The official jargon changed here from "need to know" and "need to share," to "responsibility to share." Effectively, these formulations take a step back from the principle of availability and its demand toward member states to provide information without further ado (cf. Bunyan 2006; Töpfer 2008). Moreover, the principle of availability refers to criminal law information, which are not addressed in the EUROSUR GUI. Again, it shows that EUROSUR has not been developed along existing legal categories, but makes its own definition offer.

sions and compare this procedure with the final rule in the EUROSUR Regulation.

First, however, it should be mentioned that the details on space and time ("location" and "updated") provided in the incident report allows us to deduce the possibilities and motives of the EUROSUR network in terms of a timely operational response. Although information on the "location" indicated with longitude and latitude coordinates can be relevant for operational decisions as well as for the retrospective transparency of events, it is useless when reported one day after the occurrence. Yet, the time tag does not ask for the time of occurrence, but rather refers to the information in the incident report, stating when it was last updated. This documents when the incident became an artifact in the system, or when the information was changed. The continual possibility to update e the incident report lets the EUROSUR seem more like a documentation platform and archive than as an agency supporting prompt interventions. In fact, Martina Tazzioli, who in 2014 had the chance to conduct ethnographic work in the Italian NCC after EUROSUR became operational, found that "the average time of latency between a migration event being added to a map and being displayed is of some hours and can reach two days" (Tazzioli/Walters 2016: 9). Apparently, this has not changed much since the pilot phase, when it was considered a success by Frontex and EC officials if "the stuff is inside the system within 24 hours."[26] Compliance with and the actual usage of the system is thus critical for any evaluation of EUROSUR's function as an agency supporting operational reactions.

I will now return to those temporary concessions that fostered the compliance of member states during the pilot phase and initially allowed them to maintain control over their national information.

Sharing Policies:
Maintaining Control Over One's National Information

Since the EUROSUR Regulation of 22 October 2013, all incident reports created in the IT network are sent to Frontex. While some NNCs can automatically retrieve the information, most participants enter the information manually, although the exchange of information is instituted and regulated via the EUROSUR system. For some, this high level of compliance may come as a surprise.

A look at the test phase demonstrates the gradual process of convincing member states and getting them to share information and become less reluctant toward a European standard format of communication regarding operational in-

---

26 Formulation used by an EC official in December 2012.

formation. When I interviewed the project manager responsible at Frontex during the test phase, he described the options for the exchange of information in the following way:

S.E.: Does one have the opportunity to select the information that will go into the network?

P.M.: There is the option of selecting between automatically or manually. But first, when you inject information in the system, it is injected locally, because maybe your people want to see it and maybe you want to discuss this with other people in the NCC. And then someone has to publish it. And when you publish, the information will be distributed following the sharing policies that you have established.

S.E.: And what could be the sharing policies?

P.M.: Sharing policies are defined by each node [that is, NCC]. For instance, illegal immigration will go to everybody, crime will go to France and Italy, crisis will go to everybody, so this is the sharing policy.[27]

The option to define individual information sharing policies was crucial to the acceptance of the system among member state authorities. Member states thus maintained authority over their national 'border-related information' in two ways: First, national authorities decided which information would be shared with whom – that is, the participants could exploit the system to their advantage and interests without having to comply with a central demand to provide information. A selective usage of the system was allowed; there were no strings attached, just strings of digital references were offered. Second, national border enforcement activities were not reported on the European level, which essentially would have suggested a central supervision of Schengen activities. When asked whether these different options were part of the design from the beginning, the Frontex official replied at length:

"I planned it in this way, after discussion with the member states. I got their answers, and I quickly saw that they didn't want to have a big brother. I saw also that if we establish a centralized system, the centralized system will be managing the information which will be

---

27 EUROSUR Project Manager at Frontex, personal interview (May 15, 2012).

the common denominator of everybody. And that common denominator will be very small, so 'No thank you' – we will not have a centralized system."[28]

The obstacles to sharing information are identified as conflicting interests and fear of supervision. Convincing member states to loosen their sovereign monopoly over national surveillance information and to routinely and actively share information required added value. For, if the common denominator is "very small" and members' reluctance to report their own activities is great, the system will not take off. The Frontex official describes a kind of skepticism that is typical for law enforcement agencies with regard to the exchange of information: the belief, or rather concern, "that communications amalgamation breaks down both territorial and formal organizational boundaries" (Ericson/Haggerty 1997: 393). Hence, the EUROSUR system was explicitly offered to member states as a service in which each participant could select the options that best benefitted their needs.

"We have a distributed system with the possibility to create communities of interest. And if there is one of the nodes that cannot see some type of information – so what? This node will not see it. But the others – why not?! You may create a community! Imagine that we're having 25 nodes, and there are five nodes that have customs' information – because this picture of the NCC having all the information is not real – so imagine that there are five that have customs information, and they are able to share that information between them. We will be helping them! And that will be part of their border situation, and they will have a European situational picture of their region that will be richer than that of other nodes."[29]

Future additional reporting burdens were left to the member states to decide. The incentive to do so, however, was established with reference to the value of information itself: "If I am very active and if I am sharing a lot of information with the others I will have a very rich map, so if I am very active, I will have a rich map."[30] A glance at the EUROSUR electronic map shows why this circular argument could be convincing. Engaging in the exchange of information, and sharing a great amount of information with many partners meant having more tags on one's own situational picture.

---

28 EUROSUR Project Manager at Frontex, personal interview (May 15, 2012).
29 Ibid.
30 Ibid.

Getting involved was visually rewarded with a "richer map" and the feeling of knowing what was going on at the common borders. Again, the option to define individual sharing policies was crucial to the acceptance of the system by member state authorities. Still, the idea of generating different national pictures of the situation at the external borders was not in the interest of the European Commission, and ultimately sharing policies disappeared with the publication of the final regulation.

Impact Levels: The Traffic Lights of Border Control

In addition to reporting occurrences in the form of an incident report, NCCs are requested to assign each incident an "indicative impact level, ranging from 'low' and 'medium' to 'high.'" The purpose of this procedure is primarily to assess local events with regard to their relevance for common Schengen border policies. What local occurrences weigh enough to impact Schengen responsibilities? Put differently: What local information is also relevant to others, and to what extent? In this case, "impact" is not further defined, as this could be construed as being overly demanding and perhaps even patronizing toward member states who may then no longer accept the system and could leave the test phase.

During the test phase, the assignment of impact levels was monitored by Frontex. The agency ran a so-called "consistency check" on how member states apply the impact levels. However, this consistency check had the potential to go beyond this information submitted with the incident report and to additionally enable national claims to be put into perspective. "It is not just exchange of information," noted a Frontex official, "it is also asking for information and asking the Italians: 'Why do you think that this event is high impact when we see that it is only related to a single Moroccan?'"[31] The impact level thus not only reports local urgency, but also allows for comparability. The application of impact levels can thus be considered a relatively strong insight into national affairs and border police work, and its acceptance by member states therefore surprising.

As already mentioned, this acceptance emerged gradually. During the pilot phase, the value of these procedures could be tested without having to share all of the information all of the time with all of the nodes. In fact, those events assigned a low impact were intended to remain in the member states' NCCs. Medium and high impact incidents were sent to Frontex where the "consistency check" was applied. Assigning a low impact level to an incident thus meant keeping control over the distribution of an incident report. In this sense, the rule

---

31 EUROSUR Project Manager at Frontex, personal interview (May 15, 2012).

that incidents of low impact need not be shared with Frontex did not necessarily mean that the incidents were of minor importance to overall European border management, but rather allowed member states to be active in the system *without* being monitored by others. That the draft regulation proposed that "[a]ll [read: only] events assigned with a 'medium' to 'high' impact level shall be shared with the Agency"[32] can be regarded as the top-down expectation of the European Commission to at least routinely share those incidents with Frontex that member states considered as having a moderate or significant impact on the situation at the common external borders.

However, the final regulation no longer grants the selective exchange of information, but rather prescribes that *every* incident "shall be shared with the Agency."[33] This can be judged as a positive achievement of the European Commission, which was able to convince the Council that all incident-reports go to Frontex.

"The argument on the side of the Commission in this regard – and the member agreed – was: if a migratory route is altered and a new route is being tested, it is not risked [by facilitators, S.E.] to send 30, 40 or 100 persons which then are intercepted. Rather one sends three, five, ten persons and it is watched how permeable the border is; now, these incidents would be classified as low impact. But if one was already able to *see* these incidents, new routes could be detected much faster, instead of waiting until member states report these 30, 40 or 100 persons. "[34]

Finally, the EUROSUR Regulation requires Frontex to "visualise the impact levels attributed to the external borders in the European situational picture"[35]. For this purpose, Frontex aggregates the individual impact levels in the context of the agency's risk analysis, referring both to the impact level assigned by member states and the frequency of incidents of a specific type along a defined "border section." This visualization consists of the respective border section being colored, so that different parts or dots along the external borders of the EU appear as green, yellow, or red stripes.

---

32 EUROSUR legislative proposal COM(2011) 873, Art. 9 (4).
33 EUROSUR Regulation (EU) No 1052/2013, Art. 9 (4).
34 EC official in Brussels, personal interview (December 2012).
35 EUROSUR Regulation (EU) No 1052/2013, Art. 15 (3).

Figure 9: Frontex's demonstration of border sections and impact levels

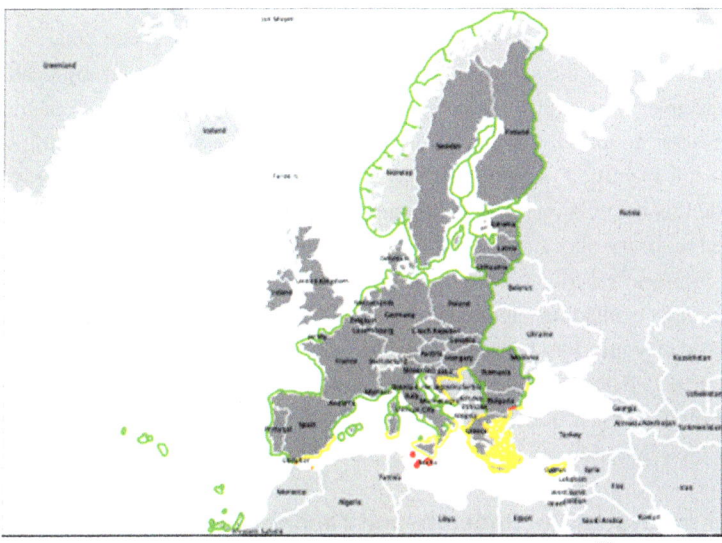

Source: European Commission, press release of November 29, 2013[36]

This means that the distinguishing aspect of an incident is no longer the national border, but the color-coded impact level. Additionally, the color codes are not applied to national borders, but to designated border sections. The EUROSUR Regulation requires each member state to "divide its external land and sea borders into border sections, and [...] notify them to the Agency"[37].

Border Guard Major Świąteka reasons that national borders would be too general a unit, as "it depends on what is happening on the other side of the border."[38] Furthermore, she considers the assignment of impact levels more of an exercise of semantic interoperability. During a presentation on EUROSUR, she stated: "It is not just to give names; we will be obliged to react accordingly. This is why EUROSUR is not just a system for the exchange of information but

---

36 European Commission (2013): EUROSUR: Protecting the Schengen external borders - protecting migrants' lives, MEMO/13/1070 (November 29, 2013), p. 3, at: https://ec.europa.eu/commission/presscorner/api/files/document/print/en/memo_13_10 70/MEMO_13_1070_EN.pdf (accessed August 15, 2019).
37 EUROSUR Regulation (EU) No 1052/2013, Art. 14.
38 BG Major Świąteka: EUROSUR Presentation (May 16, 2012).

much, much more."[39] Even if the authority of border guards is still tied to territorial borders, as depicted on the screen, their place of operation is denationalized and dynamic.

Coloring puts the self-evaluations of the member states into a supranational perspective. This allows for comparisons, while also painting a new picture of the border: no longer are state borders drawn as lines on a map, now their insecurities are identified, aggregated, and visualized as concerns rendered in color. While this new outlook affects the image of a common EU border, it is also referred to for the allocation of resources and personnel, as the EUROSUR Regulation foresees "reaction corresponding to impact levels."[40] Thus, in the process of collecting, evaluating, aggregating, visualizing and coloring pieces of information, they turn into occasions or even evidence for intervention. According to the "EUROSUR on the screen," there is always something to do: perhaps more here (red), and less there (green). In this sense, the exchange of information fuses with the suggestion of operational urgency.

Layers: System Architecture and Techno-Political Filter

The division of the EUROSUR GIS into layers surpasses the conventional use of layers in a geographical information system. Generally, data on the distribution and characteristics of defined aspects are clustered into layers to be selected for display. This is also used in the context of EUROSUR when types of border-related incidents appear as layers or sub-layers, as described above. The practical reason for layers in the GIS is that it creates the possibility to select and combine information, or to single out a single aspect for display. This is also possible with the EUROSUR application. An operator can thus select "cross-border crime" and receive a map that displays only this defined information.

Additionally, it is interesting to note that the EUROSUR layers also imply different fields of responsibility. In addition to these thematic variables, which can be displayed layer by layer, the institutional structure of sharing and processing information via the EUROSUR network is also organized in layers. The Head of Research and Development explained this during the test phase:

"The way the EUROSUR network is built up is that we will have different layers, the operational layer, and the analytical layer, which can be used by different people. For instance, if you talk about analysis, you do not want operational people to have direct access

---

39 BG Major Świąteka: EUROSUR Presentation (May 16, 2012).
40 EUROSUR Regulation (EU) No 1052/2013, Art. 16.

to that layer. I mean this is a layer which is used for analytical people to compile information, to draw conclusions, basically, to do analyses. And this analysis will then appear in the network of EUROSUR. And if we're talking about the operational information, which is real time or near real time, this is the event or incident layer, as we call it, and this is where people, this kind of operational people, can put on things that are actually happening at the external border right now. So we see it in these kinds of layers."[41]

The layers the official is describing here distinguish competences and thus operate as protected spaces in the system. Moreover, these layers do not cluster information in terms of content, but in terms of how it is obtained and processed and according to its weight in knowledge production. Louise Amoore received a similar statement from an interview with a border security software designer in 2009. Her interviewee stated: "There is real time decision making, and then the offline team who run the analytics and work out the best set of rules" (Amoore 2011: 25). This new distinction in competences has thus been built into the IT architecture of EUROSUR by way of "layers." The draft regulation specifies the three layers with regard to the information they collect and in turn provide:

(a) an events layer, containing information on incidents concerning irregular migration, cross-border crime and crisis situations;
(b) an operational layer, containing information on the status and position of own assets, areas of operation and environmental information;
(c) an analysis-layer, containing strategic information, analytical products, intelligence as well as imagery and geo-data.[42]

The final regulation, however, merely lists the three layers that make up any situational picture in the EUROSUR: the events layer, the operational layer, and the analysis layer.[43] The wording follows the formal logic of a GIS. When the regulation was passed, customizing the participants to fit the distribution of tasks and competences in the EUROSUR network was no longer debated, but taken for granted. It no longer needed to be specified, as it logically emerged from the system. It is an *infra*structure that is taken for granted.

---

41 Head of Research and Development at Frontex, telephone interview (October 28, 2011).
42 EUROSUR legislative proposal, COM(2011) 873 final, Art. 8 (2).
43 EUROSUR Regulation (EU) No 1052/2013, Art. 8 (2).

In sum, discussing the EUROSUR network initially meant developing an IT application and discussing the menu options of its graphical user interface (GUI). The development of EUROSUR focused on what this could look like and how it could be represented on a screen. Different national angles were tentatively subsumed under menu items, domains of responsibility were translated into GIS layers, and organizational hierarchies were flattened into nodes in the system. Regarding the test application, discussions were geared toward (and reduced to) the GUI, the usability of which mediated the negotiations. To a certain extent, a question of sovereign competences (in this case, the authority of one's own national information) was flanked by, reduced to or even smothered by the question of software design. Ultimately, it can be assumed that it was most likely easier to get used to menu items for the purpose of testing an IT application than to agree on common priorities for border policies in Europe. Because interaction is mainly with the platform rather than member states engaging in discussions, the exchange of information ensues smoothly. Or, as Ruben Andersson commented pointedly: "If they started talking, it would never happen" (Andersson 2016: 13).[44]

In effect, the fact that officials did not want to make these development steps public because they said that they were "premature" highlights the frailty of the inter-organizational agreement at this time rather than the technical shortcomings. What was critical about the pilot phase was not the readiness of the technology, but the compliance of the member states.

4.2 THE EUROPEAN SITUATIONAL PICTURE

The immediate purpose of the exchange of information in the EUROSUR network is the generation of the European situational picture (ESP). Frontex provides the ESP to the national authorities active in national coordination centers (NCCs) in the format of the electronic map described above. During the pilot

---

44 From the quoted passages in Andersson's essay; I assume that he had the same interview partner as I did. Certain formulations are very similar to the statements I recorded. This demonstrates nicely that Frontex officials not only "brief" social scientists (cf. fn. 4 and 5), but are themselves briefed. Certain formulations seem to be deliberately released to the public, as if their effect was expected. Dealing with the controlled disclosure of information limits ethnographic work in the (border) security domain more than dealing with difficulties acquiring access or finding interview partners.

phase, member states experienced the added value of sharing and accumulating their information by seeing it all assembled in the European situational picture. This visualization literary makes visible the added value of exchanging information, which is in turn accessible as an object and thus exploitable by participants. This having been said, the EUROSUR electronic map is about Europe's borders. Geographic features are secondary in the cartographic representation and can be changed by the individual user, that is, by each NCC. "The map is a holder of information," explains the responsible project manager at Frontex, who argued:

"We don't need to have very precise maps because we just use them as a place holder for the information. Nevertheless, in the rack that I am installing, there is one server of maps. We are providing three maps, but if one of the users wants to put their own maps, they can do it."[45]

As the official said about the test phase of the network, the background map's "open street layer," which appears by default – presenting a white European continent in front of a light blue background (figure 4) – was never changed by member states. The reason was obvious to him: "Then the events are more visible."[46] In fact, the ESP is all about the visibility and tagging of events,[47] rather than the definition of a territory. While in the territorial frame the *drawing of a*

---

45 EUROSUR Project Manager at Frontex, personal interview (May 15, 2012). – The "server of maps" offers three maps to choose from; apart from the one selected in the Frontex office, which in the system is called "open street layer," two further options exist – termed "blue marble" and "land set" – both of which are based on satellite images. The user has the possibility to manually select further configurations. Apart from the background map, it is possible to define whether bio-physical conditions should be indicated: forests, for example, can be added and would appear in green imitating biophysical appearances according to their actual color (cf. Ehrensvärd 1987: 131). The blue color representing the Mediterranean Sea is most likely also taken from the realistic tradition of imitating perception, which has been customized to the extent that it is common to talk about blue borders.
46 EUROSUR Project Manager at Frontex, personal interview (May 15, 2012).
47 Martina Tazzioli also highlights the focus on events articulated on the map and describe this gaze as an "epistemology of the event" (Tazzioli 2018: 6). Joseph Pugliese argues that the "incident-as-event is the non-normative figure that ruptures the banal unfolding of normative seriality on the screen" (Pugliese 2014: 580).

single line allowed things and people to be organized, the *accumulation* of information, as in the ESP, lets single events that are suspicious to be identified or detected against the background of data. The ESP maps insecurities, hotspots of migratory pressure, and risks as they culminate into an accumulation of incidents marked as traffic signs or colored-in border sections. In fact, the ESP is not intended to provide a cartographic representation in which territorial border lines compartmentalize, contour and identify political authority; it was meant to provide a "situational picture" that can be used by authorities to develop operational strategies. Yet, what are the peculiar characteristics of a situational picture? What does its map accomplish? What is the argument its map is trying to make?

Situational pictures can quite generally be described as tools for making decisions. They arrange information as objects of concern that represent the spatial distribution of, for instance, adversary troops in the battle field, a certain type of crime, HIV or aids, or consumer patterns on a neighborhood, country or global scale. This can be arranged above a table or in a GIS-generated map to create a dynamic depiction of an object or theme in a defined area. The purpose is to produce an overview, a panorama, with regard to the extent and distribution of a defined issue of concern, so that personnel and resources can be deployed accordingly. In the context of inter-organizational cooperation, situational pictures also provide a platform for collecting information from different actors. Situational pictures can also be used to anticipate future developments or to trace the evolution of a situation. They are a typical asset in control rooms of all kinds, where they may be wall-sized or available on different screens. In any case, contemplating the picture is expected to lead to an informed, evidence-based decision that is tailored to the situation being viewed from a distance.

EUROSUR's definition of a "situational picture" states that the picture must be represented and accessible via ICT as a "graphical interface."[48] Its content is defined as "near real time data and information received from different authorities, sensors, platforms and other sources."[49] This surveillance data is visualized as a situational picture which is "shared across communication and information channels with other authorities in order to achieve situational awareness and support the reaction capability along the external borders and the pre-frontier area."[50] What is missing is any mention of the issue being displayed in the ESP.

---

48 EUROSUR Regulation (EU) No 1052/2013, Art. 3(d).
49 Ibid.
50 Ibid.

The definition merely answers Wood's and Fels's call for a definition of the map's performance and its argument by stating the purpose of EUROSUR's situational picture as achieving "situational awareness" and supporting "the reaction capability along the external borders and the pre-frontier area"[51]. The electronic map thus embodies a widely accepted rationale that there is a virtual causal relation between the availability of information and the effectiveness of (border) policing. It assumes that authorities know (or rather see) what to do. And the argument? What argument does the ESP put forth and on the basis of what supporting documentation? Judging from the Regulation's defined aim of "situational awareness" and its respective definition as "the ability to monitor, detect, identify, track and understand illegal cross-border activities in order to find reasoned grounds for reaction measures on the basis of combining new information with existing knowledge, and to be better able to reduce loss of lives of migrants at, along or in the proximity of, the external borders,"[52] the ESP is meant to argue ("find reasoned grounds") for reaction measures.

In effect, the non-representational map of the ESP argues that certain situations, such as a high-impact, red border section or an accumulation of incidents of a certain type require reaction measures. However, these reaction measures are not specified in the regulation; they are rather described as an ability that is made possible by the situational awareness achieved by the ESP. According to the regulation, "reaction capability" means "the ability to perform actions aimed at countering illegal cross-border activities at, along or in the proximity of, the external borders, including the means and timelines to react adequately"[53]. This definition does not provide a qualitative benchmark of reaction capability either in terms of a defined timeliness of the reaction or in terms of objectives. It also does not refer to any legal basis for interventions, or mention that this definition addresses law enforcement units, whose reaction capability is a concern. Rather, it stresses that the "ability to perform actions" and "the means and timeliness to react adequately" result from the quality of the ESP. What is unsettling here is the fact that the humanitarian intention "to be better able to reduce loss of lives of migrants" is included in the "situational awareness," but is not mentioned as one of the results of this awareness. Saving lives is not part of its defined reaction capability.

---

51 EUROSUR Regulation (EU) No 1052/2013, Art. 3(d).
52 Ibid, Art. 3(b).
53 Ibid, Art. 3(c).

Overall, the generation of the object of knowledge itself, the ESP, is underlined as the means and ends of the exchange of information in the EUROSUR network. The argument, or evidence, for taking reaction measures is visually presented on the electronic map of the ESP. However, it is visualized "on the basis of combining new information,"[54] such as operational information or signals, and fused with "existing knowledge,"[55] such as available data or databases. According to the Head of Research and Development at Frontex, the ability to electronically leave their national border and see (and compare) what is happening at other parts of the external borders not only supports solidarity among authorities – in the sense that, for instance, Polish authorities *see* that the Italians have much to do – it also allows them "to understand parallels."[56] He explains:

"Normally, the member state, they should know what they are doing at their external borders [...] in that sense it isn't additional information, they know where the patrol units are, so in that sense it is nothing new. However, they can see that at the border between Ukraine and Slovakia that a new modus operandi is popping up there and, I don't know, Chinese are appearing there at the border with false documents, so they might think: 'Okay if we see Chinese at our border we might want to check a little bit further and verify whether these documents are really the correct ones.' And this tool to understand parallels is not available in Europe at the moment."[57]

However, matching data and conducting a risk analysis – factors alluded to in the definition of situational awareness – go beyond profiting from the experiences of other authorities and border guard colleagues. Moreover, they also go beyond the mere purpose of information exchange. These computerized analyses rather produce knowledge and generate scenarios. They project models of how and where the border will probably (or possibly) be subject to pressure in the future. In this attempt to understand parallels, the "emphasis is on what can be conducted 'across' items of data, on and through their very relation" (Amoore 2011: 30). However, this relation is a data correlation, and it serves to detect anomalies in a set of data. As such, it operates in a self-referential manner. The (future) risks emerge according to how the filters have been defined.

---

54 EUROSUR Regulation (EU) No 1052/2013, Art. 3(b).
55 Ibid.
56 Head of Research and Development at Frontex, personal interview (May 27, 2011).
57 Ibid.

Since the prognostic criteria and indices for data analyses are defined by the agency itself, the European situational picture is critically influenced by Frontex's services and risk analysis. In fact, a careful reading of the composition of the ESP as defined in Article 10 of the EUROSUR Regulation reveals that the ESP is, in fact, abounding with Frontex's risk analysis and processed information. Inti Schubert's observation that the generation of situational pictures enables authorities (here Europol) "to define the requirements for their intervention themselves" (Schubert 2008: 177) proves true in the case of the ESP. Although merely a coordinator, the Frontex agency is in the position to produce a dynamically developing knowledge base that serves to justify and legitimize border control, surveillance and intervention measures.

4.3 THE COMMON PRE-FRONTIER INTELLIGENCE PICTURE (CPIP)

The common pre-frontier intelligence picture (CPIP) was planned as a "service to the EUROSUR."[58] Its service consists in the contribution of information to the European situational picture (ESP). Although the CPIP was launched separate from the EUROSUR IT application, its content is ultimately visualized together with the ESP: "technically, the ESP and the CPIP are one."[59] In practice, this means that the information collected for the CPIP appears together with the ESP on the same screen in the same map. Contrary to its technical fusion and visual indistinguishability, however, the regulation lists the CPIP as a separate situational picture that is different from the ESP and the national situational pictures.[60] Moreover, its information is described as being from the "pre-frontier" and as leading to an "intelligence picture." We must therefore ask, if the differences do not appear onscreen, what kind of situational picture is this? What sort of information is this about? And where is the pre-frontier area?

Research and development for a common pre-frontier intelligence picture (CPIP) was conducted by a German company called Electronic Systems GmbH (ESG) together with the University of the German Federal Army Munich as a subcontractor, with cooperation from the subcontractor EADS. Drawing up a

---

58 EUROSUR Project Manager at Frontex, personal interview (May 15, 2012).
59 Formulation used by an EC official in December 2012.
60 EUROSUR Regulation (EU) No 1052/2013, Art. 8.

CPIP concept was one of the sub-projects of a larger contract with ESG for the EUROSUR technical study.[61] The task of the CPIP subproject consisted in proposing a way to provide member states with a comprehensive information base, while at the same time leaving their authority over information untouched. The study's final report, presented to the Commission in January 2010, provides insight into the sources and the kind of "intelligence" considered usable for the CPIP.[62]

In the report, the CPIP is intended to "provide the national coordination centres (NCCs) with effective, accurate and timely intelligence [...] in a frequent, reliable, interoperable and cost-efficient manner,"[63] In terms of the CPIP concept, not only the quality of the data is intended to matter, but also the quality of the service of providing information in and of itself. In fact, this service served two purposes: a) member states were to receive information that would be "out of scope" for them to collect, access or produce themselves; b) in addition, they were to receive new information frequently, cost-free and via reliable and interoperable channels. The advertisement directed at member states is clear: CPIP offers you more information, processed according to your interests, without extra cost or effort. The distinction between "items that are *in scope* of the CPIP and those that are *out of scope*,"[64] which the report lists in tabular form, deservers a closer look. *Out of scope* for the CPIP is any information collected within the

---

61 In January 2009, the Commission contracted Electronic Systems GmbH (ESG) to do a "Technical study on developing concepts for border surveillance infrastructure, a secure communication network and a pre-frontier intelligence picture within the framework of the European Border Surveillance System" referred to as the EUROSUR technical study [hereafter cited as EUROSUR technical study]. The study is divided into three subprojects: namely, the management concept (subproject 1), the communication information system (CIS) (subproject 2), and the common pre-frontier intelligence picture (CPIP) (subproject 3).

62 The study is designated intellectual property of the Commission, which is why approval from the Commission is required for each citation. Inquiries made directly to the ESG are also referred back to the Commission. In a conversation on the phone with a representative of the ESG, my identity as a PhD student of sociology was questioned and I was asked if I were not rather from a "leftist newspaper." All quotations cited in this work have been authorized by a spokesperson of the Commission during a personal conversion in 2016 with the concrete citations at hand.

63 EUROSUR technical study, subproject 3, p. 11.

64 EUROSUR technical study, subproject 3, p. 19, original emphasis.

sovereign territory of the member states or Schengen associated countries. For the purpose of the CPIP, no information or intelligence can be collected from within a national territory. Furthermore, information that is relevant for defense, personal data and law enforcement activities other than border control are out of scope for the CPIP.[65] Essentially, this distinction keeps the supranational level of the EU out of member states' bureaucracies. The proposed CPIP does not interfere with national administrations, security procedures or other sovereign competences. Conversely, the report envisions the "geographical area beyond the territory/external border of EU Member States and Schengen associated countries [...] with main focus on neighbouring third countries" as being "in scope" of the CPIP, thus circumscribing this area as pre-frontier. The CPIP is also designed to include information on "border management in third countries" as well as information that is processed, that is, analysed or matched, against other databases.[66] Furthermore, there is information submitted from many possible sources, like embassies, to official informants, like the immigration liaison officer (ILO), as well as types of information, like open-source intelligence (OSINT), imagery intelligence (IMINT) and signals intelligence (SIGINT). The CPIP sub-report offers a compilation of information and information channels that it would be "nice to have."

Since most of these sources found their way into the draft regulation, Hayes and Vermeulen expressed the concern "that a potentially limitless amount of third parties – coupled with the lack of meaningful oversight on the sharing of data between these parties – implies that 'function creep' will be built into the EUROSUR system from the outset" (Hayes/Vermeulen 2012: 20). Despite seemingly limitless ambitions and ideas for synergy, the actual CPIP service still was described as "a very rudimentary collecting system"[67] during the development phase. According to the EUROSUR project manager at Frontex, "the purpose of EUROSUR is to make this more, let's say, routine, and assign someone responsible, which is Frontex."[68] In the end, Frontex's Risk Analysis Unit (RAU) was tasked with establishing and maintaining the CPIP. It can be assumed that the task of composing the CPIP was not taken lightly by the Risk Analysis Unit, as it had to adapt to the expectation of a 24/7 service and thus the notion of an early warning system, while risk analysis at Frontex had actually thus far been con-

---

65 EUROSUR technical study, subproject 3, p. 19.
66 Ibid.
67 EUROSUR Project Manager at Frontex, personal interview (May 15, 2012).
68 Ibid.

cerned with long term studies, annual or quarterly reports and the formulation of risk indicators, etc.

Ultimately, the CPIP was not drafted as a separate informational layer or separate electronic map, like the national situational pictures, but as a draft of a sphere of supranational competences in border management that evolves *qua* informational affiliations and access. As a result, national territories and informational sovereignty are explicitly out of scope, while everything else that may affect the EU external border could be in scope of the CPIP. In order to concretize supranational interiority as a sovereign place for the postnational EU external border, the CPIP has been developed along the notion of the information exploitation and coverage of the pre-frontier area.

4.3.1 The Pre-Frontier: Risks, Surveillance and the Elsewhere

When asked about the specific nature of the CPIP, a Frontex official stated that it was "just exchanging information which is not coming from the border but before the border."[69] In a similar vein, the EUROSUR Regulation defines the pre-frontier area *prima facie* in geographical terms. Yet, it is also completely boundless as "the geographical area beyond the external borders,"[70] In other words, the pre-frontier is non-EU, it is the rest of the world whenever it affects the external borders of the EU. With regard to the CPIP, "border–related" does not result from having a geographical proximity to the political and administrative borders of individual member states, but from being passed through an informational filter. The pre-frontier is an "amorphous domain" (Pugliese 2014: 578) characterized *ex negativo* as not interfering with national sovereignty. Likewise, the draft regulation proposed that pre-frontier may be defined as "the geographical area beyond the external border of Member States *which is not covered by a national border surveillance system.*"[71] This statement illustrates the added value of CPIP for the member states, because it contributes information that cannot be generated with the authority and the border surveillance systems of the individual member states. The added information can be interpreted as *the* critical incentive for the member states to participate in EUROSUR and to engage in exchanging information themselves. However, as we have seen with other incentives of the development phase, the incentive has become invisible in the final regulation

---

69 EUROSUR Project Manager at Frontex, personal interview (May 15, 2012).
70 EUROSUR Regulation (EU) No 1052/2013, Art. 3 (g).
71 EUROSUR legislative proposal, COM(2011) 873 final, Art. 3 (f), emphasis added.

proposal. The pre-frontier is thus blithely defined as "the geographical area beyond the external borders."[72] Instead of a geographical place (not even of the extra-territorial kind), it is rather a network of cooperation, sources and references.

Furthermore, the notion of pre-frontier encompasses the notion of a dark field, of the unknown and of futurity. This dark field needs to be explored, illuminated, explained and put on the screen. In the indeterminability (and liminality) of the dark field, the assessment of risks and the sovereign mandate to restrict people's liberties merge easily, because the potential deviances in the dark field seem to call for action (Denninger 2008: 94-95; Aradau/Lobo-Guerrero/van Munster 2008; Ellebrecht 2014b). When relating strategic measures to risks, this brings about the "paradoxical situation that action must be taken although there is ultimately no basis for the action" (Nassehi 1997: 169-171). Pugliese describes the empowering modeling of possible risks as the "multi-layered aspect of the 'pre' – pre-frontier, pre-emptive risk, precautionary assessments and so on" (Pugliese 2014: 579). This intimate relation between pre-emption, virtual suspicion and scanning data for risks is also illustrated in the description of CPIP information.

S.E.: If you look at the different outlines and comments on the EUROSUR, then the CPIP seems to be the big thing.

P.M.: Sabrina, I told you, that you only collect information if you are going to act. If you are not going to act, why are you collecting information? So, CPIP should be a source of information that allows you to be proactive and not reactive, so that you know what is coming to you. For instance, you know that there is a group of people which are gathering in Georgia and they are planning all of them to cross to Europe, and to all, in block, require asylum – that is information that would be coming from the pre-frontier area. [...] Or you know that there is this ship which is known to have been involved in traffic of tobacco before, that is now leaving Odessa, and then the Rumanians and Bulgarians are together and say: "Okay let's see where this guy is going this time." This is CPIP. [...] Look, one of the sources is OSINT, open source, so you have information of traffic of ships and traffic of merchants, which is very much accessible. But if you are able to analyze this information you may find anomalies, in the container traffic for instance. Anecdotally, there is a JRC, joint research center project, which is analyzing the moving of 8 million containers and telling the member states: "We have identified this which seems to be doing something strange." And the hit of the cases in which they were right is about 50

---

72 EUROSUR Regulation (EU) No 1052/2013, Art. 3 (g).

per cent. When they say this container is suspect, 50 per cent of the time there is something strange. This is CPIP.[73]

The situational picture of the pre-frontier presents information "that allows you to be proactive," but instead of working with legal evidence, it works with a virtual suspicion. Policing based on collected knowledge and experience is not new ("let's see where this guy is going this time"). What is new is that this knowledge comes from a database and has been evaluated through algorithms and is no longer tied to the experience of the border guard doing the assessment. In information-based border management, a suspicion no longer develops through a concrete operational situation on a border, but within the national coordination centers and analytical institutes, in particular the Frontex Risk Analysis Unit (RAU). The "seeing like a border" called for by Chris Rumford (see for instance Rumford/Geiger 2014) is also embraced and managed by Frontex, although not cosmopolitan in outlook. The gaze on the border reality rather is "more technologically and statistically mediated and 'datafied'" (Broeders/Dijstelbloem 2016: 242). Judging by the premise of "if you are able to analyze the information" stated in the interview, the interest in and use for data and information is potentially unlimited.

The EUROSUR Regulation allows for the electronic monitoring of the pre-frontier area and therefore transfers the coordination of "the common application of surveillance tools"[74] to Frontex. The agency is thus again awarded a strong power over knowledge because it can define, or rather select, the targets to be monitored and the kind of data to be collected and processed. The task of supplying "national coordination centres *and itself* with surveillance information on the external borders and on the pre-frontier on a regular, reliable and cost-efficient basis"[75] distinctly goes beyond the act of providing a service. Rather, because Frontex is a coordinator, it is also a management tool and an authority.

Frontex can generate surveillance information through a variety of different information sources and surveillance apparatuses. First, the agency can monitor selected harbors in non-member states via satellite image.[76] Through these satellite images, Frontex can monitor the coastlines of non-member parties in order to determine potential landing sites for small boats that can be used for refugees

---

73 EUROSUR Project Manager at Frontex, personal interview (May 15, 2012).
74 EUROSUR Regulation (EU) No 1052/2013, Art. 12.
75 Ibid., Art. 12 (1), emphasis added.
76 EUROSUR Regulation (EU) No 1052/2013, Art. 12 (2a), (3b).

and migrants. Second, the agency can also evaluate shipping traffic information.[77] The evaluation of various tracking signals[78] allows them to locate vessels that are not sending signals and therefore cannot be identified. Because the monitoring and tracking of shipping traffic occurs via a comparison of signals that have already been received, all vessels that do not send signals are suspected. As a result, the line separating not-identified and potentially dangerously become fluid (Mallia 2010: 34). In addition, the suspicious lack of signals of certain boats and the SOS calls of vessels in distress are also relevant pieces of information when creating an overall picture. When visualized and integrated into discussions, this information creates opportunities for border guards to intervene (Miltner 2006: 84-85). Third, additional selected maritime areas or parts of the pre-frontier area can be monitored.[79] with "sensors mounted on any vehicle, vessel or other craft."[80] Frontex decides which areas, harbors or vessels to monitor based on its own risk analysis. Although its declared aim is to provide member states with information, it also admits that the "agency may use on its own initiative the surveillance tools referred to in paragraph 2 for collecting information which is relevant for the common pre-frontier intelligence picture,"[81] Finally, the visualization of border-related incidents in the pre-frontier area, regardless of how this occurs, – whether as dots, satellite imagery or incident reports – normalizes its somewhat extra-territorial mandate by suggesting a transformed topography of operational borders. The legal borders of policing thus become more mobile as the CPIP becomes more routine.

The self-reflexive reference to CPIP amplifies Frontex's competences. As an official of the European Parliament in Brussels said while shaking his head during the negotiations for the EUROSUR Regulation, "CPIP is Frontex," Indeed, assigned with the task of establishing the CPIP and ESP, Frontex has become not only an institutional hub through which information concerning the pre-frontier area can be collected and made graphically understandable; it has also become a

---

77 EUROSUR Regulation (EU) No 1052/2013, Art. 12 (3a).
78 Ships are to report their identity and position four times a day to Long Range Identification and Tracking System (LRIT) data centers. The implementation of LRIT is mandatory for all ships with over 300 gross tonnage as of May 2006. Information from the Vessel Monitoring System (VMS) or the Automatic Identification System (AIS) can be used without a ship's consent (Mallia 2010: 34-37).
79 EUROSUR Regulation (EU) No 1052/2013: Art. 12 (2e).
80 Ibid, Art. 12 (3c).
81 Ibid, Art. 12 (5).

service provider that has and distributes statistical information about crossings of the EU's outer borders. Thanks to EUROSUR, Frontex is no longer merely an agency acting as a neutral coordinator on behalf of a supranational state; it is rather a "centre of calculation" (cf. Latour 2003: 215-257) for its border.[82]

At the same time, the CPIP is not an information layer or a separate electronic map, like the national situational pictures, but a description of competences. CPIP is the supranational sphere of competences, agreements and access. Regarding the ESP, it lets risk analysis and operational recommendations be integrated into the way national authorities see and interpret situations along the external border of the EU. To Frontex, the CPIP is an instrument for bridging the gap between management and mandate.

4.4 EUROSUR ON THE SCREEN: THE DEPICTION OF AN EXTERNAL EU BORDER?

As Gordon Fyfe and John Law point out, a "depiction is never just an illustration. It is the material representation, the apparently stabilized product of a process of work" (Fyfe/Law 1988: 1). In this section, I began by unfolding the process of work that was necessary for developing a network that facilitates the exchange of information and analysis between border authorities in the EU. I then outlined the visualization and integration of this data on the screen as a European situational picture (ESP) and a common pre-frontier intelligence picture (CPIP) respectively, and I discussed the premises and arguments of the electronic depiction. Effectively, the EUROSUR IT network is as much a result of a process of work as it is an ongoing process of constant work on the ESP. I thus analyzed the EUROSUR on the screen as both a result and a process.

In tracing the development of the network, it quickly became clear that the challenge presented by this process of work did not consist in the technical details of the GIS's configuration, programming or software design, but rather in the acceptance of and compliance to the system by member state authorities. Still, the flexible and non-committal method used to test the IT application strongly contributed to convincing member states to consider the system in the

---

82 I used this characterization already in an earlier publication (Ellebrecht 2014b: 180). It has also been advanced by Dennis Broeders and Huub Dijstelbloem (2016: 243) in an essay publication.

first place and gradually led to an increase in trust and compliance among participants. The communication format and the rules of information exchange between member state authorities were geared toward the usability of the graphic user interface.

Indeed, an issue of sovereign competences was translated into an issue of software design and was solved as such. Correspondingly, different national angles were arranged in the GUI under menu items, domains of competence were translated into GIS layers, and different political hierarchies were flattened to nodes in the system. Ultimately, it was probably easier to get used to menu items for the purpose of testing an IT application than to agree on common priorities for border policies in Europe.

However, the EUROSUR on the screen did more than just allow the reconstruction of the process of work that went into it. The electronic map of the ESP, the "EUROSUR on the screen," not only provides an image to the added value of information exchange and not only demonstrates that all the extra work and the institutional reconfigurations are worth it, it also offers what Latour has called a "new visual language" (Latour 1986: 19) that allows the external border of the EU to be 'seen' as a supranational entity.

Indeed, it is not border guards and Frontex officials who now have the new supranational border in mind and in plain view – a supranational EU external border is not a thing that border guards or foreign ministers all of a sudden see and thereof take for granted. It is not a new thing that can be seen from one moment to the next, from the moment of signing the Schengen Agreement or its Europeanization in the Treaty of Amsterdam. It is rather the case that "the same old eyes and old minds" are now applied to the communicational format of the EUROSUR network, which allows them to naturally see the external border of the EU as a job description. The EUROSUR on the screen offers the "new fact sheets inside new institutions" (Latour 1986: 15), which allows the old heads to naturally see the common border. Incident reports and impact levels are distinct features of this new fact sheet. As boundary objects (Star/Griesemer 1989), they unite national issues at the border with ambitions of European border management. Hence, the "EUROSUR on the screen" can duly be described as a "giant 'optical device' that creates a new laboratory, a new type of vision and a new phenomenon to look at" (Latour 1986: 19).

In many ways, the EUROSUR items differ from the cartographic depiction of political borders and the treaties on them in the modern frame. First and foremost, EUROSUR's electronic map provides a situational picture and not a representational map. The electronic map displaying the European situational picture is the tangible result of both the exchange of information and institutional reconfigurations in EU border policies. It is the epitome of the system and the focal point of the regulation. The regulation, in turn, defines how situational pictures are to be produced, namely "through the collection, evaluation, collation, analysis, interpretation, generation, visualization and dissemination of information." In fact, the European situational picture is based on a reversed relationship between the notion of border and the notion of selection: the drawing of a line as a benchmark to selection has given way to the drawing together of disaggregated sources and information which visually cumulate by their geo-code; homogenous territory on the one side, constantly changing distribution and assessment of risks on the other. In this sense, Rocco Bellanova and Denis Duez aptly describe EUROSUR as a "continuous effort of mise-en-discourse" rather than "an addendum or technical fix" (2016b: 40).

This chapter has shown that EUROSUR brings about the laboratory, the vision, and ultimately the "new phenomenon to look at" (ibid). While the different NCCs and Frontex RAU are networked as the "new laboratory" producing knowledge and maps of border-related incidents, the ESP embodies the "new type of vision." This vision assembles on the screen, where it benefits from "the appearance of a neutral and depoliticized form of calculation" (Amoore 2009: 20), even though it integrates discontinuously generated data and the most diverse ways of obtaining information and suspicion. Ultimately, the ESP provides a view of the situation at the external borders and a vision of cooperation, joint tasks, and operational urgencies. The exchange of information thus produces a picture, a vision, and affords a supranational mandate to react.

5 EUROSUR on Paper – in the Official Journal of the EU

The EUROSUR on the screen mediates the "new phenomenon to look at" (Latour 1986: 19): the external border of the EU. Since this work deals with the emergence of an EU external border, the question now arises whether the technical tool described above has told the entire story of its evolution. Is the EU's external border reified via the digital geo-coded mapping of border-related events and impact levels? Does EUROSUR, in fact, successfully produce an external border of the EU by providing a network and a situational picture? In other words: is this a story of technological determinism?

If the 'new' materiality of the border was, in fact, digitally produced, how would this border acquire its legitimacy? Isn't a border also a legal entity aside from being materially and cartographically represented; not only a product of practices but also of treaties?

This chapter examines how this external EU border in-the-making turns into an official border with legal authority. It traces different attempts to acquire legality for a supranational border which would provide law enforcement officers with the quality to act. While the external border materializes on the screen, its mandate and legitimacy assemble elsewhere. But where? And as what kind of product? How does the EUROSUR development phase play into this assembling of legality? To answer these questions, this chapter turns toward the second product of the EUROSUR development phase, namely the EUROSUR Regulation, and thus to an item of secondary EU law. In terms of their status in the legal framework of the EU, regulations are "binding in their entirety and have direct effects in the Member States" (Voermans 2009: 412). In the words of the Head of the Research and Development Unit at Frontex, the EUROSUR Regulation is the tangible result of the "bigger Commission project," which he distinguished in an interview from the "practical project" of the EUROSUR network.

"We have our own EUROSUR here, within Frontex, which is a very practical project, which focuses on the development of this network. This forms part of the bigger Commission project that has different steps, and that will lead to a further gradual build-up, integration of the EUROSUR idea in this bigger conceptual picture."[1]

This chapter is interested in the details, traits and traces of the "bigger conceptual picture," and thus in the other half of the story. It discusses in how far the "practical project" of the IT network described in the previous section relates to the political process of streamlining border policies among EU member states. In doing so, I intend to explore what precisely the kind of relation is that is behind the notion of the network-forming part of the "bigger conceptual picture."

While the previous chapter dealt with the generation of compliance, this chapter focusses on how the obligations concerning the exchange of information and the cooperation between member states and the Frontex agency became acceptable and binding. Officials of the European Commission know and underline that the acceptance is always very important, and that the mere saying that this is a binding rule is not enough. Yet, how did the "bigger Commission project"[2] of EUROSUR gain acceptance among member states and in the European Parliament to the effect of legal codification. How can the relation between the binding rule of the EUROSUR Regulation, i.e. the legal thing, and the acceptance of the technical EUROSUR network, i.e. the technical thing, be described?

Do politics thus have artifacts or legislations? With this question in mind, I want to follow the course of garnering legitimacy for common EU border policies, from the signing of the Schengen Agreement in June 1985 to the adoption of the EUROSUR Regulation in December 2013. Looking at different attempts of Europeanization in the field of immigration and border control policies since the Schengen Agreement, I intend to specify what the EUROSUR project does, assembles and mobilizes, all of which did not fall into place before.

For this purpose, I trace the political and institutional development of the EUROSUR, firstly by examining its precedent initiatives between 1985 and 2013, and secondly by paying particular attention to visions and catalysts of communitarian border policies in the EU. Generally, a move from "Europeanization by objectives" to "Europeanization by service" can be observed. This development can be traced on different plateaus, which I will explore in the following

---

1 Head of Research and Development at Frontex, telephone interview (October 28, 2011).
2 Ibid.

six sections. However, the heuristic division shall not suggest that the development was directed toward EUROSUR from the beginning. Rather, different attempts at mutualizing operational standards and exchanging information can be observed.

5.1 SCHENGEN AS A POSTNATIONAL LABORATORY AND FRAMEWORK FOR NEGOTIATIONS (1985-1997)

Unlike Latour's (1986: 17) description of a process of inscription, in which "paper always appears at the end," the following development was initiated with the signing of a paper. On June 14, 1985, the representatives of the five signatory states, West Germany, France, the Netherlands, Belgium and Luxembourg, signed the "Agreement on the gradual abolition of checks at their common borders": the Schengen Agreement.[3] For the act of signing the agreement, they left the firm ground of their territorial nation-states and boarded the riverboat Princess Marie-Astrid. This took them to the middle of the river Moselle, and thus to a *condominium*, a location of joint sovereignty. The choice of location was consciously a symbolic one.[4] It was meant to signify the overcoming of the "old" nationalisms in Europe and demonstrate the courage to base policies on joint considerations rather than on national sovereignty. As elaborated above, the aim of reconciliation through economic integration had been set with the Treaty of Rome. However, even though market integration was considered a path to stabil-

---

3   The agreement was signed by Robert Goebbels (Secretary of State for Foreign Affairs) for Luxembourg, Catherine Lalumière (Secretary of State for European Affairs) for France, Waldemar Schreckenberger (Secretary of State at the Federal Chancellery) for West Germany, Paul de Keersmaeker (Secretary of State for European Affairs) for Belgium, and by Wim van Eekelen (Secretary of State for Foreign Affairs) for the Netherlands.

4   According to the former Luxembourgish secretary of state Robert Goebbels, cosigner of the agreement, the symbolism was decisive for the choice of location. German original: "Wir haben das gemacht in Schengen, weil dies das Dreiländereck ist, dort, wo der Benelux, Deutschland und Frankreich zusammenstoßen, und auf einem Schiff in der Mosel, weil die Mosel ein Kondominium ist, das heißt deutsches und luxemburgisches Hoheitsgebiet" (quoted in Herter 2010). The Luxembourgian town of Schengen, from which the 'Princess Marie-Astrid' departed, gave name to the agreement.

ity and peace among previous bellicose states in Europe, the concrete political consequences of doing away with sovereign control at national border appeared too risky to the political actors and the general public in EEC countries (Hobbing 2006: 173; Zaiotti 2011: 4, 67-89). To a certain extent, the Schengen group thus acted as an avant-garde in putting a political will on paper that hadn't garnered consensus among all EEC member states.

What did this paper stipulate? Albeit a treaty on borders, it did not determine or redraw any borders by delimitating territory (see chapter 2.1). It constituted an area for the free movement for goods, capital, services and persons, which rendered cooperation necessary (Vobruba 2012: 135; Nagy 2006: 105). Unlike territorial border treaties, the Schengen Agreement did not resolve a conflict, nor organize a consensus. Neither did the Schengen Implementing Convention (SIC) of 1990. On the contrary, both papers fueled debates and requested further work and procedures. Signatory states agreed to "open discussions" on ways of cooperation and judicial assistance,[5] "to examine any [related] difficulties,"[6] to "endeavour" or "seek to harmonize" laws and regulations,[7] to "endeavour to approximate visa policies,"[8] and to "seek means to combat crime jointly."[9] The pragmatic and consented aim was formulated as the realization of an "equal level of control [...] exercised at external borders."[10]

While the agreement enabled a common domestic market, the papers read as a recognition of the practical problems that the gradual abolition of "internal" borders could bring about, especially with regard to the mandate and organization of law enforcement. As has been noted above, the Schengen Agreement and Convention did not bring about the notion of legal authority for an external EU border or common border policies.

Unlike those contracts in modern politics that concealed national territorial borders, these two papers rather mark the beginning of displacements and mobilizations of competences in security policies in the EU. With the monopoly over the legitimate means of movement (Torpey 1998) being delegated to an arena of, "cooperation," "mutual recognition" and "shared responsibility," – as the jargon puts it – common Schengen border policies were required to work toward acquir-

---

5   Schengen Agreement, Art. 18.
6   Ibid, Art. 18 (b).
7   Ibid, Art. 13 and Art. 19.
8   Ibid, Art. 7.
9   Ibid, Art. 18 (c).
10 Schengen Implementing Convention, Art. 6 (5).

ing acceptance and legitimacy among member states and practitioners. Even though the five signatory states individually went ahead in working toward European market integration, this process was neither smooth nor easy. In fact, the implementation of the Schengen rules has been described as "tortuous," with difficulties ranging from "problems with the SIS computer system" to "concerns with transparency and democratic accountability," to public concerns or "panic [...] about immigration and drugs" (Duff 1997: 53). Commentators thus saw Schengen as either "pathfinder" (ibid: 52), "competitor" (Jeandesboz 2009: para. 2), or "laboratory" (Monar 2001: 750-752) for cooperation in the areas of border and migration control.

Of these characterizations, the laboratory metaphor has gained the most currency. This is particularly true among academic commentators, who have deployed or quoted the metaphor to illustrate the agreement's secretive preparations or to criticize the intergovernmental procedures as illegitimate in terms of EU integration. For instance, William Walters (2002: 561) notes that Schengen had been developed and implemented outside the framework of the EU. The fact that this criticism concerns the authorship of the agreement and not its legality deserves careful attention. The Schengen Agreement's form – an international agreement – was not so critical to the acceptance of its rules, as was its formation: in fact, the preparation of the Schengen Agreement was largely based on a German-French initiative carried out under strict secrecy by then Chancellor Helmuth Kohl and then President François Mitterrand. In Germany, "neither the parliament nor the responsible ministries nor the public had been informed prior to the agreement" (Siebold 2013: 43; Baumann 2006: 80-81). Waldemar Schreckenberger, chief of the German Federal Chancellery (Ger.: *Bundeskanzleramt*) at that time, recalled in an interview with Mechthild Baumann that Helmuth Kohl personally requested him to work out the Schengen Agreement. "I succeeded ultimately to engage the responsible minister in intensive work. When I determined that a representative of the minister wasn't prepared to cooperate, then he wouldn't be invited anymore" (quoted in Baumann 2008: 22). By choosing the format of an intergovernmental agreement, which did not require ratification by national parliaments, Kohl and Mitterrand chose a procedure which was not made to generate acceptance or legitimacy, but rather aimed at getting things done.

When the laboratory metaphor is evoked today, it stirs up this sense of illegitimacy, secrecy and undemocratic decisions. However, unlike this impetus, the laboratory metaphor was first deployed by the political actors involved in order to actually counter the "sense of illegitimacy surrounding the Schengen initiative" (Zaiotti 2011: 75). Zaiotti actually found that "[t]he laboratory metaphor and the family of related concepts ('testing,' 'experimenting,' 'trial,' etc.) surfaced in internal and public documents and speeches about the Schengen regime soon after the initiative was launched in the mid-1980s" (ibid). The Commission, for its parts, considered Schengen as a "separate but parallel and very relevant exercise";[11] it was considered a "testing ground" and "test-bed"[12] for the developments concerning free movement in the EU. The Commission did not consider the initiative as thwarting EU procedures and legislation. Instead, it actively tried to use it in order to accelerate EU wide integration in this regard.

"The Commission participates in the work of the Schengen Group which it finds invaluable in formulating its ideas in the wider Community context and which enables it to help ensure that Schengen is compatible with Community law and with the Community's objectives: but in no way would the Commission wish to slow down progress where progress can be made."[13]

It remains controversial whether intergovernmental cooperation in juridical and police matters is to be considered an "aberration" (Ger.: *Fehlentwicklung*, Stabenow 1995) or an "engine" for common European policies. Clearly, the Schengen Agreement and the Convention did not conceal supranational border and migration policies or an external EU border. They are, in fact, agreements for opening up a laboratory for postnational law enforcement, and they describe the first modes of functioning and equipment to be used in this setup.

---

11 Abolition of controls of persons at intra-community borders, COM(88) 640 final, para. 12.
12 Formulation used in: Written Question No. 413/89 by Mr. Ernest Glinne to the Commission of the European Community. Assessment of the Schengen agreement, OJ C 90 (9 April 1990): 11; quoted in Zaiotti (2011: 75).
13 Abolition of controls of persons at intra-community borders, COM(88) 640 final, para. 12.

5.2 IN SEARCH FOR NEW, SUPRANATIONAL HEADS (1997-2003)

When the heads of states and governments updated the Treaty of the European Union on June 18, 1997 in Amsterdam, they formalized the incorporation of the Schengen rules into the legal framework of the EU. The EU brought supranational legitimacy to the intergovernmental Schengen arrangement. With its "extensive list of working arrangements" and the then working Schengen Information System (SIS), Schengen increased the "operational capacity" of policies concerning police and judicial cooperation (Boer/Corrado 1999: 399). Monica den Boer and Laura Corrado see the Treaty of Amsterdam as a "momentum for a marriage of convenience between Schengen and the EU" (ibid), with the fiancés exchanging legitimacy for operational capacity.

The Treaty of Amsterdam redirected the efforts of the Schengen group into ambitions for an Area of Freedom, Security and Justice (AFSJ), a space instituted by way of police and justice cooperation. The latter was translated into a program for measures in Tampere, Finland in 1999. The Tampere Programme intended to render border and migration policies more coherent and more effective. It did so by taking into account that post-Amsterdam, the political and institutional setup would, in theory, facilitate communitarian policies. However, the forms of these common EU border and migration control policies and also the figures which could potentially operationalize them and enforce an external border were envisioned quite differently.

5.2.1 The Idea of a 'European Corps of Border Guards' or a 'European Border Police'

When the European Commission proposed a regulation on the European Border and Coast Guard in December 2015, observers of EU Justice and Home Affairs might have groaningly commented that this had only been a question of time.[14]

---

14 European Commission (2015): Proposal for a Regulation of the European Parliament and of the Council on the European Border and Coast Guard and repealing Regulation (EC) No 2007/2004, Regulation (EC) No 863/2007 and Council Decision 2005/267/EC, COM(2015) 671 final (December 15, 2015).

In fact, what had been proposed and has been accepted in 2016[15] is not less than a supranational border police, which derives its mandate and strategy from supranational considerations. A European border police is not a recent idea. In fact, it has been around since the Treaty of Amsterdam and thus, since the incorporation of the Schengen rules into the EU legal framework. As early as 2000, word was out about an EU-wide integrated border police. If it was, in fact, only a question of time until EU border guards would be accepted, one can raise the question of what happened in the interim. Why has it been consented to now, and what is different now from then? Is it a proposal that just had to be digested, one that needed 15 years to mature so that the heads of state could simply "rubber stamp" (Eriksson 2016) it four months after it had been tabled by the Commission?

Against the background of the previous chapter, I argue that this development has required more than time, diplomatic patience and the persistent repetition of communitarian benefits. On the basis of the analyses in chapter 4, I claim that the vision of the European border guard was lacking a visualized localization for their mandate. The European situational picture generated in the EUROSUR framework embodies this visualization. In fact, a consideration of the first proposals around an EU border guard reveals similar ideas, concepts, and even semantics to those that now support the EUROSUR project. Yet, this early vision was still lacking the "optical consistency" (Latour 1986: 15) that EUROSUR later provided with its menu items, icons and reporting sheets.

Let us turn back to the first mentions of an EU border police. In 2000, various media outlets reported that Italy and Germany foresaw an exchange of troops, aiming "to serve as a vanguard of an EU-wide integrated border police" (*Migration News* (N.N.) 2000). Kurt Schelter, minister for justice and European affairs for the federal state Brandenburg, was quoted in the British *Telegraph* proposing the "deployment up to 10,000 of Germany's 40,000 Federal Border Guards in a joint EU border patrol. This was motivated by the fact that German frontiers with

---

15 Regulation (EU) No 2016/1624 of the European Parliament and of the Council of 14 September 2016 on the European Border and Coast Guard and amending Regulation (EU) 2016/399 of the European Parliament and of the Council and repealing Regulation (EC) No 863/2007 of the European Parliament and of the Council, Council Regulation (EC) No 2007/2004 and Council Decision 2005/267/EC, in: OJ L 251/1 (September 16, 2016); [hereafter cited as Regulation on the European Border and Coast Guard Agency].

Poland and the Czech Republic are removed under the Schengen system" (Evans-Pritchard/Helm 2000). However, the intention to deploy border guards 'elsewhere' was not considered a mere geographical shift. The journalists Ambrose Evan-Pritchard and Toby Helm point to the "political sensitivities" of "stationing German border guards on Polish soil" and reported that "Berlin [was] looking at the idea of a joint EU force in which every country would participate on equal terms" (ibid). From this perspective, the communitarian vision still implicates the taming of the national. By contrast, the United Kingdom worked toward taming European and Schengen ambitions for an integrated force, while agreeing on the need for more cooperation in tackling illegal migration (Zaiotti 2011: 162-163).

In 2000, the Commission nevertheless commented with reserve on the border guard exchange between Italy and Germany. It emphasized that "such exercises were a matter for individual member states," that "there were no plans for a supranational force, and that the Commission's job was only to set common standards for dealing with asylum requests, refugees and illegal migrants" (quoted in *Migration News* (N.N.) 2000). Yet, the first official mention of the term "European Border Guard" can be traced back to the Commission's "Communication on Illegal Immigration" of November 15, 2001.[16] Therein, the Commission stresses that "the setting up of a European Border Guard" was a "core element" of a border management strategy; it also mentioned that the idea had "received strong political support" and that "exploratory work" was underway.[17] The exploratory work consisted of a) the first joint operations and b) conceptual explorations: the Commission supported a feasibility study on the idea of a European Border Police. The laboratory was thus generating its first outputs.

The "Feasibility Study for Setting-up of a European Border Police" was conducted by Italy together with Germany, Belgium, France and Spain, with 80 per cent of the financial support coming from the Odysseus Programme. The feasibility study was undertaken over a six-month period between November 2001 and May 2002 and was presented during a ministerial conference in Rome on 30 May 2002. It collected "input from a number of national experts, most of whom tended to defend their national methods and organisational structures" (Monar 2006: 196). Jörg Monar assumes that this rather protective stance toward national competences and organizational structures led to the study's proposition of a

---

16 Communication from the Commission to the Council and the European Parliament on a common policy on illegal immigration, COM(2001) 672 final (November 15, 2001).
17 Ibid, Section 4.4 (Border Management, p.17-18).

complex network of national border police forces. The form of organization was evoked as "polycentric and multipurpose system."[18] The network model was evoked as "a series of 'knots,' each of them related to specific and sector requirements/objectives."[19] The knots would specialize while the system remained flexible and elastic.[20]

In fact, the study used similar terms as would be later used in the context of the EUROSUR network. There was talk of centers and knots, for instance, which correspond to NCCs, and nodes in the system in the context of EUROSUR. At that time, however, the study's vision was not approved by member states. In the view of most national authorities involved, the proposal for a polycentric network model "was lacking in clarity, providing a mosaic of proposed structures and individual measures rather than a grand design" (Monar 2006: 196). Monar comments that "some of the participating Member states were not fully satisfied;" and he goes on to quote a Brussels newspaper article dismissing the "entire study, rather harshly, as '80 pages of waffle'" (quoted in ibid: 196-197).

Apparently, the study's network model was a strong vision that, however, was lacking its visual grip. Unlike BG Major Aleksandra Świąteka in 2012, authorities in 2003 could not *see* – and therefore could not recognize – the benefit of it all. In more abstract terms, the 2003 proposal of a European Border Police was lacking the "'optical consistency' necessary for power on a large scale" (Latour 1986: 15). As the new object to be guarded, the external border was neither considered natural, nor taken for granted institutionally. In other words, it was not rendered immutable or – as we are accustomed to in our formulation of borders – not yet natural. The EU external border could therefore not be seen, as it was not made visible, which is to say, interobjective.

In fact, the proposal of a European border police or border guard was advanced during a situation which, following Latour, can be described as an "agnostic situation" (Latour 1986: 8). Security personnel still believed in the strength of the national framework for law enforcement. However, they did not deny the eventual existence or rather necessity of an EU external border. Just, it was not taken for granted by the former national heads. In their mind, there was no picture of an EU external border. The mandate that was proposed – the guarding of a supranational border – was built on the projection, the enunciation of an

---

18 Feasibility Study for Setting-up of a European Border Police, Final Report, Rome (May 30, 2002), Section 13, p. 30.
19 Ibid, Section 14, p. 30.
20 Ibid, Section 19, p. 35-36.

"absent thing" (ibid). One the one hand, this was due to the spectral character of all borders. On the other hand, this was also due to fact that different heads of state and government and also the security personnel at the border had no "meeting ground" (ibid) for recognizing an EU external border. Peter Hobbing's description of the vested perspective on common border tasks illustrates the mistrust with regard to communitarian law enforcement at Schengen borders.

"Discussions sprang up, inside the territory, as to whether 'these foreigners on the border' would do a good job in keeping the border tight, or create loopholes that allowed organised crime and illicit migration to penetrate all the way through the Union. Right on the border, discussions went in the opposite direction: 'Why is it just us who bear all the responsibility and the financial burden?'" (Hobbing 2005: 1)

Oblivious to the apparition of a supranational border, the European Council did not find consensus on the proposal of a European border police. The Presidency's conclusion of the 2001 Laeken meeting abstained from using the term "European Border Guard" or "European Border Police" at all; and the Council's compromise has been described as "carefully worded" by commentators (Monar 2006: 195; Leonard 2009: 376-377). Echoing the prudent tone of the Schengen Convention, the Council's Laeken conclusion[21] calls on the group members to work toward an Europeanization of border surveillance and control.

Hence, ten years after the formulation of the SIC, and two years after the integration of the Schengen rules into the EU legal framework, border policies are still national in outlook. Communitarian control policies remain an objective to work toward. Actually, the Presidency's requests to the Council and the Commission is less a mandate than a vague declaration of intent, in which the Council members want to principally establish the conditions of possibility for common services of control. Council and Commission are concordantly requested to "work out arrangements for cooperation between services responsible for external border control and [...] examine the conditions in which a mechanism or common services to control external borders could be created."[22] For the time being, the attempts were merely directed toward setting the course while examin-

---

21 Presidency Conclusions on Justice and Home Affairs, Laeken Conclusion No 42, 17 December 2001, SN 300/1/01.
22 Ibid, para. 42.

ing the "conditions in which"[23] the vision of a supranational border would be visible and politically thinkable as a supranational thing.

5.2.2 The Auxiliary and Displacing Notion of Integrated Border Management (IBM)

On 7 May 2002, the Commission responded to the Laeken conclusion.[24] Its response has been interpreted as an "effort to satisfy both the advocates and the sceptics" of a supranational border police (Monar 2006: 196). In its communication, the Commission placed emphasis on both "operational synergies" and on whatever "*practical* progress which could be achieved in various fields *in the meantime*" (ibid, emphasis added). Joint operations and border guard exchanges thus occurred while the legal codification of a supranational mandate was pending. Such a mandate would provide border guards with the power to sanction on behalf of the EU. Thus, while there was a lot of integrative work going on at the actual workplaces of border guards, there was no political agreement on the common legal framework which would place this cooperation under a supranational mandate.

Effectively, the ambition for a supranational force entails going beyond the principle of mutual recognition of decisions at national borders, which was foreseen in the Schengen Agreement and Convention. Ambitions for a supranational force have to deal with the question of where this supranational authority would be based. It also raises questions of which authority would enforce whose laws and grant access to what kinds of rights; for instance, whether Greek nationals would accept a French border guard patrolling along their borders. Apart from that issue, the figure of a European border guard was required to formulate, accept and enforce common (im)migration and asylum rules (of which there are none even until today) and grant European rights. The notion of integrated border management (IBM), as introduced by the Commission's Communication of May 7, 2002, mediated between practical cooperation, which suffered from its

---

23 Presidency Conclusions on Justice and Home Affairs, Laeken Conclusion No 42, 17 December 2001, SN 300/1/01, para. 42.

24 European Commission (2002): Communication from the Commission to the Council and the European Parliament, Towards Integrated Management of the External Borders of the Member States of the European Union, COM(2002) 233 final (May 7, 2002).

test character, and the reluctance toward official harmonization (in a legal sense). By pragmatically focusing on the optimization of controlling and surveilling movement across borders, the auxiliary notion of integrated management somewhat depoliticized the communitarization of border policies.

During the 1990s, the concept of integrated border management had been elaborated as a community concept (Hobbing 2005: 2). However, rather than the converging political impetus, a "pragmatic orientation" (Monar 2006) and a managerial tone of focusing on concrete tasks and measures took hold. The border was no longer evoked as a security shield or borderline but instead as a common task of security personnel. Border enforcement is thereby "detached from the territorial logic" (Jorry 2007: 14) and targeted toward certain groups of people and certain kinds of movements deemed relevant to border control – which in this case is translated into the control of movement. For this border work, neither geography, nor law stands as a unifier, but rather common challenges and common tasks. Integrated border management is thus an integrating task.

5.2.3 The CIVIPOL Feasibility Study and the Notion of the Virtual (Maritime) Border

With regard to the idea of a European border guards, the integrative vision of the Commission's communication has been relativized by the Councils pragmatic orientation. What remains integrated, however, in a managerial sense of a comprehensive approach, are the measures to counter illegal migration – particularly by sea. It is against the backdrop of the sea, that it is possible to reverse the question of localization of an EU external border and ask for the locus of common tasks, challenges, and risks. The CIVIPOL feasibility study, which had been commissioned to examine how the EU could strengthen "controls at maritime borders in order to combat illegal immigration," is a central document in this regard.[25]

In 2002, the Commission contracted CIVIPOL, a French think tank associated with the national Ministry of the Interior, to conduct the "Feasibility study on

---

25 CIVIPOL (2003): Feasibility study on the control of the European Union's maritime borders. Final report transmitted to DG JAI on July 4, 2003. Available as Council Document 11490/1/03 (September 19, 2003); [hereafter cited as CIVIPOL study or CIVIPOL feasibility study], here: p. 4.

the control of the European Union's maritime borders." The study was completed swiftly in the first half of 2003 and then presented in Brussels on July 4, 2003. The document was of central importance, as it presented new drafts of the location as well as the type of common external borders. Different commentators have identified the so called CIVIPOL feasibility study as an inflection point in the self-conception of EU border policies. For instance, Dimitris Papadopoulos, Niamh Stephenson and Vassilis Tsianos introduce the study as an example of the "virtualisation of borders, which consists of deterritorialising border controls and externalising camps" (Papadopoulos/Stephenson/Tsianos 2008: 176). Olivier Clochard and Bruno Dupeyron trace how the externalization of EU police activities to countries of departure became thinkable through the lens of the CIVIPOL feasibility study (Clochard/Dupeyron 2007: 27-29). Statewatch analyst Ben Hayes even considers the study "a law enforcement blueprint rather than any kind of objective or broad-based 'feasibility study'" (Hayes 2003: para. 9). In fact, operational practices of border enforcement agencies as well as national legislations changed in reference to the CIVIPOL study and its concept of the "virtual maritime border,"

The study (hereafter cited in the text) describes the special characteristics of maritime borders. According to the CIVIPOL study, maritime borders are prone to three types of "illegal immigration" which it classifies according to routes or possible entries into the EU. First, there are *port-to-port routes* with harbors as entry points where illegal immigrants enter as stowaways; second, there are *focal routes,* which are "geographically favourable" resulting in 70 to 80 per cent of illegal immigration occurring in this way: "The usual practice here is that a (disposable) light boat, overloaded and having absolutely no safety equipment, makes a night crossing."[26] Third, CIVIPOL sees *random routes* which involve ships from 300 to 500 GRT and which are "chartered by transnational criminal organisations with investment capacities and local accomplices in the port of departure."[27] The study states that, although only two to three per cent of illegal immigration occurs in this last manner, it attracted the greatest public attention as several hundred migrants were involved.[28] In terms of legal instruments, the study sees that illegal immigrations are "subject to international law on two grounds": They can either be "seen from the sea" or "from the land."[29] It has

---

26 CIVIPOL feasibility study, p. 9.
27 Ibid, p. 10, emphasis added.
28 Ibid.
29 Ibid, p. 20.

been argued that seen from the sea, "the legal bases for combating illegal immigration" are to be found in the December 10, 1982 Montego Bay Convention on the Law of the Sea. On this basis of flag state liability, the interception or containment of vessels with migrants on board could be justified in different maritime zones.[30] In contrast, seen from the land, the rights of migrants were emphasized:

"the right of asylum is the criterion which distinguishes a political refugee from an illegal immigrant as regards the right to enter and stay in a European country. All the Member States or Schengen States have ratified the Geneva Convention. They are required to apply it. An illegal immigrant will therefore, naturally, claim refugee status as long as possible one way or another."[31]

In short, at sea, the operational leeway for border enforcement was considered stronger in comparison to containment possibilities at land, where the obligation of states toward individuals weighs higher. In consequence, the study recommends that physical border controls may be supported and reinforced by "an upstream 'virtual border' for the operational management of the three types of routes,"[32] which means shifting controls to ports or countries of origin and departure. With this shift in competences being generally more available via sea operations, the notion of a virtual border and the notion of the maritime border merged. Operating on the ambiguous notion of a virtual border, the CIVIPOL study advocates that border controls be relocated to possible migrant departure and transit points (such as coasts and harbors). Hayes criticizes that "[t]he underlying principle is that the EU's 'sea border' extends to any country with which it shares an ocean, basically giving it the right to police the entire sea" (Hayes 2003: para. 10). The concept of the virtual maritime border was taken up by the European Council in its "Programme of measures to combat illegal immigration across the maritime borders of the Member States of the European Union":

---

30 CIVIPOL feasibility study, p. 37.
31 Ibid, p. 20.
32 Ibid, p.53.

"The programme adopts the concept of the virtual maritime border in order to reinforce the legal borders of Member States by means of joint operations and specific measures in the places where illegal migratory flows originate or transit."[33]

The legal borders of policing seem to easily blur at sea. Subsequently, the Council's interpretation allows for operational flexibility along "the virtual maritime border": it argued that the passage of migrant vessels was not innocent, and there such passage could be intercepted both in territorial waters and contiguous zones; furthermore, if the vessel was not flying a flag, it could legally be intercepted on the high seas; lastly, joint patrols with countries of departure were considered an option if consent was given. Commentators gave the impression that the management of maritime borders invited a rewriting of the law of the sea (Hayes 2003: para. 23-28).

In fact, the CIVIPOL study documents an uninhibited will to reinterpret the possibility of enforcement practices at sea. The relocalizing of the job site of border guards, the institutional widening of competences and the use of external relations are semantically fettled in the sentence "virtual maritime border." The concept of the virtual maritime border thus rendered plausible a flexibilization of border control. Linking the concept of the virtual border to the idea of a maritime border made it possible to open up the idea of precise territorial borders in their spatial dimension and use them to entice geographical ambiguity. In the process, the reference intrinsic to border enforcement is no longer external to geographical administrative markers. The semiotic proximity of the sea and virtuality (Schroer 2006: 258-264) certainly contributed to detaching the range of European border control measures from 24 nautical miles of the contiguous zone; it also diffused its spatial reference (Ellebrecht 2014b: 177). In the argument that follows, the concept of the virtual border will appear again in connection with the notion of one that is intelligence-led. It is with this concept that the jurisdiction of law enforcement and border authorities increases with regard to geographical reference and access to information.

---

33 European Council (2003): Programme of measures to combat illegal immigration across the maritime border of the Member States of the European Union, EC 15445/03 (November 28, 2003).

5.3 COORDINATED COOPERATION ALONG THE VIRTUAL BORDER (2003-2008)

5.3.1 The Creation of Frontex: From Europeanization by Objectives to Management by Service

The CIVIPOL study further served as a basis for proposing the establishment of the "European Agency for the Management of Operational Cooperation at the External Borders of the Member States of the European Union" which has been abbreviated as Frontex (from the French phrase *frontières extérieures*). The Commission proposed its creation to the Council in November 2003. A year later the agency was established by the so called Frontex Regulation of October 26, 2004.[34] It took another year until the agency opened its headquarters in Warsaw on October 3, 2005. The stringent necessity to cooperate stemming from the Schengen Agreement and Convention was thus delegated for coordination to a community agency of the regulatory type.[35]

The creation of an agency was interpreted as "an ex post authorization of existing initiatives, and a streamlining of existing structures," with the regulation providing "little more than a window dressing exercise, giving a 'legal basis' to the *ad hoc* development of a whole host of operational bodies and measures that are already in place" (Hayes 2003: para. 2, original emphasis). Operational cooperation and the exchange of information which hitherto "all depended on the willingness of some member states to maybe share some information"[36] now depended on the knack the agency would show.

From the beginning the delegation of coordination to an agency was carefully framed as "support," "facilitation," and "service" to the member states, rather than any form of central, supranational border authority. In fact, since the establishment of Frontex "careful attention was paid to constantly refer to 'external

---

34 European Council (2004): Establishing a European Agency for the Management of Operational Cooperation at the External Borders of the Member States of the European Union, Council Regulation EC/2007/2004, October 26, 2004, in: OJ L 349 (November 25, 2004) [hereafter cited as Frontex Regulation EC 2007/2004].

35 Sarah Leonard (2009: 373-374) aptly describes Frontex as a regulatory agency, which is set out in its own legal basis, whereas executive agencies are allotted more narrowly defined tasks.

36 Head of Research and Development at Frontex, personal interview (May 27, 2011).

borders of the Member States' in order to stress as clearly as possible that the competence over the area of 'borders' remains at the heart of sovereignty of the State" (Carrera 2008: 9).[37]

The agency has been introduced as coordinator and iterates its role. However, tasked with risk analysis,[38] the role of the coordinator translates into the "competence to carry out 'coordinating intelligence-driven operations' based on risk analysis and threat assessments" (Carrera 2008: 2). While border control remained in the responsibility of member states, the management of risks and threats gained plausibility as a community task. Risk analysis, however, could be provided as a service to the member states, which allows the agency to suggest, if not recommend, technical and operational measures. Thus comments Andrew Neal that Frontex "sits alongside the (perhaps deliberately) less controversial discourse of regulation, best practice, training, coordination and management. [...] for the most part Frontex speaks 'risk' as a series of quiet, professional, technical practices" (Neal 2009: 351).

The Frontex Regulation has since been amended by the Council Decision of 2005/267/EC which established a secure web-based Information and Coordination Network for Member States' Migration Management Services, and two pieces of legislation: the Regulation on Rapid Border InterventionTeams, the revised mandate of September 2011. Both are no longer in force. The agency's personnel, budget, competences, and tasks have increased steadily. Since October 6, 2016, the abbreviated name Frontex has turned into a stand-in of sorts: Frontex now stands for the European Border and Coast Guard (EBCG) Agency.[39] This nominal transition to independence corresponds to an increase in autonomous competences: the coordinator pools means of violence (resources in the form of personnel and tools), and means of the power to decide (information and data). Furthermore in 2018, the Commission "proposed to strengthen the re-

---

37 However, already in 2006, Peter Hobbing expects that "with a growing need for operational assistance, [the agency] will develop into a body not too different from the European Border Guard originally intended" (Hobbing 2006: 184). The creation and also institutional development of Frontex has been analyzed and commented widely (cf. Carrera 2008; Fischer-Lescano/Lohr/Tohidipur 2009; Leonard 2009; Papastavridis 2010; Neal 2009; Kasparek 2010; Mungianu 2013; Perkowski 2018). For prompt analyses see the online blog *EU LAW Analysis* by Steve Peers at: http://eulawanalysis.blogspot.com.

38 Frontex Regulation EC 2007/2004, recital 6, Art. 2 (c), and Art. 4.

39 Regulation on the European Border and Coast Guard Agency of September 16, 2016.

cently created EBCG (2016) by providing the EBCG Agency [...] with its own operational tool, a standing corps of 10,000 EU border guards with executive powers that would be operational from 2020."[40]

From the beginning, Frontex was not to be dependent on information that member states were eventually willing to share, nor did the Hague principle of availability of information relate to the agency's task in any way. Rather, the idea was to set up a coherent information base, one which would be supranational in outlook while also identifying the common tasks and threats of all EU member states. Overall, through the creation of an agency, the management of border policies in Europe has increasingly been achieved by various services, rather than by objectives. Therein the agency both fulfills the roll of a coordinator while at the same time providing the grounds – decision support, trend and risk analysis, background information, statistics, equipment – for both member states' and community operations along the external borders. In addition, "support to return operations" also counts as a service to the member states.

In fact, Frontex services gained more weight in the process of integration and harmonization than they did in the attempt for legal harmonization – pursued, for instance, by the Schengen Borders Code (SBC).[41] The Schengen Borders Code presented a renewed attempt to impose standardized external border controls and to apply common rules to the practices and procedures. Yet, the SBC states *how border guards should fulfill their mandate*: that is, according to which standards and procedures border policing should occur. Conversely, one of the major tasks of Frontex consists in providing evidence for the need of supranational activities, and thus evidence for the need of those operations which they are meant to coordinate. Frontex is thus tasked with rendering plausible the supranational mandate

---

40 European Commission (2018): Proposal for a Regulation of the European Parliament and the Council on the European Border and Coast Guard, COM(2018) 631 (September, 12, 2018). The quotation is taken from the "Legislative Train Schedule" a website by the European Parliament, at: http://www.europarl.europa.eu/legislative-train/theme-towards-a-new-policy-on-migration/file-european-border-and-coast-guard (accessed October 19, 2019). For an analysis of these developments see Carrera/den Hertog (2016) and Campesi (2018).

41 European Parliament & European Council (2008): Establishing a Community Code on the rules governing the movement of persons across borders (Schengen Borders Code), EC/562/2006, March 15, 2006, in: OJ L 105 (April 13, 2006), [hereafter cited as Schengen Borders Code (2008)].

to the member states. The agency does this by conducting feasibility studies, by providing risk analysis (the criteria of which are defined by the agency itself), and through its services. The art of coordination exercised by Frontex consists in advising, giving recommendations and facilitating those tasks that are controversial in national parliaments. The mandate and the sovereign competences rest with the individual member state. In official terms, the agency does not interfere with the sovereignty of member states; in terms of service provision, competences are mediated.

5.3.2 From a "Maritime" to an "Intelligence-Led" Virtual Border

Two of the early tasks of Frontex consisted in the composition of two feasibility studies: first, the MEDSEA feasibility study on Mediterranean Coastal Patrols Network presented on July 14, 2006, and second, the BORTEC study on the technical feasibility of establishing a surveillance system (European Surveillance System) presented on January 12, 2007.

The BORTEC study has been of particular legitimizing relevance to the EUROSUR project. In the Commission's Communication "Reinforcing the management of the European Union's Southern Maritime Borders,"[42] the study was already referred to as evidence even though it was not yet presented officially to the Commission. To date, the BORTEC study remains unpublished; however, a summary is available in a working document entitled "Integrated maritime policy for the EU, Working Document III on Maritime Surveillance Systems" published by the European Commission and prepared by the Joint Research Centre in Ispra, Italy.[43]

From these documents it can be gleaned that the BORTEC study "made a thorough analysis of existing maritime surveillance systems and operators in Portugal, Spain, France, Italy, Slovenia, Malta, Greece and Cyprus,"[44] The summary gives two tables for each of the eight countries. The first table displays the authorities involved in maritime surveillance and their responsibilities. The sec-

---

42 European Commission (2006): Reinforcing the management of the European Union's Southern Maritime Borders, COM(2006) 733 final (November 30, 2006).

43 European Commission/Joint Research Center Ispra (2008): Integrated maritime policy for the EU, Working Document III on Maritime Surveillance Systems (June 14, 2008), at: https://ec.europa.eu/maritimeaffairs/sites/maritimeaffairs/files/docs/body/maritime-surveillance_en.pdf (accessed August 13, 2019).

44 Ibid, p. 23.

ond gives an overview of the technological systems in place. National plans to integrate existing surveillance systems were documented. While the data collection process took two months, the study was completed within six. Whereas the Commission's summary only gives the impression of a general inventory, the information in the BORTEC study must have been more precise in nature; the summary explicitly excluded information: 1) on the components of the systems, 2) on how the systems operate, 3) on the geographical range of surveillance coverage, 4) on the exact numbers and types of patrol boats, aircrafts and vehicles. Moreover, it can be assumed that policy recommendations were given, as repeated reference is made to their suggestions. As a supporting reference, the BORTEC study is an important document in reference to which the necessity to streamline border surveillance and control measures is supported.

The managerial premises that cooperation leads to more effective border surveillance and control and would thus be more cost-efficient – an assumption that has gained the status of self-evident by the time of the EUROSUR draft regulation – was introduced by the BORTEC study. The BORTEC study served as an exploration into the structural and political possibility of a European border surveillance and control system. In the beginning this European structure was thought to be based on: a) common border patrols and b) an information-based network, and its operational area stretched along the maritime border.

Since 2006, a reinterpretation – and extension, respectively – of the notion of a "virtual border" as introduced by the CIVIPOL feasibility study from maritime to intelligence-led is observable. In that year, the Commission published different Communications and strategy papers on priorities in the "fight against illegal immigration," which emphasize the potential benefit of "intelligent solutions" and "technological mechanisms,"[45] Contrary to earlier approaches, the emphasis on integrated border management is less on European (policy) integration, but rather on an "integrated technological approach – e-borders,"[46] which might integrate its participant in passing.

In its Communication on policy priorities in the "fight against illegal immigration of third-country nationals" of July 19, 2006, the Commission introduces the concept of intelligence-led border management described as "a process of

---

45 European Commission (2006): Policy priorities in the fight against illegal immigration of third-country nationals, COM(2006) 402 final (July 19, 2006).
46 Ibid, para. 23.

gathering and analyzing data for threat analysis and risk assessment, with a view to establishing certain risk criteria."[47]

Often e-borders are identified in the computerized handling of information which has been advanced as part of the Schengen Process since its beginning, most notable in the databases which have been created to support coordinated efforts, namely the Schengen Information System (SIS), the VISA Information System (VIS) and the European Dactyloscopy (EURODAC). These databases are mostly related to the border's filter function. When the Commission now states that intelligence-led border management "would allow border control authorities to filter out passengers who fall under one of these categories, in order to carry out additional checks,"[48] this bestows yet another quality to the generation of suspicion for law enforcement agencies.

The concept of the virtual border takes in the notion of an intelligence-driven approach to border management. This is exemplified in an article in "Focus," the in-house magazine of the AeroSpace and Defence Industries Association of Europe (ASD), in which Ilkka Laitinen, then Director of Frontex, explicitly referred to the operating value (Ger.: *Betriebswert*) of the concept of the virtual border.

"In the 21st century border management must be intelligence-driven. This is a prerequisite of all actions taken regarding borders. Effective border management does not exist without sophisticated systems of data collection and analysis followed by its timely dissemination to officers making decisions on the ground, such as the eligibility for crossing of a person or cargo. Illegal entries represent a small percentage of the overall flow across a border. Nevertheless, in real numbers it is a massive flow. That's why the concept of a 'virtual border' is so important; because the management of a border starts even while gathering intelligence or issuing a visa in a third country. The physical border is, so to say, the 'last borderline.'"[49]

Different aspects are alluded to in this quotation: a detachment from territorial logic, a different time-space relation to the notion of border management, an increasing reliance on data, and the lack of a distinction between information and intelligence. As stated elsewhere (cf. Ellebrecht 2014a), the concept of the virtual border can be considered the guiding image (Ger.: *Leitbild*) to the Europeani-

---

47 European Commission (2006): Policy priorities in the fight against illegal immigration of third-country nationals, COM(2006) 402 final (July 19, 2006).
48 Ibid.
49 Laitinen, Ilkka (2008): "Shaping European Security," in: Focus 2/2008, p.8.

zation of border control. Its ability to take in the notion of the maritime border as operational area and its operational strategy as being intelligence-led merged in the notion of the virtual border and could be recalled flexibly but in an all-encompassing manner. The virtual border set aside the need to be localized and instead called for specific forms of information (surveillance information, namely), to support its control.

This is the discursive environment when the Commission presented first ideas on a European Border Surveillance System, abbreviated as EUROSUR. In its Communication to the Council "Reinforcing the management of the European Union's Southern Maritime Borders" of November 30, 2006, EUROSUR is sketched against the backdrop of the virtual border: its operational area is the maritime border and its operational means are intelligence-led. The first paragraph on EUROSUR reads as the intent to optimize existing surveillance activities and surveillance technologies.

"EUROSUR could in a first stage focus on synergies created by linking the existing national surveillance systems currently in use at the southern maritime external borders. In a second stage, however, it should gradually replace national surveillance systems at land and maritime borders, providing a cost-efficient solution, including for example, a combination of radar and satellite surveillance at European level, taking into account on-going developments realized in the framework of GMES (Global Monitoring for Environment and Security). EUROSUR will benefit from experience at national and European level with similar surveillance systems, possible synergies with existing European surveillance systems for other purposes should also be explored."[50]

According to the Commission, EUROSUR could first take stock of existing national surveillance systems, link them in a first step and replace them in a second step through itself, which is a European Border Surveillance System. The optimizing jargon of "synergies" and "cost-efficiency" presented integrated border management as a question of technical interoperability and technological progress.

---

50 European Commission (2006): Reinforcing the management of the European Union's Southern Maritime Borders, COM(2006) 733 final (November 30, 2006), Section 2.2 (A European surveillance system, para. 24).

5.4 FROM THE EUROSUR ROADMAP TO ITS DRAFT REGULATION (2008-2011): NATIONAL INFRASTRUCTURES, SUPRANATIONAL INCENTIVES

While Monar saw that pragmatism was understood in operational terms in 2003, pragmatism post 2006 was regarded in terms of 'technological solutions.' The Commission's Border Package from February 13, 2008 can be identified as the official turning point in this regard. The so-called Border Package consisted of three communications. The first communication sketched "A comprehensive vision for an integrated European border management system for the 21st century" and called for the creation of an entry/exit registration system.[51] In the second, the Commission presented the results of a first evaluation of the Frontex agency, which served as the basis for its proposals to strengthen Frontex's responsibilities and resources.[52] The third included plans for a European border surveillance system, later referred to as EUROSUR Roadmap.[53] During the respective press conference, Franco Frattini, then Commissioner for Justice and Home Affairs, described the Border Package as a proposal, a vision for the future development of border control; however, concrete measures or implementations could only be expected after a period of five to ten years (Kasparek 2008). Generally, the Commission drew a rather satisfactory balance of the developments thus far and considered the "ambitious agenda set by the Commission and the Council in 2002 [...] completed."[54] The Schengen Borders Code of 2006 was referred to as a consolidation of the legislative framework. Cooperation was seen as institutionalized and fostered by the Frontex agency, which in the Commission's view had added an "operational dimension" to the European model for integrated bor-

---

51 European Commission (2008): Preparing the next Steps in Border Management for the European Union, COM(2008) 69 final (February 13, 2008).
52 European Commission (2008): Report on the Evaluation and Future Development of the Frontex Agency, COM(2008) 67 final (February 13, 2008).
53 European Commission (2008): Examining the Creation of a European Border Surveillance System (EUROSUR), COM(2008) 68 final (February 13, 2008), [hereafter cited as EUROSUR Roadmap, COM(2008) 68 final].
54 European Commission (2008): Preparing the next Steps in Border Management for the European Union, COM(2008) 69 final (February 13, 2008), Section 1.1 (Policy context).

der management.[55] Finally, in the spirit of "the best way to show solidarity is money,"[56] the Commission stated that the "concepts of burden-sharing and solidarity have been given real meaning by the European Border Fund (EBF) which, for the first time, allocates substantial financial resources to these policy areas."[57]

While practical effectiveness had been promoted for the purpose of integrating border policies, the next round in this narration of progress revolved around technological solutions, technical mechanisms and smart borders. In order to strike a balance between securing its citizens on the one hand, and granting freedom of movement on the other, the Commission put emphasis on "using the most advanced technology to reach the highest level of security."[58] Technological solutions were considered the most apt tools with which to strike that balance that had occupied the Schengen Process from the very beginning. "All new technologies, such as biometrics, unmanned aerial vehicles or entry-exit systems are expensive," admitted the former Director of Frontex Ilkka Laitinen, "but they will allow Europe to remain open and be ready for a fast response to constantly changing threats" (Laitinen 2008: 8).

With technological borders, there would supposedly be no trade-off between freedom and security, between an open and a secure Europe. Two initiatives were put forward under this "technological imperative" (Chapman 2004): the EUROSUR Roadmap and an outline for smart borders in the form of an entry/exit registration system. Both initiatives bet on technical solutions; in fact, they were themselves presented as "technical frameworks" or "technical mechanisms," This new tone led to criticism; Peter Hobbing, for instance, noted:

"All that seemed of doubtful value before, such as fully automated border checks, comprehensive systems of entry-exit control, air passenger surveillance and electronic travel

---

55 European Commission (2008): Preparing the next Steps in Border Management for the European Union, COM(2008) 69 final (February 13, 2008), Section 1.1 (Policy context).
56 EUROSUR Project Manager at Frontex, personal interview (May 15, 2012).
57 European Commission (2008): Preparing the next Steps in Border Management for the European Union, COM(2008) 69 final (February 13, 2008), Section 1.1 (Policy context).
58 European Commission (2008): Press release. A comprehensive Vision for an Integrated European Border Management System for the 21st Century, IP/08/215 (February 13, 2008).

authorisation, high-tech border installations including virtual fences, has all of a sudden become part of the EU's vision for the 21st century." (Hobbing 2010: 68)

The Border Package was about more than simply promoting the development and use of new technologies for surveillance and control. It set into motion the rhetoric of the *conflation* of surveillance instruments and means for policy integration: the integration of (different) surveillance systems was thus framed in terms of establishing common border policies.

5.4.1 The EUROSUR Roadmap

When EUROSUR was commissioned as part of the 2008 Border Package, the Commission set the defined aim of having a regulation ready and accepted within the current financial framework, which ran until 2013. Despite various research and development projects for smart and e-technologies, the targeted *political* result of the EUROSUR Roadmap was to establish an EC regulation. It is important to keep this in mind – particularly because, in this case, the making of the law proved to be overdetermined by the development of different technical elements used in the EUROSUR framework. This had the particular effect that neither the European Parliament nor the national parliaments were able to fulfill their function of control, because they were only involved at a time when the points had already been fixed.

Although conveyed as a vision, the communication for "[e]xamining the creation of a European Border Surveillance System (EUROSUR)" functioned not only as a Roadmap, but also as a mandate for the political, technical, informational and legal reconfigurations of border management at both national and European levels. It underscored the necessity of taking advantage of synergy between surveillance technologies and the sharing of information among border authorities in Europe. The Roadmap's stated objective was "to examine the parameters within which a European Border Surveillance System (EUROSUR) [...] could be developed."[59] Although these parameters entailed both political, organizational, legal and technical dimensions, the technical aspect of system interoperability was also rhetorically prioritized. The European Border Surveillance System itself was meant to be "a common technical framework" that was built to

---

59 EUROSUR Roadmap, COM(2008) 68 final, Section 1 (Introduction).

"support Member States' authorities to act efficiently at local level, command at national level, coordinate at European level and cooperate with third countries in order to detect, identify, track and intercept persons attempting to enter the EU illegally outside border crossing points."[60]

If one looks at the levels where EUROSUR sought to improve border protection – reaction capability at the local level, allocation of resources and personnel at the national and European planning levels, and facilitation of inter-organizational information sharing and cooperation with third countries – the envisioned political and geographical reach of EUROSUR is remarkable. The all-encompassing notion of integrated management, which tackles a task (here border surveillance and control) from a holistic perspective, was projected onto the technological possibility of integrating surveillance systems. Furthermore, EUROSUR was thought of as a tool for border guards, analysts and policy makers. The "common technical framework" was to provide those authorities responsible for border control in the Member States "with more timely and reliable information," so that they are able to reduce the "number of illegal migrations who manage to enter the EU undetected," "contribute to the prevention of cross-border crime" as well as "enhance search and rescue capacity."[61]

This technical framework was thus envisioned as a universal problem-solver, or as it was termed in official rhetoric: a multi-purpose system. The ambivalence of the declared objectives – namely, to save migrants' lives at sea and to counter unauthorized migration – evaded the technological promises of a multi-purpose system. In addition, the integrative technical framework, which was seemingly not inconsistent with this idea, was supposed to be "set up without affecting the respective areas of jurisdiction of Member States nor replace any existing systems."[62] Where the system of systems was attractive and convincing, the idea of a European Border Guard stirred up reluctance regarding the subject of convergence. At this point, it is again important to underline that the technical framework that would later take shape in the EUROSUR network (see chapter 4) had not yet been specified in 2008. The EUROSUR Roadmap was delineated as eight steps in three phases.

---

60   EUROSUR Roadmap, COM(2008) 68 final, Section 3 (General concept).
61   Ibid, Section 2.2 (Objectives).
62   Ibid, COM(2008) 68 final, Section 3 (General concept).

The first phase dealt with national infrastructures, the second phase addressed surveillance tools, and the third phase foresaw the setup of an integrated network. What appears to be a chronological sequence is actually a successive Europeanization. While the first three steps addressed those areas where neither the Commission nor Frontex have decision-making or regulatory competencies, the second and third phase (steps 4 to 8) foresaw elements where responsibility was increasingly allotted to Frontex.

From the launching of the EUROSUR Roadmap in 2008 to the legislative proposal in 2011, it was almost exclusively up to the political will of member states whether EUROSUR would take off or not. The establishment of national coordination centers (indicated as step 1) as well as the acceptance and usage of the EUROSUR network (indicated as step 2) set the course for the success of EUROSUR. However, framed as preparatory or infrastructural, this decisive development phase was seldom recognized as such.

5.4.2 The First Phase: National Infrastructures – a Means or an End?

When examining the practicalities of the first phase projected in the Roadmap, an organizational reconfiguration of border management among European national authorities comes to the fore. The first three steps subsumed under "infrastructure" entail the building of national coordination centers (NCCs) (step 1), the development of the EUROSUR network (step 2), and the coordination of relations with third countries (step 3). In a (perhaps deliberately) ambiguous manner, the notion of infrastructure captured both an institutional and a technological aspect. First, it referred to the institutional reconfigurations within member states that came with the establishment of a single central office to coordinate border surveillance. The second notion of infrastructure involved the technical connection between computers and apparatuses and may have thus referred to both the infrastructure of surveillance technology and the ICT network. Effectively, the planned infrastructure was both technical and institutional. Furthermore, step 3 expanded the meaning of infrastructure to entail "relations with third countries." Political and electronic connections were thus also subsumed as infrastructure.

The first step of setting up the NCCs had the declared aim of "providing the essential border surveillance infrastructure at national level."[63] Subsequently,

---

63 EUROSUR Roadmap, COM(2008) 68 final, Section 4.1.1.

step 1 fanned out into a recommendation for surveillance systems – that is, equipment ("one single national border surveillance system") – *and* for the organizational level of national border surveillance and control ("one single national coordination centre").[64] The establishment of the physical office of the NCC was thus a different action than the upgrade of a national surveillance system that could be managed from that office. In any case, the Commission encouraged member states to "make full use of the financial support available under the External Borders Fund (EBF) for the above *two* actions."[65]

Shortly after launching the EUROSUR Roadmap, the Commission sent out a questionnaire to member states to collect information "on existing and planned national border surveillance infrastructure, communication and information exchange systems and on the use of surveillance tools such as satellites,"[66] It is likely that it also took stock of states' willingness to upgrade existing national surveillance infrastructures. The collected information served as initial input for the development of what is called the "EUROSUR guidelines," Following the interim report, these guidelines were thought to clarify "responsibilities and duties for national coordination centres"[67]. The Commission was thereby not allowed to dictate a technical standard, nor influence the internal business of member states.

That the Commission was working at the limits of its authority in the first phase can be seen when considering how the budgetary impact of EUROSUR was calculated. In estimating the costs of EUROSUR, only the amount used for the NCC, that is, "for the technical equipment inside, personnel and building maintenance costs, computers,"[68] was taken into account. Any expenditure for surveillance systems was excluded from the cost calculation for EUROSUR.

In keeping with this budgetary distinction, the Commission did not expect the establishment of NCCs to be overly expensive. It was estimated that it could amount to a maximum of several hundred thousand euros. However, when including the expenditure that indirectly went to the EUROSUR for "national border surveillance systems" vaguely specified in the official jargon as "all the equipment and such," 50 per cent of the external border fund of 1.8 billion euros

---

64 EUROSUR Roadmap, COM(2008) 68 final, Section 4.1 (Recommendations, p. 6-7).
65 Ibid, Section 4.1 (Recommendations, p. 7), emphasis added.
66 European Commission (2009): Report on Progress made in developing the European Border Surveillance System (EUROSUR), SEC(2009) 1265 final (September 24, 2009), Section 2.1.1.2 (Measures taken during the reporting period, p. 4).
67 Ibid.
68 EC official in Brussels, personal interview (December 2012).

went toward border surveillance. The Commission's reason for keeping these two items separate, why the surveillance apparatus should not be counted in the costs for EUROSUR, although EUROSUR is (as its name indicates) a surveillance system, can be explained by its limited authority: "We excluded national border surveillance because we do not regulate this."[69]

In this first phase, however, both surveillance gadgetry as well as office supplies for the establishment of NCCs were merged under the heading of infrastructure. The official budgetary balance abstractly noted that the establishment of the NCCs was to be co-financed 75 per cent with funds from the External Borders Fund, while the remaining 25 per cent were to be provided by the respective member states. Despite lengthy procedures of applying for and receiving funds, the Commission, by its own account, was satisfied with the use of the EBF. The infrastructure, in its reference to surveillance technologies and the physical office of the NCC, was also tied to the competences assembled in a NCC. Again, neither Frontex nor the Commission had the authority to regulate the competences that member states' authorities would transfer to or locate at the NCC. The Commission, however, sketched different ways to run a NCC. These so called "policy options" implied both different technological functionalities *and* a different degree of competence for the NCC. These competencies can be mainly distinguished by the degree of centralization instituted by the office (from bureaucratic information gathering to coordination, command and control), and with regard to the kind of information processed and available at the respective NCC (from unclassified to top secret).

The EUROSUR Roadmap and its accompanying impact assessments[70] detailed four policy options running up to 2013. Policy option 1, termed the "status quo option," recalled the 2004 Hague Programme and the related communication from the Commission from May 2005 entitled "Ten priorities for the next five

---

69 EC official in Brussels, personal interview (December 2012).

70 - European Commission (2008): Examining the Creation of a European Border Surveillance System (EUROSUR): Impact Assessment, SEC(2008) 151 (February 13, 2008), [hereafter cited as Impact Assessment of the EUROSUR Roadmap, SEC(2008) 151];

- European Commission (2008): Examining the creation of a European border surveillance system (EUROSUR): Summary of the Impact Assessment, SEC(2008) 152 (February 13, 2008), [hereafter cited as Summary of the Roadmap's Impact Assessment, SEC(2008) 152].

years." However, the timeline of these priorities already suggests that "the status quo option" was not an option.

The other three policy options were staggered according to the reach of system integration. While policy option 2 focused on "upgrading and streamlining existing surveillance systems and mechanisms at Member State level," policy option 3 entails "developing common tools and applications at European level," Finally, policy option 4 "builds upon the actions proposed in the two previous options and combines them in a coherent framework"[71]. However, when considering the Impact Assessments accompanying the 2011 EUROSUR draft regulation,[72] it quickly becomes clear that the policy options include more than the reach of system integration: it is about the NCC's own resources and competences, which are linked to the type and amount of data to be assembled and handled by the office. This is also shown in a figure from the EUROSUR Impact Assessment (figure 10), in which the status quo option is no longer shown.

---

71 Summary of the Roadmap's Impact Assessment, SEC(2008) 152, (Comparison of the Policy Options). For an analysis of the EUROSUR Roadmap and its relation to the development of Frontex see Jeandesboz (2008).

72 The EUROSUR legislative proposal has been accompanied by three Impact Assessments of together 114 pages, including 8 ANNEXES with cost estimates, list of expert groups, etc.
 - European Commission (2011): Impact Assessment accompanying the Proposal for a Regulation of the European Parliament and of the Council establishing the European Border Surveillance System (EUROSUR), SEC(2011) 1536 final (December 12, 2011), (40 pages), [hereafter cited as EUROSUR Impact Assessment, SEC(2011) 1536 final];
 - European Commission (2011): Executive Summary of the Impact Assessment accompanying the Proposal for a Regulation of the European Parliament and of the Council establishing the European Border Surveillance System (EUROSUR), SEC(2011) 1537 final (December 12, 2011), (9 pages), [hereafter cited as Executive Summary to the EUROSUR Impact Assessment SEC(2011) 1537 final];
 - European Commission (2011): Impact Assessment accompanying the Proposal for a Regulation of the European Parliament and of the Council establishing the European Border Surveillance System (EUROSUR), SEC(2011) 1538 final (December 12, 2011), (65 pages), [hereafter cited as Compilation of Annexes to the EUROSUR Impact Assessment, SEC(2011) 1538].

Figure 10: Policy options, EUROSUR development (official illustration)

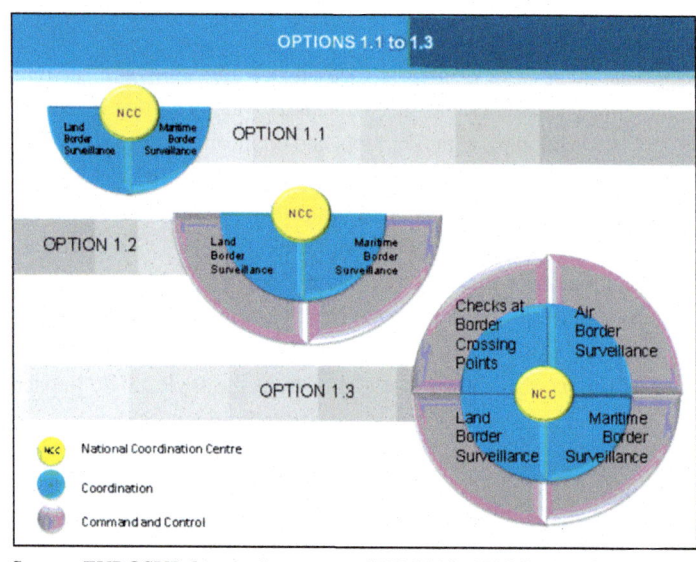

Source: EUROSUR Impact Assessment SEC(2011) 1536 final, p. 23

Furthermore, the selection of information from a certain area is displayed along with the competences as a circle, which suggests that these matters were logically related and strive for completion. It is also suggested that the option is not an either-or situation but a continuum, a possible successive upgrade and expansion – if nothing else, the achievement of a level of common technical frameworks as technical completion.

"There were different approaches. For the context of EUROSUR, merely land and maritime surveillance had been determined to be included. It was also an option to include border checks, which several member states opted for; or thirdly, to further include air border surveillance. This would result in a full command and control center, and this will be expensive, and there are a few member states which also did that."[73]

Thus, the more competences national authorities decided to transfer to the NCC, the more expensive the NCC would be. However, it is not the competence of command and control that costs, but the technologies needed to assemble all the

---

73 EC official in Brussels, personal interview (December 2012).

necessary surveillance and information at the center. In August 2011, member states' decisions concerning these policy options stood as summarized in table 1.

Table 1: Policy options as applied by 18 member states in 2011

Policy Option	NCC competences	Countries
1	NCC coordinates (at least) the surveillance of land and maritime surveillance	Italy, France, Netherlands, Belgium and Poland
2	NCC has command and control competences for (at least) land and maritime suveillance	Cyprus, Spain, Hungary Lata, Romaina, greece, Slovenia and Slovakai
3	NCC has command and control competencies for border control	Bulgaria, Estonia, Germany, Latvia, Lithunia, Portugal and Finnland

Source: EUROSUR Impact Assessment SEC(2011) 1536 final, p. 23

Technical equipment and the power to command and control are what related the ordinary task of setting up business offices to the political and technical competencies based and collected at these centers. Policy options were not only conditioned by technology; merging the two was already a political decision in itself. In this case, technology became a substitute for policy. The option of partially funding national surveillance systems for the NCC via the EBF served as an incentive to choose policies that might reduce the exclusive competence of member states in the information and operational environment of borders in favor of a computerized network or of integrated systems for monitoring and surveillance.

Various other sensitive political decisions also needed to be made in order to establish a NCC. What authorities were to be present at the center? What competences needed to be assigned to the NCCs? What data needed to be shared and to what level of secrecy? Was the handling of personal data supposed to be supported in the EUROSUR network? Should the data be transferred manually or automatically to the system? Should the NCC be a national command and control center and thus run 24/7? All these options had to be decided by national authorities when establishing their NCC. The listing of policy options, however, suggested that member states could simply opt for either one, and it distracts from the fact that all these tensions and decisions between national authorities must be already solved, avoided or overthrown in order to establish an NCC.

Table 2 illustrates some of these decisions and alludes to the differences in tone toward the EU among the member states.[74] The table also illustrates what was easily forgotten later on: That the establishment and setup of an NCC is an entirely different procedure from its connection to the EUROSUR network (see the second and third column in table 2). The neat schedule provided by Frontex in its 2015 report on the functioning of EUROSUR stands in sharp contrast to the more than 50 pages concerning policy options in the Commission's Impact Assessments of 2011.[75] Furthermore, the Frontex report again conflates technical and political infrastructure. Bureaucratically speaking, EUROSUR provided financial support for the technical NCC infrastructure. Developed as a technical framework, political decisions fell short and were cloaked as "infrastructure" in the first step of the EUROSUR Roadmap. The question of whether there should be a national surveillance system was overwritten by the question of what kind of technology. Moreover, the table shows that being connected to the EUROSUR network cannot be equated with establishing an NCC.

---

[74] The table has been compiled in December 2016 and, for most parts, quotes member states answers to questionnaires by the European Commission; the boxes are thus filled in quite heterogeneously. The information in the third column indicating the NCC's connection to the EUROSUR network has been taken from the 2015 Frontex Report "The functioning of EUROSUR," at http://statewatch.org/news/ 2016/mar/eu-frontex-report-on-eurosur-functioning-12-2015.pdf (accessed December 5, 2016). All other information have been taken from the Compilation of Annexes to the EUROSUR Impact Assessment, SEC(2011) 1538: Annex 4.2 (Overview of coordination of the NCCs with other national authorities and third countries, p. 27-29), Annex 4.3a (Classification level of information shared in NCCs, p. 30), Annex 4.4 (Costs of setting up, upgrading and maintaining NCCs and FSC (2007-2010), p. 33), Annex 4.5 (Annual staff in NCCs and FSC (2007-2010), p. 34).

[75] EUROSUR Impact Assessment, SEC(2011) 1536 final, p. 19-39; Executive Summary to the EUROSUR Impact Assessment SEC(2011) 1537 final, p. 4-5; Compilation of Annexes to the EUROSUR Impact Assessment, SEC(2011) 1538, p. 25-52.

Table 2: NCC set-up and connections

Node / Country	NCC setup	Connection to EUROSUR network	Costs (in EUR) 2007-2010	Responsible authority for NCC	Classification level of information shared in NCC's (Sep. 2011)	Coordination with third countries	Staff figure (2010)
FSC	2008	21.09.2011	2,238,499				2
Poland	2010	21.09.2011	201,01	Chief of Polish Border Guards	Up to 'Restricted'	Mainly Russia, Belarus & Ukraine	12
Finland	2005	18.10.2011	6,638,798	Finnish Border Guard	Up to 'Secret'	Y	19
Spain	2009	03.11.2019	3,084,768	Guardia Civil	Up to 'Secret'	Morocco, Mauritania, Senegal, Cape Verde, Gambia, G. Bissau, Algeria	19
Slovakia	2007	15.11.2011	18,894,418	Presidium of police force	Up to 'Confidential'	Ukraine	30
Italy	2011	22.11.2011	32,540,000	Ministry of Interior	Only unclassified	North African Countries	3

Node / Country	NCC setup	Connection to EUROSUR network	Costs (in EUR) 2007-2010	Responsible authority for NCC	Classification level of information shared in NCC's (Sep. 2011)	Coordination with third countries	Staff figure (2010)
France	2010	29.11.2011	597,00	General Secretary of the Sea; Service du Premier Ministre	Protected, but unclassified	N	11
Greece	2013	18.05.2012	0	Ministry of Citizen Protection	Up to 'Top secret'	Albania, FYROM, Turkey, Egypt	
Lithuania	2011	31.05.2012	0	State Border Guard Service	Protected, but unclassified	Russian Fed., Rep. of Belarus	
Portugal	2009	15.06.2012		SEF	Up to 'Secret'	YES (Undetermined)	6
Cyprus	2010	25.06.2012	320,00	Cyprus Police - (Port and Marine Police Unit)	Protected, but unclassified	N	28

Bulgaria	2010	17.07.2012	500,00	Ministry of Interior, Chief Directorate Border Police	Protected, but unclassified	Serbia, FYROM, Turkey, Ukraine, Russia, Georgia	42
Hungary	2011	20.07.2012	0	Police	Up to 'Restricted'	Ukraine, Serbia	
Romania	2010	28.09.2012	22,51	Romanian Border Headquarters	Only unclassified	Turkey, Georgia, Russian Fed., Ukraine	
Norway	—	05.10.2012	No data provided	NR		NR	
Latvia	2007	31.10.2012	605,45	State Border Guard	Protected, but unclassified	Russian Fed., Rep. of Belarus	11
Estonia	2009	09.11.2012	292,30	Police and Border Guard Board authorities	Up to 'Restricted'	Russian Fed., Rep. of Belarus	13

Node / Country	NCC setup	Connection to EUROSUR network	Costs (in EUR) 2007-2010	Responsible authority for NCC	Classification level of information shared in NCC's (Sep. 2011)	Coordination with third countries	Staff figure (2010)
Slovenia	2007	05.12.2012	200,00	Ministry of Interior – Police	Protected, but unclassified	Italian LCC (Trieste) within FRONTEX EPN	
Malta	2008	14.12.2012	7,528,588	Armed Forces of Malta	Only unclassified	Worldwide	50
Croatia		25.03.2014					
Denmark		25.04.2014	No data provided	?		No Response	
Iceland		30.04.2014	No data provided	?		No Response	
Luxembourg		04.06.2014					
Sweden		24.06.2014	No data provided			No Response	

Czech Republic	27.06.2014					
Switzerland	09.09.2014					
Liechtenstein	17.09.2014					
Germany	15.10.2014	2008		Federal Police (Bundespolizei)	Up to 'Restricted'	N
Belgium	21.10.2014	2007	1,170,000	MIK – coast guards	Up to 'Top Secret'	All European EU-countries via MOC	9
Netherlands	13.11.2014	2011		Min. of Home affairs and Kingdom relations	Up to 'Restricted'	N
Austria	25.11.2014					

Legend
Green: member states participating in the first pilot phase
Orange: member states participating in the "big pilot" phase
Blue: member states which joint post post the acceptance of the EUROSUR Regulation

Sources: see fotenote 74, p. 160

However, in later documentation, it is only the connection to the EUROSUR network that is documented and communicated as the decisive element. As such, the political reconfigurations at the national level are rendered invisible. Institutionally, however, the inconspicuous establishment of NCCs is justified with reference to the role and responsibility of Frontex. The agency is in charge of only the development of the network, and as such only reports from the connected NCCs to the EUROSUR network. As a result, the establishment of the NCCs is not documented as being part of the political setup of EUROSUR, even though NCCs are extolled as the "backbone" of the system.[76] In this process, it was obviously possible to transform something taboo into something attractive. While conducting my interviews, I was told different anecdotes about "fights" among law enforcement authorities in several member states concerning the establishment of the NCCs. Accordingly, the more advanced the application of the EUROSUR network became, the more diffuse the initial skepticism became. In the end, authorities even "started fighting for the NCC"[77] for the assumed reasons of status and recognition.

When a member state decides to establish an NCC, it is then equipped with a server that connects it to the EUROSUR network. The commissioning of the server is staged as a symbolic act, for which the responsible Frontex official specially arrives. It thus seems no coincidence that the "big computer rack" hosting different servers for the EUROSUR application played a recurring role in many different conversations with Frontex officials, be it when joking that EUROSUR could not be delivered "in your pocket," or by showing a photograph of two men in work clothes carrying a computer rack. At this point in time, the EUROSUR test application was already on the server. The EUROSUR project manager at Frontex even talked about the computer rack and network as a gift to member states: "My biggest satisfaction is hearing the member states say: 'thank you very much for what you are doing,' because I am providing them with *something* for *free*, and something that is useful."[78] As a gift, the material artifact stood for the possibility to connect to the EUROSUR network, to exchange as well as receive information. However, the gift also brought on a backlash, quite in the

---

76 Cf. for instance, the description on the Frontex website "The backbone of Eurosur is a network of national coordination centers (NCCs)," at: http://frontex.europa.eu/intelligence/eurosur/ (accessed February 4, 2017), as well as EUROSUR draft regulation: p. 2 and 29.
77 EUROSUR Project Manager at Frontex, personal interview (May 15, 2012).
78 Ibid.

Maussian (2016 [1925]) sense, because it concomitantly represented an expectation to actually connect to the EUROSUR network, to use it and feed it with information. In this way, the network instituted a relationship of mutual obligation that would ultimately be more beneficial for the donor. Moreover, a further spin was given to this gift-induced dependency: Frontex not only provided the network as a gift; it also remained part of the equation by using the network itself, as the following interview excerpt demonstrates.

Head of R&D (Frontex): Basically Frontex is also part of the EUROSUR network, also a kind of NCC although not national, but we are at the same level. It is very flat. We are not in charge, it is flat, a flat platform. And we are also only one of the participants in that exchange schema. But we have taken it upon us to develop the EUROSUR network, which means basically the technical installations that are needed to be present in the NCCs for making the exchange of incident-related information possible. This is developed here.

S.E.: What kind of technical equipment is that?

Head of R&D (Frontex): It is basically a big computer rack that is duplicated in each of the member states to make this exchange from a technical point of view possible; [...] there is no database, it is just exchange of the information.[79]

The role of Frontex and the impact of the EUROSUR are played down here by the rhetorical analogies between technological elements and political structures. Frontex routinely stresses its coordinating role in the context of the EUROSUR project ("We are not in charge"), which also suggests that the hierarchies within EUROSUR are flat ("it is flat"), and epitomizing "it" as the communication platform itself ("it is flat, a flat platform"). The flat platform embodies and presents as plausible Frontex's claim of being "on the same level." Furthermore, the "technical installations" are reduced to the big computer network, while the process of defining menu items and border-related incidents, which is the guts of the installation (see chapters 4.1. and 4.2), is excluded.

In sum, in the first three years of the EUROSUR development phase, the institutional reconfiguration in member states toward establishing NCCs, as well as the potential of the electronic EUROSUR network, were systematically trivialized and played down: the technology at stake in the European surveillance system was portrayed as "just a big computer rack" (and not as an integration of

---

79 Head of Research and Development at Frontex, personal interview (May 27, 2011).

national surveillance systems), "just a network" (and not as a proposal for a mandatory European communicational format), "just the equipment for an office" (the NCC) (and not as surveillance technology or as the acquisition and centralization of competences), "just exchange of information," (and not as a database or an increase in power). Moreover, only after the institutional changes were set in motion was EUROSUR's legislative proposal issued. After the infrastructure was laid, the EP and national parliaments became involved, and while the paper's formulations were still being discussed, the political and institutional reconfigurations were already being taken for granted. Establishing an NCC ostensibly meant connecting to a computerized network for information exchange. The network was an incentive to access a new arena of information and intelligence that was – and this is where we find the optical device – supranational in outlook. Effectively, the arena of European competences took shape as a technical innovation in the field of border surveillance and not as an encroachment on exclusive national competences.

5.4.3 The Second Phase: Surveillance Tools – Incentive, Subterfuge or Qualitative Change of Border Management?

Effectively, the Roadmap's second phase can be described as an arena of supranational services, incentives and devices. As such, its relation to the first phase is not chronological but rather structural and political. While the first three steps addressed member states' competences, the second phase sketched how EUROSUR could generate surveillance information and thus produce an "added value" for member states – namely, that of surveillance information generated at the supranational level. The second phase concentrated on surveillance tools, both in terms of research and development (step 4) and their common application (step 5), as well as the common pre-frontier intelligence picture (CPIP) (step 6). The Commission explicitly invited research and development projects on border surveillance within the framework of the Seventh Framework Programme for Research and Technological Development (FP7) with a view to EUROSUR as a potential "end-user." The Commission Staff Working Paper of January 28, 2011 mentioned nine border surveillance projects it recommended taking "into account when developing EUROSUR"[80]. Generally, the Roadmap's recommenda-

---

80 European Commission (2011): Determining the technical and operational framework of the European Border Surveillance System (EUROSUR) and the actions to be taken

tions revealed the extensive understanding of surveillance that underpinned the EUROSUR project and its sole focus on maritime surveillance.

"The 7th Framework Program for research and development (security and space themes) should be used to improve the performance *and use* of surveillance tools, to increase the area covered, the number of suspicious activities detected as well as to improve the identification of potentially suspicious targets *and the access* to high resolution observation satellite data."[81]

Simply put, this framework states that this technology's capability must be improved (development, engineering), *and* the number of end users increased (market). Moreover, the power, reach and effectiveness of surveillance should also be increased by expanding "the area covered," raising "the number of suspicious activities detected," and by improving "the identification of potentially suspicious targets," This surveillance gaze is deep and wide and should be further improved in resolution. Surveillance expands the idea of what it may be able to reveal and thereby achieve in our imagination. It is fostered both by a proliferation of its tools as well as its ends. In this vein, EUROSUR has also been portrayed as a surveillance behemoth that, with its drones, radar surveillance and so forth, is advancing the militarization of borders (cf. Lemberg-Pedersen 2013: 152-153; Monroy 2011).

However, it is virtually impossible to document the concrete and measurable influence of FP7 projects in border surveillance on EUROSUR. Nevertheless, a significant, indirect influence can be assumed when listing different FP7 projects in which the EUROSUR is the "end-user" along with their defined objectives and the volume of funding they received. Taking this approach, Hayes and Vermeulen conclude that, by 2012, the EU had provided more than 170 million Euros in funding to 16 projects that promised direct or indirect synergy with the EUROSUR system (Hayes/Vermeulen 2012: 60-64). These included the development and testing of unmanned aerial vehicles (UAVs) and satellites for use in civil-security applications.

Similarly, Martin Lemberg-Pedersen presented EUROSUR as an "example of outsourced research and development in border control systems, which in-

---

for its establishment, SEC(2011) 145 final (January 28, .2011), Section 5.4 (Research and development to improve the performance of surveillance tools).
81 EUROSUR Roadmap, COM(2008) 68 final, Section 4.2 (Recommendation, p. 8-9), emphasis added.

volve a substantial amount of sub-contracting" (Lemberg-Pedersen 2013: 156-157). Based on his own calculations and the remodeling of contracts and grants per project, he regards EUROSUR as subsidizing the arms industry, and argued that the influence of private security companies on the governance of borders has been "more pervasive [...] than mediatized political discourses categorizing immigration as a security threat" (ibid: 157).

There are essentially two issues at stake. First, there is the question of to what extent the diverse new surveillance technologies that were proposed to serve EUROSUR are changing operational practices and value orientation, and thus the quality of border work. There have been initial general enquires into the question of how these new technologies of surveillance and production of suspicion are impacting enforcement practices (see for instance den Boer 2011). However, as the period of investigation does not include when EUROSUR became operational, an evaluation of the effects of surveillance technologies on border policing goes beyond the reach of the material of this study.

The second issue is that private military companies were able to influence the definition of political problems, because private military contractors "can no longer content themselves with being mere technical experts. They become security experts shaping understanding of and decisions about security" (Leander 2005: 612). Because of competition in the security technologies market and for funding, technologies not only have to be good, they also have the following paradoxical effect:

"The competition for market shares pushes PMCs to become lobbyists, security advisers and public-opinion-makers. [...] They create a demand for the services they offer by making clients [in this case policy makers and legislators] aware of the many threats they need protections against." (Leander 2005: 612)

In the market for security technologies, supply and demand is distorted by the factor "risk" which, however, is calculated, assessed and provided as needs assessment by the suppliers themselves. This can result in lock-in effects that make it rather difficult to reverse the technological upgrading of borders.

For the case of EUROSUR, sources also suggest that the supply-side of security companies and security research projects intended to define the setup and thus the abilities of the system. According to one Frontex source, the agency concluded from tests that satellite surveillance was not contributing to improving maritime response, and that the main reason was the time of latency. Satellite imagery was considered virtually useless for operational purposes in which moving targets were to be detected between waves. An official of the European Commission also admitted that companies were preferable that do not develop their own technology, as "they don't want to sell you something all the time." According to another Brussel's official, the development and use of drones in EUROSUR projects had only been incorporated into the EUROSUR draft regulation on request from the Directorate-General Enterprise and Industry (DG-ENTR). However, the Directorate General for Migration and Home Affairs (DG Home) wanted to keep a low profile and did not want to attract public outrage for having mentioned drones, which in any case were not decisive for the success of EUROSUR. Effectively, Anna Leander's words resonate in so far as the technical experts not only generate their own demand, but lobbyists and advisers to policy makers do so as well to an extent where political decision-makers have to make a conscious effort to decide against technological solutions.

In the end, the question to be asked is what technologies were and are behind the notion of advanced solutions in the case of EUROSUR. Presented as a "system of systems," the dominant reception of EUROSUR has primarily revolved around surveillance technology, particularly around drones and satellite surveillance. However, the most important technology of the EUROSUR framework is the ICT application of the EUROSUR network. From the beginning, EUROSUR has 'played' with an extensive understanding of surveillance that includes monitoring technologies, data processing and the assembling and integration of much information.

The promise of creating better awareness and a more timely response enables us to subsume variable notions of surveillance into a central idea, thus diverting criticism of big bad systems, while achieving almost clinical silence and seclusion in order to build trust in and compliance with an IT system for the exchange of operational information. In either case, the entire legal text of the EUROSUR Regulation was predetermined by technical semantics and functionalities. In this vein, the Commission described the draft regulation as "the result of summarizing 1500 pages of technical specifications in 21 articles" (quoted in Bellanova/Duez 2016: 28).

5.5 "THIS IS A BEAUTIFUL SITUATION HERE" – EUROSUR'S DRAFTING PROCEDURES AND THE PILOT PHASE (2011-2012)

When the draft regulation was launched by the Commission on December 12, 2011, the European Parliament and the Council began negotiating their respective positions in preparation of the *trialogue* between the European Council, European Parliament and European Commission. Between December 2011 and December 2012, they staked out their positions parallel to the so-called "big pilot," the testphase of the EUROSUR network. This parallel adjustment of a piece of legislation and a piece of technology has been considered "a beautiful situation":

"There is some beautiful situation here; we are developing a system which is in a test phase, and at the same time, there is a legislative proposal in parallel. The legislative proposal is taking the ideas from this system, and we may propose changes to the legislative proposal based on the use of the EUROSUR, of this system. So I think this is a beautiful situation here. Now, we have here an application, this application which is very much in line with the legislative proposal."[82]

Considering the time line, the result of this suitable regulation is not surprising. Because "the legislative proposal is taking the ideas from this system," the application consequently seems to be "in line with the legislative proposal." In fact, as the previous chapter has illustrated, what much of the regulation describes is software architecture. However, this statement also implies that legislation is the authority by which to set standards and with which to be in line. The "beautiful situation" of developing both an IT application and legislation in parallel was thus, in fact, regarded as a rather comfortable and gainful one for the success of the EUROSUR project.

When voting on the EUROSUR Regulation, member states were expected to be less under the impression that they were voting on a binding EU law, and more that they were reconfirming what they had already developed and what they were already using in daily practice. Their acceptance thus appears in a somewhat depoliticized light: it is a user's acceptance of technology, and not a member state's willingness to further integrate and accept Europeanization to the effect of legal codification. An official from the Commission and hence a figure

---

82 EUROSUR Project Manager at Frontex, personal interview (May 15, 2012).

representing the legislative body similarly noted in December 2012, the system and the legislation were consciously developed in parallel "in order to trial and error, in order to test things. That way we were able to integrate feedback from the technical development of the EUROSUR network into the legislation, and we are still able to do so."[83] To a certain extent, this echoes the laboratory metaphor deployed in the early days of the Schengen process. When applied to technology, the metaphor seems even more plausible.

Technology requires test phases "in order to trial and error, in order to test things." In the case of legislation, however, the officials at DG Home by their own accounts know that "if you go too far and want to define too much, things are not accepted." In the case of EUROSUR, however, the Commission has said that it witnessed a common spirit, in the sense that it honorably mentioned that the member states had committed themselves to EUROSUR and that all of them put effort into the project. The Commission stated that it was important that member states maintained a sense of ownership and responsibility. However, ownership and responsibility were thought of almost exclusively with reference to the development and setup of the EUROSUR network. In terms of legislation, the influence of member states was minimized, particularly meaning the question of subsidiarity – that is, the question of whether the EU was in charge in this matter – was only directed at national parliaments after the NCCs had been established, the EBF had been used and the network application was up and running, as the following section describes.

5.5.1 National Parliaments and the Principle of Subsidiarity

After the European Commission proposed the EUROSUR legislation in December 2011, member states were called upon to clarify the issue of subsidiarity – that is, to determine in their own national parliaments whether the EU had competency in this area.[84] In the case of the proposed EUROSUR Regulation, only the Swedish parliament, the Riksdag, had concerns regarding the competency of the EU. In a reasoned opinion, it stated that "it is not sufficiently clear that the goals of the proposed measures cannot be achieved at national level. Nor is it clear that the goals of the proposed measures can better be achieved if undertak-

---

83 EC official in Brussels, personal interview (December 2012).

84 Cf. Article 5 (3) of the Treaty of the European Union (TEU) and the Protocol on the Application of the Principles of Subsidiarity and Proportionality.

en at EU level."[85] The Swedish Riksdag was thereby the only institution to officially call into question the widely accepted premises of a causal relation between the quality of border surveillance and control and the quantity of shared information and data. The basic idea of EUROSUR that situational awareness would better be achieved at the level of the EU was thus not shared by the Swedish Riksdag.

At the time of the legislative proposal, the Commission, by contrast, argued that EUROSUR was in line with the principle of subsidiarity, as it "follows a decentralized approach, with the national coordination centres for border surveillance forming the backbone of the EUROSUR cooperation."[86] The Commission supported its argument by weighing the amount of information and data against the quality of analyzing it. While "in quantitative terms most information would be managed in the national coordination centres, without Frontex being able to see this information,"[87] the EU level was fostered in qualitative terms of situational awareness. In fact, sharing and interlinking systems and information in the supranational format of EUROSUR was thought to bring *true added value to border surveillance.*"[88] The Commission argued that

"[b]etter information sharing will help to identify targets such as boats used for irregular migration and cross-border crime more accurately and therefore allow a more targeted timely and cost-efficient use of available equipment for interception. This is an objective which cannot be sufficiently achieved by the Member States alone and which can be better achieved at Union level."[89]

5.5.2 Drafting Procedures in the European Parliament and the European Council

Before the *trialogue* between the European Council, European Parliament and European Commission could be opened in December 2012, the Council and Par-

---

85 Swedish Riksdag (2011): Reasoned Opinion of the Riksdag, Statement 2011/12: JuU29 Appendix 4.
86 EUROSUR Impact Assessment, SEC(2011) 1536 final, Section 3.5 (Subsidiarity, p. 11).
87 Ibid.
88 Ibid.
89 Ibid.

liament first needed to negotiate their individual positions. The rapporteur in the European Parliament was Jan Mulder from the Liberal Party, with Ska Keller from the EP Greens functioned as shadow rapporteur. When the EUROSUR Regulation was proposed, the Council was under the Polish presidency. Then, during the first six months of the drafting procedure, amendments were formulated under Danish presidency, while the final draft issued by the Council in December 2012 was submitted under Cypriot presidency.

In both the European Parliament and the European Council, the most controversial issue was to what extent "the saving of migrants' lives" should be part of the EUROSUR provisions. From the "first documents coming out of the Danish Council Presidency and the European Parliament before the summer of 2012," Jorrit Rijpma and Mathias Vermeulen conclude that "both institutions wanted to ensure *that EUROSUR would improve the capacity* of FRONTEX and the Member States to save lives of migrants" (2015: 464, emphasis added). However, the issue of saving migrants at sea was not difficult and controversial in terms of capacity; it was not debated whether migrants could better be rescued with larger or smaller vessels, or whether they were spotted at sea easier by binoculars or satellite- or thermo-cameras. The question was rather whether a humanitarian objective was meant to be part of the surveillance system at all. The European Parliament intended, if nothing else, to attach a humanitarian end to the proposed improvement of capacities and it proposed the following wording for recital 2 of the EUROSUR Regulation:

"The practice of travelling in small and unseaworthy vessels has dramatically increased the number of migrants drowning at the southern maritime external borders. EUROSUR should considerably improve the operational and technical ability of the Agency and Member States to detect and track these small vessels, *leading in the mid-term to a considerable reduction of the loss of migrants and refugees at sea.*" (quoted in Rijpma/Vermeulen 2015: 464, emphasis added)

The final regulation, however, provides a formulation that relativizes the responsibility toward persons and vessels at sea. The ability to detect vessels is still formulated as an objective, but the aim of tracking is no longer mentioned in the introductory recital, whereby any impression of potentially witnessing distress at sea is avoided. The final official commitment is indirect at best and plainly evasive at worst: "to detect such small vessels and to improve the reaction capability of the Member States, thereby *contributing* to reducing the loss of lives of migrants."[90] As information alone can already be declared as a contribution to saving lives at sea, an actual effort to rescue persons at sea is not part of the commitment fostered by EUROSUR. Reaction capabilities thus rather serve the hunter who is hoping not to be required as a friend.

The compromise text put forth by the Danish Presidency proposed that the information that would go into the European situational picture (ESP) and the Common Pre-frontier Intelligence Picture (CPIP) would "reflect information that would be relevant for the protection of lives of migrants" (Rijpma/Vermeulen 2015: 464). A consequence of this amendment would have been that distress calls would be visualized on the electronic map of the ESP. Moreover, the Danish presidency even went one step further and proposed to link operational obligations to the availability of information on migrants endangered at sea by proposing to broaden the definition of "reaction capability" in Article 3(b) to also imply "protecting lives of migrants at the external borders."[91] In the Council, however, "the compromise text was not well received, in particular by the southern Member States, who feared that the EUROSUR Regulation would only increase their responsibilities for intercepted migrants and asylum seekers, rather than alleviate the burden" (ibid). These proposals were thus withdrawn from the new draft which the Cypriot Presidency tabled at the first *trialogue* meeting with the EP rapporteur in December 2012.

The Commission, for its part, felt that the negotiations with the European Parliament and Council had run smoothly and easily, and an EC official assumed that this would not have been the case without the pilot project. For this reason, it is worth looking again at how the EUROSUR network was accepted by the users during the test phase of the so-called "big pilot."

5.5.3 How Did the System Take Off?

According to aggregated data on the activities in EUROSUR in 2012 provided to me by Frontex, there was a constant increase in information entered in the EUROSUR network in 2012. In total, Frontex created 4,484 "artifacts," while the Member States entered 3,062 pieces of information. According to the information at hand, the system started to really pick up after July 2012. While there

---

90 EUROSUR Regulation (EU) No 1052/2013, Recital 2, emphasis added.
91 European Council (2012): Proposal for a regulation of the European Parliament and of the Council establishing the European Border Surveillance System EUROSUR – Note to working party on frontiers/mixed committee, EC 11437/12 (June 20, 2012).

were 1,342 entries registered under the name of Frontex in July 2012, member states' artifacts amounted to only 273. Within six months, that is, by January 2013, the entry of artifacts increased threefold for Frontex and more than ten times for member states. Of the total number of 7,584 artifacts created, 32 were maps, 1,757 were documents and the majority of 5,757 were incidents.[92]

Although the sample period is too short to draw conclusions, it can be noted that Frontex was more active in the system than the other nodes. The second basic trend that can be seen in the charts is that incident reports were used the most. However, considering the usage by (new) participants, an observer to the big pilot phase stated that caution should be used when reading the figures, stressing that these did not allow for reliable statements to be made just yet. The observer told me:

"In the current situation, member states enter a lot of data when they are first connected, but then it levels out pretty quickly because Frontex is not yet always able to provide feedback. They all faithfully do their part in the beginning, then they don't get anything back [...]. But that's hopefully over now – that the member states had to enter in something for EUROSUR and for another Frontex system that was built at the same time, meaning they had to enter the same information for Frontex two times and were wondering why they had to do that twice and what Frontex was doing on the other end [...] but that is being fixed now."[93]

The observer mentions the well-known risks that frequently emerge when new technologies are introduced in organizations. On the one hand, there is a reluctance to accept extra or double work. On the other hand, a neglect of, or even a disregard for, new technologies can quickly set in when nothing is offered in return – for example, if the surplus value is not available or evident.

As to the practical acceptance of EUROSUR, which was critical for its development, the following occurred. Political acceptance, which had long been secondary to issues of usability, became more important, because the draft regulation that was presented more or less parallel to the "big pilot" already proposed a political compromise. This made it unlikely that the system would be generally rejected at that point: not only had a mandatory use of the system been proposed,

---

92 Data on EUROSUR activity from July 2012 to January 2013, provided by Frontex via Email on February 1, 2013 (Repository S. Ellebrecht).
93 Own conversation protocol, December 2012; the quotation has been authorized in 2016.

the member states, as users of the system, were now involved in negotiating the means of communication while the medium was being set up. Losing their status as users would have meant losing their ability to help shape the draft regulation.

Beyond the development phase, when looking at the report about the functioning of EUROSUR that was tabled by Frontex in December 2015, it can be concluded that double work was resolved, while the general trend of usage continued: "the incidents reported into JORA (Joint operations reporting application) are being fed by Frontex into the Eurosur network application."[94] Frontex remained the most active node in the system with "64,355 events uploaded in the application" between November 2011 and November 2015.

In total "the Eurosur network application has recorded a total of 117,721 events, while 9,125 documents were stored in its repository. In terms of events most reported in the Eurosur network application, these are firstly related to 'irregular migration' (over 90,000), followed by 'related cross-border crime' (over 20,000). Only a minority of events are related to the 'crisis' category (just over 100)."[95]

5.6 EUROSUR AS AN ITEM OF LAW: THE FINAL REGULATION OF 22 OCTOBER 2013

When EUROSUR was commissioned as part of the 2008 Border Package, it was foreseen to be completed in a regulation within the ongoing financial framework running from 2007 to 2013. The procedure toward the EUROSUR Regulation

---

94 Frontex Report to the European Parliament and the Council on Art 22 (2) of the Regulation EU 1052/2013, The functioning of EUROSUR, (December 1, 2015), [hereafter cited as Frontex Report on the functioning of EUROSUR (2015)], p.10. The report states: "From the beginning of the Eurosur network implementation, emphasis was put on the integration between the existing JORA incident reporting and the Eurosur network application. Frontex ensured early that there is no duplication of incident reporting during Frontex coordinated Joint Operations, which contributed significantly to the compilation of a reliable and coherent European Situational Picture" (p. 12). Against the background of unauthorized sources, this assessment seems to profit strongly from its ex-post perspective. For a recent comparison of the activities in EUROSUR and JORA, see Martina Tazzioli's (2018) astute analysis.

95 Frontex Report on the functioning of EUROSUR (2015), p.18.

was quick and neat. The publication of the Roadmap in February 2008 was followed by a period during which political and technical feasibility studies were carried out. By 2012, the EU had provided funding worth over 170 million euros to 16 research and development projects that promised synergies with the EUROSUR system (Hayes/Vermeulen 2012: 60-64). In addition, the development of the IT application for the EUROSUR network began in November 2009. Structures and definitions that provided themselves in the network's test phases were included in the legislative proposal tabled by the Commission on December 12, 2011.

At this point in time, the member states were requested to clarify the issue of subsidiarity, that is, to determine in their own national parliaments whether the EU had competency in this area. After the Council of the European Union and the European Parliament had determined their positions on the proposed legislation, the *trialogue* between Council, Parliament, and Commission was inaugurated under the Cypriot presidency. The ultimate aim was to adopt the regulation by October 2013. And so it happened. The ordinary legislative procedure ended with the Council of the European Union adopting the regulation on October 22, 2013 without discussion.[96] Two weeks earlier, the European Parliament had approved the EUROSUR Regulation, by 479 votes to 101, with 20 abstentions.[97] As a consequence, the exchange of information and interagency cooperation has been carried out on the legal basis of the EUROSUR Regulation since December 2, 2013.

What does this item of law do? In simple terms, it renders interactions obligatory, which were previously subject to change or dismissal. These interactions concern the exchange of information and operational coordination between border agencies in Europe. The EUROSUR Regulation provided Frontex and member states with a binding "communicational format" aimed at underpinning border surveillance and control practices, data collection and analysis, as well as op-

---

96 Council of the European Union, *Council adopts regulation establishing the EUROSUR system*, 15031/13, press release, October 22, 2013, at: https://www.consili um.europa.eu/uedocs/cms_data/docs/pressdata/en/jha/139099.pdf (accessed August 26, 2019).

97 European Parliament News, EU border surveillance: MEPPs approve Eurosur operating rules, press release, October 10, 2013, at: http://www.europarl.europa.eu/news/en/news-room/20131007IPR211624/html/EU-border-surveillance-MEPs-approve-Eurosur-operating-rules (accessed October 12, 2013).

erational cooperation and planning. For this purpose, the EUROSUR Regulation has rendered the following components compulsory:

"(a) national coordination centres;
(b) national situational pictures;
(c) a communication network;
(d) a European situational picture;
(e) a common pre-frontier intelligence picture;
(f) a common application of surveillance tools"[98]

These elements are results of the EUROSUR development process and yet heretofore *did not exist*. By means of the EUROSUR Regulation these elements are not only accepted, but are rendered official, legitimate, and mandatory. Basically, the EUROSUR Regulation obliges member states to have a national coordination centre and to contribute information to the European situational picture (ESP) by operating the EUROSUR network from this bureau. To a certain extent, the regulation encompasses a software architecture and fixes the definitions on menu items, reporting formats, layers, informational sources and modes of visualization as agreed upon during the development phase. The regulation covers the composition of situational pictures, the necessary communication routines to stipulate the network, as well as the structure and the sources of the final ESP, which, to a degree, brings us back again to the beginning of this chapter – to the EUROSUR network and its devising actors. However, due to the provision, the technical framework has turned into a legal framework for the exchange of information and operational coordination. By means of the regulation, EUROSUR is no longer merely a tool or network but also a set of obligations.

While the previous chapter has shed light on the packing of a black box, namely that of the EUROSUR network, the item of law, the regulation, cannot be unpacked as it is no black box which would substitute, accelerate or delegate anything (Latour 2014: 272-273). In fact, Latour considers an item of law a very different object from a technological artifact. While, for instance, a speed bump (the example is Latour's 1994: 38-40) replaces the police patrol, that is, speed control is delegated to a material artifact, a corresponding item of law – be it on speed limits or the official rules for installing speed bumps – neither controls nor delegates. It rather states that the kind of mobilization and mediation inscribed in the

---

98 EUROSUR Regulation (EU) No 1052/2013, Art. 4 (1).

speed bump is lawful. An item of law does not replace or coagulate an interaction, nor is anything accelerated, delegated or innovated by a legal text. Unlike technical mediation, an item of law does not stabilize an interaction but renders the stabilized set of interactions official and binding. It turns them into an obligation and lends an atmosphere of legal authority to the arrangement, very much in the Weberian sense of an impersonal and rational order.

How does it accomplish this? Rather than making a detour, law bases itself on a constant invocation of other, precedent legal documents: decisions and signatures of this and that date in such and such place. "The legal document 'cools down' the hot process of production: it is the extensity that emerges from the intensive ordeal, which is composed entirely of associations" (McGee 2014: 146). Correspondingly, a legal document is not a black box, it cannot be unpacked as it requires itself to be spread around, to be distributed and to be associated and cross-referenced to other procedures and texts. At this point, when the object is propagated by the treaty, associations are not only objectified, but justified – in the case of borders often to the extent of naturalization and fetishization. As an item of law, EUROSUR can be spread, visited, researched, consulted and referred to by policy makers.

6 EUROSUR: IT's Mediation

What exactly is referred to, when the acronym EUROSUR is deployed by policy makers and those involved in "the progressive establishment of a European model of integrated border management"[1]? What kind of object is EUROSUR? Does EUROSUR refer to the situational picture, and thus to a GIS-generated map, which border guards and analysts see on their screen when wanting to inquire about the latest from the border? Does EUROSUR, as an umbrella term, refer to the technical upgrade and integration of border surveillance of EU member states, as expressed in the phrase 'system of systems'? Is EUROSUR the electronic network installed between national coordination centers (NCCs)? Does it, as such, refer to a setup designed for the purpose of inter-organizational communication and information exchange? Is it a concretization of the 'flanking measures' to the Schengen Agreement and its Convention? Is it, thus, another inter-governmental arena; or can it rather be characterized a communitarian heterotopia (Foucault 1986 [1967]), indicating common concerns while at the same time displaying the crisis of precisely that common entity?

In a sense, EUROSUR is all of the above. However, in more pragmatic terms it has been portrayed as "just a network, nothing else."[2] And in fact, developing this network, all the other reconfigurations have been mediated. EUROSUR is thus not an object, but a trigger. It is the mediator for several reconfigurations in EU border management.

Part II of this book started off with the intention to trace, analyze and discuss the contribution of the European Border Surveillance System, EUROSUR, to the emergence of a supranational EU border. The exploration has focused upon the

---

[1] Executive Summary to the EUROSUR Impact Assessment SEC(2011) 1537 final, p. 2.
[2] Head of Research and Development at Frontex, personal interview (May 27, 2011).

development phase of EUROSUR running from February 2008 to December 2013. During a period of just under six years, two results – or, in fact, products – were yielded: first, the IT application of the EUROSUR network and second, the EUROSUR Regulation. Both products revolve around the exchange of border-related information between EU member states and Frontex for the purpose of generating a common European situation picture (ESP) visualized in an electronic map. The EUROSUR development phase has been explored for those inscriptions that made it into software *and* regulation, such as for instance, menu items of the GUI that are at the same time mentioned in the regulation as obligatory element of the situational pictures.

Generally, the analysis referred both to the making of a cartographic depiction and of a legal text as mediators of the external EU border. Their interplay: the IT application provides the classifications to sort and valuate border-related information and offers a standardized communication format for the exchange of information. The regulation turns this standard into an official procedure, and allots the respective competences.

EUROSUR not only facilitates the exchange of information nor does it merely produce an electronic map; the processes instituted by EUROSUR rather contributes significantly to the formation, acceptance and validity of an external EU border while. The development process of these two products proposed, tested and eventually stabilized the material basis for a new taken for granted idea of an external EU border: While the IT application and its GIS produce chains of references which are supposed to increase and guarantee situational awareness, the regulation describes this accumulation of information as chains of obligations.

These chains of references and chains of obligations have been set up anew with their interrelation mediating the supranational border mandate; (new) chains of reference have been established with regard to "situational awareness," and the provision of a "situational picture," A new truth about what concerns the border is onscreen and guiding the allocation of personnel, resources and the legitimization for interventions. In turn, the regulation fixes the maintenance of these references as an obligation. As the 'result' of these reconfigurations and new fact sheets, new chains of references and new obligations of reporting and assessing the border become tangible to and exploitable by participants. This picture of the external EU border appears plausible, and finds adoption. Chains of obligations and chains of references thus work together and establish a very powerful system whose output changes the assumed geographical and informational limits of border policing.

As both software and regulation are set up for the purpose of generating a European situational picture, their parallel development has provided for the possibility of a dual claim: the ESP produces a both truth claim and a legitimacy claim. In this case, politics thus have artifacts and legislations, their power, however, "does not lie in themselves. It lies in their associations; it is the product of the way they are put together and distributed" (Joerges 1999: 5). Subsequently, EUROSUR – as process, trigger, object and system – constructs that which is legitimately taken to be the border and the need for protection, together with the authority to regulate movement. From the previous two chapters, EUROSUR's mediation can be summarized by the following five aspects:

- *Europeanization.* Since cooperation and information exchange have been cautiously valued and rejected by member states from the very beginnings of the Schengen Process, the development of EUROSUR has produced a degree of integration that did not previously exist and that even seemed heretofore unrealistic. A "detour" – through the development of a communication platform for the exchange of information – mediated member states' willingness to accept obligations concerning the reporting and operationalization of border surveillance and control.
- *Composition of a new visual language.* The most powerful mediation is achieved by way of visualization of the information exchanged in EUROSUR in the European situational picture (ESP). The electronic map of the ESP, the "EUROSUR on the screen," not only provides an image to the added value of information exchange, it also offers what Latour has called a "new visual language" (Latour 1986: 19), that allows the external border of the EU to be naturally 'seen' as a supranational entity. Just as at the turn from medieval to the modern age when "maps depicted political authority as homogeneously territorial and linearly bounded *even before* political practices and institutions were operationalized as such" (Branch 2011: 2, emphasis added), the mapping practices instituted by EUROSUR have been analyzed with regard to the crafting of the supranational authority they evoke. The IT network not only facilitates the exchange of information, but also mediates the integration of border policing in Europe by translating local occurrences into "border-related incidents." It composes a novel and binding association of informants, isolates or rather black-boxes the discontinuous generation of data, and delegates the outline of an external EU border and its supranational mandate to the visualization of information on a screen. In this way, all kinds of information – risk analyses, geodetic data, daily news, police information and (live) monitoring data – are combined

and visualized as 'one' on the screen. EUROSUR does not mediate the formation of an external EU border by demarcating a cartographic space, but by visualizing and geo-referencing risk analyses, incident reports and the attribution of impact levels.

- *Appropriation/Assembling of supranational competences.* The European situational picture not only depicts the occurrences along the external borders of the EU. It rather outlines and projects the area of supranational concern along a tailored body of processed surveillance data. Thereby, EUROSUR triggers that the ideas about the appropriate and legitimate forms of European political authority differ them the territorial logic. The supranational notion of the virtual border is perpetuated by surveillance information that is analyzed along self-determined prognostic criteria, and which acquires the status of "situational awareness" once visualized in the European situational picture. Gathering, aggregating, and evaluating data is the basis for risk analysis and thus the distribution of resources and personnel along a frontier, but also for individual checks and other measure carried out by border service staff. The appropriation of EU competences is not mediated via territory, but via information and data management. Surveillance is the supranational realm of competences, providing risk assessments as a service and the *better* (the supranational) overview.

- *Increase in competences for Frontex.* In this context, the Frontex agency is given an enormous power to define and set the agenda. Since the prognostic criteria and indices for data analysis are defined by Frontex itself, the European situational picture is critically influenced by the agency's services and risk analysis. By developing the technical network, by providing pre-frontier information and risk analysis, by visualizing the surveillance information in the ESP, and by administering the common application of surveillance, Frontex has acquired the position to produce a dynamically developing knowledge base that serves to justify and legitimize border control, surveillance and intervention measures. At the same time, its institutional competences merely appear in disguise with reference to the function of a 'coordinating' agency or a 'service' to the member states.

- *Infrastructural take on immigration and asylum policies.* Mediated through the production of a situational picture, the emerging EU border locates its enforcement areas by tracing vessels. As a result, the operational area is rendered dynamic. The border of policing is not so much limited by reference to geography, but rather mobilized by reference to ever-changing migratory routes and moving vessels. As a result, routes, vehicles and infrastructures both of mobility and surveillance are emerging as the relevant means of power.

This chapter has highlighted EUROSUR's quality as an optical device that provides the "new visual language" (Latour 1986: 19) to naturally see the external EU border. The European situational pictures changes the self-conception of border enforcement. The latter is centrally mediated by information management and the notion of suspicion and less by territory and the notion of inside-outside. Furthermore, it is sorting out the *bona fide* from the *mala fide* movement. This kind of external EU border tackles the "crimmigrant" (Aas 2011) and their means of transport.

It should be stressed that, to date, no European asylum legislation or migration law exists. In the visualization of the situational picture, however, "unauthorized border crossing" first appears as a risk and then takes on the status of "border criminality" in the incident report. EUROSUR thus sketches a unified view of violations of immigration rules, although common immigration laws are absent. While the legal border of policing finds mobilization and mandating via EUROSUR, the legal borders of rights remain scattered. Technically the attempt is being continued to integrate the motives of hunter and friend by rendering their work interoperable in the EUROSUR system. Stefan Kaufmann considers this active ambivalence – the *power to flexibly change* from an authoritarian mode of governing to a humanitarian mode – characteristic of the contemporary border regime. The following chapters explore how the migrant vessel by its versatile nature paradoxically allows for this flexibility.

**The Refugee Boat –
Vehicle, Moving Target,
Integrating Figure of EU Bordering**

Part III: The Refugee Boat – Vehicle, Moving Target, Integrating Figure of EU Bordering

In the context of the southern external borders of the EU, migrant vessels stand, on the one hand, for the risks of border crossing by sea, and on the other, for the challenges of border control. Examining EUROSUR's legitimizing narrative, the previous chapter demonstrated that the reference to small boats both works to claim necessity to save migrants' lives at sea and to justify the need for better surveillance. Those dinghies, fishing boats or freighters represent, in a nutshell, risks and challenges from the standpoint of border crossing *and* from that of border surveillance and control. In order to decipher and explain the possibility of this oscillating reference to the vessels commonly used for migration by sea, this part of the book focuses on the vehicle itself.

For the following three chapters, I take up William Walters' impetus to examine "the missing vehicles" in the context of migration and border control, taking seriously "the symbolic work that vehicles do – both incidental and calculated" (Walters 2011: 6) as well as the materiality of the boat as a socio-political and judicial entity. Modifying Latour's "Where are the missing masses?," Walters claims that the vehicles used for migration, have by their "behavior or nature […] a comparable role" (Latour 1992: 225) to that of humans for the realization and reception of (unauthorized) migration. If true, the socio-technical arrangements aligned to the phenomenon of unauthorized maritime migration could be traced back to its vehicular facilitator. For the purpose of operationalizing Walters' claim, the following chapters examine the vehicle used for migration by sea as a site in its own right.

The intention of the site-specific analysis is not to portray the history of a site, in this case of the refugee boat or migrant vessel, but rather to construct the emergence of a supranational EU border from the perspective of the small boat. The analysis thereby goes beyond emphasizing the impact of migrant vessels on EU border policies. It aims to understand and highlight the difference the boat makes. Walters' claim to focus on the vehicles of migration corresponds to the methodological premises of this study. It allows tracing the role of the vehicle pertaining to networks of commercialized migration as well as to the technical functioning and legal justification of border surveillance and control.

Chapter 7 starts with an analysis of the vehicular characteristics of boats and ships and their differences. It then explores their very first appropriation in the context of unauthorized and clandestine migration in the context of the Indochina Refugee Crisis.

Chapter 8 examines the appropriation of the vessel in the context of seaborne migration to Europe across the Mediterranean Sea, with the reception of the image of the small, overcrowded and unseaworthy vessel given a discursive analysis. Finally, chapter 9 investigates the role the vessel plays in distinguishing the migrants' legal status. The analysis focuses on those arguments that rely on the vehicle as vessel: as stateless, as in distress, as a suspicious one "that is doing something strange,"[1] and that is thus a target of surveillance. This allows the testing of the hypothesis that a prioritization of the vehicle in legal reasoning (while at the same time bypassing or postponing any need to address the human cargo) facilitates operational practices that otherwise would have been difficult, if not impossible, to justify. To conclude, these trajectories are analyzed with regard to the boats' role in the emergence of a supranational external EU border.

---

1 EUROSUR Project Manager at Frontex, personal interview (May 15, 2012)].

7 Site Inspection: On Boats and Ships, their Appropriation for Flight and Migration

7.1 WHAT CHARACTERIZES BOATS AND SHIPS AS VEHICLES?

Described as "a small buoyant structure for travel on water"[1] a boat can essentially be characterized by its ability to traverse bodies of water. To float on water is a boat's property and condition. Yet, "travel on water" points, in fact, to more than the mere floating; first, it points to a directional movement, and second, to transportation. For, it is not the boat that travels; cargo or passengers travel *by water*, while the boat moves and carries *across water*. With its agency consisting in its ability to float and to transport cargo, the navigable boat thus allows for taking the liquid route. Facilitating mobility and transportation is an essential characteristic of any technology of movement; vehicles generally enable increased independence from a fixed place. Yet, what distinguishes boats and ships from other technologies of movement and transportation is the medium they are devoted to: the sea.

The sea – as the medium to be crossed and by which the boat is carried – places its own stamp on the journey and requires the vehicle to be fabricated in a certain way. While the sea, together with Archimedes' principle,[2] governs the

---

[1] Merriam Webster, sub voce "boat," at: https://www.merriam-webster.com/thesaurus/boat (accessed March 29, 2019).

[2] Archimedes' principle indicates that a body floats if its weight is equal to the weight of the liquid (water) it displaces with its volume. The force that drives the vessel down into the water (weight) equals the force that drives it up (buoyancy which is proportional to the displaced volume). The form of the bow plays a significant role, as it de-

watercraft's fabric and basic design, its functional use determines its size and facilities. Fishing vessels, canoes, yachts, dinghies are small, light and easily maneuverable vessels used for pleasure boating or fishing; they are suited for inland and coastal waters. The unwieldy container ships, tanker ships or cruise ships are deployed on international seagoing voyages; their enormous volumes are matched by (equally) massive bows. Overall, the relation between size, shape and utilization arranges itself around the capacity to float.

From the late 15th century onwards, this capacity made the modern venture of navigation possible. Maritime vessels were used to explore the globe, to enhance trade, to expand spheres of influence and to displace, exploit or exchange whatever found ashore. Considered iniquity or even blasphemy in ancient and pre-modern times, seafaring later took on a promising connotation (Makropoulos 1998: 56-57). The sea itself was no longer regarded from a distance as an arbitrary force, adverse to (spatial) orientation and characterized by unpredictability and "anomy" – that is, without legal force or binding effect (ibid: 56). In the course of the modern times, the sea could rather be experienced by sailing across it. Taking inspiration from the practice of seafaring adventures, the sea was seen as a challenge, as an element to be braved and mastered by means of navigation. Nautical metaphors thus changed fundamentally in meaning (Blumenberg 1997). Seafaring became the epitome of human curiosity and of a justified pursuit of happiness (Makropoulos 1998: 57). To this date, the ship stands for the extension of "the faculty and scope of human cognition and action" (Makropoulos 1997: 11).

It is noteworthy that the notion of 'ship' is not infused by acceleration in overcoming distances unlike other vehicles such as the airplane or car (Siegfried 2005; Geisthövel 2005). Seafaring rather symbolizes, first and foremost, the *practical* possibility of freedom.[3] It is not velocity that distinguishes boats and ships from other vehicles, but the possibility and (technical) suitability of an otherwise impossible endeavor: the crossing of the sea. In addition to being a technology of movement, boat and ships are enablers and facilitators, the latter in the most literal sense of the word. Similarly, Rebekka Ladewig (2005: 64) sees the common characteristics of all ships – maritime ships, airship, spaceships – in the

---

termines how much water is displaced, e.g. in the case of bulbous bows. This will also determine how much additional cargo weight can be transported by the vessel.

3   In fact, while aviation symbolizes a rather intellectual freedom, navigation has been regarded as the practical venture through which freedom could be achieved (Makropoulos 1998: 56).

fact "that they enable humans by their concessive, enveloping and protective character, to move through elementary (natural) spaces and open them up as spaces of action and play." In a sense, the proverbial ocean of opportunity can only be accessed by means of boats and ships. Lastly, boats, ships and vessels stand for the passage, middle passage, the transit, the route itself (Certeau 2013 [1984]: 121; Gilroy 2000). They transmit, transport and transgress; they not only facilitate but initiate.

In thinking about boats and ships there is always an encounter with the changing nature of the sea, its unpredictability, its perils and promises. Imaginations on the nature of the sea concomitantly evoke the phenomenology of seafaring, of being on board a vessel, which, in turn, underpin any imagining of boats and ships. Michel Foucault (1986 [1967]: 27) depicts a boat as "a floating piece of space, a place without a place, that exists by itself, that is closed in on itself and at the same time is given over to the infinity of the sea […]." It is in this context, that Foucault characterizes the ship as the "heterotopia par excellence," as "greatest reserve of the imagination" (ibid). While in Ladewig's portrayal the relation between water and craft emphasizes access to opportunities and the protective character of the vessel, Foucault depicts it as a "piece of space" without external reference and completely at mercy of the ubiquitous sea. While the ship promises to cross the sea, to bring about an unknown, yet promising future, the sea advises caution. The ship promises, the sea admonishes.

7.1.1 The Medium of the Sea

Any maritime crossing fundamentally depends on the medium of the sea and its (weather) condition. In fact, while the vessel crosses the ocean, the water carries the craft. Even if the progress in navigational technologies – from compass to GPS, from wooden sailing ships to post Panamax ships – masks the intimacy between water and craft, the place element (Ger.: *Ortselement*) nevertheless requires alignment. The sea is a functional necessity and an essential threat to any vessel.

Following Simmel's way of describing and analyzing space, the sea can be described as a purely sensual formation, which does *not* form itself in space.[4] It is surface or turmoil. Applying Deleuze's and Guattari's (2013: 479) portrayal of the qualities of the sea, seafaring can be envisioned as an encounter with affects.

---

4   While the border famously is defined as "sociological fact, that forms itself in space" Simmel (1997 [1908]: 144).

Accordingly, seafaring can be described as an *experience of space* rather than an overcoming of it. According to the French philosophers "the sea is the smooth space par excellence" (ibid). As opposite to striated space, smooth space is mainly characterized by its incommensurability with measures and defined properties.

"Whereas in the striated forms organize a matter, in the smooth materials signal forces and serve as symptoms for them. It is an intensive rather than extensive space, one of distances, not of measures and properties. […] Perception in it is based on symptoms and evaluations rather than measures and properties. That is why smooth space is occupied by intensities, wind and noise, forces, and sonorous and tactile qualities, as in the desert, steppe, or ice." (Deleuze/Guattari 2013: 479)

It follows that the sea cannot be bound. Moreover, as aesthetic impression and lived experience, the ocean is undifferentiated; it does not show any landmarks to which the eyes can hold onto. With the sea being a smooth space, the seagoing vessel becomes itself a (land)mark, point of reference and sign of life. While the sea swallows and blurs, the vessel, its direction, route and cargo indicate the relations at stake.

7.1.2 On Boats, Ships and their Differences

According to a basic definition provided by the *Columbia Electronic Encyclopedia*, a boat is a "small, open nautical vessel propelled by sail, oar, pole, paddle, or motor." It follows that the "use of the term boat for larger vessels, although common, is somewhat improper, but the line between boats and ships is not easy to draw."[5] With regard to their utilization, however, boats are neither intended nor suitable for the open sea, which is both reflected by and due to their small bow. This relative unseaworthiness blends into legal definitions of both the term "boat" and "ship."

The dominant negative classification for "ship" is that "on the one side, (motor)boats, floating docks, pontoons, and seaplanes […] are not considered ships" neither are "boats or any yachts which are propelled by sails or oars" (Rah 2009: 59).

In her comparative examination of the meaning of the term "ship" in German, British, US-American, French and Greek legal texts, Heidi Engert-Schüler

---

5 Columbia Electronic Encyclopedia, sub voce "boat," at: http://www.infoplease.com/encyclopedia/history/boat.html (accessed March 29, 2019).

(1979: 59) extracts the overall definition that a ship "is an item of a not minuscule size [Ger.: *Gegenstand von nicht unbedeutender Größe*], which is suitable and dedicated for the sea" [Ger.: *zur Schifffahrt geeignet und bestimmt*]. The tautological definition – a ship is a vehicle capable of navigation – links the characteristics of a ship to its technical suitability (Ger.: *Eignung*) for the high sea. Yet, Engert-Schüler already conducts her analysis under the premise that the term ship refers to a sea-going vessel on international voyage (ibid: 26-29).

A ship is imagined against the background of the high seas which it crosses. Boats, in contrast, are used in lakes, coastal and internal waters. In our imagination, boats move in a placid, recreational scene; they are goods and chattels, the economical basis of local fishermen or sports equipment, linked to adventures. One of the few conceivable images of a small boat on the high seas is that of a life boat. A boat does not cross an ocean, nor does it push a frontier. It stays local as it generally returns to its place of departure. Ships, in contrast, are used to change location. Likewise, Engert-Schüler stresses that the prime characteristic of seafaring is not transportation but the change of location (1979: 58). The intention of seafaring, however, the crossing-over, the change of location may as well be pursued on a boat. This is to say that the suitability to travel the open sea (Ger.: *Eignung*) does not by implication comply with its dedicated purpose (Ger.: *Widmung; Nutzung*). A boat may be found on the open sea, too; yet, does it *ipso facto* turn into a ship? And what difference would it make?

In fact, international law attaches a variety of legal consequences to the factual finding that an "item is a ship" (Engert-Schüler 1979: 25). The rights and obligations defined in international maritime law apply to ships and not to boats, such as for example the right to innocent passage (Rah 2009: 15). However, technical qualifications do not suffice for the legal recognition of a watercraft to be a ship. Cargo has its bearing on the classification of vessels, too: the 1974 International Convention for the Safety of Life at Sea (SOLAS) defines a vessel that "carries more than twelve passengers" as a "passenger ship"[6] – *regardless of size*, as Patricia Mallia (2010: 35) points out.

According to the rights and obligations under the Law of the Sea,[7] a watercraft is only treated as a ship when flying a flag. The flag indicates the nationality of

---

6 SOLAS, Chapter I, Regulation 2(f).
7 The 1982 United Nations Law of the Sea Convention (LOSC) is the most comprehensive interstate agreement on the rules and obligations concerning international seafaring. 91 countries have signed the LOSC; in 2013 the European Union also signed it.

ships (Gavouneli 2006: 206-209; Rah 2009: 17-18). By flying a flag, a ship indicates that it is registered with the respective state. However, ships cannot be registered with just any state and thus fly its flag. Art. 91 (1) of the Law of the Sea Convention (LOSC) stipulates that "[t]here must be a genuine link between the State and the ship." When a ship bears a flag, it thus indicates a consented legal relationship: the flag bearing said state holds both legal authority over that vessel and its cargo as well as responsibility for it. By flying a flag, a vessel displays its jurisdictional reference, that is, the laws that apply on board as well as those of the state which then is obliged "to effectively exercise its jurisdiction and control in matters administrative, technical and social, ranging from the construction, equipment and seaworthiness of ships to the manning, labor conditions and the training of crews on board."[8] A vessel is thus considered a ship when identifiable, that is, localizable with regard to its legal position in international relations.

What is relevant in this context is the question whether for the factual finding "item is a ship" flag state regulations should be recognized or not. In this regard, Sicco Rah deduces from the LOSC that "vessels that are not legally entitled to flying a flag [...] may not be regarded as ships." (Rah 2009: 16) In contrast, Engert-Schüler argues that the reference to flag state is not appropriate, as not every item that wears a flag turns into a ship (Engert-Schüler 1979: 25). By means of her comparative analysis of legal texts, she proves that the suitability for the high seas and not the registration with or reference to a flag state is the most significant feature of a ship in legal understanding (ibid: 25-26, 59). Reviewing the understanding of the term ship in both the texts of the LOSC, in different multilateral international agreements, as well as in German maritime law, Inken von Gadow-Stephani minimizes the definition even further: she argues that one should act on the assumption of a ship "if an item serves the locomotion on water" (2006: 19-26, here: 26). She accordingly defines "ship" as an item "that can move by floating" (Ger.: *der sich schwimmend fortbewegen kann*) (ibid: 23). This definition does not distinguish between boats and ships. Gadow-Stephani places emphasis on the mere ability of the floating movement on water – and not to the suitability for the high seas. Thus, she does not see the prerequisite for the applicability of rights in a technical qualification, but a physical ability and moving presence on water.

Ultimately, ships are not considered independent legal entities. This holds true despite diverse (metaphorical) conceptions of a ship as legal territory, and contrary to common references to the rights of a ship (Rah 2009: 15). Ships are

---

8   LOSC Art. 94.

no subject of international law. As vehicles they are rather "merely movable objects [Ger.: *lediglich bewegliche Sachen*] in the ownership and possession of states or international organizations" (Gadow-Stephani 2006: 19). It follows that the rights of a ship are rights which states grant each other (Rah 2009: 21).

By implication this also means that the recognition of a vessel as ship brings state politics to the table. When, in turn, the vessels used for maritime migration are regularly depicted as boats, this might also serve to circumvent international politics. This aspect will be elaborated further below.
When addressing the characteristics of boats and ships as technologies of mobility, its technical specifications and requirements can be distinguished from the legal terminology of the term ship as well as from the metaphorical reference to boats and ships. In all three contexts, boats and ships are treated unequally although a clear definition of their distinguishing features is lacking. The only recurring distinction between boats and ships is their size as the technical condition of seaworthiness. Other technical classifications blend into legal references, and vice versa. Together they serve as a basis for claiming or rejecting obligations and competences toward the vehicle and its passengers. As this study is interested in the reference to boats and ships in the context of EU border surveillance and control practices, it is not important to distinguish between boats and ships by definition; nor will I maintain a defined separation between boats and ships. This section rather reveals that the description of a vehicle is simultaneously a negotiation of competences and obligations toward its (in)animate goods.

7.2 APPROPRIATION OF BOATS AND SHIPS FOR FLIGHT AND UNAUTHORIZED MIGRATION

As vehicles, boats and ships generally assist in traversing maritime distances. If, however, the purpose of the change of location is flight or clandestine migration, this later appropriation impacts upon the condition of the itinerary, its organization, its departure and arrival, the fate of the human cargo and on the vehicle itself. Seaborne escape and migration is hardly "travel by water."

Correspondingly, the suitability of the vessel is not only directed to seafaring alone. The purpose of flight or clandestine migration has its own bearings on the suitability of the vessel. Boats and ships that are appropriated for the purpose of flight or clandestine migration are compromised by a dual, yet ambivalent, sometimes conflicting suitability (Ger.: *Eignung*): for the purpose of clandestine seaborne migration small boats are, for instance, more suitable than ships, as it is more difficult to detect boats amid the waves. In terms of seaworthiness, however, small boats are not suited for the open sea. Furthermore, the condition and thus seaworthiness of a vessel is thwarted by the profitability of commercialized migration.

The following section illustrates and examines the implications of dual suitability. Under the premises that the vessel appropriated for flight and clandestine migration incorporates this dual suitability, a site-inspection, which focuses on the practicalities and experiences of flight and migration by boat, gains strategic relevance. Starting with the earliest appropriation of boats and ships in the context of the Indochina Refugee Crisis, I intend to explore the characteristic difference the boat makes as a means of movement in the context of unauthorized migration.

7.2.1 Boats and Ships as Appropriated during the Indochina Refugee Crises

Since the systematic use of vessels for the purposes of escape during the Indochina refugee crisis, the "refugee boat" can be considered a particular *type* of vessel: a vessel classified by its (human) cargo. The boat, in turn, gives name to the passengers it transports: the boat-people. Moreover, the vehicle leaves its mark on the person: even after disembarking "an encounter with travel follows you around. Long after your journey is finished you remain a boat person" (Walters 2011: 5).

The term "boat-people" was coined during the Indochina Refugee Crisis following the Vietnam War. The communist takeover of the three Indochinese countries Vietnam, Cambodia and Laos in 1975 forced approximately three million people to seek refuge in neighboring Southeast Asian countries over the next two decades.[9] According to UNHCR's statistics, about one fourth of these refugees, which amounts to 796,310 persons, were Vietnamese refugees who escaped by boat.[10]

---

9   Various studies on the Indochina Refugee Crises attempt to quantify and classify the number of refugee during that period Robinson (1998: 2), Davies (2008: 85), Thompson (2010); Wain (1981: 42). However, all note that these numbers can only be minimum estimates, as thousands are believed to have perished en route and in the hands of pirates.

10 UNHCR (2000): The State of the World's Refugees: Fifty Years of Humanitarian Action, Chapter 4 (Flight from Indochina: 79-105, here p. 98 and 102) at:

When forces of the communist North marched into Saigon in April 1975, American forces attempted to evacuate Vietnamese people by airlifting them from the rooftop of the American embassy. Between April 21 and 29, 1975, 35,000 Vietnamese were to be flown out (Vo 2006: 65). The Pentagon "positioned more than two dozen aircraft carriers, destroyers, and merchant marine vessels off the Vietnamese coast" (Robinson 1998: 18). When on April 30, Saigon was taken by the communists, airlifts became impossible, and escapees used "supply and patrol boats, landing craft, fishing boats, trawlers, tugs, ferries, and anything that could float" (Vo 2006: 70) to flee Saigon. The then US President Gerald Ford ordered the ships of the U.S. Seventh Fleet to drop anchor outside Vietnamese territorial waters and take escapees on board (ibid: 3). The exodus was an emergency evacuation, with scarce logistical resources and no time left.

Reports of the sea being crowded with "overloaded fishing boats and other small craft" (Thompson 2010: 28), of Vietnamese fishers setting their boats on fire to force the US Navy to take them on board illustrate the precipitous exodus that the Vietnamese reportedly called "the running" (ibid: 27). The staggering number of 60,000 refugees over several days is tangibly illustrated in depictions of the US Navy having to hoist people aboard using cargo nets instead of ladders, which proved infeasible given the scores of people trying to climb them. Moreover, the limit of persons to be taken aboard US ships was raised several times (Vo 2006: 70).

Considering the haste in fleeing Saigon aboard "anything that could float" (Vo 2006: 70), the appropriation of boats and ships in this context occurs within the framework of an emergency situation: for the appropriation of boats and ships this meant that the characteristic of "floating" was enough. In this situation, boats were not a means of first or last choice, but rather *the* last resort. The fact that during evacuation no attention was paid to ensure the escape of high-risk persons, that is, "Vietnamese who work for any element of the US mission" (Robinson 1998: 17), illustrates not only the time pressure and urgency of the evacuation but also its indiscriminate operationalization. There was no triaging or classification; there were contingents of Vietnamese to be fitted on ships. Those taken on board US ships were taken to the US military base in Guam, where arrangements had been made to process 50,000 Vietnamese. Most of them were relocated to the US.

---

http://www.unhcr.org/4a4c754a9.html (accessed August 27, 2019), [hereafter cited as UNHCR Report (2000): Flight from Indochina].

Overall, in that situation, the sea was the last open route, and floating vehicles the only suitable option to take said route. However, those sea-lifted Vietnamese refugees were never described by the term boat-people, neither by the American forces nor by UNHCR. The Vietnamese were referred to as refugees, evacuees, or simply as the Vietnamese people. The appropriation of boats and ships in this context was spontaneous and functional rather than strategic. Even though fishing boats and other watercraft had been used to escape, and even though this image of fleeing Saigon by sea determined the image of the evacuation, this scenario did not elicit the term "boat-people." The peculiar hybrid of the "boat-people" is not the product of an emergency situation and does thus not carry its notion of urgency and final run.

7.2.2 "Boat-People": An Evasive Term

However, following the ad-hoc mass evacuation, the mode of escaping by boat continued. While UNHCR registered 378 boat escapees landing on neighboring shores in 1975, their number increased to 5,247 in 1976, and rose further to 15,690 over the next few years (Wain 1981: 42).

In retrospect UNHCR described its "initial reaction" as "to treat these movements as the aftermath of war rather than as the beginning of a new refugee crisis."[11] Yet, the increasing number of individuals fleeing Vietnam by sea rendered a clarification of their refugee status and the subsequent processing necessary; especially so, since neighboring Southeast Asian states were increasingly reluctant toward allowing Vietnamese refugees to land on their shores. Already in 1975, UNHCR mentioned difficulties in "ensuring that Indochinese people seeking asylum by boat would be rescued at sea or provided with asylum upon arrival in Southeast Asian states" (quoted in Davies 2008: 89).

Despite these concerns, UNHCR did not grant *prima facie* refugee status[12] to the people leaving Vietnam. Even more irritating was that "there was no mention

---

11 UNHCR Report (2000): Flight from Indochina, p. 81.

12 "*Prima facie* refugees is a term used to identify a large number of people fleeing events in which they may not have actively participated, but fear the consequences for themselves and those around them if they do not flee, it also takes into account those that have been personally threatened or persecuted. In contrast to individual refugee status granted under the 1951 Convention, *prima facie* refugee status is used in situations where individual screening is not possible, though this does not preclude eventual individual screening for refugee status." (Davies 2008: 20).

of refugees at all in the earliest communications between UNHCR and Southeast Asian states in the immediate aftermath of the Vietnam war" (Davies 2008: 90). In 1975 and 1976, the Indochinese were regarded and referred to as displaced persons by UNHCR and Southeast Asian officials alike (ibid: 91; Robinson 1998: 20-25).

The year following, the term boat-people came to be used in negotiations between Southeast Asian government officials and UNHCR. The first official documents referring to Vietnamese refugees as "boat-people" were UNHCR's Weekly Notes in 1977 in which the organization summarized "the increasing denial by Southeast Asian states to 'boat-people' arrivals unless the UNHCR guaranteed that the asylum seekers' asylum would be temporary only" (quoted in Davies 2008: 93, fn. 38). In October 1977, Thailand, the Philippines and Indonesia requested during different meetings of the United Nations General Assembly to treat the problem of the so-called boat-people as a global one. Arguing that allowing boat-people to land might attract an even greater influx, Southeast Asian governments justified their rejection of Vietnamese refugees (ibid: 93).

The term boat-people thus was either inadvertently or purposefully used in a period during which both UNHCR and the receiving neighboring countries avoided calling or classifying the Vietnamese as refugees. UNHCR's continuous efforts to have Southeast Asian governments sign international refugee law, namely the 1951 Refugee Convention and its 1967 Protocol, limited the pressure UNHCR could possibly put on those countries' governments with regard to taking on the increasing number of Indochinese attempting to arrive by boat. Considering this, it seems plausible that UNHCR therefore refrained from granting *prima facie* refugee status and from using the term "refugees." The United States, in contrast, pushed toward calling the people fleeing Vietnam, Cambodia or Laos, refugees. In response to UNHCR's evasive rhetoric, the US representative Haugh was considered to rather "dropped [...] large hints about what he found missing from the discussion" (Robinson 1998: 22).

"The refugee [...] fled from his homeland as an individual who had been deprived of his human rights and it was noteworthy that the High Commissioner directed his program of international protection and material assistance to the refugee as an individual and that each project was geared to the rehabilitation of the refugee and the restoration of his faith and hope in humanity." (quoted in Robinson 1998: 22)

However, Davies (2008: 94) points out that commentators also interpreted the US's prompt recognition of a *prima facie* refugee status as a justification for waging war against communism in the region. The many refugees were taken as proof of an inhumane and authoritarian communist regime.

In this atmosphere of terminological vagueness, typical of negotiations, the term boat-people might have been "inadvertently coined," as Martin Tsamenyi (1983: 348) argues. As it were, the term became utilized as it put, in a descriptive fashion, a visual image into language. Moreover, the term summed up the practical common denominator of those Indochinese who fled by boat as their classificatory characteristic and attribute: they came by boat; or rather, they were in a boat and needed to land somewhere. As UNHCR and Southeast Asian government officials came to use the term "boat-people" to avoid using the obliging term "refugee," the periphrasis boat-people also echoes this hesitation and indicates a latent doubt of the refugee status of persons on board a certain type of vessel. At first glance, this might appear to merely suspend the refugee debate; yet, it restructured the international response toward the emerging Indochinese refugee crisis and its protagonists: the boat-people. In fact, the concrete setting of 'a group of people in a boat at sea' opened up new arguments and provided time and space for negotiations.

Meanwhile, Thailand, Malaysia and Indochina increasingly turned away boats from their shores; this pushback put pressure on the international community to address the issue as a global one. At the same time, boat-people ended their state of uncertainty at sea by provoking a distress situation. Barry Wain reports in his monograph *The Refused* that it was a "common but dangerous practice to hole their boats so they would be allowed to land" (Wain 1981: 65). Yet, the reluctance of Southeast Asian states to admit Indochinese boat-people not only occurred in avoidance of legal obligation and in keeping local hostility toward the Indochinese at bay. It was also an expression of a growing skepticism that the new government in South Vietnam was not only actively "exporting refugees" (Thompson 2010: 162) but was also profiting from it. And, in fact, an unofficial "pay-as-you-go policy" (Robinson 1998: 41) perpetuated the exodus of ever more Vietnamese, most of them ethnic Chinese who were "invited" to leave and charged for this option. Underlining their doubt in the genuine refugee status of the boat-people, Southeast Asian officials thus started to refer to them as "illegal migrants."

When in 1978 "several of the boats arriving on the shores of countries in Southeast Asia were not small wooden fishing craft but steel-hulled freighters chartered by regional smuggling syndicates and carrying over 2,000 people at a time"[13] the increasing irritation led to forceful refusals. Southeast Asian countries argued that a prerequisite for a temporary asylum of refugees on their shores was the guaranteed permanent resettlement in other countries of the international community. Temporary asylum was thus traded against permanent resettlement. The two situations involving the freighters *Southern Cross* and *Hai Hong*, which I will address in the section following, catalyzed this kind of international policy arrangement, which became known under the phrase "an open door for an open shore."

7.2.3 The Southern Cross and the Hai Hong Incidents

The voyages of the coastal freighters *Southern Cross* and *Hai Hong* came to be remembered as "the first organized refugee movement involving a non-Vietnamese vessel" (Wain 1981: 18)[14]. The incident of the *Hai Hong* was tangible evidence that the transport of refugees had turned into an organized and profitable business. And still, this did not clarify but rather intensify the international debate over the refugee status of the persons on board.

The refugee pick-up of the *Southern Cross* was arranged by the Vietnamese businessman Tay Kheng Hong. Tay used his business and government contacts and convinced the managing director of Seng Bee Shipping, Chong Chai Kok, and the Finnish sea captain, Sven Olof Ahlqvist, who possessed a Singaporean employment pass, to use the 850-ton Honduras-registered freighter for the commercial transport of Vietnamese passengers. When the *Southern Cross* left Singapore on August 24, 1978, it was empty and supposedly going "to collect a cargo of salt" in Bangkok (Wain 1981: 18). Instead, the freighter docked in Ho Chi Minh City, formerly Saigon, and picked up 1,250 people who had paid the Vietnamese authorities six to eight pieces of gold (ibid: 21), which roughly amounts to 1,500 Euros today. The involvement of local authorities at the very least is demonstrated in the below description of the logistic arrangements for embarkation:

---

13 UNHCR Report (2000): Flight from Indochina p. 82.
14 The description of the two voyages mainly follows Barry Wain's detailed examination. The earliest account of the two incidents dates from 1979 and is provided by Bruce Grant's (1979) investigation *The Boat People*. Larry Clinton Thompson's (2010) account offers further insights of the US perspectives on both the freighters' incidents as well as on the Indochinese Exodus in general.

"[T]he *Southern Cross* had received red-carpet treatment when it went to collect its cargo. A Vietnamese government pilot launch came alongside; the pilot boarded the *Southern Cross* and guided it up the twisting Saigon River to a berth in Ho Chi Minh City. The ship was supplied with fresh water and vegetables, guarded by troops patrolling the wharf and guided by the same pilot to the collection point in the following day. The pilot and three armed soldiers spent the night on board. In Ho Chi Minh City, Tay had been taken to a restaurant for a meal with civilian officials. On its departure the *Southern Cross* was allowed to fly the red-and-yellow Vietnamese flag, had the benefit of the pilot's services until it was two hours in the open sea and was not challenged by Vietnamese security patrols." (Wain 1981: 21)

The refugee-freighter was escorted by government officials out to the open sea. Once it reached international waters, the Captain radioed that his freighter had rescued 1,220 Vietnamese "in international waters from four large fishing junks" (Wain 1981: 18-19) and wished to put them ashore immediately in Malaysia. The Malaysian government refused permission for the vessel to land and escorted it out of its territorial waters again. Singapore, too, refused to accept the vessel. The crew of syndicates, which had already left the freighter when the distress call had been sent, rejoined the ship together with a load of additional water, food and fuel sent by the shipping company as the vessel was stranded at sea. Almost one month after its departure, on September 21, 1978, the *Southern Cross* had drifted into Indonesian waters, where Ahlqvist "beached deliberately on Pengibu Island" (ibid: 19). Even though Indonesian authorities suspected that the captain of the ship might attempt to solve the dilemma over the refugees by purposely grounding the vessel in order to capitalize from the situation with regard to insurance; however, "a trade in refugees never occurred to them – or to anyone else" (ibid). Doubt was cast on the patterns of navigation, rather than on the status and the circumstances of the passengers. This changed with the second set of deceptive maneuvers the same group of syndicates launched with the *Hai Hong*.

Tay again organized a freighter through his contacts at Seng Bee Shipping, employed the Indonesian Sunsun Serigar as new captain and registered the "aging coastal freighter" (Wain 1981: 16) with Panama for a month. It had been arranged that 1,200 refugee passengers would be picked up by the *Hai Hong*. This time, there was no red-carpet treatment; Vietnamese officials instead expected the *Hai Hong* to take an additional 1,300 passengers aboard. They enforced their demand by threatening to arrest the crew and its captain and by blocking the ship's exits. On October 24, 1978, the heavily overcrowded *Hai Hong* left the port of Saigon with approximately 2,500 passengers on board, the vast majority being ethnic Chinese.

With engine trouble and a typhoon endangering the voyage, the captain corrected his northward course and directed the *Hai Hong* toward Indonesian archipelagos. When on November 2, 1978, the captain of the *Hai Hong* radioed to the Eastern South Asia regional office of UNHCR in Malaysia, he briefly reported "that he was in Indonesian waters with more than 2,000 refugees on board" (Wain 1981: 23; Thompson 2010: 150). Later the same day, the captain sent another radio message to the UNHCR office in Kuala Lumpur in which he provided more details:

"He said the *Hai Hong* was Panamanian-registered, Singapore-owned. [...] [I]t had been en route from Singapore to Hong Kong when, on October 23, it had developed engine trouble near Lincoln Island in the Paracels. The following day it had been boarded by more than 2,000 refugees from between 10 and 15 smaller boats." (Wain 1981: 23)

The reported chronology, however, attracted suspicion. Why would a captain wait an entire week to inform UNHCR after having picked up such a large number of refugees, and why would he first change his course? Furthermore, most practical doubts emerged as it seems implausible that "2,000 Vietnamese [had] managed to gather at one place in the middle of an ocean, 225 miles from the coast of Vietnam, as Typhoon Rita stirred the seas and sent much larger vessels scurrying for shelter" (Wain 1981: 23). This and further inconsistencies lead to official investigations. Both the Australian and Southeast Asian governments as well as UNHCR were deeply disturbed by the level of commercialized and organized refugee trade for which the voyage of the *Hai Hong* provided evidence. In his short statement of November 3, Rajagopalam Sampatkumar, Regional Representative of UNHCR, expressed concerns about an illicit market of people trafficking from southern Vietnam which would jeopardize UNHCR's assistance for "genuine refugees." Amongst policy makers in Canberra it was even concluded "that the *Hai Hong* venture must fail and that its failure must stand as deterrent to any similar enterprises in the future" (ibid: 27).

On November 6, the *Hai Hong* was driven from Indonesian waters. When on November 9, the freighter dropped anchor again, it did so twelve miles off the Malaysian Port Klang. At that time, it was flying the Malaysian flag.[15] While

---

15 During the investigation, it turned out that the *Hai Hong* was formerly "registered in the Malaysian port of Penang" (Wain 1981: 29) under its original name, *Golden Hill*.

Sampatkumar made efforts to board the *Hai Hong* and assess the situation of the people on board, the government in Kuala Lumpur ordered the ship out of Malaysian waters. It was made clear that "if the ship proved obstinate the government would take all steps necessary to force it beyond territorial waters" (Wain 1981: 32).

Meanwhile pictures and documentaries of the *Hai Hong* – of more than 2,000 thirsty and devastated people, cramped on a scrap-metal vessel in the middle of the ocean – began to spread in Western media. Shock and sympathy might have triggered the relatively quick commitment to "take" the boat-people from the *Hai Hong* and resettle them as refugees. Word was again passed to UNHCR. Sampatkumar, who, in fact, was increasingly worried about UNHCR's poor access to the freighter and the poor health of some of the *Hai Hong* passengers, seemed to reverse his opinion overnight. UNHCR officially declared that it considered the passengers of the *Hai Hong* as refugees (Wain 1981: 32-33). It was added from UNHCR headquarters that "in the future, unless there are clear indications to the contrary, boat cases from VietNam be considered prima facie of concern to UNHCR."[16] With 657 *Hai Hong* passengers resettled in Germany, 604 in Canada, 897 in the United States, 222 in France, 52 in Switzerland, nine in New Zealand and eight in Australia, the new category of the humanitarian refugee was created.

The shift in perspective is remarkable: the humanitarian eye was not geared toward refugees from war or an authoritarian regime, but toward people on a boat. While official political discourse in the region evaded and protracted the decision on the refugee status, Western policy makers rather discussed the situation aboard the *Hai Hong*, the dangers of the seaborne escape, the bad condition or unseaworthiness of refugee vessels. The boat was referred to as a mirror of the misery of the Vietnamese people. Their immediate neediness consisted in being aboard an overcrowded and unseaworthy vessel. The urgency to do something was manifest in the bad condition of the vessel.

With the voyage of the *Hai Hong* ending successfully for the Vietnamese refugee, two more ships followed: the *Tung An* with 2,300 Vietnamese on board, and the *Huey Fong* with more than 3,000 passengers on board. And again, the situation on board was protracted until coastal states received assurance that the refugees would be resettled elsewhere after disembarkation (Thompson 2010: 151). Yet, these were almost the final larger ships from Vietnam. "Thereafter,

---

16 Quoted in UNHCR Report (2000): Flight from Indochina, p. 83.

refugees turned to flight in smaller craft and at a much greater risk, hoping to sneak ashore in one or another Southeast Asian country" (ibid). Robinson assumes that the "organizers learned that big ships drew too much attention and began to abandon them for smaller vessels" (Robinson 1998: 32). Similarly, Grant notes that the "attraction of the freighters was that they were safer, minimizing the dangers of piracy and death at sea. The use of cargo ships gave the whole exodus a higher profile, and led to a more thorough investigation of the system that brought paying refugees out of southern Vietnam" (Grant 1979: 116). Likewise, Singapore's Prime Minister, Lee Kuan Yew, commented in 1979 that the "latest exodus of 'boat-people' and 'ship-people' [was] the result of acts of cold calculation, measured in gold" (quoted in Thompson 2010: 162). And in fact, the profitability of trafficking refugees is more evident in the cases of cramped freighters.

During the late 1970s the image of rickety and cramped vessels became an emblem for grief and suffering in the Western media, which ultimately catalyzed the establishment of the humanitarian refugee and justified resettlement quotas. Escape by boat was taken as proof of neediness and refugee status. Yet, among Southeast Asian countries, it is precisely the neediness of Vietnamese boat-people which was contested. Until today, and also transferred to the European context, both trajectories meet in the expression boat-people and the image of the overcrowded and unseaworthy refugee boat.

7.3 WHAT DIFFERENCE DOES THE BOAT MAKE?

With unauthorized migrants and refugees on board, boats and ships can thus be distinguished with regard to the level of international politics they can trigger. Boats not only "sneak ashore" (Thompson 2010: 151) and thus signify the possibility of an unauthorized, unsighted entry, they also escape open international diplomacy if not conflict.

Ships and freighters not only attract more attention due to the mere number of passengers they can carry. They also involve, by means of their technical and legal references, legal obligations, business ties, and the question of state jurisdiction over the vessel and its cargo. Yet, does it in fact make a difference, whether refugees are on a boat or ship?

Lee Kuan Yew's statement cited above in fact implies at least a symbolic difference between "boat-people" and "ship-people." A freighter is a bold hint to the commercialized structure of facilitated maritime migration, and the genuine status of the refugee is ever more questioned on a ship than on a boat. In these cases, the state of the vessel as unseaworthy – and in this case unseaworthiness can be due to the fact that the vessel is simply too small for the high seas or due to its poor condition, being rusty, rickety, made of scrap metal – becomes a proxy for the neediness of the passengers on board. The vessel signifies urgency, while the recognition of an eventual refugee status is protracted.

Size and seaworthiness, the two main distinguishing features between boats and ships, are thus turned on their heads by the appropriation of vessels in the context of flight and migration: while the size of the ship (it cannot be small) and the seaworthiness qualify a vessel for international voyages, a small or unseaworthy boat is what qualifies its passengers for international protection.

What can be observed for the case of the refugee boat is a dual, yet ambivalent, sometimes conflicting suitability (Ger.: *Eignung*) which not only responds to the nature of the sea, but also to the nature of international refugee policies.

8 Seaborne Migration: Europe's Boat Migrants and their Refugee Vessels

In the context of maritime migration to Europe, vessels also play a role as vehicular facilitators. The following exploration of the appropriation of boats and ships in the context of unauthorized Mediterranean crossings will illustrate that the vessel is a focal point in many ways. Boats and ships are not only central to the practical endeavor of maritime migration to Europe; they are also a crucial asset for the organization of this specific journey which provides for a particular access to the legal and administrative territories of the EU.

If the program of a watercraft can be phrased as "to carry across water," migration disturbs this aim. The program "get people into Europe by sea" requires a certain type of vessel. Tracing this program means asking for the vessels' relation to the phenomenon of unauthorized migration to Europe. This in turn means portraying the vessels' share in the illicit market of smuggling migrants, describing its strategies to remain undetected, exploring the circumstances on board as well as the vessels relation to the migrants' death toll in the Mediterranean Sea.

The following three sections focus on the ambivalent features that both stem from and are reflected by the condition, appropriation and image of the migrant vessel as "refugee boat," "ghost ship" or "cargo freighter." In order to decipher and understand how politics approaches these different ambivalent features, the following sections outline the rumors, the factual findings, the indicators and images concerning boats, ships, and their migrant passengers, as well as the symbolic work they do. Moreover, they examine how far the condition and image of the vessel blends into the status ascribed to maritime migrants heading for Europe. If Mathias Bös (1997: 135) is right stating that "categorizations of migrations are determined rather by political processes than by migrants' characteristics," the question is: what are the political processes leading to the category of boat migration and boat refugees?

8.1 BOATS AND BORDER ENFORCEMENT IN THE MEDITERRANEAN

As a mode of migration and circulation between countries bordering the Mediterranean Sea, maritime crossings have been quite regular. The mode of crossing the Mediterranean by boat preceded the efforts of European countries to regulate the phenomenon. This is to say that the appropriation of boats for migration has been one of the Mediterranean's "historical uses" (Pugh 2000: 31) and did not emerge as a subversive strategy or illegal practice, but as a regional practicality. What emerged, however, was the commercialization of unauthorized Mediterranean crossings, along with border control and surveillance practices. This section is about the boat mediating the two.

8.1.1 Boats for Migration: From "Historical Uses" to First Schengen Targets

In the 1960s, irregular migration was a rather tolerated practice in the Strait of Gibraltar. The distance of only 14 kilometers between Tarifa and Tangier could be crossed using small fishing vessels. The only hindrances were either strong currents or ship traffic (Carling 2007b: 22). Another historic route was the trip by boat from Tunisia or Libya to Italy. With fishermen commuting between Tunisia and Sicily to sell fish on their mutual local markets, and many Sicilian-Tunisian marriages and thus family visits, going back and forth by boat across the Sicilian Channel used to be a rather common practice.[1] Moreover, would-be migrants only needed a valid passport to travel to Italy, as the Tunis-Palermo and Tunis-Trapani ferries traveled back and forth in the Strait of Sicily (Ben-Yehoyada 2011: 19). For both countries, Italy and Spain, irregular migration and the informal economy were closely related; the corresponding networks aligned both labor and transportation. This is well illustrated by the case of the Tunisia-Sicily connection:

"Other Tunisians found both work and a ride to Italy on Sicilian trawlers that anchored in Tunisian ports. Sicilian captains in search of cheap fuel or undisturbed fishing in Tunisian waters often hired Tunisian crewmen to mediate the exchanges. The Sicilian fishing fleet

---

1 Gloria Cipolla, Cooperazione Internazionale Sud Sud (CISS), personal interview in her office at the CISS in Palermo, Sicily (March 25, 2011).

played a dual role for would-be migrants: Its easily approached sailors got the Tunisians aboard the trawlers, and then its vessels carried them across the channel. In the business of clandestine migration, transporters and passengers were somewhat interchangeable. Many of the Sicilian fleet's Tunisian crewmen were originally passengers, who later arranged for the passage of friends and relatives, who still later became coworkers on the trawlers." (Ben-Yehoyada 2011: 19)

With informal transportation networks up and running between Mediterranean countries, trips "did not require much secrecy, if any" (Ben-Yehoyada 2011: 19). This changed, however when the Schengen acquis stipulated stricter control of the exterior borders. By joining the Schengen group in the early 1990s, Italy and Spain committed themselves to aligning their migration, visa and border control policies with the Schengen acquis.[2] Until their borders were waived, both countries introduced major legal reforms.[3]

---

2   On November 27, 1990, Italy signed the Schengen Agreement. Spain and Portugal followed on June 25, 1991 while Greece joined on November 6, 1992. However, border controls between these countries and other Schengen members only got waived when checks had been tightened at the then external border of the Schengen area. For Spain and Portugal, this was March 26, 1995; for Italy October 26, 1997; for Greece March 26, 2000.

3   Spain: The very first law to regulate immigration policies in Spain was passed by the government in July 1985. Presented as an urgent bill, the 'Law about the rights and freedoms of foreigners in Spain' (Ley Orgánica 7/1985 sobre derechos y libertades de los extranjeros en España, known as the Ley de Extranjería [Foreigners' Law]) was hardly debated in Parliament and passed "by virtual unanimity" (Moreno Fuentes 2000: 10). The urgency was declared with reference to joining the Schengen states by January 1986. The new law foresaw restrictive immigration policies and a strong focus on border control. "The new Law also defined the presence in Spanish soil without the necessary authorisation, as an offence punished with expulsion from the territory" (Moreno Fuentes 2000: 10-11). The resolution proposal of April 1991 initiated a series of decisions and directives: regularization of irregular foreign workers (1991, 1996, and 2000), employer sanctions, the introduction of a quota for foreign workers in 1993. In 1991, visa requirements were introduced for Latin American and Moroccan nationals. Due to these restrictions on labor immigration, asylum claims were used to work in Spain, as asylum petitioners still had the right and possibility to work while their claim was reviewed (Cornelius 1994: 351). This, again, led to the 1994 reform of Spain's asylum law. The previous regulation, which was considered generous and left

In anticipatory adjustment, the "Europeanisation" (Moreno Fuentes 2000: 2) of immigration policies shaped Spain's national policies at a point in time when the issue of immigration had not even reached the national agenda (Cornelius 1994; Moreno Fuentes 2000; Kreienbrink 2004). Kreienbrink shows that in the 1980s, Spain's immigration and border policies were hardly defined, and even in the 1990s, Spain's economic focus on the tourist economy thwarted strict mobility regulations (2004: 73-86, 91). For Italy, too, Kitty Calavita (1994: 320) found a "relative absence of public debate on this issue [immigration]," as immigrant black labor formed a substantial part of the Italian economy, and in many places was considered complementary to the local workforce (ibid: 311). During the 1980s, both countries had transformed from countries of emigration to countries of immigration (Bade 2000; Boswell 2005: 2-3). However, the emergence of national immigration policies was fostered by the new task of securing maritime borders as Schengen borders.

Overall, and significantly, the institutional incentive to codetermine EU policy in this emerging policy field, namely border surveillance and control, preceded the experience of migration as an actual problem. Moreno Fuentes accordingly comments on the case of Spain:

"In the absence of a nationally specific stand on immigration the 'Europeanisation' of this area of policies represented not only the participation of Spanish officials in the committees created to coordinate and define a common European immigration policy, but also the somehow thoughtless acceptance of European policy objectives within the legislation implemented at the national level. The result was a very restrictive policy that did not correspond to the early stages of the migratory processes that were affecting Spain." (Moreno Fuentes 2000: 2)

---

it at the state's discretion to grant asylum for humanitarian reasons, was abolished and asylum was restricted to the political refugee of the Geneva Convention (Kreienbrink 2004: 189-235). Italy: In 1990, the Italian government passed the Martelli Law (named after the then justice minister Claudio Martelli), Italy's first immigration legislation, which enacted visa requirements for North African nationals and was communicated as strict and discouraging of immigration. However, commentators also considered it a hidden regularization program (Calavita 1994: 318). The Italian debate was generally more concerned with undocumented migration, rather than with asylum (Turner et al. 2006: 88-92). Southern European countries turned both into countries of immigration and into gatekeepers of the EU – not only in terms of geography but also in terms of policies.

Effectively, Spain and Italy were the last countries in Western Europe to introduce visa requirements for North African nationals and only did so in compliance with the Schengen Acquis: Spain in May 1991 and Italy in 1990. The significance of introducing visa requirement for Northern African nationals to the emerging external EU border must not be underestimated. By introducing these visa requirements, Northern Mediterranean states decided to be European countries and to pronounce Schengen membership while putting less emphasis on their hitherto regional economic ties. However, legalizations in Spain and amnesties in Italy indicate that a clean break was neither possible in terms of enforcement, nor was it politically or economically desirable.

One Means of Transport, Multiple Itineraries

Since the early 1990s, the Schengen-induced increased border control measures have been discussed as contributing factors to the changing patterns of (maritime) migration. In fact, intensified sea patrols and tightly enforced borders seldom dissolve migratory intentions but rather lead to displacement effects (Haas 2006, 2008), a diversion of routes, as well as the emergence of transit migration (Simon 2006; Mehdi Lahlou 2006). Several commentators argued that the new visa requirements together with the enforcement of Schengen borders not only resulted in more queuing for visas, but fueled "a rapidly expanding economy of illegal migration services" (Carling 2007b: 11).[4]

Furthermore, boat migration was diverted to the Canary Islands to the effect that in "2003 and 2004 unauthorized arrivals by boat along the Spanish coasts were split almost equally between the Canary Islands and the Spanish mainland" (Carling 2007b: 14). Moreover, boats increasingly departed to the Canary Islands from West African countries, particularly Mauritania (approx. 800 km) and Senegal (approx. 1,400 km). When in 2006, boat migration to the EU reached its first peak with a total of 72,035 arrivals, the majority of migrants landed on the Canary Islands, which according to Lutterbeck amounted to 33,126 persons (Lutterbeck 2010: 130). The Atlantic route toward the Canary Islands was said, however, to cause an unequally higher migrant mortality. Already in 2009, members

---

4   Alison Mountz and Ronja Kempin describe the mutual interrelation between border enforcement and human smuggling as "geographically relational" (Mountz/Kempin 2014: 86). They even push the argument to the extent of stating that "enforcement measures and human smuggling industries tend to escalate in symbiotic fashion: as one intensifies, so too does the other" (ibid: 85).

of the Red Cross mentioned to me during a personal interview that for every person that arrives, 1.5 have died at sea.

At the same time, the composition of migrant nationalities on board the vessels diversified at the beginning of the new millennium; which among other aspects, also implies that the business spread. This latter effect was more pronounced than any increase in the total number of migrants. In 2003, the Moroccan Ministry of Interior reported that for the first time, the number of sub-Saharan clandestine migrants had outnumbered the number of national clandestine migrants, the difference being 12,400 to 23,851 (quoted in Mghari 2005: 201). In 2008, Hein de Haas noted with regards to EU bound migration from North African countries, that "(r)ather than an increase *per se,* the major change has been that, after 2000, sub-Saharan Africans started to join illegal Mediterranean crossings and have now overtaken North Africans as the largest category of irregular boat migrants" (Haas 2008: 13-14, emphasis original). This trend continued to 2012 (Bruycker/Di Bartolomeo/Fargues 2013: 6). Ten years later, in 2018, sea arrivals' most common countries of origin are Mali, Afghanistan, Irak and Syria.[5] These dynamic aspects need to be remembered when quoting aggregated numbers on maritime migration to Europe.

8.1.2 From Counting Boats to Classifying Migrants as "Arrivals by Sea" to Counting "Illegal Border Crossings"

In the years that followed Spain's newly received Schengen membership, the number of boats intercepted at sea increased more than a hundredfold. While in 1991, four so called *pateras* were reportedly intercepted in Spanish coastal waters, 1,020 were reported in 2002 (Kreienbrink 2004: 210). More boats also meant more immigrants. In that same period, detentions increased from 477 to 16,670 (ibid). However, the increasing numbers of *pateras* and immigrants not only documented the increase of migratory flux but also resulted from increasing ambitions of the Guardia Civil del Mar, which had just been founded in 1991 (Kreienbrink 2004: 210) to detect and seize vessels and passengers. Moreover, this was spurred by a continued increase in border surveillance and more sophisticated technology in the Integrated System of External Vigilance (SIVE, in the

---

5 UNHCR (2018): Desperate Journeys. Refugees and migrants arriving in Europe and at Europe's borders. January-December 2018, at: https://www.unhcr.org/desperate journeys/ (accessed October10, 2019).

Spanish: *Sistema Integrado de Vigilancia Exterior*)[6]. Hence, the numbers collated in table 3 are not only a description of the phenomenon of migration, but also of the activities of border surveillance and control. This demonstrates well the argument that I made above with regard to the epistemological challenge of thinking about (political) borders: political borders are not generated by way of practices of subversion; it is rather that subversion is itself defined by way of bordering and by those classifications that mediate bordering.

With regional migration being part of the informal economy, boat migration turned out to be the most visible part that could be tackled (cf. Genova 2013).

Kreienbrink, who documents one of the earliest reports of data on unauthorized maritime immigration to Spain, captioned his table "seized '*pateras*' and persons apprehended thereof" (Kreienbrink 2004: 210). Here, the new move in border enforcement finds expression: *pateras* are seized and their passengers apprehended. Even though the possibility of boat-migrants with a valid visa is not excluded in this formulation, the discursive link between arriving in *pateras* and being apprehended is revealed. Of course, this link has not been set by Kreienbrink. The author's table merely documents the emerging lens of sorting out EU-bound migration. In a very practical sense of stopping and interdicting the continuation of a directional movement, the seizure of *pateras* has turned into *the* performance of border control. Implementing the Schengen acquis meant stopping *pateras*. In the context of freedom of movement within Schengen, *pateras* became the reference point for problematizing access to the Schengen area.

Theories of globalization and conceptions of postnational political forms trip up on the modern territorial border. Likewise, any national administrative logic of quantifying migration crumbles vis-à-vis data collection on seaborne migration. Acknowledging eventual biases emerging from territorial, that is, administrative references, different authors also include apprehensions in North African countries, such as Morocco or Libya (cf. for instance Fekete 2003).At the same time, classifications are unclear: what to count in order to document border control activities and what kind of migration actually violates the border? Boats, migrants, Moroccans on a tourist visa, persons per boat? The numbers in table 3 document early tentative classifications of Spain's Europeanized border enforcement.

---

6 The effects of the SIVE have been discussed by Carling (2007b) and Kaufmann (2008).

Table 3: Boats to Europe (1991-2004)

Year	vessels intercepted *	persons detained **	ratio (rounded) ***
1991	4	477	112
1992	15	616	41
1993	33	1925	58
1994	34	352	10
1995	130	1800	14
1996	339	1.573	5
1997	399	887	2
1998	557	2.995	5
1999	475	3.569	8
2000	807	15195	19
2001	1060	18517	17
2002	1020	16670	16
2003	942	19.176	20
2004	740	15.675	21
* in Spanish waters, by Spanish border guards ** apprehensions, persons detained off the vessel *** persons detained/vessels intercepted			

Sources: Numbers quoted in Kreienbrink 2004: 201; Lutterbeck 2006: 63; Mehdi Lahlou 2006: 117

Returning to the quantifying representation of the phenomenon, in 2006, Lutterbeck, too, quotes the number of "[i]nterceptions of vessels and undocumented immigrants in Spanish waters," providing the number of detained persons to capture the number unauthorized migrants (Lutterbeck 2006: 63). Carling argues that the "only way of quantifying the unauthorised migration flow is to refer to apprehensions along these borders" counting "the number of interceptions of unauthorised migrants along the Spanish coasts" (Carling 2007b: 20). His methodology is accepted and applied widely.[7] In a sense, both Lutterbeck and Carling construct the border along Spanish enforcement activities. While Lutterbeck quoted both the number of boats and the number of immigrants intercepted *in Spanish waters*, Carling skips the numbers of vessels, but provides the number of interceptions *along the Spanish coast*, thereby quantifying persons which had been picked up at sea and detained on Spanish territory. Successively, reporting the number of boats is replaced by a reference to the location of interception.

Only speculation can be advanced about why Kreienbrink did not mention any territorial restriction to the sample, and why Carling and most of his successors, skip the number of boats. However, I dare to speculate: The lack of a geographical reference in Kreienbrink's account might result from considering this information as superfluous, as it was taken for granted that sea patrolling only occurred in territorial waters, be it due to legal compliance or limited enforcement capacities, or in reflection of the practices of boat migration.[8] The lack of geographical information may also be explained by the focus of discursive attention: it was not the legality and scope of border security that was up for debate, but the fulfillment of Schengen obligations, which were symbolically communicated and performed by the stopping of boats. Despite the legal vagueness of whether border surveillance and control practices amount to enforcement jurisdiction, the data on 'boats' and 'persons detained' are used to sketch the proportion of the issue at stake. At the same time, the issue at stake found localization "at sea," and "on boats."

This hypothesis is further supported by the lack in substantial knowledge which could be generated from the number of boats within the frame of Europe bound maritime migration. The number of unauthorized migrants could not be extrapolated from the number of boats, especially because boats were known to commute. With migrants being forced to swim the rest of the way, boats were reused for transport purposes.

---

7   Michael Jandl (2004) also proposed a methodology to estimate "illegal migration" in Europe; however, his approach is not as widely applied as Carling's methodology.

8   The Spanish Guardia Civil generally operated close to the Spanish coast. This tactic was reportedly deployed in order to avoid that facilitators threw their passengers over board once detected (Kreienbrink (2004: 210). This alludes to quite a different operational philosophy than the one in place post-**SIVE** or during Frontex Joint Operations, when the ideal of intervention 'already at the shores of third countries' is pursued.

In fact, in a strict methodological sense, a trend analysis cannot be derived from the data presented, as it is based on triangulation and thus on different labels and methods of quantification. Often triangulation is aptly used to cross-check data and gain the most plausible numerical information. In this case, the triangulation of data, sources and their utilization also reveals the insecurity concerning the new labels of border enforcement and migrant illegality. Deciphering the classifications used in the collated table 3 reveals how the sorting machine in the Mediterranean was successively programed.

Consequently, the issue at stake – Europeanization of border management and Schengen compliance – was projected onto the migrant vessel, and connected boat migration and the image of "black young men jam-packed in a fishing vessel" to border violation and illegality. This had consequences for the way boats were treated by authorities - in fact, boats seem to be far more than means of transportation, which could be counted to determine the volume of traffic. During her field work in Libya, Sicily, Lampedusa and Malta, legal anthropologist Silja Klepp (2011) came across numerous traces of boats as flexible resources. Klepp remembers the following anecdote from an official at the Lampedusa boat cemetery:

"In 2003 and 2004 there were always repeated requests from Libya and Lampedusa for stolen boats, which were then brought back to Libya by the Italian navy. As soon as they realized that that the boats arrived back on Lampedusa fully laden with migrants, they began working to destroy the boats immediately. Ever since, he [the official]'s been convinced that the Libyan government was hidden behind the organization of maritime migration. In 2005 the delegation of the Libyan army came to Lampedusa to look after their boats. The Libyans had always repeatedly asked for their boats, but he always kept them away from the ship's graveyard because he didn't want to give the boats back." (Klepp 2011: 224-225)

The migrant vessels are as much a resource for strategic businesses as for symbolic politics: in order to prevent Libyan authorities from engaging in the smuggling business, the boat cemetery official – in a preventive manner – keeps the vessels hidden. Meanwhile, the request by the Libyan government for 'its own boats' can duly be interpreted as diplomatic provocation. This corresponds with the idea of a boat cemetery, and with the public destruction and burning of boats which, during the 1990s, had been decreed by the Berlusconi administration several times and appeared to commentators as the "equivalent to destroying an enemy's logistic assets" (Pugh 2004: 57). Finally in 2015, these vessels acquired the status of a strategic military target. In May 2015, the EU's foreign policy chief, Federica Mogherini, asked the United Nations to "authorise military action to destroy boats used to smuggle people from Africa to Europe" (Melvin 2015). A military mission, dubbed EU NAVFOR Med (European Union Naval Force - Mediterranean), has been planned "to intercept and board what are deemed to be 'hostile' vessels, preferably before they have left Libyan waters" (*The Economist* (N.N.) 2015b). Further description of the plans mentioned the confiscation and destruction of boats, possible in harbors or on land "by helicopter gunships or even special forces" (ibid). *The Economist* also reported that NATO offered to help if requested; there is, by contrast, little mentioning of the proceedings with regard to the migrants on board.

The small boats, the *pateras,* function as initial evidence in a process of problematization (Foucault). Moreover, just like the sailing ship disappeared again off the map once the new world was founded (Certeau 2013 [1984]: 121); counting boats disappeared again once the Mediterranean had been transformed into Europe's imagined southern maritime border. Furthermore, attention is not only geared to irregular migration itself, but peculiarly toward this particular mode of travel: by sea. In fact, this is the very attribute which gives name to migrants' quantifications: arrivals by sea. With this label detached from any legal or territorial reference, arriving on board these vessels, refugees and migrants land on EU shores as if they came out of nowhere. The labeling is most non-committal and almost without reference. The only localizing reference made: by sea, dispenses any political vector.

Today, information on the boats or freighters on which migrants travel is no longer provided numerically, but rather in terms of the vessel's condition. The political implications of these conditions – overcrowded, small and unseaworthy – will be dealt with in the next section (8.2). For the moment, it is important to emphasize that despite the iterated description of the kind of migration – "they arrive by boat" – migration dynamics have changed significantly throughout the past 30 years.

The Frontex agency has increasingly developed its Risk Analysis Unit (RAU), which is tasked with producing reports on the situation along the external borders. Since 2010, Frontex publishes Annual Risk Analysis (ARA). Frontex provides quickly accessible and neatly visualized data on its website, to the effect that there is hardly any news on migration to Europe which is not flanked by data of the agency or its visualizations. Frontex counts the number of illegal border crossings and distinguishes them by routes.⁹. While the Schengen regulations brought a new logic of classification to the Mediterranean space, Frontex analyses have formalized the knowledge on Europe-bound migration through the lens of its illegalization. Likewise, Frontex's classification of distinguishing between different routes supports Bös's hypothesis that rather than migrants' characteristics, it is political processes which determine how we count.

8.1.3 Deaths at Sea: Quantifying the Migrants' Death Toll

This also holds true for the counting of migrant fatalities in the Mediterranean. As unauthorized migration occurs clandestinely, fatalities *en route* are hardly quantifiable. Both boats and bodies might be involved in unsighted accidents. In 2009 UNHCR's answer to a frequently asked question states that the "exact death toll will probably never be known as some of the flimsy vessels used by boat-people just disappear without trace."[10]

In 2019, however, the UNHCR provides comprehensive data on what is now called "the Mediterranean Situation," including the number of land arrivals, sea arrivals, and dead and missing, as well as data on the most common nationalities of Mediterranean sea and land arrivals.[11] This is not self-evident, but the result of increased public and political pressure with regard to the availability of data on the situation of refugees and migrations crossing the Mediterranean following (a) the 2013 Lampedusa incident referred to in the introduction, (b) the increase in Mediterranean crossings during the refugee crisis following the war in Syria in 2014 and 2015, and (c) the *Mare Nostrum* operation, which triggered a discussion on the legality and effectiveness of border enforcement and rescue operations, thereby generating a demand for data to prove or refute the various claims. In February 2017, when I submitted the manuscript of this book as a PhD thesis, the only comprehensive data available on migratory movements across the Mediterranean was provided by the Frontex: the agency identified migration routes, provided numbers and maps and explained where the migratory pressure was the

---

9 Cp. Frontex, Website: Migratory Routes Map, at: http://frontex.europa.eu/trends-and-routes/migratory-routes-map/ (accessed October 19, 2019).

10 UNHCR (2009): Irregular Migration by Sea: Frequently Asked Questions, May 28, 2009, at: https://www.unhcr.org/subsites/euasylum/4a1e48f66/irregular-migration-sea-frequently-asked-questions.html (accessed 14.10.2019).

11 The information is constantly updated and available at: https://data2.unhcr.org/en/situations/mediterranean.

strongest, and which route was currently used the most. The number of dead and missing was not provided. This section describes the state of official non-knowledge at that time.

In practical terms of producing data, estimates of the number of deaths at sea have been based on different sources: "on survivors' accounts of the number of passengers" (Carling 2007a: 330), on distress calls to UNHCR or coastal authorities, on projections based on bodies found ashore, or lately, also on estimates of border guards who have been deployed during Frontex Joint operations (cf. Meyer 2015).[12] In essence, "[f]atalities are counted as the sum of bodies discovered and persons registered as missing" (Carling 2007a: 331). In terms of generation and processing of data, the number of persons registered as missing is frequently added to the number of fatalities in order to compensate for those deaths which remain unsighted and unregistered. Generally, numbers of maritime migrant fatalities can be regarded minimum estimates.

Apart from the practical problem of quantifying incidents which occur out of sight, quantifications often carry an administrative bias, as only bodies found on European shores are included. Liz Fekete commented in 2003 that "the 'nautical graveyards' are increasingly in African territorial waters ensuring that the problem is hidden even further from the European gaze" (Fekete 2003: 3). Similarly, Henk van Houtum criticized that the deaths, which is to say the names of individuals and causes of death, are "made absent, unrepresented, and invisible" (van Houtum 2010: 968). Out of sight is hence not only out of mind, but also out of official statistics, and thus political concern.

The fact that the numbers of deaths which occur during maritime migration to Europe are not officially counted had been criticized by activists, researchers and the European Parliament (EP). The most explicit critique has been formulated in a 2007 report titled "The human costs of border control," by Thomas Spijker-

---

12   When the German government provided data on the number of victims along the European external borders for the first time in 2012, it was emphasized that this data was not to be considered part of official statistics. The numbers would be based on information provided by federal police officers who had been deployed to support the work of Frontex. According to this information, 180 refugees had died during an attempt to enter the EU in an unauthorized manner. It was also highlighted that 3,300 persons had been rescued during Frontex operations during the same time period (Meyer 2015).

boer, written on request of the EP. His study assesses "the relationship between irregular immigration, increased border control, and the number of casualties at Europe's maritime borders" (Spijkerboer 2007: 127). While different scientists have identified border control as contributing merely indirectly to the number of fatalities,[13] Spijkerboer comes to conclude that the rising number of migrant fatalities is "a result of increased border control" (ibid). Duly acknowledging that there is no consistent evidence base from which to derive such claims, Spijkerboer rather points to the paradox of the situation, namely that border control practices are thought of as both a counter measure and a cause of migrants' death. He argues that a reliable data base would not only allow for validity checks against political claims, but would also allow open discussions on the legality of (supranational) border control.

"Getting more and more precise data would enable us to discuss the validity of the proposition often made by European governments, holding that border deaths can be combated by combating irregular migration. As matters stand now, it seems more likely that the reverse is true: border deaths increase as a consequence of intensified border control. This effect of increased border control has bearings on its legality which have yet to be assessed." (Spijkerboer 2007: 139)

Despite the declared political relevance of data on this topic to border policy in Europe, the paucity of any official count of migrants' deaths had *not* been overcome in 2015. In 2014 Spijkerboer and Last wrote a report for the IOM; they noted that "[a]gencies that deal directly with migrants attempting to cross the southern EU border without authorization, such as the national coast guards and Frontex, do not include data on deaths in their annual reports or statistics" (Last/Spijkerboer 2014: 96). Considering the fact that Frontex hosts an entire Risk Analysis Unit, which collects and processes various border related data from member states and international agencies such as EUROPOL and European Maritime Safety Agency (EMSA), this official non-knowledge is hardly intelligible. The explanation might be found in the political weight of the numbers. To officially register cases means to officially accept liability. Governments would

---

13 Carling approaches this question with a quantitative research design and concludes that "it is difficult to claim that the control measures are directly responsible for the increasing number of fatalities. Apparently, the growth in the number of deaths results from an increased number of migration attempts, combined with a constant or slightly falling risk of dying on the way" (Carling 2007a: 340).

have to relate to those numbers. Even though causal responsibility of EU border enforcement practices with regard to fatalities cannot be verified, this does not relinquish EU governments from doing something about the death toll.

"The obligation of a State to take appropriate steps to safeguard lives is not conditioned on a causal relationship between the State's actions and someone's death. Rather, the obligation is triggered by the State's *knowledge* that a particular life is at risk and that same State's *ability* to do something about it." (Spijkerboer 2007: 138, emphasis added)

The relation between *knowledge* on a particular risky pattern and the *ability* to mitigate the risk is also illustrated in the example of road fatalities. In that case, the prevention of movement by repression is reported to be successful, that is, an increase in control pressure is claimed to reduce the number of road fatalities. This is the impetus of European states' argument that fighting migration means fighting related deaths: an intensification of border control would thus reduce the migrants' death toll. A government is not responsible if someone died while crossing the road, yet, if the street had been known to be busy, a traffic light or zebra crossing could have been installed to prevent such a death. Applied to border control, the question is whether increased surveillance increases the risk of trips going wrong or in the bolstering of their safety. Again, it is the decision between hunter and friend which suggests an answer in this case.

Kiza considers the increase in the number of fatalities a possible Achilles' heel "of the EU strategy of a criminalization and securitization of migration" (Kiza 2008: 213), as the escalation, more than the actual number, would impeach the effectiveness and legality of border policies in the Mediterranean.

The available data on refugees and migrants who died on their way to Europe has been collected by activists or NGOs in an attempt to document and denounce states' border control practices. NGOs document and count the number of deaths they attribute to EU border policies and practices. Even though these have turned into "the primary sources of data on border related deaths in the Mediterranean" (Last/Spijkerboer 2014: 96), their statistics are far from functioning as a monitoring mechanism. Recent accounts of the death toll by the Migration Policy Center (Bruycker/Di Bartolomeo/Fargues 2013) and IOM (Brian/Laczko 2014b) thus criticize the fact that governments do not monitor the impact of their practices themselves.

The international non-governmental organization UNITED for Intercultural Action (UNITED) has started listing the deaths of refugees and migrants, which it considers related to European states' immigration and border control policies and practices.[14] The UNITED list of deaths compiles the dates migrants were found, the number of fatalities, the causes of death, countries of origin and the sources which reported on the incident. UNITED thereby provides a starting point for long-term research on the matter.[15] The list not only includes deaths that occurred at the border but also those that can be attributed to the migratory journey: death in the Sahara or in transit countries, death or suicide in detention centers, death as a stowaway, as victims of racist attacks in Europe, or homeless. While the list functions as a reminder and as a monitoring instrument, these cases are included to illustrate the range of effects attributed to EU border policies, even if the fatality did not occur at or along the geographic border. Last and Spijkerboer have filtered the UNITED list of deaths for those cases which have directly occurred "during the attempt to cross a southern EU external border" (Last/Spijkerboer 2014: 92). They counted 14,600 out of the 17,306 cases UNITED listed between 1993 and November 2012.

The second alternative source is the blog of "Fortress Europe," initiated by Gabriel del Grande, an Italian journalist and writer. Between 1988 until October 2014, the blog listed 21,439 deaths.[16] Working with this data, the Migration Policy Center (MPC) has produced two reports, narrowing down the numbers to those cases that relate to maritime crossings (Bruycker/Di Bartolomeo/Fargues 2013; Fargues/Bonfanti 2014). Their methodology resulted in counting "15,016 dead and missing persons [...] from January 1998 till September 30, 2014" (Fargues/Bonfanti 2014: 5).[17] Already in 2008, Ernesto Kiza argues that the mass

---

14 On June 20, 2015, the International Refugee Day, UNITED published an updated list of deaths, and states that between 1993 and 2015 "at least 22,000 refugee deaths can be attributed to the 'Fatal Policies of Fortress Europe,'" at: http://unitedagainstrefugeedeaths.eu/about-the-campaign/about-the-united-list-of-deaths/ (accessed August 25, 2015).

15 The documentation of UNITED has been used by Carling (2007a) and Kiza (2008), who examined the relation between border enforcement and migrant fatalities.

16 Gabriel del Grande, Blog "Fortress Europe" at: http://fortresseurope.blogspot.de/ (accessed February 1, 2017). In October 2019, the Italian site of the blog, which provides translations to 20 languages, lists reports to February 2016.

17 Comparing the list on the Fortress Europe blog to the UNITED list of death, Last and Spijkerboer found a more extensive coverage of the Egyptian (Sinai)-Israeli border and the Sahara in the Fortress Europe blog and a more comprehensive coverage of Greece and Spain in the UNITED list of death (Last/Spijkerboer 2014: 92), which stresses again that quantifying the death toll always remains partial.

victimization in the Mediterranean shows an "ever clearer escalation dynamics" (Kiza 2008: 213). This trend has continued to aggravate until today. In 2013 Bruycker and colleagues found that

"the maritime route to Europe is amongst the most dangerous in the world. Moreover, the last section [the boat passage, S.E.], at the gate of the EU, is the most lethal, and mortality during the journey has increased considerably in the last decade (Bruycker/Di Bartolomeo/Fargues 2013: 4).

Likewise, IOM concludes that in 2014, the Mediterranean has been "the deadliest sea in the world for migrants" (Brian/Laczko 2014a: 20), with deaths related to the crossing making for 75 per cent of all migrants' death in that year.

8.1.4 What Contributes to the Trip Being Increasingly Lethal?

Available data suggests that the number of fatalities rises and falls in roughly the same way as the number of arrivals by sea. This rather general description updates Carling's 2007 finding to June 2015.

Yet, what does the relation between arrivals and fatalities tell us? Does it suggest a mere proportional relationship in the sense that the number of fatalities depends on the number of persons who migrate by sea? Is the risk of dying at sea normally distributed? In order to assess this question, we can first look at whether the risk of dying at sea has changed over time – that is, whether certain periods of time were more lethal than others despite the general trend. Carling (2007a: 331-336) proposes calculating a migrant mortality rate (MMR), which shows the relation between dead and missing and departures. Following Carling, departures are estimated as the number of dead and missing plus the number of arrivals (ibid: 332).

There are several restrictions with regard to the reliability of the data and thus also problems with regard to the validity of an MMR. Both the number of arrivals as well as the number of dead and missing persons might be underrecorded. This could also vary in degree at different points in time. For instance, during the 1990s, undocumented migration to Spain was estimated to be almost 50 per cent of the general migratory influx (Carling 2007a). However, and in strong contrast, in 2011, Frontex officials estimated that 98 per cent were detected before arriving at European shores. Consequently, only two per cent of arrivals were undocumented.[18] As discussed above, the number of dead and missing can only be taken as a minimum estimate. Both factors, however, change the MMR. If detections work well and most arrivals are counted, but the number of deaths at sea is not reported accurately, the statistical risk of dying at sea decreases. Likewise, if the quality of data on deaths at sea remains the same, while arrivals succeed undetected, the calculated risk is higher than empirical observations lead us to believe. In any case, the question of what contributes to the trip being increasingly lethal cannot be found using the MMR.

An evaluation of the contributing factors suffers from both the classical out-of-sight-out-of-mind problem related to issues at sea, and the secrecy of border enforcement's operational information. Overall, six different explanations have been proposed as contributing factors to the increasing victimization of migrants in the Mediterranean: first, the condition of the vessels; second, the the smuggling business; third, EU border enforcement measures and policies; fourth, the involvement of authorities; fifth, self-endangerment, and sixth, diffusion of responsibility.

However, when considered more closely, these explanations interfere with each other in an odd way and reveal the possible political interpretations which are implicitly there. The vessel, for instance, has been identified as a serious risk both in policy research, such as by UNODC, and in academic research as well as in investigative journalism. The causes of fatal accidents have been attributed to the poor state of many vessels, or to the fact that these kinds of small fishing boats or inflatable dinghies are not made for sea voyages. Ernesto Kiza, for instance, researched the victimization of migrants *en route* for the case of the southern EU borders between 1999 and 2004. Kiza demonstrates that "the vehicle most used in the context of undocumented migration from South to North is [...] simultaneously the most problematic and dangerous" (Kiza 2008: 237). Based on data from UNITED, Kiza's study documents an increase in the use of boats for clandestine seaborne migration (ibid: 213-323, 241). In comparison to other means of transport (he further accounts the categories walking, swimming, container, lorry, and others), between 80 and 96 per cent of cases in the sample period used boats (ibid: 238). According to Kiza, three problems are related to the utilization of boats in this context. First, the carrying capacity of the vessel is usually exceeded; second, the poor condition of the vessel itself (leakages, engine failure); and third, a lack of qualified operators on board the vessels (ibid:

---

18 Head of Sea Border Sector at Frontex and colleague, personal interview (May 27, 2011).

239). These deficiencies are, however, either attributed to economic reasoning, that is, commercialized migration facilitation, or to border enforcement measures. Italy provides an instructive example in the latter case. There, "ultra-modern speedboats (zodiacs) of the *'scafisti'* [smugglers]" have been replaced by hardly seaworthy fishing vessels (ibid: 337-338). Likewise, in Spain, it could be observed that the deployment of seaworthy *pateras* which were hitherto used for regional fishing and had been appropriated for migration purposes, have been replaced by *pateras* which were 'adjusted' by deteriorating the vessels state to the business of transporting migrants clandestinely (ibid: 338). It has been suggested that the condition of the vessel was adjusted to and provoked by border enforcement measures and the narrow admission requirement of 'being almost in distress.' Moreover, tight border controls increased the number of deaths as the maritime journeys were forced to take more dangerous detours. In addition, tougher border controls increased the costs of being transported. Different forms of self-endangerment have been advanced with regard to the increasing death toll in the Mediterranean. Different officials mentioned to me that migrants would deliberately provoke a distress situation in order to force border guards to take them on board. Other forms of self-endangerment include panic aboard the vessels, or throwing navigational equipment aboard when being spotted by a helicopter or aircraft. Technical problems to send a rescue call were also mentioned.

Yet again, this contradicts the observations of journalist Wolfgang Bauer during his attempt to across the Mediterranean in a boat among Syrian refugees. According to Bauer, the transportation business has developed into an economically competitive market, and bad service might result in passengers denouncing smugglers or middlemen to authorities. Furthermore, with the money for the trip being left with middlemen, trips are often only paid after the successful completion of the journey. Smugglers thus have an interest in organizing a safe trip. For every person making the journey attracts five new clients.[19]

Ultimately, the diffusion and, at times, avoidance of responsibility for rescue at sea, which Silja Klepp already observed in 2007 in her ethnography on the maritime boundary in the Mediterranean, remains difficult to pinpoint. At the same time, public discourse has become used to blaming fatalities to the unseaworthiness of boats, the greed or cruelty of smugglers, and an argument that has been foregrounded since 2015: the pull-factor of rescue measures. Overall, access to the operational field has proven difficult for researchers. This is precisely why it

---

19 Journalist Bauer, telephone interview (June 2014).

is so difficult to verify or denounce the claim that better surveillance and a better exchange of information would contribute to saving lives at sea. If there is hardly any reliable, official data, and if, at the same time, democratic and public control is limited by reference to the operational nature of border enforcement, this means that the relation between border policies and enforcement measures and the loss of lives at sea cannot be officially assessed. However, the fact that Frontex stated that 98 per cent of boats were detected raises questions of why an increasing number of people die while at the same time more boats are being spotted. Finally, with regard to the justification of EUROSUR, it is remarkable that among all the reasons discussed in media and academia, the alleged lack of surveillance and of interagency cooperation and good communication has not been mentioned as a factor contributing to the increasing death toll.

8.1.5 The Passage: ... at Sea ... on Board, and Under Cover of Darkness

In the context of flight and migration by sea, the small boat not only stands for a means of transport, but also for the *condition of being transported*. Testimonies of this "modern Odyssey"[20] are, however, rare. For example, even though legal anthropologist Silja Klepp conversed with different migrants, she only cites two testimonies of the actual experience of being on board a migrant vessel, and those are rather evasive. A woman with whom she met several times in Hal Far on Malta assures "she had been asleep for the entire time of the journey of four night and four days" (Klepp 2011: 219). Another migrant Klepp spoke with didn't want to talk too long about the sea journey and gave a staccato memory of the passage:

"We spent three days and three nights on the water. For two days and nights we met no one at sea, but then a Tunisian fishing boat supplied us with a few bottles of water and bread. During all of the crossing we prayed to Allah. Especially the darkness of the night made us afraid. Then we saw other fishing boats. We thought we were on the way to Italy, and drove on in the same direction. We had a compass with us. But then we found ourselves in the port of La Valletta, and the police and an ambulance were waiting for us." (quoted in Klepp 2011: 219)

---

20 Journalist Bauer, telephone interview (June 2014).

The anthropologist reflects that it became successively clear to her, "that to all who cross the Mediterranean this way, it means a traumatic experience of which no one easily speaks" (Klepp 2011: 219). By contrast, Ruben Andersson's research in Senegal revealed that testimony is not only an individual's story, but also a sellable thing, a product of specific expectations, namely "stories of deaths and suffering at sea" (Andersson 2010: 40). Not to mention these are also products in increasing demand, "[j]ournalists, police, academics, aid workers and research students [...] have combed the terrain for interviews with migrants and repatriates" (ibid). There is enough reason and opportunity to only tell one's story for money: "For a small sum, I'll give you three or four guys," was the 'special offer' made to the anthropologist, "10,000 cfa (15€) is enough, since you are a research student" (ibid). Journalists had reportedly paid tenfold.

Trauma-related speechlessness on the one hand, commodified and exoticized suffering on the other – and in-between: the passage, without witness.

The passage seems to be a *dark field* in every sense of the word. In fact, darkness is as much a prerequisite to a successful, that is, undetected embarkation, as it is the disquieting condition of several hours of the journey. While embarkation can only be unreeled under cover of darkness, darkness aboard a vessel merges up and down, vanishes orientation, and renders the horizon invisible. Under cover of darkness equally means to be at its mercy. The sea carries this ambivalence between functional necessity and essential threat, too. The water covers the tracks of routes, but also causes deaths at sea to vanish. It carries the boat, but might as well swallow the vehicle along with its passengers.[21] Recon-

---

21   This sensation is powerfully worked out in Nam Le's short story "The Boat," Nam Le describes the atmosphere of darkness at sea as a "black syrup" (Le 2008: 233) and a "viscid space without reference or light or sound" (Le 2008: 233) and follows the experiences of a girl, called Mai on board a foundering vessel in the South China Sea. I consider it necessary to provide an impression of the probable condition on board a refugee-vessel, and this condition and even the imagination of these conditions blend into the political handling of the phenomenon. For it is a lived experience and not merely an attested trauma. In order to evoke a possible atmosphere, I shall 'import' fiction: "Finally the storm arrived in force. The remaining light drained out of the hold. Wind screamed through the cracks. She felt the panicked limbs, people clawing for direction, sudden slaps of ice-cold water, the banging and shapeless shouts from the deck above. The whole world reeled. Everywhere the stink of vomit. Her stomach forced up, squashed through her throat. So this was what it was like, she thought, the

sidering Habib Buhari's statement against this background, it becomes apparent that the only emotion mentioned refers to the darkness of the night. Water and bread, prayer and compass are tools for the passage. There is no mention of hunger or thirst, uncertainty, panic or hope. The profound experience of being existentially at mercy of the dark sea underpins his halting account of the passage. In reports to the European spectator, these sensations are translated into soundbites: "When I was on board the vessel, I thought I was dead," stated a migrant in a documentary of 'their journey' on German television – and at this point I would not need a reference as it is a ubiquitous and random quote. The passage which "depending on the places of embarkation and destination [...] can last anywhere between 2 hours and 30 days" (UNODC 2011: 30) remains hidden from view.

ZEIT-journalist Wolfgang Bauer was the first journalist to actually cover the seaborne passage. He provided insights into the organization of crossings from Egypt. Together with the photographer Stanislav Krupar, Bauer clandestinely joined a group of Syrian refugees trying to get from Egypt to Italy by boat across the sea (Bauer 2014). The documentary starts with an interesting decision: based on rumors about the different conditions of vessels deployed for the trip, the journalists decided not to start from Libya or Tunisia, but from Egypt. From Libya or Tunisia "the distance to Italy is shorter, but the boats are extremely dilapidated. The Egyptian smugglers have to travel a larger distance, but therefore deploy better ships" (ibid: 14). On first account, the crossing seemed to be the

> moment before death. She closed her eyes, swallowed compulsively; tried to close out the crawling blackness, the howl of the wind. She tried to recall her father's stories – storms at sea, waves ten, fifteen, meters high! – but they rang shallow against what she'd just seen: those dense roaring slabs of water, sky churning overhead like a puddle being mucked with a stick. She was crammed in by a boatload of human bodies, thinking of her father and becoming overwhelmed, slowly, with loneliness. As much loneliness as fear. Concentrate, she told herself, And she did – forcing herself to concentrate, if not – if she was unable to – on the thought of her family, then on the contact of flesh pressed against her on every side, the human warmth, felling every square inch of skin against her body and through it the shared consciousness of – what? Death? Fear? Surrender? She stayed in that human cocoon, heaving and rolling, concentrating, until it was over" (Le 2008: 231-232). The blanket atmosphere of the elements, of water and wind, and of an omnivorous darkness, the narrowness, the smell, the bodily surrender, these descriptions cut through the soundbites sought after by media coverage.

most disturbing part of the journey. In his report, Bauer quickly relativizes this concern: "We thought that the sea is the greatest danger on our journey. Yet the greatest danger lurked: on land" (ibid). The journalist then provided a fascinating insight into the business of commercialized migration facilitation and its different legs: different means of transport, different hideouts, different profiteers, kidnapping, protection racket and the permanent uncertainty about when the vessel will be ready.

The refugees are in an awkward manner both clients and commodities on which 'local migration lords' base their businesses. The crossing itself, however, did not succeed. Their boat was detected in Egyptian territorial waters, all passengers were detained and the journalists had to reveal their identity and were deported to Turkey.

In a telephone conversion, Bauer described the moment his group was able to "change the medium from land, with all its diffuse uncertainties, to the sea into a boat" as a "great moment." Most of the fellow passengers had a blissful smile on their face when finally being on board. At last, the journey was no longer a pretense of concealment or "a game of hide-and-seek." All the diffuse feelings, the uncertainty, was washed-up since "the boat is very concrete." This was particularly so, since while waiting and hiding, being in vulnerable diffuse fear, it had always been unclear whether there will be a boat at all, that is, whether the final leap will be possible and dared at last. "So in the beginning," states Bauer,

"there is less fear. When you're first on the boat, you have first and foremost a feeling of relief. Being on the boat is like being on the rail, an apparent automatism, no more hiding. It's a kind of congratulatory moment. That changes, of course, depending on the progress of this modern Odyssey."[22]

Yet again, the European spectators' knowledge about the precise nature of this course remains dark. Whatever occurs during passage, when turning up on Europe's public horizon, it is in the form of an overcrowded boat. Individual testimonies, the passengers themselves remain mute and visually aggregated to a boatload of people, to the visual image of the cramped and unseaworthy small boat. All that which is not known is compensated by the taken-for-granted, explanatory image of the migrant vessel, to which I will now turn.

---

22 Journalist Bauer, telephone interview (June 2014).

8.2 "WHEN YOU SEE THE BOAT, THE BOAT TELLS THE STORY"

The statement heading this section was given toward the end of an interview conversion with two Frontex officials from the Sea Borders Sector in the agency's headquarter in Warsaw. The scheduled time for the interview ran out, and the PR officer entered the room as to guide me to the next interview she had scheduled for me. "Do you see your job adequately represented in the media coverage," was the final question my interview-guideline prompted; and despite the shortage of time, it provoked a twenty minute answer. The two Frontex officials answered in an engaged manner, stating that the mandate of Frontex was poorly understood. They felt that the media coverage was wrongly focused. Reports would focus on humanitarian issues while it was criminal networks that border management was dealing with. Underlining the fact that migrants were victims and that the facilitators were the targets of border control and surveillance activities, the officers provided printouts of photographs of drugs detected on board a small vessel and of crowded boats. They mentioned different stories of migrants who, during debriefing, described their situations as vulnerable. According to the Frontex officials, the majority of migrants have no idea about what they got themselves into. Thus, they would end up in a situation at mercy of facilitators, who, in a low risk/high profit business, took advantage of migrants' aspirations. One of the officers stated that the amount of money which was generated through these illegal networks was shocking to him, and that considering Frontex's limited budget and capacities, he always felt one step behind.[23] While the officers of the Sea Border Sector presented their images of the issue at stake as corrective to one-sided media coverage, the PR officer joined in providing demonstrative evidence, stating that migrants were taken in by facilitators. Referring to the photographic material on Frontex's website, she concluded:

"If you look at the photos, some of which are on our website, you can see the boats that people come on. [...] I mean this is, when you see the boat, the boat tells the story. And sometimes the boats are supposed to have hundreds of people. I mean, it's self-explanatory."[24]

---

23 Head of Sea Border Sector at Frontex and colleague, personal interview (May 27, 2011).

24 Press officer at Frontex, conversation aside from the interview with the officials from the Sea Border Sector at Frontex (May 27, 2011).

According to the Frontex officials, the boats clearly indicate the carelessness of the facilitators, the profitability of the smuggling business, as well as migrants' cluelessness. In a similarly obvious way, the boat represents the misery of the migrants on board. "The boat tells the story." Yet, what story is this exactly? And how does it become involved in politics?

In the EU media, the condition of the migrants' vessel as unseaworthy, small, overcrowded, wooden or rusty is referred to as an almost explanatory variable. In fact, the standard reference to the condition of the boat is not infrequently the explanatory punchline to any news about seaborne migration. Maegan Hendow, for instance, writes that the passage turns "a dangerous trek for the old and over-capacity boats used for the journey" (2013: 193). In her article on "Tunisian Migrant Journeys," she underlines the lack in safety of the maritime trip to which the condition of the vessels – "overcrowded and often dilapidated" (ibid) – contributes to a large extent. The amount of agency attributed to the vessel is noteworthy. It is the vessel whose capacity is exceeded, and to whom the trip is dangerous. At the same time, the safety of many trips is, in fact, compromised by the condition of the vessel and the number of people on board. Yet, this image not only describes a condition, it is explanation and rubric.

Apart from the factual deficiencies of migratory vessels – which I am explicitly not denying – images of crowded and unseaworthy vessels have become an archetypal image, an icon, almost used as taken-for granted explanation rather than individual testimony. Pictures and photographs are used as interchangeable images. This section deciphers within the taken-for-granted suggestion quoted from the Frontex officials. It takes apart the obvious idea about the scrupulous smuggler, the unseaworthy and crowded boats, and the migrant at mercy – at mercy of the smuggler, the boat and the sea. In order to do so, I will take issue with its three recurring attributes – overcrowded, small and unseaworthy – and ask for their problematization and appropriation in politics. Concomitantly, the following explorations decipher the "vehicle-body entanglements" (Walters 2011: 6), which the strangely undividable hybrids of the refugee boat and the boat-people represent: A crowd of people bound to, put into, dependent on and visually integrated with their means of transport. Analyzing this depiction of transport, the image of the crammed, unseaworthy, and small vessel, can reveal how the politics of pity and risk (Aradau 2004) underpin the emergence of an EU border mandate.

8.2.1 Overcrowded – "The Boat is Full"

If something is full, matters are beyond enough; a limit is met, almost exceeded. Crammed vessels indicate the scarcity of space, to the extent that more (for the case of vessels additional passengers or cargo) means shipwreck and an end to all. The almost over-capacity vessel is both a visual and verbal metaphor. Along with the expression "Das Boot ist voll" ("The boat is full") comes an impetus of scarcity of space, resources and capacities, which has prominently, yet controversially characterized the asylum debate in Switzerland since the Second World War and reappears then and again in the German public debate on migration and asylum policies. Even though this allusion appears askew and inadequate vis-à-vis jam-packed migrant vessels in the Mediterranean, a careful consideration reveals overlaps and their absurdities.

What turned into a metaphor of political rhetoric, *Das Boot ist voll*, is the title of a book by the Swiss journalist and writer Alfred Häsler (2008 [1967]) in which he critically engaged with Swiss refugee policy during the Second World War.[25] In Switzerland, the reception of particularly Jewish refugees was a controversial issue during war-time, with the metaphor of the lifeboat igniting public controversies. Eduard von Steiger, a member of Swiss government, introduced the expression during a talk in Zürich, where he metaphorically compared Switzerland to a lifeboat:

"Who has to commandeer a strong, already occupied lifeboat with limited capacity and limited inventory while a thousand victims of a shipwreck scream for rescue, it seems hard to measure when he can't take them all." (quoted in Häsler 2008 [1967]: 170)

The emphasis Steiger stressed was that of an ethically bitter, but necessary decision; as the lifeboat has limited capacities, reception must be limited too.[26]

Even though the metaphor was controversially discussed in Swiss parliament, it hit the mark of the Swiss self-image as caring, humanitarian, yet reasonable and neutral (Häsler 2008 [1967]: 160-185).[27] After the war, the emphasis of

---

25 The English edition appeared in 1969 titled "The lifeboat is full".
26 An approximate 20,000 political refugees, most of them Jews, had been refused entry into Switzerland or had been taken back beyond the border, another 14,500 entry permits had been refused. At the same time protection was granted to an approximate 60,000 civilians (de Weck 2008 in Häsler 2008 [1967]: XVIII-XVIII).
27 Cf. Kreis (2006) for a discussion.

the lifeboat metaphor was shifted toward the humanitarian aspect. "Switzerland imagined and presented itself as a humanitarian haven that had given protection to those who had needed it" (Falk 2010: 85). This impetus was particularly conveyed by a poster made by the Swiss painter Victor Surbek.[28] The 128x271 cm poster presents Switzerland as an open lifeboat, the Swiss flag is set on the right side of the vessel behind four strong, rowing, helmeted Swiss soldiers.

The sea is depicted as rough and dark. On the left side, three rescued persons, two adults and one child, sit wrapped in blankets. In the middle of the vessel, another rescued, bare-chested person is lying on the lap of someone else, mimetically representing the Pietà (the Christian allegory of pity). Even though there is not much room left in the lifeboat, a strong man stretches out his hand to someone drowning. The poster "was used for an exhibit that was displayed in several Swiss cities just after the war. The aim of the poster was to collect money for the war-damaged countries of Europe" (ibid). The self-portrayal was condensed in the verbal and visual metaphor of the lifeboat, and this allowed for both the performance of a humanitarian image and the justification of its limits. The lifeboat is the materialized necessity to triage the needy.

In his 1967 book, Häsler took issue with the Swiss self-portrayal of a humanitarian neighbor to Nazi Germany and criticized the self-righteous justification of legitimate rejection. Against the background of the Indochina refugee crisis in 1979, Häsler challenged Swiss asylum policies again. He published an article in *Die Weltwoche* entitled "Unser Boot ist nicht voll" (Engl.: *Our boat is not full*), in which he urged for the Swiss government to accept more refugees (Kreis 2006: 342). The Swiss self-portrayal as lifeboat with limited capacities was rendered absurd, in view of these images of crammed refugee boats in the middle of the sea. When faced with these boats, the legitimacy to worry about one's own vessel, which rather resembled a container ship than a lifeboat, was rendered problematic. The question of whose capacities are actually exhausted has been picked up by several caricatures since then. Yet, in addition to the impetus of comparison, which had been fostered by these cartoons and images, the new agency of the refugees, who themselves attempt to save their lives by taking boats, became apparent. As refugees and migrants themselves took boats to save their lives, the depiction of the lifeboat was fundamentally jarred. Even though the image of the (nearly) over-capacity lifeboat was challenged, the metaphor remained an established part of the Swiss asylum debate (Kreis 2006).

---

28 Francesca Falk (2010, 2011) has analyzed Surbek's poster convincingly; and I follow her analysis here. Surbek's poster is reproduced in her publications.

In the early 1990s, the metaphor was also used in Germany. Initially, it was only deployed in the right-wing political discourse, such as on the election poster of the National Democratic Party of Germany (NPD). However, in August and September 1991, leading German newspapers such as *Der Spiegel* and *Frankfurter Allgemeine Zeitung* introduced the metaphor into mainstream discourse (Pagenstecher 2008a).

Yet again, even though the metaphor prevailed, the image of the refugee related to it changed fundamentally. This was triggered and reflected by the Benetton Poster by Oliviero Toscani which recalled the 1991 Vlora incident. Even though the metaphor of the overcapacity boat prevailed, the visual image fundamentally confounded its very own metaphor, giving it just another spin.

Catachresis I: Masses on Vessels – The 1991 Vlora Incident

When the cargo ship Vlora landed in the Albanian port of Durrës to unload sugar from Cuba on August 7, 1991, approximately 10,000 Albanians took over the ship and forced the captain, Halim Milaqi, to take them to Italy. It was reported that tens thousands of Albanians were waiting at the port of Durrës "in the hope of going on board ships that would take them to Italy"[29]. "My father called me," an Albanian pizza baker is later quoted in *Der Spiegel*, "he told me that 50,000 people besieged the port of Durres" (N.N. 1991: 122). The next day, the Vlora approached the coast of Puglia and forced its way into the port of Bari with an estimated 10,000 Albanian nationals on board.[30] After being allowed to disembark for humanitarian reasons, the passengers were led to La Vittoria Sports Stadium and detained there. When the Italian authorities organized immediate repatriations, clashes broke out between the Italian police and the Vlora passengers. While being detained, the Albanians used iron bars and pieces of the stadium's building material to fight the police. Water and food supplies were dropped into the sports arena from a helicopter. The situation was dramatic, *Der Spiegel* reported "a Dantesque inferno" (ibid). The masses of Durrës who, rather than waiting for a Swiss life boat, hijacked a random cargo freighter to make their way, were finally repatriated by an "armada of ferries, troopships and aircrafts" (ibid). The harsh and prompt deportation of the majority of the Vlora's passengers by

---

29 Parliamentary Assembly of the Council of Europe (PACE) Report on the Exodus of Albanian Nationals (1992: para. 23). The PACE Report is only available in excerpts at: http://migrantsatsea.org/tag/vlora/ (accessed February 1, 2017).
30 Ibid, para. 25.

the Italian government was interpreted as a signal to the Schengen group (Pagenstecher 2008b: 609) that Italy was about to join.

The takeover of the Vlora in Durrës was captured in a photograph by the Albanian Telegraphic Agency (Pagenstecher 2008b: 610), which became known for recalling the disembarkation at Bari on August, 8, 1991. It was used under this heading in the context of a controversial commercial campaign, which printed "realistic" photographs, for instance, of blood-soaked clothes, victims of war, or HIV carriers.[31] "Regardless of the controversy discussed in press agencies, press councils and feuilletons regarding whether one should advertise using misery and death for fashion, the image of migration was listed as one of the most dreadful images of the decade" (ibid: 609). This was in spite that fact that the artist who desigend the "Vlora-poster," Oliviero Toscani, might have used the photograph in a sarcastic, provocative and ambivalent manner (Scorzin 2010: 103-104) by pointing to the absurdity of whose boat was full. The image became emblematic for Europe's redefined view on refugees and migration.

The depiction differs fundamentally from the image of the refugee that underpinned the Geneva Convention and the Cold War period. It was no longer families or heroic political refugees which were on the move and needed protection (Salomon 1991). Flight and migration was rather identified with undifferentiated, yet insurrectionary masses.[32] Chimni's essay is classic in describing the shift in perception with regard to the figure of the refugee post the Cold War. He shows that the "image of a 'normal' refugee – white, male, anti-communist" led to a justified rejection with regard to the 'masses from the global South' who were "here for no good reason, […] abused hospitality, and […] [whose] number were too large" (Chimni 1998: 357). This "myth of difference" was centrally based on the notion of masses. The notion of masses blurred any difference between migration and flight, as well as individual biographical and legal issues. While individuals are attested to a capacity to act and speak, as well as an individual biography and a reason to migrate, "masses are portrayed as elemental"

---

31 For a visual impression of the 1992 campaign of United Colors of Benetton by Oliviero Toscani see the poster collection at the Museum für Gestaltung Zürich, at: https://www.eguide.ch/de/objekt/united-colors-of-benetton/ (accessed December 20, 2019).

32 For the transformation of the construction of the figure of the refugee since the Geneva Convention, see Salomon (1991). Katharina Inhetveen aptly describes the dominant self-conception in Europe: "one isn't a refugee, one was a refugee" (Inhetveen 2010: 150).

(Johnson 2011: 1029).[33] They therefore appear overwhelming, as existential threats to the receiving countries.

Moreover, public imagination of the refugee and migrants as masses goes in line with alienation, distancing, and a form of othering. The gaze at masses has a distancing effect. In this sense, Susanne Luedemann commented that one who "writes on masses cannot be and does not want to be part of it" (Luedemann 2012: 105). The notion of masses is based on a gaze from a distance, as viewed from the land or even from above. With regard to masses on vessels, it includes the possibility of observing the shipwreck from a distance, wondering why they even embarked under these conditions with an almost scientific curiosity (Blumenberg 1997). It is this curious-yet-distant gaze that allows one to evaluate and assess: the refugee status, the intention of migration, the reasons to move, the trustworthiness of the refugee, the organization of the journey. The relation between the observer and the masses has been described as a "relation of distanced criticism, even condemnation" (Luedemann 2012: 105). The crowd that empowers itself disputes the idea of the individual who is fleeing for reasons of political prosecution, that is, the refugee of the 1951 Geneva Convention.[34] Thereby, the image of the masses allows for justifying the necessity to limit admission. In the sense, the image 'masses on vessels' triggered EU bordering, even though their boat was indeed, much more overcapacity than their ships of state.

Just as Surbek's poster provides both justification and a portrayal of humanitarian and restrictive asylum policies, the image of the Vlora illustrates a similar ambivalence: the grief of the many is obvious, but the reference to their sheer

---

33 In fact, Johnson argues that this link to the elemental and the savage has only been unpacked as regards (non-white) refugees from the South: "It is in the commentary on refugees in Africa and Asia that references begin to refer to 'floods,' 'flows,' and 'hordes' of refugees. Rather than individuals, refugees began to represent masses of people moving across borders – not fleeing persecution, as outlined in the Convention, but fleeing violence and war, intimidating in their numbers" (Johnson 2011: 1023).

34 The Geneva Convention defined that refugee status may be granted to a person who as a "result of events occurring before January 1, 1951 and owing to well-founded fear of being persecuted for reasons of race, religion, nationality, membership of a particular social group or political opinion, is outside the country of his nationality and is unable or, owing to such fear, is unwilling to avail himself of the protection of that country; or who, not having a nationality and being outside the country of his former habitual residence as a result of such events, is unable or, owing to such fear, is unwilling to return to it." United Nations (1951) Convention on the Status of Refugees, Art.1 A (2).

numbers limits admission capacities. Thus, it might not be by chance that journalist Michael Schwelien (2004) used the photograph as book cover to his 2004 monograph, "Das Boot ist voll. Europa zwischen Nächstenliebe und Selbstschutz" (Engl.: *The boat is full. Europe between humanitarianism and self-protection*). Whose vessel – Europe's ship of state or the migrants' boat? Yet, there is one further catachresis in the context of Europe bound flight and migration: migrants and refugees appear as a mixed flow in overcrowded fishing vessels – no longer as an event, but as established phenomenon. In this context, the active insurgent masses are transformed into an immobile crowd. Aboard small fishing vessels, boatloads of African migrants travel toward Europe.

Catachresis II: Europe's Other aboard Overcrowded Pateras, Cayucos, or Rubber Dinghies

Careful consideration reveals that it is merely the image of masses which is maintained, rather than an actual comparability in numbers. As we have seen above, in the 1990s, *pateras* boats from Morocco to Spain were reported to carry between ten and 30 passengers. During the first decade of the new millennium the number of passengers per vessel ranged between approximately 150 and 400. According to Fargues and Bonfanti (2014: 2), between 1998 and 2013 there was an annual average of 44,000 migrants who arrived on boats. Yet, the depiction as masses was and still is present, and supports and reproduces the myth of invasion (Haas 2008).

Migrants appear "tightly packed" in overcrowded vessels and as a result, there is a visual depiction of masses which is maintained, and which suggest that there are "too many of them." The "visual type" (Walters 2014: 7) of the overcrowded vessel suggests that there are too many migrants on board, both for the vessel to be seaworthy as well as for European receiving states. Furthermore, the image of the boatload of people makes it difficult to distinguish them visually as individuals. Integrated with and stuffed into the vessel, they present one image and also one case to Europe's public imagination.

When they become visible on Europe's public horizon, their boat is not almost full, but already overloaded. This fundamentally differs from the lifeboat scenario. While rescue and humanitarian assistance follows criteria of need, the crowd necessitates sorting them out. The notion of being overcrowded thus provides the basis for the myth of difference (Chimni 1998) and also provides the justification for screening, sorting, and debriefing migrants. Moreover, when characterized as "armada of the poor and desperate" (ZDF 2014), boat passengers are both victim and threat in one and the same boat. Therefore, the oscillating reference to migrants and refugees is possible because they appear as undifferentiated boatloads.

In addition, the image of a "collective body of migrants appearing on western shores offers up a spectacle of clandestinity," whereby those considered illegal appear as irrational savages, incomprehensible to such a point that they can be studied (Andersson 2010: 43). The depiction of a cramped vessel in the middle of the sea stirs up fear *and* incomprehension. As emphatic emotion ("What if I was in their place?"), there is the fear that an overcrowded boat might capsize. The fear emerges vis-à-vis an existential threat. Yet, rather than a fellow feeling, this empathy is based on pity and commiseration. From the perspective of the EU-based spectator, incomprehension (rather than catharsis) dominates the gaze on the image. "No wonder, they don't reach if they travel under these conditions. How reckless, and yet, how desperate must they have been?" could be the inner monologue of the European spectator. Apart from the questioning of identity and legality which serves to somewhat "localize" the person, there is a general devaluation of the entire endeavor of maritime migration. The view of the overcrowded vessel from land recalls sensibilities similar to the antic and premodern perspective, which valued seafaring as outrageous and blasphemous (Makropoulos 1998: 56-57). Meanwhile, orderly and safe maritime endeavors on registered, seaworthy, and technically advanced ships stand for the justified pursuit of happiness and the exploration beyond one's own horizon. These different gazes, the antic and premodern valuation of seafaring and the modern version of enlightenment, are both present when seaborne migration is assessed by onlookers, who the evaluate the endeavor using the boat as an indicator.

Migratory ambitions on overcrowded and small fishing boats are at odds not only with politics, but also with reason and physical possibilities. Hence, that which ought not be moving, raises questions of legality and rationality. Empathy, a profound lack of understanding, and fear can equally and simultaneously be evoked by this image. Suspicion and unease dominate the seaward gaze.

Finally, the attribution "cramped vessel" is also used as an image that entices urgency. As such it is appropriated by migrants and facilitators. The journalist Wolfgang Bauer reported on three-level vessels, on which migrants hid below deck until they were close to a European state's coast. Only then, Bauer told, did migrants request to stand on deck, thus *performing* the image of the overcrowded vessel. The visual image of a cramped vessel turns into a warning signal and an SOS. The self-explanatory character which Frontex attested to the vessel – if you see the boat the boat tells the story – is taken up to craft an image of urgency and victimization. Thereby the vessel transforms into a kind of passport substitute, with 'overcrowded' providing for the just documentation to be identified as worth of access and assistance. Assuming that European spectators take the boat as an explanation, the organization of the trip will consider the following question: 'If the boat is detected, what story needs to be evoked'?

8.2.2 Small, Open Fishing Vessels

The site inspection at the beginning of this chapter examined the difference between boats and ships with regard to technical and legal classifications. The size of a vessel has been worked out as the recurring distinction between boats and ships, with the size of a vessel determining the technical condition of seaworthiness. While ships are built to go on international sea voyages, boats are rather made for coastal waters and thus remain imagined in the local or regional. Furthermore, the Hai Hong incident presented in chapter 7 has illustrated that ships repurposed for commercialized migrate can trigger diplomatic conflicts between governments and UNHCR, while boats can be dealt with as a regional phenomenon. Hence, in the context of the Hai Hong incident, a symbolic difference between "boat-people" and "ship-people" could be observed. This is also true with regards to the political attention paid to their arrival: while boats may remain in the realm of the unknown or wanted ignorance, ships cannot be denied. At first glance, small boats appear as the medium of choice to clandestine migration. The general framing of small boats is revealed in the following UNODC assessment:

"Beyond their easy availability, fishing vessels are less likely to raise suspicion given that there is a legitimate reason for this type of vessel to be out at sea. Finally, fishing vessels often do not require registration domestically or internationally, and are not required to have satellite or other tracking systems on board, meaning that smugglers can use them with very little risk of being connected to them. Where vessels are unseaworthy and not intended for reuse, there is no risk to the smuggler in assigning an unskilled person, possibly even a migrant, to captain and navigate the boats. Fishing vessels used to transport migrants generally end up at the bottom of the sea and were never intended for use in more than one journey."[35]

Additionally, small boats are a technical challenge to border surveillance, because they are difficult to detect amid the waves. In cases where the vessel's en-

---

35 UNODC (2011): Smuggling of Migrants by Sea, p. 29 at: http://www.unodc.org/documents/human-trafficking/Migrant-Smuggling/Issue-Papers/Issue_Paper_-_Smuggling_of_Migrants_by_Sea.pdf (accessed August 27, 2019).

gine is above water, radar does not always detect it.[36] Small boats are thus imagined as being able to sneak ashore. The image of the small boat supports a notion of clandestinity. In turn, this condition seems to be an essential requirement to avoid detection. The same holds true for the different registration requirements and the technical equipment required for larger vessels, such as the Long Range Identification and Tracking System. It seems probable that dockyards exist where these transponders are dismantled.[37] In these cases, the attribution "small" does not mean "boat," rather it is ships which are technically invisibilized and thereby disassociated from politics.

The kind of adventure undertaken with a vessel strongly depends on its size: the sailboat stands for expedition, the small boat for the local earning a living. The image of the small fishing vessel with African migrants thus made it appear like a regional phenomenon. The fishing vessel is supposed to stay in local African territorial waters and be used for earning a living. However, the vessels used for maritime EU bound migration seem to be ships in the technical and administrative sense of the word, and it was only through the SOLAS description that one speaks of a ship starting at 12 passengers (cf. chap.7.1). The attribute "small" can be interpreted as a political perspective, which classifies the kind of migration undertaken with these vessels as irrational. Just as these kinds of boats are not meant for international voyages, their passengers are meant to remain "local" and "at home."

The 2007 Marine I Incident

Strangely enough, the documentation of the 2007 *Marine I* voyage starts with its distress call. Little to nothing seems to be known about the organization of the vessel or the business behind its voyage. It was merely reported that the *Marine I* was an Italian built prawn trawler (Brothers 2007a). Even accounts on the vessel's point of departure are inconsistent. International newspapers assumed that the vessel "set off from the troubled West African nation of Guinea or from Ivory Coast in early December, and was probably destined for the Canaries" (ibid).

In later accounts, Conakry, Guinea is cited as the port of embarkation (Wouters/Den Heijer 2010: 2; Kumin 2014: 306). There is no mention of flag state affiliation or the owner of the vessel. Kees Wouters and Maarten Den Heijer merely note that it was "not clear under which flag the ship was sailing, nor who the owner was" (Wouters/Den Heijer 2010: 2). Only the Spanish journalist,

---

36 Head of Research and Development at Frontex, personal interview (May 27, 2011).
37 Journalist Bauer, telephone interview (June 2014).

Nicolás Castellano, assumed in an interview with legal theorist Sonja Buckel that the crew, who apparently left the vessel prior to the distress call, had been Russian (Buckel 2013: 247). She reports that the flag flown by the *Marine I* upon the arrival of Spanish authorities hangs framed in the Regional Coordination Center for the Canary Islands as a reminder of the incident (ibid: 243).[38] Whether the flag is Italian or from Ivory Coast cannot be determined from her photograph.

The distress call which subjected the *Marine I* and it passengers to interstate agreements was sent on January 30, 2007. Engine failure was stated as its reason for calling distress. The *Marine I* was on the high seas and was allegedly transporting 369 migrants of African and Asian origin (Brothers 2007b). As the responsible search and rescue (SAR) authority, the Senegalese responded that it did not have the adequate equipment to assist such a large vessel in distress. Mauritania also refused responsibility as it had not signed the SAR Convention.[39] Several days after the distress call, on February 4, 2007, the Spanish maritime rescue tug Luz de Mar reached the *Marine I* and "provided immediate relief by handing out supplies of water and food" (Wouters/Den Heijer 2010: 2). However, another eight days were needed before the vessel was brought back to port.

For six days, the Spanish government negotiated with the Senegalese and Mauritanian authorities. On the 10th of February, an agreement between Spain and Mauritania was reached: The Mauritanian authorities agreed that – for humanitarian reasons – the Luz de Mar would tow the *Marine I* into the port of Nouadhibou. In exchange, Spain guaranteed that none of the *Marine I* passengers were to remain in Mauritania. For that purpose, Spain was requested to provide airplanes on which the migrants could be repatriated. Only when the airplanes reached Nouadhibou would the cargo ship be allowed to enter the port. Moreover, the *Marine I* was only allowed to dock for four hours, during which time the migrants had to be triaged into three groups and transported off accordingly. The first group was created for persons "of African origin," which were to be repatri-

---

38 The Marine I incident has been documented and analyzed in detail by Sonja Buckel (2013: 243-289) and by Wouters and Den Heijer (2010). Further accounts have been provided by Thomas Gammeltoft-Hansen (2011: 129-130) and Judith Kumin (2014: 306-307). I mainly follow Buckel's account in the below elaborations.

39 Amnesty International (2008): Mauritiania: Nobody wants to have anything to do with us, Arrests and collective expulsions of migrants denied entry into Europe, July 1, 2008, at: https://www.amnesty.org/en/documents/afr38/001/2008/en/ (accessed August 29, 2019).

ated to Guinea-Conakry. The second group was reserved for those Asian migrants who agreed to return voluntarily. Finally, the third category was supposed to include the unmovable rest: those persons who would not accept return, and thus be transferred to Spain for repatriation (Buckel 2013: 245-246).

The dominant reasoning underpinning this categorization was repatriation and its logistical requirements. In doing so, the agreement clearly ignored the possibility that persons in need of international protection could be among the passengers on board the *Marine I*. The principle of non-refoulement didn't apply as the grounds for its application (presence of those in need of international protection) was not considered in the first place. The firm claim that all passengers were illegal immigrants was paired with the demonstrative rejection of any room for interpreting their political status. The willingness of the Spanish government to pay 650,000 Euros to Mauritania, rewarding the cooperation in the case of the *Marine I*, further highlights the atmosphere that must have determined the negotiations – the endeavor of the *Marine I* could under no circumstances be successful. The same attitude could be traced among Southeast Asian states in the case of the Hai Hong incident. Similar to the procedures in 1978, the first negotiations concerned the opening of a port to the migrants' vessel.

As provided for in the agreement of February 10, 2007 between the government of Spain and its Mauritanian counterpart, the passengers of the *Marine I* disembarked in Nouadhibou on February 12. The Spanish journalist Nicolás Castellano, who witnessed the arrival of the *Marine I*, reported in an interview that the situation on board was disastrous. The migrants were lying down, packed like sardines, the vessel was full of rats and the passengers were in a fragile state of health (quoted in Buckel 2013: 246-247). Yet, after a first medical treatment, two groups of 35 persons each were immediately flown out. The remaining 299 passengers of the *Marine I* were kept in a hangar for screening purposes. Only two days after disembarkation the great majority of them, 276 persons, had signed 'voluntary repatriation agreements' which repatriated them to either India or Pakistan. "During the interviewing and registration by IOM, these passengers had declared that the reason for their departure was fear of ostensible persecution as a result of the conflict in Kashmir" (Wouters/Den Heijer 2010: 3). Nevertheless, passengers were never asked whether they were in need of international protection. Authorities involved assumed "that these people were illegals" (Buckel 2013: 247). By April 23, 2007 most *Marine I* passengers had been repatriated.

The remaining 23 migrants who refused voluntary repatriation were kept in a fish processing plant in Nouadhibou port for another three months until July 23, 2007. During these months, they were guarded by Spanish security forces. During the entire five months, a total of 1,330 Spanish police officers had been deployed in Mauritania to monitor the impromptu detention facilitation. Detained in the fish processing plant in the port of Nouadhibou, Mauritania, the 23 immobilized migrants were kept in a "limbo juridico," a legal grey zone. They were de facto under Spanish jurisdiction, but withheld from any rights provided in the Spanish legal system or in international human rights. This was also clarified by the UN Committee Against Torture decision of November 21, 2008.[40]

On July 23, 2007, the detention of the 23 migrants in the Mauritanian fishing plant ended. The logistics that organized the confinement of the 23 migrants suggests that these passengers, under no circumstances, were allowed access to the Spanish legal system. Thirteen persons had been flown out to Pakistan on a Spanish plane. The remaining ten were flown to Gran Canary. From there a group of four was flown to Portugal where they received work and residence permits (Buckel 2013: 257). The other six persons were taken to the Spanish enclave Melilla. Two of them received asylum while the other four remained in Melilla for another three years (their asylum application had been refused). Nonetheless, the Spanish administrations were reluctant to expel them due to humanitarian concerns but also issued the three persons no papers. Finally, in June 2010, the last two passengers of the *Marine I* were hospitalized in a Barcelona based psychiatry ward that specialized in traumatic refugee experiences (ibid: 257-258).

The case of *Marine I* has been described by journalist Nicolás Castellano as "the greatest scandal of border control in terms of human rights" (quoted in Buckel 2013: 286). And in fact, the case of the *Marine I* reveals a de facto extension of Spanish jurisdiction in the form of control over the ship's passengers. At the same time, there was also a suspension of law and a refusal of access not only to Spanish territory, but also to the legal system upon which the Spanish policemen based their authority to restrict the liberties of the migrants. The legal borders of policing where thus extended not only to Mauritania but also attached to the duration of 'processing' the passengers. Meanwhile, the legal borders of rights were out of reach for the migrants and thus seemingly removed. The tension between the legal border of policing and the legal border of rights was unilaterally resolved in favor of Spanish authorities. This can be described as a classic strategy of offshoring: increase in competences (profit) as well as evasion of

---

40 J.H.A. v. Spain, CAT/C/41/D/323/2007, UN Committee Against Torture (CAT), 21 November 2008.

legal restrictions or obligations. Literature primarily described this as extraterritorial (border) control measures.

The question, however, is how the proceedings could be possible. And this is where the vessel comes in again. The *Marine I* had sent a distress call, and as the vessel was in distress, Spanish authorities got involved in a rescue operation. The Committee against Torture noted that the Spanish state "maintained control over all persons on board the *Marine I* from the time the vessel was rescued and throughout the identification and repatriation process that took place at Nouadhibou"[41] Despite the exercise of jurisdiction, rights were not made available to the detained former passengers of the *Marine I*. According to Amnesty International, the conditions of detention were "grueling." The human rights organization reported "that the Spanish authorities exercised significant psychological pressure on the 23 individuals requesting asylum in Nouadhibou […] in order to break their physical and moral resistance."[42] When criticized for the inadequate detention, the Spanish government replied to Amnesty International that

"although it had no jurisdiction in the matter, [the intervention] occurred with the sole aim of fulfilling its humanitarian duty to come to the rescue of the boat [*Marine I*] and to save the passengers and crew. This is why one cannot call its conduct into question or demand it assumes responsibilities and takes actions that are outside its jurisdiction."[43]

The distress situation of the *Marine I* was declared the justificatory basis for Spanish intervention. The humanitarian obligation turned into a substitute for sovereignty. At the same time, further responsibility was rejected. Hence, the case of the *Marine I* also points to a blurring of interception and rescue operations. While interception operations can at any moment and in any location turn into rescue operations, the jurisdiction over vessel and passengers does not cease with the termination of the distress situation. Rather, the rescue operation mobilizes the legal borders of policing by uncoupling them from the place and time of distress. Yet, this is only possible when the law of the sea is decoupled from in-

---

41 J.H.A. v. Spain, CAT/C/41/D/323/2007, UN Committee Against Torture (CAT), 21 November 2008 (emphasis added).
42 Amnesty International (2008): Mauritiania: Nobody wants to have anything to do with us, Arrests and collective expulsions of migrants denied entry into Europe, July 1, 2008, at: https://www.amnesty.org/en/documents/afr38/001/2008/en/ (accessed August 29, 2019), p.31.
43 Ibid, p. 30.

ternational refugee law (Buckel 2013: 273), thereby allowing for a fragmented reading of legal obligations and legal competences.

The negotiations over a vessel pending in international waters remind us of the *Hai Hong* bargaining in 1978. At that time, western countries agreed to resettle the boat-people to which Southeast Asian countries opened their shores. Temporary access to territory was traded for access to asylum and permanent resettlement. Yet, the negotiations over the *Marine I* and its passengers go beyond the diplomatic bargaining which could be traced in the Hai Hong case. In the case of the *Hai Hong*, western countries appeared as a third party, as an international community. The idea of burden sharing underpinned Southeast Asian governments' pressure on western governments and their stubbornness toward UNHCR. Even if the migrants on board the *Marine I* represented global inequalities, the call for burden sharing couldn't be redirected. Both cases demonstrate that being on board a vessel, migrants' access to rights is protracted and subject to negotiation.

Looking back at the role UNHCR took during the Hai Hong incident, opinion seemed to changed overnight and all Indochinese refugees on board the *Hai Hong* were declared *prima facie* refugees. The organization's stance in the case of the *Marine I* was quite different. The organization did not get involved in any negotiations with potential receiving states, nor did it comment on the refugee status of passengers. Apart from an UNHCR letter to the Spanish government of April 20, 2007, where UNHCR attested that among the 23 remaining passengers of the Marine I there was none in need of international protection, the organization was hardly involved in the procedures. After UNHRC attributed all passengers with prima facie status in the case of *Hai Hong*, the organization might have evaded any similar signal that would allow for linking the vessel to a prima facie refugee status. In fact, in 2011, a UNHCR official stated in an interview with Buckel that the Spanish government wanted to "evade the impression that one only needs to hop into a boat to arrive in Spain" (quoted in Buckel 2013: 257). The vessel which came to indicate the need of international protection after the Hai Hong incident was not to be provided again with recognition of legal status.

News about larger vessels and freighters either stir up indignation with regards to the circumstances and conditions on board, or outrage over nonexistent captains and the cowardice and cruelty of facilitators (cf. the below section). Meanwhile, the sensation stirred up by small boats rather relates to incomprehension, pity, and the angst of being close to death. The small boat is the image of bare life when evoked in the sense of the raft of the medusa; the image of the sacrilegious attempt to overcome nature; and the image of one's own determination when evoked in an archaic sense. Consequently, the image of the small boat allows for an oscillation between two dispositions: blaming migrants for the most irrational of journeys and depoliticizing the savage refugee.

8.2.3 Unseaworthy – a Technical Description?

Toy boats, nutshells, one-way-ships,[44] the tenor is pretty much clear: this vehicle is not made for overcoming *any* space. This kind of boat shouldn't be used to cross the sea in the first place. When examining the characteristics of boats and ships as vehicles in chapter 7, I've shown that boats weren't considered suitable for the high seas or international voyages, but remained locally bound in conception *and* dedicated purpose (Ger.: *Widmung*). The appropriation of these vessels for Europe bound migration thus counters the image of "ought-to-be-traffic." The attribute of "unseaworthy" points beyond the technical description; it also hints at moral and political implications.

The condition of the vessel allows for the classification of seaborne migration as a humanitarian issue. Lutterbeck, for instance, states that "irregular migration across the Mediterranean has also become a serious humanitarian issue, as the would-be immigrants often travel in unseaworthy and overloaded vessels and accidents are frequent" (Lutterbeck 2010: 127). If the vessel is in bad shape, the condition of being transported is grueling. However, worse conditions increase the chances of being rescued. Thus, the condition of the vessel is provoked by an atrocious and inhuman double bind: the vessels ought to be strong enough to carry a certain amount of people, yet, if the vessel should succeed, its condition can only be marginally acceptable, that is, barely strong enough to make the whole journey. In fact, even during the Italian operation *Mare Nostrum*, the condition of the vessels used along the central Mediterranean route worsened. Before the operation was launched, Italy's Defense Minister Mario Mauro reportedly stated that:

"the ships would be escorted to the nearest safe port, in compliance with international law. If there aren't any migrants in need of medical assistance […] and if the ship is able to sail, it will be taken to the safest and nearest port, not necessarily Italian." (quoted in ANSAmed (N.N.) 2013)

---

44 All three expressions have been used by Frontex officials during interviews conducted for this study, as well as in German and international press releases.

Even though a careful reading of this statement reveals that access to Europe requires a life-threatening state of either vessel or passengers, the poor condition of the intercepted vessels was interpreted as an indication of the unscrupulous and rough business conducted by facilitators. The image of the unscrupulous smuggler was pushed further in January 2015 with the incidents of the freighters *Blue Sky M* and *Ezadeen*, which were carrying more than 1,300 Syrian refugees. After these two freighters were stopped in the Mediterranean, new labels began to surface. The ships were described as "crew-less freighters," "spectral vessels," and the "new tactic" of smugglers was attested a "new dimension of cruelty" (cf. Spalinger 2015; Frances D'emilio 2015). The smuggling business was described as scrupulous, cynical, and inhuman. Across the international press, it was reported that the use of cargo ships was a new trend whereby the abandoning of the vessels was the new tactic of smugglers. For the first time since the enforcement of Schengen borders in the Mediterranean, media attention was solely geared toward the freighters and the organization of their journeys.

On December 30, 2014 the Moldovan-flagged cargo freighter *Blue Sky M* drew attention as "a passenger sent a distress call […] when the ship was off Greece. Greek authorities scrambled a navy frigate and helicopter, but the captain said the vessel wasn't in distress and didn't require assistance" (*Associated Press* (N.N.) 2014). In Italian waters the ship was boarded by coast guards officials who were lowered from a helicopter. A female passenger had reportedly called the Italian Coast Guard, stating that freighter was alone and needed help. After the coast guards found the *Blue Sky M* on automatic pilot, the "spectral vessel" tagline began to spread. The assessment of the Italian coast guard commander Filippo Marini particularly helped paint a dramatic picture and pointed to the vessel itself as a new threat. According to Marini, "despite strong winds and high waves, Coast Guard officers were lowered onto the ship's bridge and managed to regain of the steering about a half-hour before it was due to strike the coast" (Frances D'emilio 2015). The language appeared rather militarized with Marini comparing the vessel to a bomb: "Certainly it's very dangerous because a ship with no one on the command bridge is like a bomb that will strike up against the reefs" (ibid). The state of the "abandoned vessel" was described as ready for the scrap heap. By January 2, 2015 news of the *Ezadeen* spread as another episode of this "new tactic," Marini's bomb metaphor had already transformed into a piece of information: it was recalled that the *Blue Sky M* was set on a "collision course for a stretch of Italy's southern coast" (Povoledo/Cowell 2015). The narrative was mimicked for the Sierra Leone-flagged *Ezadeen*:

"For the second time in three days, the Italian authorities found themselves racing on Friday to rescue hundreds of migrants from an aging freighter that traffickers had pointed toward Italy and then abandoned, leaving the ship to plow through wintry seas at top speed with no one at the helm, heading straight for the coastline." (Povoledo/Cowell 2015)

The information provided was contradictory – rescuers were reportedly "able to board the ship only after it ran out of fuel and stopped" (ibid). By the afternoon it had apparently been towed to a dock by an Icelandic ship operating in the Frontex mission *Triton* (Spalinger 2015). Despite several inconsistencies, the episode was taken as "further confirmation that traffickers had hit on a new tactic to extract ever greater profits from human misery while eluding apprehension" (Povoledo/Cowell 2015). Even though the image of an unseaworthy vessel would usually provoke at least some humanitarian considerations, the characterization of the vessel as "abandoned" and "spectral" channelled all public interest toward the vessel and the business of commercialized migration facilitation. No distinction was made between captain, crew and smugglers. Moreover, information on the vessel and its registration, often difficult to get, was available in this case. The Moldovan-flagged *Blue Sky M* belonged to the Romanian based company Fairway Navigation Ltd, and the Sierra Leone-flagged *Ezadeen* was owned by the Syrian businessman Youssef Mohamad Lebbadi, whose shipping company is based in the port city of Tarus (Jakob/Gottschlich/Braun 2015). The fact that the *Ezadeen* was employed as a cattle ship was used to further underline the victimization of refugees by facilitators. The profit margins of a facilitator are estimated to be one million dollars per steel-hulled vessel, with passengers being charged up to 6,000 dollars each (Povoledo/Cowell 2015). Facilitators are described as cowardly and cruel.

By framing the *Blue Sky M* and the *Ezadeen* as "ghost ships" and "spectral vessels," Frontex sets a particular moral valuation of the incidents. And even though it won't be possible to know whether Frontex has chosen this precise narrative deliberately or unwittingly, the characterization of ghost ship recalls the S.S. Jeddah affaire of August 1880. For this incident, the label of the ghost ship and the valuation of the captain being coward and cruel, were first coined.[45]

---

45 During the night of August 7 and 8, 1880, the S.S. Jeddah, a British streamer with 778 men, 147 women, 67 children, and 600 tonnes of cargo (sugar and timber) was damaged to the point where water started flowing into the engine room. This caused a serious distress situation. The Captain Lucas Clark abandoned the ship with his first officer on a life boat, which was picked up by another steamer and brought to Aden.

Cowardly and cruel – such is the moral assessment that is meant to be evoked by the tale of the spectral vessel – a narrative which in its application to the incident of the Blue Sky M and the Ezadeen diffuses rescue responsibilities and the refugee question at Europe's borders and one-sidedly blames facilitators and seafarers.

However, in April 2015, investigations of the German news magazine *Panorama* found that the *Blue Sky M* had been navigated by seafarers who "used their professional skills to save the passengers from war" (Buchen 2015). A passenger is quoted as noting that the captain had carefully navigated the ship along the coast. Moreover, the journalists' investigations exposed that the *Blue Sky M* was "seaworthy without any reservation [Ger.: *ohne Einschränkungen seetauglich*]" (ibid). The Italian prosecutor in Lecce confirmed this valuation.

When confronted with the *Panorama* investigations, the Frontex press officer argued that Frontex information at that time was not as good as the magazine's information. This did, however, not lead to public corrections by the European agency. This situation also demonstrates that Frontex, with poor information, apparently assumed that the ship was unseaworthy and ready for the scrap heap. The focus on freighters and their allegedly poor state was set by Frontex and has been echoed by the international press. In fact, the unseaworthy vessel and the criminal networks fall in the operational field of the agency, while asylum policies or humanitarian issues don't fall in the auspices of border enforcement, not even in its coordination efforts. By channeling the discourse toward spectral ves-

---

> Meanwhile the abandoned passengers on board the Jeddah ceaselessly bailed water out of the ship, pumping four days and nights. They set new sails and with the right wind, the Jeddah drifted toward the coast where the British steamer S.S. Antenor spotted it and towed it to Aden. Two days later, on August 10, 1880, Captain Clark telegraphed Singapore that the Jeddah sunk with 953 pilgrims on board and that all passengers had perished. One day later, on August 11, 1880 a second telegram was sent by the Captain of the Antenor which had towed the Jeddah into the harbor of Aden. This one reported that all lives had been saved. The fact that Captain Clark had abandoned his ship in distress was publicly condemned. Commentators revealed sheer indignation and called Clark's behavior of the lowest modes of action and especially of cowardice. "The maritime court in Alden judged Clark guilty. He had failed to apply the simplest judgment on that day and had showed a 'shameful lack of courage' as well as 'massive misconduct.' The owner of the harbor added that the captain committed the greatest inhumanity" (summarized from and quoted in Kreitling 2015, also cf. Moore/F. R. G 2000).

sels, Frontex contoured its target and mandate, and thus positioned itself in the fight against criminal facilitation networks. Meanwhile, nothing was reported about the whereabouts of the passengers. With the exception of the alleged captain, no individual testimony was covered in media reports. Passengers' reasons for fleeing were not even speculated upon. Although the Syrian passengers most probably have all been granted refugee status, it was not in the interest of Frontex to have this message disseminated. Scandalizing the cruelty of smugglers and the condition of the vessel as unseaworthy, Frontex set the agenda and diverted possible signals of group refugee status. Furthermore, as Frontex had just launched the joint operation *Triton*, which replaced the Italian rescue operation *Mare Nostrum*, a general discussion about the legality and proportionality of EU border enforcement measures and rescue obligations was adamantly avoided.

The *Panorama* journalists concluded that Frontex would surely be content with its power to define the incident. The incident of the Blue Sky M shows "how far Europe's border protectors go in the propaganda fueled fight against illegal migration. Obviously, they want to pass the responsibility for the death of many refugees onto the smugglers" (Buchen 2015).

This episode further demonstrates that "unseaworthy" is not a mere technical description, but implies discussions of ownership, responsibility and sometimes even suggests a moral valuation.

8.3 WHAT STORY DOES THE BOAT TELL?

"If you see the boat, the boat tells the story" – this explanatory and evaluative shortcut condenses around the boat, what cannot be understood nor classified as one: the complex circumstances, the different motives of migration and the varying itineraries. While UNHCR's description of "mixed flow" warns not to treat all passengers equally only because they arrived by equal means, the suggestive explanation that the condition and image of the vessel is supposed to provide reduces all rhetorical differentiation to a subtly evaluative assessment. The diverse itineraries get reduced to their cramped presence at sea.

While section 8.1 focused on the metric dealings with boats, their passengers and deaths at sea, section 8.2 examined the visual and verbal metaphor of the small, overcrowded and unseaworthy refugee boat. It could be shown that numbers hardly contribute to the public or political valuation of the situation in the Mediterranean. Migratory endeavors as well as asylum requests are rather assessed and "explained" with reference to the condition of the vehicular facilitator. Overcrowded, unseaworthy, small – all three adjectives are attributed to those vessels repurposed in the context of European-bound flight and migration. Even though the analysis in section 8.2 meant to challenge the supposedly self-explanatory image of the overcrowded depilated migrant vessels, I am not denying the poor state of most of these vehicles. Rather, I wish to illustrate that there is an oscillating reference behind the supposedly self-explanatory image. As a result, different "stories" are evoked parallel to one another, allowing for the oscillating reference to refugee boats, migrant vessels and their passengers, which in the process translates the unsuitability of the vessel into different evaluations of the migratory endeavor itself.

Again, what story does the boat tell? – An intimate, anti-modern relation? A tale of limited capacities, of subversion, of humanitarian urgency or of profit-oriented appropriation?

All three attributes: small, overcrowded and unseaworthy, share the impetus that this maritime journey is not meant to occur. An overcrowded or small boat, and explicitly unseaworthy vessel, is not made for international voyages nor for any directional movement on water. These vessels are not built for the amount of people they carry and they are not meant for being used to travel to Europe. Size and seaworthiness – the two main distinguishable features between boats and ships – are turned on their head in the context of flight and migration.

The vessel's suitability no longer embodies the nature of the sea, but responds to the nature of international refugee policies as well as the nature of a surveillance apparatus and EU border enforcement measures. A vessel's flexible suitability integrates and reflects the ambiguities and contradictions of European border policies. The unseaworthiness of the vessel is the substitute "passport" to passengers' admission into Europe and their subsequent access to rights.

The tale of limited capacities evoked by referring to the "overcrowded" has two facets: it entails the narrative of urgency and humanitarian need while at the same time questioning the admission capacities of receiving states. The reference to sheer numbers and masses de-individualizes migrants and refugees to boatloads of people of which there are "just too many." The portrayal of an undifferentiated mass thus allows for distancing and evaluation. Both the profitability of the smuggling business and the victimization of smuggled migrants is evoked by the mere reference to the condition of the boat as crowded and unseaworthy. While the victimization removes political agency, the condition of the vessel carries the implication of reckless endeavor, of a "you should have stayed where you came from" accompanied by a shake of the head.

The reference to small fishing vessels suggests an intimate relation between the vehicle and its passengers to the regional or "local" appropriation. Fishing vessels are supposed to stay local and earn their owners a living. They intimately relate to the area where they are from, exactly like the refugees, who are evoked with a constitutive connection to their homeland (Inhetveen 2010: 157). Small boats are decisively not part of international politics, and thus cannot count on the rights and obligations state grant each other.

Arriving by boat, migrants' itineraries and their complicated organizations are effectively reduced to the sea passage. Their itineraries are aggregated to arrivals by sea. The conditions under which one is being transported obscures the reasons for migration and can be used as purifying, to attribute pity or to argue for repatriation. The different images of vessels and their attributes are entangled in politics through the stirring up of emotions such as fear and pity, or by enticing suspicion and calculations of risk. These emotions and the explanations they suggest don't only seem plausible to the general public; they merge in an unstated way and leave one irritated, uncertain, and unsettled when faced with the standard image of the migrant vessel as an open boat stuffed with young black people, mostly men. Empathy, a profound lack of understanding, and fear can equally and simultaneously be evoked by this image.

9 Seaborne Bordering: Legal Negotiations on Boats and Boat Migrants in EU Border Policies

The previous section examined the powerful image of the refugee boat by describing the extent to which the vessel's recurring attributes of being small, overcrowded and unseaworthy go beyond a mere technical assessment of a vessel's suitability to move on water. I have illustrated that the image together with the vessel's attributes call forth assumptions and fantasies about the condition and origin of its passengers and their political status, as well as the organization of the journey, thus opening up the possibility to valuate and classify the status and ambitions of migrants and refugees arriving in Europe. This chapter focuses on legal reasoning advanced in EU border policies toward migrants and refugees encountered at sea.

When in 2000 (and explicitly in 2004) Michael Pugh considered it justified to apply the term boat-people to the context of maritime migration to the EU, he did so in order "to distinguish their status in law and political discourse" (Pugh 2004: 51). Yet, what distinguishes the status of boat-people from that of other migrants and refugees? Pugh's formulation suggests that it is, in fact, the vehicle that makes the difference. However, others observe a blurring (Inhetveen 2010: 155) or nullifying (Budz 2009) effect of the vehicle on the legal status of its passengers. This section explores the vessel's share in the legal argumentations of EU border enforcement measures.

Against the background of the seemingly self-explanatory image of the refugee boat, it felt almost naive to ask a Frontex official working with the Sea Border Sector about how he could know at sea whether a vessel was used for unauthorized migration. Yet, there was no mention of the crowd of people crammed on deck or the condition of the vessel. "They do not fly a flag" was the taken-for-granted answer that the official provided. In further interviews and when analyzing legal documents related to sea voyages, I affirmed that the relevant legal ground for intercepting vessels with migrants and asylum seekers on board is *the vessel's* "absence of nationality" (Papastavridis 2009: 159). Would a flag then prevent a migrants' boat from being intercepted or pushed-back? Legally speaking: maybe. Empirically deducing: rather not.

And still, could the vessel provide the legal ground for border police intervention, while the target and concern of border guards sits inside the vehicle? What does this legalistic separation – a distinction between legal reasoning *in rem*, that is, concerning the vessel itself, and legal reasoning *in personas*, that is, concerning the crew and passengers of a vessel – allow for? Which legal status is attached to the means of transport – the boat? Which legal status is, in turn, attached to its passengers? Furthermore, how does the legal reasoning *in rem* interfere with the *in personas* reasoning?

For the purpose of working out the vessel's share in legal reasoning, the analysis concentrates on those arguments which rely on the vehicle itself, justifying the interception of "stateless vessels," of "vessels in distress," and of "suspicious vessels." This allows for testing the hypothesis of whether a prioritization of the vehicle in legal reasoning allows for operational practices which otherwise would have been difficult if not impossible to justify. Focusing on the boat, is not to say that persons are no longer considered a part of the relation. Rather, I intend to understand how the reference of having been on board "such a boat" effects migrants' classification and administration in Europe.

In order to explore how the liquid sea and the movable environment of the boat can determine the legal status of migrants – who then are even called seaborne or boat migrants – the relation between territorial border enforcement and the different maritime spaces needs to be assessed. Section 9.1 discusses the extent to which maritime spaces converge with, or diverge from, the notion of territorial borders. As maritime interceptions are a common state practice in the Mediterranean, section 9.2 examines its legality as a border enforcement practice at sea. The section also goes into the three most virulent characterizations of the vessel that legitimize interception: the stateless vessel, the vessel in distress and the suspicious vessel. Section 9.3 summarizes the preceding three chapters on the refugee boat as vehicle, moving target, and integrating figure of EU bordering. The final section analyses the share of the refugee boat to the crafting of an external EU border.

9.1 MARITIME SPACES AND TERRITORIAL BORDER ENFORCEMENT

Political geographer Victor Prescott identified two characteristic differences between maritime borders and land borders: first, maritime borders are rarely demarcated; second, they are more permeable than land borders (Prescott 1987: 25). It follows that in practical terms, border enforcement along maritime borders is more challenging than along land borders.

In terms of national jurisdiction and thus the range of state authority, border enforcement can occur at a port or within the territorial waters of a coastal state, the breadth of which is restricted to twelve nautical miles by Art. 3 of the 1982 LOS Convention. However, Art. 33 (1) LOSC compensates for the practical difficulties of maritime border enforcement by allowing for certain control practices to be expanded up to 24 nautical miles.

"In a zone contiguous to its territorial sea, described as the contiguous zone, the coastal State may exercise the control necessary to:
(a) prevent infringement of its customs, fiscal, immigration or sanitary laws and regulations within its territory or territorial sea;
(b) punish infringement of the above laws and regulations committed within its territory or territorial sea."

Border surveillance and control can be enacted inside the territorial waters[1] *and* in the contiguous zone. The competences of a state extend to 24 nautical miles off the baseline of its coast.[2] Meanwhile, the legal border of individual's rights is not explicitly expanded; as the obligations of a coastal state only fully apply in its territorial waters. Thus, the purpose of the contiguous zone explicitly consists in providing for the possibility of effective border control along blue borders (Rah 2009: 61). For the maritime space of the contiguous zone this means that state powers are extended to it, while at the same time the contiguous zone is no longer state territory.

---

1   According to Art. 3 of the Law of the Sea Convention (LOSC), the breadth of the territorial sea, to which the sovereignty of a coastal state extends, can be extended to twelve nautical miles.
2   LOSC, Art. 33 (2).

However, as in the exercise of state power on land, these control measures must equally consider the principle of proportionality and non-discrimination; they also have to satisfy humanitarian obligations and the principle of non-refoulement. Andreas Fischer-Lescano, Tillmann Löhr and Timo Tohidipur advance the territorial argument in a non-geographical interpretation: they argue that border control measures "have a functional territorial reference point since they are linked to the enforcement of state jurisdiction," regardless of where they are carried out. It follows that border enforcement measures continue to be linked to a territorial frame, even in extraterritorial areas. "The factually substantiated territorial reference significantly relativises exterritoriality and means that sovereign measures linked to border control activities fall within the ECHR's scope" (Fischer-Lescano/Lohr/Tohidipur 2009: 277). According to Fischer-Lescano and colleagues, extending the legal border of policing without simultaneously extending the legal border of rights externalizes responsibilities while provoking a "lack of efficient access to legal protection" (ibid: 295) on the side of refugees encountered at sea.

Effectively, border zones and designated danger zones are areas where the competences of policing are exceptional. The exceptional competences allotted to border guards or border police for the geographic location of the political border *and limited to it*, have been stressed by Kaufmann et al. (2002), Kaufmann (2006: 42), and Mau (2010: 59). No reasonable suspicion is required for intervention and identification checks by the police. Enforcing the border, the liberties of persons can be limited. Access to rights can be rejected to those not carrying the right documents. Borders are thus "border zones of limited rights" (Basaran 2011: 7). The tension between the legal borders of rights and the legal borders of policing characterizes border zones (ibid: 6-8), because it entails a lawful way of limiting the liberties of citizens and foreign nationals. The relation between the legal border of policing and the legal border of rights is generally asymmetrical in areas dedicated to sorting people and granting access, that is, border zones.

On land, this asymmetry between policing and rights is restricted to a certain geographical area – the geographical location of the borderline and 30 kilometers of hot pursuit. At sea, however, this asymmetry is, in principle, limited to the legal construct of the contiguous zone.

Yet, the contiguous zone not only extends the legal borders of policing geographically, it even strengthens them by extending competences while tying rights and obligations to the territorial waters and to land. This one-sidedness of this maritime zone can be used to the advantage of the coastal state in its control and enforcement capabilities. This radical split is at the bottom of so called pushback and interception operations. Before discussing the reasonings that sustain so called interception or pushback operations, I shall go into a brief excursus on the maritime zone of the high seas and its notion of the freedom of the sea.

The first to claim that the sea was a free space was the Dutch philosopher Hugo Grotius (1583-1645). In *Mare Liberum*, Grotius argued that the sea was international rather than merely at the disposal of the capable sea powers. He claimed that "no part of the sea can be considered as the territory of any people whatsoever" (Grotius 2001 [1609]: 34) but as a common property which "all men might use [...] without the prejudice to anyone else" (ibid: 2). According to Grotius, all nations should be able to undertake and profit from ocean-going trade and at the same time grant mutual non-interference. The assumption that directional movement occurs for the purpose of trade and commerce underpinned Grotius's claim. The emphasis on movement and on the principle of non-interference with innocent passages at sea is key to what Grotius understood as the freedom of the sea. In other words, no authority should control access to the sea. The claim was revolutionary for the early 17th century. *Mare Liberum* not only undermined the Pope's world order, it also opposed the British maritime mastery.[3] It thus provoked several responses.

In 1635, the British polymath John Selden (1584-1654) published *Mare Clausum,* which divided the sea into exclusive spheres of interest and power. In 1703, Cornelis van Bynkershoek mediated the two positions arguing that possession of the sea was principally possible, but that a state's dominion and possession over the sea ended "where missiles [...] exploded" (quoted in Prescott 1987: 16). In the early 18th century, the range of a cannon shot was roughly three miles long. Bynkershoek's cannon shot rule has been referred to as argumentative basis for the legal construct of the territorial waters. However, the mediation it offered was too variable (ibid: 16-17), and states continuously tried to expand their spheres of influence and possession at sea. Even though different empirical examples can demonstrate states' eagerness to appropriate the sea, the international customary law of the freedom of the sea is frequently brought against these ambitions. The stipulation twelve nautical miles in the Law of the Sea Convention of 1982 is a refining of territorial waters and thus state authority and jurisdiction, states dominion and possession is restricted geographically. Until this date, the

---

3   The Catholic Church promptly indicated *Mare Liberum* as it undermined the papal world order (Raya).

freedom of the sea is enshrined in Art. 87 of the LOS Convention. It declares that the high seas are "open to all States, whether coastal or land-locked." It provides among other things for the freedom of navigation.[4]

The freedom of the sea opposes the taking of possession, the territorialization, and the striating of the sea by stressing that the sea is "the spatial extension resource, principally useful as a domain for movement" (McDougal/Burke 1962: vii). Grotius claim that "the seas are by their very nature a domination-free sphere of trade routes [Ger.: *herrschaftsfreie Handelsstraßen*], which cannot be subjected to state appropriation" (Gadow-Stephani 2006: 39) implies that there is no supreme authority, no monopoly ruling over the legitimate means of movement at sea.

The notion of a space of movement free from dominion, and the principle of territorial sovereignty grounded on some sort of measured spatial extension stress different premises. While in the latter case, rules apply "within" a certain area, the former is concerned with movement itself. And while in the latter, movement as such can be interdicted, the former may merely define the "traffic rules." When movement across maritime borders is surveilled and controlled, these two principles – the freedom of the sea and territorial order – confront each other. Meanwhile, boats and ships navigate between them, integrating and challenging both principles.

Overall, it is important to keep in mind that the contiguous zone already compensates for the practical difficulties of maritime border surveillance and control. In *strictu sensu* of the 1982 United Nations LOS Convention, which the EU joined in August 2013, border enforcement measures can only legitimately occur within the territorial waters of a coastal state and its contiguous zone. In fact, the contiguous zone is a maritime construct granted in order to address the practical difficulties of maritime border enforcement. With the contiguous zone providing

---

4   Ships enjoy freedom of navigation, even in territorial waters of a third coastal state, provided their passage is innocent and that there is a genuine link between the vessel and a flag state. Apart from providing for the freedom of navigation, Art. 87 (1) of the LOS Convention lists: "(b) freedom of overflight; (c) freedom to lay submarine cables and pipelines, subject to Part VI; (d) freedom to construct artificial islands and other installations permitted under international law, subject to Part VI; (e) freedom of fishing, subject to the conditions laid down in section 2; (f) freedom of scientific research, subject to Parts VI and XIII."

already exceptional competences beyond the territorial border-line, anything beyond 24 miles has nothing to do with border enforcement measures.

And still, despite the right to innocent passage and the principle geographical limitation of border enforcement measures to the contiguous zone, the LOS Convention encompasses no provisions from which refugee boats or migrants' vessels could profit. It is instead composed of rights and obligations which states grant each other (Rah 2009: 21). Moreover, considering the history of the Freedom of the Sea and the Freedom of Navigation, these ideas and norms have been formulated without any bearing on (small) vessels or on the case of flight and migration as a purpose of seafaring. To a certain extent the discussions around the legality of maritime interceptions connects with these loopholes.

9.2 LEGITIMIZING MARITIME INTERCEPTION AS A BORDER ENFORCEMENT PRACTICE

Ever since operational border enforcement along Schengen borders has been coordinated by the Frontex agency, maritime border enforcement practices of European Mediterranean states have changed. Under the premise of "proactive" and "integrated border management," border enforcement measures have also been implemented beyond the contiguous zone, and thus occur where border enforcement is not supposed to occur. On the high sea, or in foreign waters, border enforcement measures encompass interceptions or pushback of migrants' vessels in designated "operational areas." Monitoring, control and recovery efforts are geared toward the small, crowded and barely seaworthy boats as condensed moment of suspicion, unease and insecurity. In fact, the interception "of boats carrying irregular migrants is the primary tool by means of which States attempt to stem the number of arrivals at their shores and thus fulfill their main policy aim" (Mallia 2010: 18) in the area of immigration control.

Yet, it is debatable whether maritime interception is to be considered a legitimate border enforcement practice. Both the available official description of "interception" as well as practitioners' early assessments of practices that were subsumed under this term, reveal a disconnect between a common state practice at sea and the legal provisions in place. This section examines how these gaps are being closed by reference to the three most virulent characterizations of the vessel that legitimize interception: the vessel's statelessness, its being in distress and its being suspicious.

It should be noted that there is no official definition of interception as a policing practice or border enforcement measure. There rather is a description of a modus operandi.

In June 2000, UNHCR's Executive Committee described past and current state practices and thereof derived a provisional definition of interception. The "definition" should not be read as affirmation by UNHCR of the respective control practices. The Executive Committee found that interception encompasses "all measures applied by a State, outside its national territory, in order to prevent interrupt or stop the movement of persons without the required documentation crossing international borders by land, air, or sea, and making their way to the country of prospective destination."[5]

The most important aspect of this definition is that it provides for an alternative location to control the movement of persons other than the administrative territorial border or the national territory. Moreover, the definition reveals that interception occurs with the sole intention to stop unauthorized mobility. With this intention defining it, interception rather appears as a policy than a practice. In fact, it entails "all measures applied by a State, outside its national territory," to prevent that someone without the necessary authorization enters its territory. Barbara Miltner underlines that this definition "reflects and emphasizes the *extraterritorial* character of interception" (Miltner 2006: 79, original emphasis).

This forward displacement, or extra-territorialization, is not derived from the practical difficulties of maritime border control. Rather, it occurs to fend off obligations, which are triggered when refugees and migrants are encountered or picked up at sea. The ExCom correspondingly observed that in "most instances, the aim after interception is return without delay of all irregular passengers to their country of origin."[6] Effectively, access to the legal border of rights is restricted or even made impossible by relocating, that is, by pushing the frontier further off territory. While in 2000 the stock-taking definition of interception also entailed administrative instruments such as the non-issuing of a visa, the Executive Committee narrowed this description to active practices in 2003. It stated that

---

5   Executive Committee of the High Commissioner's program, 18th Meeting of the Standing Committee (EC/50/SC/CPR.17), June 9, 2000: Interception of Asylum-Seekers and Refugees: The International Framework and Recommendations for a comprehensive Approach, at: https://www.unhcr.org/4963237411.pdf (accessed September 2, 2019), Section B (i) (Defining interception, para. 10).

6   Ibid: Section B (ii) (Description of interception practices, para. 12).

"interception is one of the measures employed by States to:
- prevent embarkation of persons on an international journey;
- prevent further onward international travel by persons who have commenced their journey; or
- assert control of vessels where there are reasonable grounds to believe the vessel is transporting persons contrary to international or national maritime law;
- where, in relation to the above, the person or persons do not have the required documentation or valid permission to enter; and that such measures also serve to protect the lives and security of the travelling public as well as persons being smuggled or transported in an irregular manner."[7]

Implicitly, the notion of interception revolves around control practices at sea, with regard to vessels repurposed for facilitating migration. Similar to the 2000 definition, interception is first and foremost thought of to tackle the movement of undocumented persons. Interception is thus not part of overall immigration or mobility policies, but tackles a particular segment, that is, those cases which have no legitimate means of movement in the first place.

Even before 2015 and the operation *Mare Nostrum*, the legality of maritime interception practices in the Mediterranean has been analyzed and debated widely (Gavouneli 2006; Miltner 2006; Fischer-Lescano/Lohr/Tohidipur 2009; Trevisanut 2010; Tondini 2012; Coppens 2012; Papastavridis 2013). Generally, interceptions on the high seas without flag-state consent are considered a violation of the principle of free navigation on international waters under the LOS Convention.[8] Effectively, however, a number of legal constructs have been advanced, which allow for the maritime interception of migrants while at the same time circumventing the principle of non-refoulement.

In fact, considering a statement given by a commander of the Armed Forces of Malta (AFM) already in 2005, it seems as if legal reasoning was constructed for a state practice that already functioned all too well. In an interview with Silja Klepp, the commander concedes that "the current status of international law […] doesn't really facilitate this type of interception operations" (Klepp 2011: 295).

---

7 Executive Committee of the High Commissioner's Program/Standing Committee (2003): Conclusion on Protection Safeguards in Interception MeasuresConclusion on Protection Safeguards in Interception Measures, at: https://www.unhcr.org/3f93b2894.html (accessed October 19, 2019).

8 The argument is also advanced by Brouwer/Kumin (2003: 14); Basaran (2011: 74).

He briefly mentions the different legal statutes which have been advanced to justify maritime interception: the Palermo protocols – "about the fact that they still believe in flag state permission and these are not wearing a flag" – the LOSC and the crimes listed – namely slavery, piracy, illegal transmission – actually "attract international jurisdiction,"[9] including the Vienna Convention's concerning drug trafficking. According to the commander, the facts which have been used to justify interception don't really match with the situation of encountering migrants and refugee vessels at sea. The statement of facts under which interception occurs is thus unclear (ibid). With regard to maritime interceptions of migrants' vessels, the AFM commander concluded that

"[t]here is no body of international law which covers it. Now again we have said that stateless vessels on the High Sea are subject to anyone's jurisdiction, but A you have to have something in your national law which covers it and Malta hasn't and B you have to talk about proportionality." (quoted in Klepp 2011: 295)

The commander further explains that Malta could only legitimately intervene in the case of rescue (Klepp 2011: 296). Similarly, Matteo Tondini (2012: 62-64), strategist and former military legal adviser to the Italian Navy, states that the SAR regime is the only available legal instrument to contribute to the legality of interception. Beyond that, if competences cannot be mobilized under criminal law nor for humanitarian reasons, there is a third reason: the suspicion of smuggling migrants, which works on the notion of risk and proactivity. These three legitimizing constructs will be considered in detail in the following subsections. All three deduce the legality of interception from different traits of the vessel: its legal, situational and techno-legal traits.

9.2.1 The Stateless Vessel

The legality of interception was first established on the grounds that vessels are stateless. As described by the AFM official cited above, it had been argued that on the high sea, ships without a flag are subject to anyone's jurisdiction. They may, in accordance with Article 110 (1d) of the LOS Convention, be stopped, boarded and seized. Because the rights of international maritime law are rights which states grant each other and thus based on reciprocity and mutual recognition, vessels without a flag cannot count on these rights nor on the protection by

---

9   LOSC, Art. 99-108.

any state. In other words, stateless vessels cannot rely on the principle of non-interference. Rah adds that "no rights of a foreign state are violated when such vehicles [vessels with no flags] are stopped" (2009: 21).

If a migrant vessel was flying a flag and if there was a genuine link between the vessel and the flag state, the vessel could, in principle, profit from the right to innocent passage in the territorial waters of a coastal state. It could also profit on the principle of non-interference and the freedom of navigation on the high sea. In fact, "the act of carrying migrants on the high seas is not an international crime as such" (Papastavridis 2009: 163). Yet, despite these principle legal provisions, flying a flag is not part of the optional equipment for a vessel repurposed for unauthorized migration. If it were for legalistic reasons, the genuine link between a ship and the flag state required by Article 91 (1) of the LOS Convention is not only implausible but also inexpedient.

Flag state registration is implausible since the watercraft used for seaborne migration – wooden fishing boots, inflatable boats, dinghies, unregistered freighters – would regularly not meet the requirement to fly a state's flag. UNODC reported that the fishing vessels used for smuggling "often do not require registration domestically or internationally, and are [also] not required to have satellite or other tracking systems on board."[10] Flag state registration is inexpedient with regard to the purpose of the journey. Neither the facilitators, nor the migrants, nor the refugees would claim the protection of a state (as flag state). Which flag could they possibly fly, which would render their movement on water acceptable, and which would meaningfully help to identify the vessel? If a flag could be flown to indicate the need for protection (for example, a "Nansen-flag"), the migrants' vessels could fly the flag of the European Union. However, I dare hypothesize that procedures at sea would remain as they are, with or without flag, as the absence of the vessel's nationality is not the issue at stake, but "merely" the basis for interception.

This question or rather omission of a plausible answer demonstrates the absence of nationality as legitimate ground for intercepting migrant vessels. It belongs to a straw man argument, as the stateless vessel ground builds upon a set-up implausibility. In fact, the reference to a state would rather increase the risk for mi-

---

10 United Nations Office on Drugs and Crime (UNODC) (2011): Smuggling of Migrants by Sea, at: http://www.unodc.org/documents/human-trafficking/Migrant-Smuggling/Issue-Papers/Issue_Paper_-_Smuggling_of_Migrants_by_Sea.pdf, (accessed August 25, 2015), p. 29.

grants and refugees alike for being identified with that state and deported to it. Flag state protection thus helps the "tourists" (Bauman 1997: 83-93), who do not – by their very movement – contest the authority over the legitimate means of movement. Hence, grounding the legality of maritime interception on the statelessness of the migrants' vessel allows one to overlook the possible need of protection of its passengers. A stateless vessel is argued to be legitimately intercepted on the high seas, and be taken or pushed back to its place of embarkation. The principle of non-refoulement can effectively be circumvented by prioritizing the boat as object of legal reasoning. This legal narrative avoids the elephant in the boat.

Being on board "such a vessel" therefore entails risking (Bauman 1997) and asking for international protection. As a legal figure, the vehicle shows similarities with Agamben's (1998 [1995]) *homo sacer*: the seizure and even destruction of the vessel can occur exempt from punishment as it does not violate the rights of a foreign state or private owner. The migrants' vessel doesn't form part of the international order of (flag) state affiliation. Consequently, Herman Meyers argues that the statelessness can be understood as "allocationlessness" (Meyers 1967: 309), as no rights or duties are attached to a vessel without flag. Moreover, its perceived condition reduces it to a piece of material that barely floats. It is not treated as territory and thus, the vessel's deck does not provide its occupants with rights. The migrants' vessels are a *bare thing*, which according to "generally end up at the bottom of the sea and were never intended for use in more than one journey."[11] Effectively, the hybrid "migrants' vessel" or "refugee boat" is vested with a double statelessness – its passengers are not infrequently traveling without papers on a stateless vessel. For this hybrid, access to rights is (at the very least) protracted and set at an angle. The competences of law enforcement authorities over the vessel, by contrast, are ample and declared straightforward. It has been stressed that the passengers of a stateless vessel are not automatically stateless and that the absence of nationality of the vessel should not affect the nationality of the individuals on board (Meyers 1967: 309; Papastavridis 2009: 163). However, with state practices and their legal reasoning resorting first and foremost to the vehicle, and plainly omit the human cargo, the vulnerability of the migrants on board is augmented. Enforcement jurisdiction over the vessel *in rem* allows for one to nullify the principle of non-refoulement applicable to passengers in search for international protection.

---

11 United Nations Office on Drugs and Crime (UNODC) (2011): Smuggling of Migrants by Sea, p. 29.

9.2.2 The Vessel in Distress

A vessel without nationality legally justifies the hunter's engagement in border enforcement. A vessel in distress alarms allies to assist or rescue passengers from a capsizing vessel. Interviewees in this study have mentioned that interception operations can easily turn into search and rescue operations.[12] This is an apt description when looking at patrol activities in the Mediterranean. Since many vessels used by migrants and refugees to cross the Mediterranean travel in substandard condition and are overcrowded, distress situations are common.[13] In 2009, the European Commission even conceded that "[m]ost of the maritime operations coordinated by Frontex turn into search and rescue operations."[14] When patrol vessels encounter boats or ships in distress, they are obliged – just like all other ships or coastal states – to "go to the aid of ships in distress regardless of where they are" (Brouwer/Kumin 2003: 14).

---

12 Similarly, Thomas Gammeltoft-Hansen quotes a Spanish navel captain who in 2007 saw that the encounter "may provoke capsizing, either deliberately as migrants seek to provoke a rescue operation, or involuntarily if the weight of those on board the often overcrowded ships shifts too much to one side" (quoted in Gammeltoft-Hansen 2011: 141). The researcher thereof concludes that "[i]n practice, interception operations may quickly change to a situation of search and rescue" (ibid). The reasons he advances are: first, the bad condition of many vessels and second, the difficult situation of encounter between intercepting and migrant vessels.

13 For instance, in 2011 UNHCR published a table with documented distress incidents at sea involving refugees and migrants for the period between January 1, 2011 and October 31, 2011. For the investigated period of nine months, UNHCR documented 39 incidents of distress at sea in different regions of the world. In 23 incidents the location of distress had been the Mediterranean Basin, which means that almost 60 per cent of the distress incidents were documented for the Mediterranean Basin which increases the probability of border patrols encountering or being called by a vessel in distress and thereby being obliged to rescue. Yet, in the case of the Mediterranean incidents, the circumstances of the distress situation remain mostly unelaborated.

14 European Commission: Proposal for a Council Decision supplementing the Schengen Borders Code as regards the surveillance of the sea external borders in the context of the operational cooperation coordinated by the European Agency for the Management of Operational Cooperation at the External Borders, November 27, 2009, COM (2009) 658 final: section 2 (Reasons and Objectives).

This obligation follows from Article 98 (1) of the LOS Convention, which mandates that every vessel, official and private, to "render assistance to any person found at sea in danger of being lost" and "to proceed with all possible speed to the rescue of persons in distress, if informed of their need of assistance."[15] Seline Trevisanut clarifies that although Article 98 "is located in the LOSC section on the high seas, the duty to render assistance applies in all maritime zones" (Trevisanut 2010: 526) as the duty "could not disappear just because of the crossing of a maritime frontier" (ibid: 527, fn. 8).

In fact, the international search and rescue regime operates beyond the principle of territory, which typically structures international relations and agreements. It imposes duties on all coastal and seafaring states independent of the maritime zone and encourages them to coordinate their search and rescue services (Gammeltoft-Hansen 2011: 141). Unlike in the case of territories, search and rescue (SAR) zones can also overlap, as is the case of the Maltese and the Italian SAR zones (Trevisanut 2010: 524).[16]

While enforcement measures are restricted to a defined territorial area, humanitarian duties such as rescue operations request universal application and thus exceptions to territorial references in law enforcement measures. While the specific geographical location is central for ascertaining the competences and duties of law enforcement vessels vis-à-vis a vessel in question and its passengers, the humanitarian operation of rescue at sea enables and even requires interference, regardless of geocodes or juridical-administrative references. Therefore, border enforcement activities effectively depart from their designated operational purpose and domain by responding to a distress call. To a certain extent, distress situations rescind the spatial restrictions to law enforcement competences. A distress situation both obliges and authorizes its witnesses. However, they only do so temporarily and for the purpose of the respective rescue operation.

---

15 In 2014 the EU has taken a similar formulation into: Regulation (EU) No 656/2014 of the European Parliament and of the European Council of May 15, 2014: establishing rules for the surveillance of the external sea borders in the context of operational cooperation coordinated by the European Agency for the Management of Operational Cooperation at the External Borders of the Member States of the European Union: Preamble (14).

16 "Malta has unilaterally declared this zone and has not negotiated its delimitation with neighboring States. As a result, the extension of the Maltese SAR zone is equivalent to 750 times its territory" (Trevisanut 2010: 524) Moreover, its extension coincides with the Maltese Flight Information Region (Klepp 2011: 341).

Distress situations at sea trigger the legal framework of the 1974 International Convention on the Safety of Life at Sea (SOLAS)[17] and the 1979 International Convention on Maritime Search and Rescue (SAR Convention)[18], both of which fall under the Law of the Sea Convention (LOSC). The SAR Convention defines the actual distress phase as a "situation wherein there is reasonable certainty that a person, a vessel or other craft is threatened by grave and imminent danger and requires immediate assistance."[19]

Practitioners' statements that interception operations can easily turn into search and rescue operations suggest that while patrolling, border guards would not only detect vessels but assess whether the vessel in question was in a situation where "immediate assistance" was required. Their assessment of the situation would thus change subsequent proceedings with the vessel and its passengers. If the vessel is not found to be in a distress situation, interference with the vessel occurs in the framework of border enforcement measures. The lack of a flag or the suspicion of smuggling migrants (cf. below) would legitimize the exercise of jurisdiction over the vessel (and its passengers).

Without distress, focus is on the rights and the security of states and thus the competences of law enforcement agencies vis-à-vis migrant vessels. In case of distress, emphasis shifts to the safety of migrants and refugees on board. If the vessel is found to be in distress, a rescue obligation according to the LOSC and SAR Convention would be triggered. The translation from hunter to friend thus partly depends on the assessment of the hunter himself. At the same time, the humanitarian character of rescue often conflicts with migration control objectives that underpin border enforcement measures (Miltner 2006: 82).

A common definition of distress shared by EU member states seems particularly important for joint operation contexts. Yet, while some member states consider all migrants' vessels to be in distress due to their bad condition, overcrowding, or the lack of a professional navigator, others argue that migrants are not in distress

---

[17] International Convention for the Safety of Life at Sea (SOLAS) (adopted November 1, 1974, in force May 25, 1980); in: United Nations (ed., 1980): Treaty Series 1184/18961: 278-453.

[18] International Convention on Maritime Search and Rescue (SAR Convention) (adopted April 27, 1979, in force June 22, 1985), in: United Nations (ed., 1985): Treaty Series 1405/23489: 118-256.

[19] SAR Convention, Annex, Chapter 1 (1.3.11).

until their vessels actually start sinking.[20] These diverging interpretations of the SAR provisions result in conflicting operational practices between national border enforcement units. Even the European Commission criticized in 2009 that "these rules are not interpreted or applied uniformly by the Member States."[21] It even noted that "the fact that the operations become search and rescue operations removes them from the Frontex coordination and Community law."[22] In addition to these differences in operational practice, the legal basis for intervention and subsequent obligations change based on the fact there is a "vessel in distress."

According to the SAR Convention, "rescue" is defined as an "operation to retrieve persons in distress, provide for their initial medical or other needs, and deliver them to a place of safety."[23] Rescue fends off the loss of lives at sea. As with other emergency operations, it prevents something worse from happening in a life-threatening situation. The description evokes a relatively straightforward yet temporary operation: rescue persons from danger at sea and take them to a place of safety in which the "grave and imminent danger" no longer exists. Yet, "the relatively straightforward issue of the disembarkation and subsequent return to their country of origin of sailors rescued at sea" (Gammeltoft-Hansen 2011: 142) has become twisted with the presence of unauthorized migrants and refugees on board vessels.

The change stems first and foremost from the disembarkation duty and the controversies about what constitutes a place of safety. In 2004, the IMO adopted amendments to the SAR and SOLAS Convention.[24] These were intended to con-

---

20 Among legal analysts this is not a clear-cut issue, either: Violeta Moreno-Lax (2011: 22-23) argued in 2011 that unseaworthiness entails distress. Coppens (2012: 345) summarizes that for "some EU member states, the vessel must be on the point of sinking while, for others, it is sufficient for the vessel to be unseaworthy. Some member states require a request for assistance from the people on board while others do not."

21 European Commission (2009): Proposal for a Council Decision supplementing the Schengen Borders Code as regards the surveillance of the sea external borders in the context of the operational cooperation coordinated by the European Agency for the Management of Operational Cooperation at the External Borders, November 27, 2009, COM(2009) 658 final , Section 2 (Reasons and objectives).

22 Ibid.

23 SAR Convention, Annex, Chapter 1 (1.3.2).

24 Both amendments were adopted by the International Maritime Organization (IMO), and entered into force on July 1, 2006. See Maritime Safety Committee, 78/26/Add. 1

trol inconveniences for rescuing ships or captains and was supposed to clarify what constitutes a place of safety. The amendments stipulate that the state responsible for the SAR zone should also ensure, as soon as possible, a safe haven (place of safety) for the disembarkation of rescued persons.

Effectively, the crux of disembarkation resides in the state's responsibility for those being rescued. Disembarkation not only terminates the actual rescue phase,[25] it is also measured by the safety of the rescuees; a place of safety "is also a place where the survivors' safety of life is no longer threatened."[26] Further obligations open up for the rescuing state with regard to unauthorized migrants – the same migrants the state had otherwise wanted to prevent from illegally crossing the border. When applied to refugees and asylum seekers, safety bears different meanings than when applied to shipwrecked persons in general. In the case of refugees, safety entails the right to seek asylum, which complicates the notion of a place of safety. The life-threatening situation of a fugitive isn't resolved when the distress situation is terminated – it's the reason for his or her being *en route* in the first place. In principle, if refugees are on board, their safety is only achieved when "effective protection" is provided (cf. Legomsky 2005).

In order to not be burdened with that obligation, state practices have extended to rescuing or assisting boats in foreign SAR zones and to disembarking migrant passengers in their place of embarkation. Rescue transforms the operation from being a humanitarian obligation to an instant mandate. This provides a basis for interference where border patrols have no enforcement jurisdiction. Rescue is repurposed and submitted to the objectives of border policies.

Different experts of international refugee law argue that the rights of migrants and refugees on board these vessels cannot be circumvented by declaring border enforcement as a series of rescue operations. And yet this is what actually happens. The distress situation of the vessel provides a legitimizing narrative for circumventing the principle of non-refoulement. The principle of refoulement

---

Annex 3 and 5 respectively. "The purpose of these amendments and the current guidance is to help ensure that persons in distress are assisted, while minimizing the inconvenience to assisting ships and ensuring the continued integrity of SAR services" (Rah 2009: 120-121).

25 "A place of safety is a location where rescue operations are considered to terminate" (SAR Convention).

26 "and where their basic human needs (such as food, shelter and medical needs) can be met" (Maritime Safety Committee; IMO (2004): Guidelines on the Treatment of Persons rescued at Sea, Resolution MSC.167(78), adopted on May 20, 2004), para. 6.12.

becomes part of operations when distress is the basis of intervention. Distress also empowers immediate assistance to a vessel or other craft and tow or escort it back to a place of safety, often the shores of the country of embarkation, while ignoring the fact that on board the vessel are passengers with mixed legal statuses (Coppens 2013: 2). Hence, when disguised as assistance, even operations of hindrance can find a legitimizing narrative. Violeta Moreno-Lax sees a *mala fide* implementation of maritime law by EU member states and a "direct breach" of their protection obligations vis-à-vis asylum seekers (Moreno-Lax 2011: 26). However, this doesn't occur in an alleged grey zone, but rather via the fact that legal border policing is stretched out by a humanitarian mandate to conduct sea rescues. It is, in fact, the reference to the vessel (in distress) that appears as mobilizing and empowering.

Mare Nostrum and the Legitimizing Narrative of Saving Lives at Sea

Italy's large-scale rescue operation *Mare Nostrum* launched 15 days after the Lampedusa shipwreck of October 3, 2013 has fostered this argumentative construct. *Mare Nostrum* lasted for a little more than a year, from October 18, 2013 to October 31, 2014. Before the operation was launched, defense minister Mario Mauro explained the operation's intention:

"the ships would be escorted to the nearest safe port, in compliance with international law. If there aren't any migrants in need of medical assistance [...] and if the ship is able to sail, it "will be taken to the safest and nearest port, not necessarily Italian." (quoted in ANSAmed (N.N.) 2013)

These procedures, however, were not what made the news. Even though a careful reading reveals that Mauro's announcement invited a worsening of the vessels' condition, the most important operational difference to conventional maritime border control was the official extension of the operational area to 70.000 square miles of sea – three times the region of Sicily.

Most importantly, in terms of equipment and personnel, operation *Mare Nostrum* spoke rescue. According to the Italian Defense Ministry, Italy deployed five Italian navy ships "either patrollers or corvettes – with wide range and medical care capabilities," One amphibious Landing Platform Dock (LPD) vessel with "specific command and control features, medical and shelter facilities for the would-be migrants."[27] Additionally, three aircrafts, one equipped with Forward Looking Infrared (FLIR), up to nine helicopters "to be readily deployed to Lampedusa or Catania," and two unmanned aerial vehicles (UAVs) of the type Camcopter S-100 surveilled the sea from above. The coastal radar network and the Italian AIS (Automatic Identification System) are shore stations that routinely support operations and have been used during *Mare Nostrum* as well. Furthermore, submarines have been deployed to investigate the smuggling business and other criminal activities. *Mare Nostrum* operated on a monthly budget of 9 million euros and was supported with 900 officers – 300 per shift. In total, 150,810 migrants were rescued during the operation.[28]

The fact that a large number of seaborne migrants could potentially find space on board an Italian navy ship was a novel idea. With assets acknowledging the need for rescue capacity, *Mare Nostrum* was prepared to function as a search and rescue operation – it expected to take on board those spotted at sea. However, the approach attracted criticism from other European member states. Opponents considered *Mare Nostrum* a pull factor as "the migrants in the boats and their smugglers could be fairly certain that they would be rescued by one of Mare Nostrum's ships" (*IRIN News* (N.N.) 2015a). The British Foreign Office minister Baroness Anelay, for instance, argued that the operation "only encouraged more people to make the treacherous journey" (quoted in ibid) Overall, the discussion about *Mare Nostrum* challenged and even reversed established arguments and practices of maritime border enforcement:

- Since the early days of Schengen, opponents of restrictive EU border policies used to argue that EU policies provoked, increased and perpetuated the smuggling business; it's now the opponents of a humanitarian rescue operation who argue that a humanitarian approach would fuel the smuggling business.
- Furthermore, the acceptance of where border enforcement should legitimately occur changed: When the Frontex operation Triton was launched to

---

27 Ministero della Difesa (2014): Operation *Mare Nostrum*, at: http://www.marina.difesa.it/EN/operations/Pagine/MareNostrum.aspx (accessed November 17, 2014).

28 The cited information on *Mare Nostrum* has been summarized in August 2015 according to the website of the Italian Ministry of Defense. Additional information, some of which differs from the Ministry's account have been provided by (Andres 2014: 28), and in quite a comprehensive graphic of *The Guardian* (Kirchgaessner/Traynor/Kingsley 2015).

replace *Mare Nostrum*, NGOs and the critics of EU border policies argued in a way unthinkable before. They requested that *Triton* be provided with more equipment and an extended operational area. European coastal services should expand their activities during the *Mare Nostrum* operation. So, those who before vehemently claimed that Frontex had nothing to search for in foreign waters or even on the high seas now support, in addition to an expansion of the mandate, Frontex's presence beyond territorial waters.

- Since *Mare Nostrum*, the occurrences at sea no longer happen out of sight. A variety of private individuals and non-governmental organizations, such as SOS Méditerranée and Sea Watch, interfere with border surveillance and border enforcement in the Mediterranean. As a result, not only is the information monopoly on the part of border enforcement agencies broken, news of rescue *ships* – rather than boats – with migrants on board is also increasingly reaching public attention. This intensifies the focus on the image of the small refugee boat and thus the marginalization and depoliticization of the people on board.

Going back to the legitimizing construct of the vessel in distress, on the whole it appears that, on the one hand, the purpose of migration control has become impossible thanks to vessels in distress. On the other hand, vessels in distress empower intervention by providing a mandate to do so. Accordingly, the rights of states and ships are no longer bound to maritime legal zones but are subordinated to distress. The vessel in distress thus mobilizes law enforcement competences. In a distress situation, the goal of patrol vessels transforms from immigration and border control to salvage. This mediation (translation) fits the law enforcement vessel with a mobilization of its operational area, that is, a situational geographical extension of the (legal) possibility to intervene.

According to Latour, translation refers to the "the creation of a link that did not exist before and that to some degree modifies two elements or agents" (Latour 1994: 2). In this case, the migrants' vessel translates the law enforcement vessel into a rescue vessel – the hunter into a friend. Even though seaborne migrants deploy the vessel as a technology of movement, their vehicle (as a thing) also becomes integrated into EU border policy reasoning providing the (situational) mandate to intervene.

9.2.3 The Suspicious Vessel

Considering the merging of interception and rescue operations, it can be stated that an enforcement vessel operates as a dual service vessel with a paradox objective. When this dual service vessel identifies or encounters an unseaworthy vessel, flagless under reasonable suspicion of smuggling migrants, this third argument ultimately legitimizes the latter's interception. In fact, with the entry into force of the Migrant Smuggling Protocol, maritime interception on the high seas or in foreign waters was rendered "a legitimate tool" for border control and enforcement (Miltner 2006: 105), as reasonable grounds to suspect that a vessel is engaged in smuggling already provide for the search, boarding and seizure of persons and cargo of such a vessel.[29] Instead of focusing on the act of illegal immigration as such, this third legal reasoning focusses on its facilitation. The hunter is not chasing migrants, but smugglers.

In fact, the Protocol against Smuggling of Migrants by Land, Sea and Air states as its purpose to "prevent and combat the smuggling of migrants, as well as to promote cooperation among State Parties to that end, while protecting the rights of smuggled migrants."[30] Thereby, the Migrant Smuggling Protocol intends a remarkable balancing act: while the *facilitation* of illegal border crossing is declared a crime in international law, the criminal liability of the facilitated migrants is explicitly excluded from the Protocol, with the migrant being declared an "object of [such] conduct,"[31] namely of smuggling.[32] Smuggling refers to the mere physical movement, the transportation of persons across international borders "on a payment-for-service basis" (Mallia 2010: 10). The service ends with the arrival of migrants at a destination (ibid: 11).

---

29 Protocol Against the Smuggling of Migrants by Land, Sea and Air, supplementing the United Nations Convention Against Transnational Organized Crime, Report of the Ad Hoc Committee on the Elaboration of a Convention against Transnational Organized Crime on the work of its first to eleventh sessions, U.N. Doc. A/55/383 (2000), Annex III, [hereafter cited as Migrant Smuggling Protocol], Art. 8, p. 5-6.
30 Migrant Smuggling Protocol, Art. 2, p. 2.
31 Ibid, Art. 5, p. 3.
32 "Smuggling" is defined in Art. 3(a) of the Migrant Smuggling Protocol as "the procurement, in order to obtain, directly or indirectly, a financial or other material benefit, of the illegal entry of a person into a State Party of which the person is not a national or a permanent resident,"

Effectively, border surveillance and enforcement practices pursue facilitation networks by tackling their vehicular indicator as the final link of the facilitation chain: the vessel boarded by migrants who travel without authorization by the state of destination. Even though the offense "is constituted by the act of the illegal crossing of an international border" (Mallia 2010: 11), it is the profit that is made out of its facilitation which gives way to a criminalization of the conduct of smuggling. However, as Papastavridis stresses "the act of carrying migrants [...] is not an international crime as such; the only conduct that is criminalized is the 'smuggling of migrants' and solely for the States parties to the respective Protocol" (Papastavridis 2009: 163).[33] Yet again, if the facilitation networks were non-commercial, the unauthorized migrants would still be tackled by border enforcement, yet the point of intervention could only be the territorial border, or in the case of seaborne migration, in the contiguous zone or the territorial waters. Interception *en route* would principally not be legitimate.

Nonetheless, with the entry into force of the Migrant Smuggling Protocol, maritime interception on the high seas or in foreign waters could be justified by reference to the (potential) crime of smuggling (Miltner 2006: 105). This legal frame criminalizes the commercialized facilitation and tackles the facilitator. However, the legalistic frame allows for systematically neglecting empirical knowledge about this type of migration. Although the inmates in this narrative are victims, their rights can be circumvented by preventing smuggling, understood as the transport in boats for money.

The suspicious fact in this scenario is the boat, particularly when seen to be overcrowded. However, when captured by satellite imagery, small boats are already suspicious even before someone has entered them. Thereby, border management is equipped with a different operating logic. The generation of suspicion no longer occurs during patrol activities, but in the mode of "proactive" border enforcement. While the stateless vessel and the humanitarian ground refer to a concrete, individual situation, smuggling tackles structures, a business, and a type of migration. Hence, this activity occurs prior to situations in which vessels are intercepted or rescued. Surveillance and the suspicion of smuggling legitimize to have a look in the first place. The vessel remains the moment of condensed suspicion, its tracking, tracing, monitoring, and identification is part of border surveillance activities. In fact, as I have elaborated in chapter 3, the Euro-

---

33 Even though Papastavridis refers to the high seas, his claim that the transport of migrants is not a crime as such also holds for land and air routes.

pean Border Surveillance System, EUROSUR tackles vessels rather than migrants.

The small, overcrowded and unseaworthy boat is regarded as a condensed suspicious fact by European border authorities, and mobilizes both control and rescue measures. The reference to something "suspicious," "strange," "abnormal" or "unidentified" traveling toward the Schengen area is regarded as a legitimate factor for further monitoring and eventual interception. As vehicle of migration, the refugee boat impacts upon, if not determines, the agency and the legal status of the persons it carried. The double statelessness of vessel and refugee allows for a patronizing treatment of the refugee-boat hybrid, which oscillates between pity and encroachment.

9.3 THE REFUGEE BOAT: VIRTUALLY (AT) THE BORDER

Tracing the construction of an external border to the EU from the perspective of the refugee boat has allowed us to explore the tones, connotations and fantasies, as well as the institutional and legal reasoning, along which the refugee boat has turned into a moving target for EU border policies. As such, the refugee boat hybrid acts as an integrating figure in the construction of a supranational EU border. Itself the only landmark at sea, a *mobile in mobili*, it mobilizes repressive state practices *and* humanitarian intervention alike, the hunter and the helper.

Exploring the international response to the earliest case of the Vietnamese "boat-people," it could be shown that the term had been introduced by political actors with the evasive intention not to discuss and decide the refugee status of the persons on board. At the same time, the situation on board the vessel was taken both as indication for the facilitation business and, in certain dramatic cases, it was in turn used as evidence for the humanitarian refugee status to apply. This kind of oscillating reference could also be demonstrated in the context of Europe-bound flight and migration since the beginning of the Schengen Process. It could be demonstrated that all three attributes: small, overcrowded and unseaworthy, share the impetus that this maritime journey is not meant to occur. At the same time, the vessel as stateless, in distress and suspicious provides the legitimizing narrative for interception or operations of hindrance at sea. In this manner, the vessel not only facilitates a subversive trip or option of last resort, but contributes significantly to the mobilization and justification of EU border enforcement measures.

The analysis of EUROSUR already allowed to trace this mobilization and mandating of EU border enforcement measures. However, while EUROSUR virtually indicates where reaction capability is needed, the vessel counts as a valid reason for interception. Serhat Karakayli and Enrica Rigo argue that the "ever vessel suspected of transporting 'illegal' migrants is considered *a virtual border* when its nationality is unknown or uncertain." (Karakayli/Rigo 2010: 124, emphasis added). They see the virtual maritime border as "one example […] of externalization of the European Union's frontiers" (ibid). In fact, it is not one of its examples. It is its driving force. The concept of the virtual border mobilizes both a more flexible approach to the geography of border controls and an expansion of the competencies of border police.

Overall, analyzing the refugee boat as mediator, it turns out that these vessels not only facilitate unauthorized maritime journeys; they are not only utilized as technologies of movement and mobility, but are also a moving target as well, a vacillating reference and integrating figure of EU bordering. The vessel facilitates, juxtaposes and negotiates the migrants' access to Europe, while also mobilizing and legitimizing the control of its access – that is, the practices of border surveillance and control. In this way, the vessel thereby mediates EU bordering.

The migrant vessel's mediation can be summarized by the following aspects:
- *Europe's other: valuating the other by their means of movement.* The hybrid of the refugee boat mediates Europe's *other* as a versatile figure. This versatility does not consist in the fact that the vessel moves on water, nor does it refer to the mixed flow of people on board. The vehicle and the attributes attached to it in the European public view, which is to say, as small, overcrowded and unseaworthy, allow for flexible valuations of the phenomenon and the people on board. It could be demonstrated that all three attributes applied to the vessel share the impetus that this maritime journey is not meant to occur. While the gaze of pity and risk is applied to the migrants, the vehicle arouses suspicion and allows for de-individualization and depoliticization of the persons on board who appear as a boatload of people.
- *Mobilization and legitimization of enforcement measurements.* With regard to EU enforcement of maritime borders, a prioritizing of the vessel in legal reasoning could be traced. This allowed for enforcement measures which otherwise would have been impossible to justify. In the territorial logic, border enforcement at sea can only legitimately occur in the territorial waters or the contiguous zone of a coastal state. By reference to the migrants' vessel as "stateless," "in distress" or "suspicious," interception and opera-

tions of hindrance found their legal construct. The legitimate reason for interceptions is found in the vessel itself, in fact, more in its condition as unseaworthy and overcrowded than in its position or purpose. Although it subverts border surveillance and control, the migrant vessel paradoxically triggers the emergence of common EU measures of border enforcement.

10 The Emergence of Viapolitics

The stated objective of this study has been to examine the formation of an external EU border since the 1985 Schengen Agreement. Starting from a characterization of the Schengen Process and reviewing how this political process has influenced the methodological and epistemological premises of border studies, it could be shown that most analyses of Europe's border(s) reflect upon the new border *as* something: *as* social practices of control, *as* subversion and movement, *as* institutional integration, *as* exception, or *as* the network-centric organization of security personnel in Europe. These analyses discuss Europe's borders in terms of Schengen's variable geometry, in terms of institutional Europeanization, in terms of its rules on paper and its contestations on the ground.

Building upon these assessments, this study has, however, taken a different methodological stance. Rather than examining the EU border *as something*, it analyzes the construction of an external EU border *via* two of its empirical construction sites: EUROSUR and the refugee boat. Gauging the formation of an external EU border by examining two of its mediators, this study offers a detailed analysis of the drawing together and networking of a border that remains under permanent construction. The two site inspections do not tell the story of a specific site, but trace and analyze the qualitative imprint EUROSUR and the refugee boat have had (and continue to have) on the external EU border.

The Latourian concept of mediation has been central to the research process and analysis. In fact, *Mediated Bordering* – the title of this book – both implies a methodological conviction and points to the most important empirical observations of this study.

The methodological conviction is rooted in the spectral character of any border. If a border *as such* does not exist or appear geographically, institutionally, or materially, if it is only available in proxies, we have to study these proxies, construction sites, and mediators in order to trace and understand how this "thing" or "network" that is socially effective in the form of a political border is programmed.

This methodological argument entails a twofold statement concerning (a) the direction of analysis and (b) the notion of praxeography. The preposition *via* – used and highlighted above – indicates both: with regard to the direction of analysis, the research object is studied *via* its proxies or mediators, similar to a train going to Berlin *via* Frankfurt, and similar to receiving information *via* satellite or *via* email. The preposition *via* contains both the notion of a point of passage and that of a medium – in the sense of a facilitator, means, gateway, corridor, route, carrier, or channel. The directionality that the preposition suggests is important for this methodology, which explores the kind and quality of the EU's external border (the site of effect) *via* an inquiry into the sites of intervention: EUROSUR and the refugee boat. For "what circulates when everything is in place cannot be confused with the set-ups that make circulation possible" (Latour 2013: 32). Secondly, *via* alludes to a praxeographic notion that does not focus on individual practices or situations but on relations, processes of stabilization, and the empirical process of mediation itself. This post-foundational methodology has been vindicated, as it has proved to reveal the kind and quality of an emerging EU external border without becoming trapped by questions about the where (*ground*) and what (*substance*) of political borders. Instead, it bases its findings on the many reasons and mediators *via* which the border is constructed, stabilized, experienceable, and researchable.

Analyzing the EU's external border *via* the development process of EUROSUR revealed quite a peculiar process of co-production. The IT application and the EU regulation – EUROSUR on the screen and EUROSUR on paper – have been developed in parallel, co-producing each other and providing for both a new spatial truth claim (supranational border work follows migratory pressures) and a legitimacy claim (a regulation to justify the border policing mandate in those terms and a mandate to intervene at calculated hotspots).

Conducting research on the EU's external border *via* the refugee boat has shed light on various (legal and symbolic) constructs used to legitimize interventions at sea and to evaluate migratory endeavors without the legal reference of a common European immigration and asylum law. Focusing on the refugee boat made it possible to trace how boat migration provided the oscillating reference that could be flexibly used to reject migrants, intervene in a range of maritime spaces, question the status of refugees, and argue nationally while mobilizing supranational resources to control the means of movement.

The analyses of both EUROSUR and the refugee boat have pointed to considerable ambivalences in EU border policies between which the two sites oscillate. More than an effect of EU border policies and operational practices, this oscillation appears to be its paramount characteristic. It is itself durable and institutionalized. The following ambivalences are thus systemic and reappear in different disguises, while bordering is mediated between them.

First, there is the ambivalence between the transcendence of borders, on the one hand, and the proliferation of control practices, on the other. The functioning logic of EUROSUR mediates between these two ambivalences by concentrating the full floodlights of surveillance on the issue of "migratory routes" and migratory pressure" while keeping Europe's map free from internal borders.

Second, the ideal imperative of the Schengen Agreement – liberty through freedom of movement – came with the promise of cooperative, and thus enhanced, security. The security promise, however, has been unfolded as a powerful parasitical twin imperative. As a consequence, the interests of internal security take precedence over the project of European integration and are considered a precondition of the latter.

The third ambivalence arises from the fact that, legally speaking, there is no common European external border. According to the Schengen Agreement, a member state that shares a border with a non-EU state has a duty to strengthen the security of its national frontier. The double-encoding of these borders as both national and European creates a tension, as does the lack of a common European immigration and asylum policy. There are some significant national differences: While unauthorized, illegal immigration is a criminal offence in one member state, in others it is treated as merely an administrative offence. The refugee boat in distress at sea calls out for the integration of all these differences; it constantly demands a European answer. EUROSUR collects, visualizes and offers the material to this very answer: it tracks and visualizes volume, frequency, routes and other data concerning "border-related events"; thereby allowing Frontex to provide member states with a European view on tasks and challenges at the common border. As an agency and as a coordinator, Frontex has no mandate to deal with individual persons at external borders nor does it have a mandate to interfere with any immigration or asylum procedures; Frontex and EUROSUR thus tackle routes, boats and other vehicles, or offer its services for the "logistics" of return flights. We thus witness viapolitics when Frontex gains competences while legal harmonization or political consensus among member states are declared to be stagnating.

Fourth, the reference to territory with regard to the border-policing mandate and the application of rights is itself ambivalent. A great deal of flexibility is used to take advantage of this incongruity between rights and territory. It is not only border control that is affected, but also the administration of migration and asylum – access to spaces of rights thus also appears stratified. While territorial frontiers once determined territorial sovereignty and therefore territorial competences, this has now definitively been superseded by cross-border cooperation on internal security, which constructs extra-territorial areas – transit zones, reception centers, the high seas as a pre-frontier area – while also defining operational areas using risk analysis. While the sovereign power to decide about access is mobilized and to a certain extent deterritorialized, access to individual rights is tight to someone entering national territory or national databases on arrival.

At sea, and this is the fifth ambivalence I want to highlight, European border management switches flexibly between monitoring and repelling migrants, on the one hand, and carrying out rescue missions, on the other. The helper can only arrive when the hunter has failed, as in the Lampedusa incident of October 2013 that I described in the introduction.

EU border policies are thus not ambivalent but flexibly and strategically oscillate between these ambivalences. Bordering, as it occurs, mediates these ambivalences. This allows for the integration of what is meant to be kept separate: the transcendence of borders and the proliferation of their surveillance and control; an increase in freedom of movement *and* security, national competences and supranational power, state sovereignty and refugee rights, the ambitions of friend and enemy, hunter and helper.

The findings and results of this study (summarized above and in chapters 6 and 9.3) support a proposition first advanced by William Walters (2011, 2014, 2015): the notion of viapolitics. They may even enable the further development of his theses and arguments. To theorize viapolitics, Walters calls us to pay attention to the symbolic, the political and the material dimension of vehicles in the context of migration policies and public discourse on migration and border control. He argues that viapolitics "orients us to see migration from the middle, that is, from the angle of the vehicle and not just the state" (Walters 2014: 1). More than a conceptual proposition or theory, Walters notion of viapolitics calls for us to pay attention to particular objects of inquiry, and thus for a certain methodological sensibility. Such is the title of the lecture when he first introduced the notion of viapolitics "Where are the missing vehicles?". The lecture's title took up the Latourian impetus to integrate material artefacts into the study of phenomena and applied it to the study of migration and migration policies.

The claim of symmetrical anthropology, namely that we must come home from the tropics and apply an equal level of curiosity to "the whole shebang" at home (Latour 1993: 101), and that in pursuing this course, we need to pay as much attention to artefacts as to humans and to acknowledge them as actants (Callon/Latour 1994) and quasi-objects (Serres 2007: 224–234), is, in fact, already present in the public imagination of migration: Not only is there a clearly stated agency when aircrafts fly, ships sail, and boats carry migrants; vehicles also overdetermine the identity of their animate and inanimate goods and those who transport them. In the case of migration however, the question is not whether the vessel or the captain sails, whether the car or the driver drives, whether the pilot, the passengers, or the aircraft flies, i.e. which actant or hybrid is moving or migrating. In the case of migration, animated goods *already appear entangled* and move as a strangely indivisible hybrid. Balibar's hints about the "empirico-transcendental question of *luggage*" (Balibar 2002a: 91, emphasis in original; cf. chap. 2.2.1) point to this reconfigured agency that differentiates between carrier and carried, between technology of movement and the passively mobile cargo. From a viapolitical angle, the carrier, the technology of movement the infrastructures are kept under control in order to indirectly govern movement.

The example of the visual and verbal image of the overcrowded and unseaworthy migrant vessel (cf. chap. 5.1.4) provides the proof of his claim: the legal status of the passengers of a refugee boat or migrant vessel is not infrequently deduced from and determined by the vessel. The vehicle-body entanglement, this hybrid of boat person and refugee boat, functions as a deliberately non-committal yet all-pervasive point of reference in political rhetoric. Visually integrated with their means of transport and the "masses" on board, migrant passengers are deindividualized and depoliticized. The image evokes legal and moral classifications: the irrationality of the journey, the illegality of its passengers, and renders the vehicle a legitimate object of intervention. From the perspective of the European spectators, this image mediates both the possibility of intercepting the vessel and thereby expanding the legal borders of policing, while at the same time disconnecting the vessel's passengers from the legal border of individual rights. The mode of viapolitics becomes apparent as an indirect constellation which systematically condones the "the elephant in the boat", i.e. the individuals on board.

The example of the boat people and the refugee boat allow us to see the classificatory process that the imagined explanation and evaluation trigger, even to the extent that the vessel provides a substitute classificatory identity when no nationality can be advanced or documented. The point of acknowledging vehicles as mediators of migration is to underline that they not only transport people but also distort and transform their identity and status. Walters notes that migrants are not only "specified [...] by institutional and legal categories but in their bodily existence by their forms of transportation. The boat people. The wet backs. The stowaway. The hobo. In all these cases an encounter with travel follows you around" (Walters 2011: 5). Yet, the moment the decision for a means of transport has been taken, or must be taken in a certain way, velocity, frequency, route, and experience, four of the six facets of mobility Tim Crewell (2010: 22-26) puts forward, are largely determined.[1] Consequently, for those on the move viapolitics have asymmetrical effects, as this mode of politics governs populations without addressing the individual.

Just as "nationality is an ascribed status that *cannot be established without reference to documents*" (Torpey 1998: 256, original emphasis), mobility is a mediated capability that is established by differentiated means of movement – vehicular, technological, administrative. Torpey already warned that "people have to some extent become prisoners of their identities, which may sharply limit their opportunities to cross jurisdictional spaces" (ibid). When nationality and identity are neither available nor helpful, as can be the case in unauthorized migration or flight, classifications are made by reference to the means of movement. In this set-up, the way you move replaces the need for political localization. The vehicle carries a person and replaces her or his passport.

What renders this constellation of mediated mobilities distinct is that it will not be found in passports or ID cards nor in biometrics, all of which play an essential role in the operationalization of border control. It is rather in the realm of capabilities, that movements are regulated. As a result, vehicles, transportation, logistics as means of movement not only characterize the kind of migration and determine the condition of the journey. They also essentially determine the path to rights and the possibility of avail oneself of them.

When juxtaposing Walter's proposition with Torpey's argument, it is not the passport or ID card that may be necessary to gain access to rights and democratic participation (ibid: 239–243, 255–257). In viapolitics, it is the kind of vehicle that determines access to a certain corridor of rights and of privileges. To put it another way: if Walter's claim holds true, vehicles would unfold a similar effect on refugees and migrants as passports, ID cards, and biometric information. Going by the description that the state holds a monopoly over the legitimate means of movement, as it has stripped "individuals and private entities" of their legitimate means of movement (ibid: 239), it can be hypothesized that the access to rights and/or privileges can be regulated by means of traffic and transportation policies. In this sense, the question of who regulates and authorizes the means of

---

1   Creswell identifies "six facets of mobility, each with a politics: the starting point [motivational force], speed, rhythm, routing, experience, and friction" (Creswell 2010: 26).

movement probes the operationalization of political borders, and it does so without needing the concept of the territorial state.

In consequence, *can we take the concept of viapolitics beyond the methodological gaze, orientation, or sensibility* that it bestows to the study of migration and border policies? Are there viapolitics in a globalizing world? And, if so, what relation to political borders would this mode of politics sustain? In order to explore this mode, I shall delineate it from notions of territorial politics and of biopolitics. Having researched the practices and policies of EU bordering, I argue that these three modes of politics – territorial politics, biopolitics, and viapolitics – generally come into effect in the operationalization of borders, and in a range of constellations.

Conventionally, borders are associated with territorial politics. Viapolitics differ from territorial politics in so far as they do not project power onto a delineated space but rather onto infrastructural means of movement (gateways, corridors, routes) and mobile means of movement (vehicles, other carriers or technologies of movement). This entails that viapolitics do not operate along an inside-outside distinction. A notion more apt to describe viapolitics is the on-and-off binary, alluding to notions of – online/offline or off the road/on the road or *en route*. Moreover, viapolitics do not know territory, nor do they discuss belonging: Viapolitics identify routes, corridors, and gateways to rights, obligations, and markets. While territorial politics are based on the "notion of camp as a safe place where no enemy could infiltrate because the borders of a specific space are under control" (Bigo 2006: 90), viapolitics are not afraid of the enemy entering a territory, but of him entering an airplane.

Logistics is the ideal-typical set-up of viapolitics, and it appears that viapolitics project their ambitions onto seamless movement or its interdiction (cf. particularly Cowen 2014: 76–88) – it is just that things get a little more complicated when the cargo is animated.

In contrast to biopolitics, viapolitics do not target individuals but their means of movement or the technical systems that enable movement. Superimposed upon the delineation of a territory is the definition of criteria that authorize coming and going. The attribution of deviance can thus impose a border on a person. While, from a territorial perspective, borders mark the range of jurisdiction in congruence to terrestrial expanses, the biopolitical angle captures the sites of selection. We are in the mode of biopolitics when populations are not only regulated at the border, but when the site of the border is "regarded as a privileged institutional site where political authorities can acquire biopolitical knowledge about populations and their movements, health, and wealth" (Walters 2002: 572–573). From the angle of biopolitics, bordering authorities protect the physical body of an individual and the political body of a nation by embracing the body and shielding it form attacks and risks.

In the mode of viapolitics, by contrast, the deindividualized person is addressed by means of traffic rules (Waitz 2014: 96; Augé 2008: 113, 121). This fits in with the way EUROSUR maps the external EU border. An important finding of this study is that the digital displaying the European Situational Picture (ESP) differs fundamentally from an analogous map of EU territory (chapters 4 and 6). It does not represent a spatial geography but detects, tracks, and identifies targets of intervention. The fact that border-related information is classified and visualized by icons which, in their design and idea, are based on traffic signs, might only be an illustration. Nonetheless, it does support the notion of politics that are designed to prevent individual negotiations.

While in territorial politics and biopolitics the notion of states penetrating or embracing society aptly describes the logic of state power (Torpey 1998: 244-245), viapolitics unfold its ambitions by spying, tracking, and analyzing data on movements and their facilitations (Tazzioli 2018; Broeders/Dijstelbloem 2016; Mountz/ Kempin 2014; Amoore 2009, 2011). Likewise, EUROSUR does not target migrants, nor does it search for refugees at sea. As a form of invisible profiling, it does not need to embrace subjects – which the state does in the biopolitical mode – it rather targets suspicious constellations by analyzing "surveillance information" or, as the jargon puts, it "pre-frontier intelligence". EUROSUR thus talks the language of viapolitics.

Going by these proposed descriptions of viapolitics, it can be concluded that the external EU border is strongly governed in the mode of viapolitics – a mode characterized by a projection of power onto the infrastructures and means of movement (and not onto the people that move), a mode determined by a surveillance gaze that tracks and archives (Tazzioli 2018) and which is thus depersonalized and depoliticized. A power oscillating between authoritarian power and humanitarian care, in the sense of being on or off. Ultimately, the Schengen Process can be considered both an expression of as well as a trigger and catalyst to the emergence of viapolitics.

Bibliography

Aas, Katja Franko (2011): "'Crimmigrant' bodies and bona fide travelers: Surveillance, citizenship and global governance," in: Theoretical Criminology 15, pp. 331-346. https://doi.org/10.1177/1362480610396643

Aden, Hartmut (2014): "Koordination und Koordinationsprobleme im ambivalenten Nebeneinander: Der polizeiliche Informationsaustausch im EU-Mehrebenensystem," in: dms – der moderne staat – Zeitschrift für Public Policy, Recht und Management 7, pp. 55-73. https://doi.org/10.3224/dms.v7i1.16236

Agamben, Giorgio (1998): Homo Sacer: Sovereign power and bare life, Stanford: Stanford University Press.

Agamben, Giorgio (2000): Means without End: Notes on politics, Minneapolis: University of Minnesota Press.

Agamben, Giorgio (2005): State of Exception, Chicago: University of Chicago Press.

Agnew, John (1994): "The Territorial Trap: The Geographical Assumptions of International Relations Theory," in: Review of International Political Economy 1, pp. 53-80. https://doi.org/10.1080/09692299408434268

Agnew, John (2008): "Borders on the mind: re-framing border thinking," in: Ethics & Global Politics 1, pp. 175-191. https://doi.org/10.3402/egp.v1i4.1892

Alliès, Paul (1980): L'invention du territoire, Grenoble: Presses Universitaires de Grenoble.

Amoore, L. (2011): "Data Derivatives: On the Emergence of a Security Risk Calculus for Our Times," in: Theory, Culture & Society 28, pp. 24-43. https://doi.org/10.1177/0263276411417430

Amoore, Louise (2009): "Lines of Sight: on the visualization of unknown futures," in: Citizenship Studies 13, pp. 17-30. https://doi.org/10.1080/13621020802586628

Andersson, Ruben (2010): "Wild Man at Europe's Gates: The Crafting of Clandestines in Spain's Cayuco Crisis," in: Etnofloor 22, pp. 31-49.

Andersson, Ruben (2016): "Hardwiring the frontier? The politics of security technology in Europes 'fight against illegal migration'," in: Security Dialogue 47, pp. 22-39. https://doi.org/10.1177/0967010615606044

Andres, Jacqueline (2014): "Mare Nostrum: humanitäre Operation oder Deckmantel militarisierter Migrationspolitik?," in: Ausdruck 1, pp. 28-29.

ANSAmed (N.N.) (2013): "Immigration: Italy launches Mare Nostrum, 400 more saved," October 15, at: http://www.ansamed.info/ansamed/en/news/sections/generalnews/2013/10/15/Immigration-Italy-launches-Mare-Nostrum-400-saved_9466386.html (accessed February 2, 2017).

Anzaldúa, Gloria (1987): Borderlands. The new mestiza = La Frontera, San Francisco: Spinsters/Aunt Lute.

Aradau, Claudia (2004): "The Perverse Politics of Four-Letter Words: Risk and Pity in the Securitization of Human Trafficking," in: Millennium - Journal of International Studies 33, pp. 251-277. https://doi.org/10.1177/03058298040330020101

Aradau, Claudia/Lobo-Guerrero, Luis/van Munster, Rens (2008): "Security, Technologies of Risk, and the Political. Guest Editors' Introduction," in: Security Dialogue 39, pp. 147-154. https://doi.org/10.1177/0967010608089159

Associated Press (N.N.) (2013): "Witness: Boat migrants used bottles to stay afloat," October 4, at: https://eu.usatoday.com/story/news/world/2013/10/04/witness-boat-migrants-used-bottles-to-stay-afloat/2922215/ (accessed October 15, 2019).

Augé, Marc (2008): Non-places. An Introduction to Supermodernity, London and New York: Verso.

Bach, Maurizio (2010): "Die Konstitution von Räumen und Grenzbildung in Europa. Von verhandlungsresistenten zu verhandlungsabhängigen Grenzen," in: Monika Eigmüller/Steffen Mau (eds.), Gesellschaftstheorie und Europapolitik. Sozialwissenschaftliche Ansätze Zur Europaforschung, Wiesbaden: VS Verlag für Sozialwissenschaften, pp. 153-178. https://doi.org/10.1007/978-3-531-92008-5_8

Bade, Klaus J. (2000): Europa in Bewegung. Migration vom späten 18. Jahrhundert bis zur Gegenwart, München: Beck.

Balibar, Etienne (1998): "The Borders of Europe." In: Robbins Cheah (ed.), Cosmopolitics: Thinking and Feeling Beyond the Nation, Minneapolis: University of Minnesota Press, pp. 216-229.

Balibar, Etienne (2002a): Politics and the Other Scene, London: Verso.

Balibar, Etienne (2002b): "World borders, political borders," in: PMLA 117, pp. 71-78. https://doi.org/10.1632/003081202X63519
Balibar, Etienne (2004): Europe as Borderland. The Alexander von Humboldt Lecture in Human Geography, Nijmegen.
Balibar, Étienne (2009): "Europe as borderland," in: Environment and Planning D: Society and Space 27, pp. 190-215. https://doi.org/10.1068/d13008
Balzacq, Thierry (2005): "The Three Faces of Securitization: Political Agency, Audience and Context," in: European Journal of International Relations 11, pp. 171-201. https://doi.org/10.1177/1354066105052960
Balzacq, Thierry/Guzzini, Stefano/Williams, Michael C./Wæver, Ole/Patomaki, Heikki (2015): "What kind of theory – if any – is securitization?," in: International Relations 29, pp. 96-136. https://doi.org/10.1177/0047117814526606
Balzacq, Thierry/Hadfield, Amelia (2012): "Differentiation and trust: Prüm and the institutional design of EU internal security," in: Cooperation and Conflict 47, pp. 539-561. https://doi.org/10.1177/0010836712462781
Balzacq, Thierry (2008): "The Policy Tools of Securitization: Information Exchange, EU Foreign and Interior Policies," in: JCMS: Journal of Common Market Studies 46, pp. 75-100. https://doi.org/10.1111/j.1468-5965.2007.00768.x
Basaran, Tugba (2011): Security, law and borders: At the limits of liberties, London: Routledge. https://doi.org/10.4324/9780203841921
Bauer, Wolfgang (2014): "Das Drama der Flüchtlinge." In: *Die Zeit - Zeit Magazin*, pp. 12-23.
Bauman, Zygmunt (1997): Postmodernity and its discontents, Cambridge: Polity Press.
Baumann, Mechthild (2006): Der deutsche Fingerabdruck. Die Rolle der deutschen Bundesregierung bei der Europäisierung der Grenzpolitik, Baden-Baden: Nomos.
Baumann, Mechthild (2008): "Der Einfluss des Bundeskanzleramts und des Bundesministeriums des Innern auf die Entwicklung einer europäischen Grenzpolitik," in: Uwe Hunger/Can M. Aybek/Andreas Ette/Ines Michalowski (eds.), Migrations- und Integrationsprozesse in Europa, Wiesbaden: VS Verlag für Sozialwissenschaften, pp. 17-33. https://doi.org/10.1007/978-3-531-91168-7_2
Beck, Ulrich/Grande, Edgar (2007): Cosmopolitan Europe, Cambridge: Polity.

Bellanova, Rocco/Duez, Denis (2016): "The Making (Sense) of EUROSUR: How to Control the Sea Borders," in: Raphael Bossong/Helena Carrapiço (eds.), EU borders and shifting internal security. Technology, externalization and accountability, Cham: Springer, pp. 23-44. https://doi.org/10.1007/978-3-319-17560-7_2

Benedikt, Clemens (2004): Diskursive Konstruktion Europas. Migration und Entwicklungspolitik im Prozess der Europäisierung, Frankfurt am Main: Brandes & Apsel.

Ben-Yehoyada, Naor (2011): "The Clandestine Central Mediterranean Passage," in: Middle East Report, pp. 18-23.

Berger, Alois (2013): "Eurosur - Dein Feind und Helfer," Deutsche Welle, October 10, at: http://dw.com/p/19xf5 (accessed October 1, 2015).

Bigo (1994): "The European Internal Security Field: Stakes and Rivalries in a Newly Developing Area of Police Intervention," in: Malcolm Anderson/Monica den Boer (eds.), Policing across national boundaries, London: Pinter Publishers, pp. 161-173.

Bigo, Didier (1996): Polices en réseaux. L'éxpérience européenne, Paris: Presses de la Fondation nationale des sciences politiques.

Bigo, Didier (2000): "When two become one: Internal and external securitisations in Europe," in: Morten Kelstrup/Michael C. Williams (eds.), International relations theory and the politics of European integration. Power, security, and community, London: Routledge, pp. 171-204. https://doi.org/10.4324/9780203187807-8

Bigo, Didier (2002): "Security and Immigration: Toward a Critique of the Governmentality of Unease," in: Alternatives: Global, Local, Political 27, pp. 63-92. https://doi.org/10.1177/03043754020270S105

Bigo, Didier (2006): "Protection: security, territory and population," in: Jef Huysmans/Andrew Dobson/Raia Prokhovnik (eds.), The politics of protection. Sites of insecurity and political agency, New York: Routledge, pp. 84-100.

Bigo, Didier (2014): "The (in)securitization practices of the three universes of EU border control: Military/Navy – border guards/police – database analysts," in: Security Dialogue 45, pp. 209-225. https://doi.org/10.1177/0967010614530459

Bischoff, Christine/Kafehsy, Sylvia/Falk, Francesca (eds.) (2010): Images of Illegalized Immigration: Towards a Critical Iconology of Politics, Bielefeld: transcript. https://doi.org/10.14361/transcript.9783839415375

Blumenberg, Hans (1997): Schiffbruch mit Zuschauer. Paradigma einer Daseinsmetapher, Frankfurt am Main: Suhrkamp.

Boer, Monica den/Corrado, Laura (1999): "For the Record or Off the Record: Comments About the Incorporation of Schengen into the EU," in: European Journal of Migration and Law 1, pp. 397-418. https://doi.org/10.1163/157181 69920958685

Bös, Mathias (1997): Migration als Problem offener Gesellschaften. Globalisierung und sozialer Wandel in Westeuropa und Nordamerika, Opladen: Leske and Budrich.

Boswell, Christina (2005): Migration in Europe. A paper prepared for the Policy Analysis and Research Programme of the Global Commission on International Migration (GCIM), at: https://pdfs.semanticscholar.org/a443/31ac8507 66c64699e604b72482b4875bf22f.pdf (accessed October 15, 2019).

Bourbeau, Philippe (2011): The Securitization of Migration: A study of Movement and Order, New York: Routledge. https://doi.org/10.4324/97802038 29349

Bowker, Geoffrey C./Star, Susan L. (2000): Sorting things out. Classification and its consequences, Cambridge: MIT Press.

Branch, Jordan (2011): "Mapping the Sovereign State: Technology, Authority, and Systemic Change," in: International Organization 65, pp. 1-36. https://doi.org/10.1017/S0020818310000299

Braun, Michael (2013): "Über 100 Flüchtlinge ertrunken," In: *Die Tageszeitung* October 3, at: http://www.taz.de/!5057919/ (accessed June 4, 2015).

Brian, Tara/Laczko, Frank (2014a): "Counting Migrant Deaths: An International Overview," in: idem (eds.), Fatal Journeys, pp. 15-43.

Brian, Tara/Brian, Tara/Laczko, Frank (2014b): Fatal Journeys: Tracking Lives Lost during Migration, Geneva: International Organization for Migration (IOM), at: http://publications.iom.int/bookstore/free/FatalJourneys_CountingtheUncoun ted.pdf (accessed October 19, 2019).

Broeders, Dennis/Dijstelbloem, Huub (2016): "The Datafication of Mobility and Migration Management: The Mediating State and Its Consequences," in: Irma van der Ploeg/Jason Pridmore (eds.), Digitizing Identities: Doing identity in a networked world, New York: Routledge, pp. 242-260. https://doi.org/ 10.4324/9781315756400-13

Brothers, Caroline (2007a): "Immigrants open new path to Europe," in: *The New York Times*, February 15, at: http://www.nytimes.com/2007/02/15/world/ asia/15iht-immigrants.4608811.html (accessed August 28, 2015).

Brothers, Caroline (2007b): "South Asians Taking Risky Route to Europe: Via Africa," in: *The New York Times*, February 19, at: http://www.nytimes.com/ 2007/02/19/world/europe/19migrants.html (accessed August 28, 2015).

Brouwer, Andrew/Kumin, Judith (2003): "Interception and Asylum: When Migration Control and Human Rights Collide," in: Revue canadienne sur les réfugiés 21, pp. 6-24.

Brouwer, Evelien R. (2008): Digital borders and real rights: Effective remedies for third-country nationals in the Schengen Information System, Leiden: Martinus Nijhoff Publishers. https://doi.org/10.1163/ej.9789004165038.i-568.22

Bruycker, Philippe de/Di Bartolomeo, Anna/Fargues, Philippe (2013): Migrants smuggled by sea to the EU: facts, laws and policy options. Migration Policy Center Research Report 2013/0, at: http://www.migrationpolicycentre.eu/docs/MPC-RR-2013-009.pdf (accessed October 19, 2019).

Buchen, Stefan (2015): "Flüchtlingsschiff: Wie Frontex die Wahrheit verdreht," in: *Panorama*, at: http://daserste.ndr.de/panorama/archiv/2015/Fuehrungsloses-Fluechtlingsschiff-Wie-Frontex-die-Wahrheit-verdreht-,schleuser164.html (accessed February 2, 2017).

Buckel, Sonja (2013): "Welcome to Europe," Die Grenzen des europäischen Migrationsrechts. Juridische Auseinandersetzungen um das "Staatsprojekt Europa," Bielefeld: transcript. https://doi.org/10.14361/transcript.9783839424865

Bunyan, Tony (2006): "The 'principle of availability'," in: Statewatch Analysis, at: http://www.statewatch.org/analyses/no-59-p-of-a-art.pdf (accessed October 19, 2019).

Burgess, J. Peter (2009): "The New Nomos of Europe," in: Geopolitics 14, pp. 135-160. https://doi.org/10.1080/14650040802578690

Buzan, Barry/Waever, Ole/Wilde, Jaap de (1998): Security: A new framework for analysis, Boulder: Lynne Rienner.

Calavita, Kitty (1994): "Italy and the New Immigration," in: Wayne A. Cornelius/Philip L. Martin/James F. Hollifield (eds.), Controlling Immigration. A global perspective, Stanford: Stanford University Press, pp. 303-329.

Callon, Michel/Latour, Bruno (1994): "Don't Throw the Baby Out with the Bath School! A Reply to Collins and Yearle," in: Andrew Pickering (ed.), Science as Practice and Culture, Chicago: University of Chicago Press, pp. 343-368.

Cameron, Angus (2011): "Ground Zero – the semiotics of the boundary line," in: Social Semiotics 21, pp. 417-434. https://doi.org/10.1080/10350330.2011.564391

Campesi, Giuseppe (2018): "European Border and Coast Guard (Frontex): Security, Democracy, and Rights at the EU Border," in: Oxford Research Encyclopedia of Criminology and Criminal Justice, pp. 1-32. https://doi.org/10.1093/acrefore/9780190264079.013.354

Caparini, Marina (ed.) (2006): Borders and Security Governance: Managing borders in a globalized world, Wien, Zürich: LIT.

Carling, Jørgen (2007a): "Migration Control and Migrant Fatalities at the Spanish-African Borders," in: International Migration Review 41, pp. 316-343. https://doi.org/10.1111/j.1747-7379.2007.00070.x

Carling, Jørgen (2007b): "Unauthorized Migration from Africa to Spain," in: International Migration 45, pp. 3-37. https://doi.org/10.1111/j.1468-2435.2007.00418.x

Carrera, Sergio/den Hertog, Leonhard (2016): "A European Border and Coast Guard: What's in a name?," CEPS Paper in Liberty and Security No 88, Brussels: Centre for European Policy Studies.

Carrera, Sergio (2008): "The EU border management strategy: FRONTEX and the challenges of irregular immigration in the Canary Islands," in: CEPS Working Document No. 261 of March 22, 2007, Brussels: Centre for European Policy Studies. https://doi.org/10.2139/ssrn.1338019

Castells, Manuel (2008): The Rise of the Network Society, Malden: Blackwell. https://doi.org/10.1002/9781444319514

Celikates, Robin (2010): "Die Demokratisierung der Demokratie. Etienne Balibar und die Dialektik von konstituierender und konstituierter Macht," in: Ulrich Bröckling (ed.), Das Politische denken. Zeitgenössische Positionen, Bielefeld: transcript, pp. 59-76. https://doi.org/10.14361/9783839411605-003

Certeau, Michel de (2013 [1984]): The Practice of Everyday Life, Berkeley: University of California Press.

Ceyhan, Ayse/Tsoukala, Anastassia (2002): "The Securitization of Migration in Western Societies: Ambivalent Discourses and Policies," in: Alternatives: Global, Local, Political 27, pp. 21-39. https://doi.org/10.1177/03043754020270S103

Chapman, Gary (2004): "Shaping Technology for the 'Good Life': The Technological Imperative versus the Social Imperative," in: Douglas Schuler/Peter Day (eds.), Shaping the network society: The new role of civil society in cyberspace, Cambridge: MIT Press, pp. 43-56.

Chimni, Bhupinder S. (1998): "The Geopolitics of Refugee Studies: A View from the South," in: Journal of Refugee Studies 11, pp. 350-374. https://doi.org/10.1093/jrs/11.4.350

Clochard, Olivier/Dupeyron, Bruno (2007): "The Maritime Borders of Europe: Upstream Migratory Controls." In: Emmanuel Brunet-Jailly (ed.), Borderlands. Comparing border security in North America and Europe, Ottawa: University of Ottawa Press, pp. 19-40. https://doi.org/10.2307/j.ctt1ckpchh.6

Coppens, Jasmine (2012): "Migrants in the Mediterranean. Do's and Don'ts in Maritime Interdiction," in: Ocean Development & International Law 43, pp. 342-370. https://doi.org/10.1080/00908320.2012.726834

Coppens, Jasmine (2013): "The essential role of Malta in drafting the new regional agreement on migrants at sea in the Mediterranean basin," in: Journal of Maritime Law and Commerce 44, pp. 1-22.

Cornelius, Wayne A. (1994): "Spain: The Uneasy Transition from Labor Exporter to Labor Importer," in: Wayne A. Cornelius/Philip L. Martin/James F. Hollifield (eds.), Controlling Immigration. A global perspective, Stanford: Stanford University Press, pp. 331-369.

Cowen, Deborah (2014): The Deadly Life of Logistics. Mapping Violence in Global Trade, Minneapolis and London: University of Minnesota Press. https://doi.org/10.5749/minnesota/9780816680870.001.0001

Cremers, Ehrhardt (1989): Grenze und Horizont. Protosoziologische Reflexionen zu einer Phänomenologie und Soziologie sozialer Grenzen. Hagen: Dissertation Fernuniversität Hagen.

Cuttitta, Paolo (2006): "Points and Lines: A Topography of Borders in the Global Space," in: Ephemera: theory and politics in organizations 6, pp. 27-39.

Cuttitta, Paolo (2007): "Le monde-frontière: Le contrôle de l'immigration dans l'espace globalisé," Cultures & Conflict 68, pp. 61-84. https://doi.org/10.4000/conflits.5593

Darling, Jonathan (2009): "Becoming Bare Life: Asylum, Hospitality, and the Politics of Encampment," in: Environment and Planning D: Society and Space 27, pp. 649-665. https://doi.org/10.1068/d10307

Davies, Lizzy (2013): "Italy boat wreck: scores of migrants die as boat sinks off Lampedusa," in: *The Guardian*, October 3, at: http://www.theguardian.com/world/2013/oct/03/lampedusa-migrants-killed-boat-sinks-italy (accessed June 4, 2015).

Davies, Sara E. (2008): Legitimising Rejection. International Refugee Law in Southeast Asia, Leiden: Martinus Nijhoff Publishers.

Deleuze, Gilles/Guattari, Félix (2013): A Thousand Plateaus: Capitalism and Schizophrenia, London: Bloomsbury Academic.

den Boer, Monica (2011): "Technology-led Policing in the European Union: An Assessment," in: Eveline de Pauw/Paul Ponsaers/Kees van der Vijver et al. (eds.), Technological-led policing, Antwerp: Maklu, pp. 41-57.

Denninger, Erhard (2008): "Prävention und Freiheit. Von der Ordnung der Freiheit," in: Stefan Huster/Karsten Rudolph/Huster-Rudolph (eds.), Vom Rechtsstaat zum Präventionsstaat, Frankfurt am Main: Suhrkamp, pp. 85-106. https://doi.org/10.5771/9783845207773

Derrida, Jacques (2006): Specters of Marx: The state of the debt, the work of mourning and the New International, New York: Routledge.

Dion, Mark (ed.) (2003): Mark Dion - Encyclomania; [anlässlich der Ausstellung Mark Dion - Encyclomania in der Villa Merkel, Galerien der Stadt Esslingen, dem Bonner Kunstverein und dem Kunstverein Hannover], Nürnberg: Verlag für Moderne Kunst.

Duff, Andrew (1997): The Treaty of Amsterdam: Text and Commentary, London: Federal Trust.

Ehrensvärd, Ulla (1987): "Color in Cartography: A Historical Survey," in: David Woodward (ed.), Art and cartography. Six historical essays, Chicago: University of Chicago Press, pp. 123-146.

Elden, Stuart (2010a): "Land, terrain, territory," in: Progress in Human Geography 34, pp. 799-817. https://doi.org/10.1177/0309132510362603

Elden, Stuart (2010b): "Thinking Territory Historically," in: Geopolitics 15, pp. 757-761. https://doi.org/10.1080/14650041003717517

Elden, Stuart (2011): "Territory without Borders," essay presented as part of symposia at the Harvard International Review, at: http://hir.harvard.edu/archives/2843 (accessed September 29, 2015).

Ellebrecht, Sabrina (2014a): "The European Border Surveillance System EUROSUR: The Computerization, Standardization, and Virtualization of Border Management in Europe," in: OSCE Yearbook. Yearbook on the Organization for Security and Co-operation in Europe (OSCE), Baden-Baden: Nomos, pp. 231-243. https://doi.org/10.5771/9783845252698_231

Ellebrecht, Sabrina (2014b): "Verdacht auf See: Zwischen Befugnissen und Signalen," in: Kriminologisches Journal 46, pp. 168-183.

Engert-Schüler, Heidi (1979): Völkerrechtliche Fragen des Eigentums an Wracks auf dem Hohen Meer, Frankfurt am Main: Metzner.

Ericson, Richard V./Haggerty, Kevin D. (1997): Policing the risk society, Oxford: Clarendon Press.

Eriksson, Aleksandra (2016): "MEPs fast-track EU border guard plan," in: euobserver, May 31, at: https://euobserver.com/migration/133629 (accessed February 3, 2017).

Evans-Pritchard, Ambrose/Helm, Toby (2000): "EU plans border force to curb crime and migrants," in: *The Telegraph*, October 12, at: http://www.telegraph.co.uk/news/worldnews/europe/poland/1370046/EU-plans-border-force-to-curb-crime-and-migrants.html (accessed February 3, 2017).

Falk, Francesca (2010): "Invasion, Infection, Invisibility: An Iconology of Illegalized Immigration," in: Christine Bischoff/Sylvia Kafehsy/Francesca Falk (eds.) (2010): Images of Il-legalized Immigration: Towards a Critical Iconology of Politics, Bielefeld: transcript., pp. 83-99.

Falk, Francesca (2011): Eine gestische Geschichte der Grenze. Wie der Liberalismus an der Grenze an seine Grenzen kommt, Paderborn: Wilhelm Fink. https://doi.org/10.30965/9783846752029

Fargues, Philippe/Bonfanti, Sara (2014): "When the best option is a leaky boat: why migrants risk their lives crossing the Mediterranean and what Europe is doing about it," Migration Policy Centre Policy Brief 2014/05, at: http://cadmus.eui.eu/handle/1814/33271 (accessed September 29, 2015).

Febvre, Lucien (1988): "'Frontière' Wort und Bedeutung," in: Lucien Febvre/Ulrich Raulff (eds.), Das Gewissen des Historikers, Berlin: Wagenbach, pp. 27-37.

Fekete, Liz (2003): "Death at the border. Who is to blame?" Institute for Race Relations, Comment, at: http://www.irr.org.uk/news/death-at-the-border-who-is-to-blame/ (accessed April 4, 2015).

Fischer-Lescano, Andreas/Lohr, Tillmann/Tohidipur, Timo (2009): "Border Controls at Sea: Requirements under International Human Rights and Refugee Law," in: International Journal of Refugee Law 21, pp. 256-296. https://doi.org/10.1093/ijrl/eep008

Foucault, Michel (1986 [1967]): "Of Other Spaces," in: Diacritics 16, pp. 22-27. https://doi.org/10.2307/464648

Frances D'emilio (2015): "New Tactic: Smugglers Put Ships on Autopilot," in: *Associated Press*, January 2, at: http://www.dailystar.com.lb/News/World/2015/Jan-03/282945-new-tactic-smugglers-put-ships-on-autopilot.ashx (accessed February 2, 2017).

Fyfe, Gordon/Law, John (eds.) (1988): Picturing Power: Visual depiction and social relations, London: Routledge.

Gadow-Stephani, Inken von (2006): Der Zugang zu Nothäfen und sonstigen Notliegeplätzen für Schiffe in Seenot, Berlin: Springer. https://doi.org/10.1007/3-540-30519-X

Gammeltoft-Hansen, Thomas (2011): Access to asylum: International refugee law and the globalization of migration control, Cambridge: Cambridge University Press.

Gavouneli, Maria (2006): "From Uniformity to Fragmentation? The ability of the UN Convention on the Law of the Sea to accommodate new uses and challenges," in: Anastasia Stratē/Maria Gavouneli/Nikolaos Skourtos (eds.), Unresolved issues and new challenges to the law of the sea: Time before and time after, Leiden: Martinus Nijhoff Publishers, pp. 205-233. https://doi.org/10.1163/ej.9789004151918.i-356.70

Geisthövel, Alexa (2005): "Das Auto," in: Alexa Geisthövel/Habbo Knoch (eds.), Orte der Moderne. Erfahrungswelten des 19. und 20. Jahrhunderts, Frankfurt am Main: Campus, pp. 37-46.

Genova, Nicholas de (2013): "Spectacles of migrant 'illegality': the scene of exclusion, the obscene of inclusion," in: Ethnic and Racial Studies 36, pp. 1180-1198. https://doi.org/10.1080/01419870.2013.783710

Gilroy, Paul (2000): The black Atlantic. Modernity and double consciousness, Cambridge, MA: Harvard University Press.

Grant, Bruce (1979): The Boat People: An 'age' investigation with Bruce Grant, New York: Penguin.

Grotius, Hugo (2001 [1609]): The freedom of the seas, or, The right which belongs to the Dutch to take part in the East Indian trade, Cark: The Lawbook Exchange.

Guild, Elspeth (2001): Moving the Borders of Europe.

Guiraudon, Virginie (2003): "The constitution of a European immigration policy domain. A political sociology approach," in: Journal of European Public Policy 10, pp. 263-282. https://doi.org/10.1080/1350176032000059035

Haas, Hein de (2006): "Trans-Saharan Migration to North Africa and the EU: Historical Routes and Current Trends," in: Migration Information Source, the online Journal of the Migration Policy Institute (MPI), at: http://www.migrationpolicy.org/article/trans-saharan-migration-north-africa-and-eu-historical-roots-and-current-trends (accessed August 24, 2015).

Haas, Hein de (2008): "The Myth of Invasion: the inconvenient realities of African migration to Europe," in: Third World Quarterly 29, pp. 1305-1322. https://doi.org/10.1080/01436590802386435

Häsler, Alfred A. (2008 [1967]): Das Boot ist voll. Die Schweiz und die Flüchtlinge 1933-1945, Zürich: Diogenes.

Hayes, Ben (2003): "Cover-up! Proposed Regulation on European Border Guard hides unaccountable, operational bodies," in: Statewatch Analysis, at: http://www.statewatch.org/analyses/no-19-eu-border-police.pdf (accessed February 3, 2017).

Hayes, Ben (2005): "SIS II: fait accompli? Construction of EU's Big Brother database underway," in: Statewatch Analysis, at: http://www.statewatch.org/news/2005/may/sisII-analysis-may05.pdf (accessed April 18, 2016).

Hayes, Ben/Vermeulen, Mathias (2012): "Borderline. EU Border Surveillance Initiatives. An Assessment of the Costs and ITs Impact on Fundamental Rights," Berlin: Heinrich Böll Foundation, at: https://www.statewatch.org/news/2012/jun/borderline.pdf (accessed October 19, 2019).

Heckmann, Friedrich (1996): "Internationale Migrationsdynamik und Schengen," in: Friedrich Heckmann/Verónica Tomei (eds.), Freizügigkeit in Europa. Migrations- und europapolitische Aspekte des Schengen-Vertrages, Bonn: Europa-Union, pp. 11-18.

Hedetoft, Ulf (2003): The Global Turn: National encounters with the world, Aarhus: Aalborg University Press.

Hempel, Leon/Carius, Michael/Ilten, Carla (2009): "Exchange of information and data between law enforcement agencies within the European Union," Discussion Paper 29, Berlin: Zentrum Technik und Gesellschaft, at: http://www.ztg.tu-berlin.de/pdf/Nr_29_Hempel_Carius_Ilten.pdf (accessed October 19, 2019).

Hendow, Maegan (2013): "Tunisian Migrant Journeys: Human Rights Concerns for Tunisians Arriving by Sea," in: Laws 2, pp. 187-209. https://doi.org/10.3390/laws2030187

Herter, Gerwald (2010): "Das Europa der Bürger. Interview mit Robert Goebbels, Mitunterzeichner, über 25 Jahre Schengener Abkommen," in: Deutschlandfunk, June 14, at: http://www.deutschlandfunk.de/das-europa-der-buerger.694.de.html?dram:article_id=68648 (accessed October 19, 2019).

Hess, Sabine/Kasparek, Bernd (eds.) (2010): Grenzregime. Diskurse, Praktiken, Institutionen in Europa, Berlin: Assoziation A.

Hess, Sabine/Tsianos, Vassilis (2010): "Ethnographische Grenzregimeanalyse," in: Sabine Hess/Bernd Kasparek (eds.), Grenzregime. Diskurse, Praktiken, Institutionen in Europa, Berlin: Assoziation A, pp. 243-264.

Hobbing, Peter (2005): "Integrated border management at the EU level," CEPS Working Document 227, Brussels: Center for European Policy Studies, pp.1-26.

Hobbing, Peter (2006): "Management of External EU Borders: Enlargement and the European Border Guard Issue," in: Marina Caparini/Otwin Marenin (eds.), Borders and security governance: managing borders in a globalised word, Zürich: LIT, pp. 169-191.

Hobbing, Peter (2010): "The Management of the EU's External Borders: From the Customs Union to Frontex and E-Borders," in: Elspeth Guild (ed.), The Area of Freedom, Security and Justice ten years on. Successes and future challenges under the Stockholm Programme, Brussels: Centre for European Policy Studies, pp. 63-72.

Huysmans, Jef (2000): "The European Union and the Securitization of Migration," in: JCMS: Journal of Common Market Studies 38, pp. 751-777. https://doi.org/10.1111/1468-5965.00263

Huysmans, Jef (2008): The politics of insecurity. Fear, migration and asylum in the EU (The new international relations series), London: Routledge.

Inhetveen, Katharina (2010): "Der Flüchtling," in: Stefan Moebius/Markus Schroer (eds.), Diven, Hacker, Spekulanten. Sozialfiguren der Gegenwart, Berlin: Suhrkamp, pp. 148-160.

Jakob, Christian/Gottschlich, Jürgen/Braun, Michael (2015): "Fluchtwege aus Syrien: Die letzte Reise der "Blue Sky M"," in: *Die Tageszeitung*, January 7, at: http://www.taz.de/!5024601/ (accessed October 1, 2015).

Jandl, Michael (2004): "The Estimation of Illegal Migration in Europe," in: Studi Emigrazione/ Migration Studies 41, pp. 141-155.

Jeandesboz, Julien (2008): "Future development of the FRONTEX and the creation of Eurosur. Analysis of the Commission Communications," Briefing Paper, Brussels: European Parliament, at: http://www.europarl.europa.eu/Reg Data/etudes/note/join/2008/408295/IPOL-LIBE_NT(2008)408295_EN.pdf (accessed October 19, 2019).

Jeandesboz, Julien (2009): "Police Logics and Intelligence Lead Logics in a Risk Society," at: http://www.libertysecurity.org/article2489.html (accessed November 15, 2012).

Johnson, Corey/Jones, Reece/Paasi, Anssi et al. (2011): "Interventions on rethinking 'the border' in border studies," in: Political Geography 30, pp. 61-69. https://doi.org/10.1016/j.polgeo.2011.01.002

Johnson, Heather L. (2011): "Click to Donate: visual images, constructing victims and imagining the female refugee," in: Third World Quarterly 32, pp. 1015-1037. https://doi.org/10.1080/01436597.2011.586235

Jorry, Hélène (2007): "Construction of a European institutional model for managing operational cooperation at the EU's external borders. Is the FRONTEX Agency a decisive step forward?," CEPS Research Paper No 6, Brussels: Centre for European Policy Studies, at: https://www.ceps.eu/wp-content/ uploads/2009/08/1483.pdf (accessed October 19, 2019).

Karakayali, Serhat/Rigo, Enrica (2010): "Mapping the European Space of Circulation," in: Nicholas de Genova/Nathalie Peutz (eds.), The Deportation Regime: Sovereignty, space, and the freedom of movement, Durham: Duke University Press, pp. 123-144.

Kasparek, Bernd (2008): "Perfektion des Grenzregimes. Das Border Package der EU-Kommission," in: ak - analyse & kritik - Zeitung für linke Debatte und Praxis.

Kasparek, Bernd (2010): "Laboratorium, Think Tank, Doing Border: Die Europäische Grenzschutzagentur Frontex," in: Sabine Hess/Bernd Kasparek (eds.), Grenzregime. Diskurse, Praktiken, Institutionen in Europa, Berlin: Assoziation A, pp. 111-126.

Kaufmann, Stefan (2006): "Grenzregimes im Zeitalter globaler Netzwerke," in: Helmuth Berking/Ulrich Beck (eds.), Die Macht des Lokalen in einer Welt ohne Grenzen, Frankfurt am Main: Campus, pp. 32-65.

Kaufmann, Stefan (2007): "Einleitung. Netzwerk - Methode, Organisationsmuster, antiessenzialistisches Konzept, Metapher der Gegenwartsgesellschaft," in: *id.* (ed.), Vernetzte Steuerung. Soziale Prozesse im Zeitalter technischer Netzwerke, Zürich: Chronos, pp. 7-21.

Kaufmann, Stefan (2008): "Technik als Politik. Zur Transformation gegenwärtiger Grenzregimes der EU," in: Comparativ. Zeitschrift für Globalgeschichte und vergleichende Gesellschaftsforschung 18, pp. 42-57.

Kaufmann, Stefan/Bröckling, Ulrich/Horn, Eva (2002): "Einleitung," in: idem (eds.), Grenzverletzer. Von Schmugglern, Spionen und anderen subversiven Gestalten, Berlin: Kadmos, pp. 7-22.

Kaunert, Christian/Léonard, Sarah/Pawlak, Patryk (eds.) (2012): European homeland security. A European strategy in the making?, New York: Routledge. https://doi.org/10.4324/9780203122457

Kirchgaessner, Stephanie/Traynor, Ian/Kingsley, Patrick (2015): "Two more migrant boats issue distress calls in Mediterranean," in: *The Guardian*, April 20, at: https://www.theguardian.com/world/2015/apr/20/two-more-mediterra nean-migrant-boats-issue-distress-calls-as-eu-ministers-meet (accessed February 3, 2017).

Kiza, Ernesto (2008): Tödliche Grenzen - die fatalen Auswirkungen europäischer Zuwanderungspolitik. Eine theoretisch-empirische Untersuchung von Todesfällen illegalisierter Migranten im Kontext neuer Migrationsdynamiken und restriktiver Migrationspolitiken, Vienna: LIT.

Klepp, Silja (2011): Europa zwischen Grenzkontrolle und Flüchtlingsschutz. Eine Ethnographie der Seegrenze auf dem Mittelmeer, Bielefeld: transcript. https://doi.org/10.14361/transcript.9783839417225

Kreienbrink, Axel (2004): Einwanderungsland Spanien. Migrationspolitik zwischen Europäisierung und nationalen Interessen, Frankfurt am Main: IKO.

Kreis, Georg (2006): "Die Metapher des Rettungsboots: zum Wert historischer Argumentationen," in: Schweizerische Zeitschrift für Geschichte 56, pp. 338-348.

Kreis, Georg (2010): "The relativity of Borders: Assessing a Central EU Problem," in: David Tréfás/Jens Lucht (eds.), Europe on trial. Shortcomings of the EU with regard to democracy, public sphere, and identity, Innsbruck, Piscataway: Studienverlag, pp. 84-97.

Kreitling, Holger (2015): "Das Vorbild für die grauenhaften Geisterschiffe," in: *Die Welt*, February 12, at: http://www.welt.de/geschichte/article137358986/Das-Vorbild-fuer-die-grauenhaften-Geisterschiffe.html (accessed September 4, 2015).

Kumin, Judith (2014): "Policy Adrift: The challenge of mixed migration by sea," in: Susan F. Martin/Sanjula S. Weerasinghe/Abbie Taylor (eds.), Humanitarian crises and migration. Causes, consequences and responses, New York: Routledge, pp. 306-324. https://doi.org/10.4324/9780203797860-15

Kwon, Miwon (2002): One place after another. Site-specific art and locational identity, Cambridge: MIT Press. https://doi.org/10.7551/mitpress/5138.001.0001

Ladewig, Rebecca (2005): "Das Raumschiff," in: Alexa Geisthövel/Habbo Knoch (eds.), Orte der Moderne. Erfahrungswelten des 19. und 20. Jahrhunderts, Frankfurt am Main: Campus, pp. 57-67.

Last, Tamara/Spijkerboer, Thomas (2014): "Tracking Death in the Mediterranean," in: Brian/Laczko (eds.), Fatal Journeys, pp. 85-107.

Latour, Bruno (1986): "Visualization and Cognition. Thinking with Eyes and Hands," in: Henrika Kuklick/Elizabeth Long (eds.), Knowledge and Society. Studies in the Sociology of Culture Past and Present, Greenwich: JAI Press, pp. 1-40.

Latour, Bruno (1992): "Where are the missing masses? The sociology of a few mundane artifacts," in: Wiebe E. Bijker/John Law (eds.), Shaping technology/building society: Studies in socio-technical change, Cambridge: MIT Press, pp. 225-259.

Latour, Bruno (1993): We have never been modern, New York: Harvester Wheatsheaf.

Latour, Bruno (1994): "On Technical Mediation. Philosophy, Sociology, Genealogy," in: Common Knowledge 3, pp. 29-64.

Latour, Bruno (1999): Pandora's hope. Essays on the reality of science studies, Cambridge: Harvard University Press.

Latour, Bruno (2002 [1993]): Aramis, or the love of technology, Cambridge: Harvard University Press.

Latour, Bruno (2003): Science in action. How to follow scientists and engineers through society, Cambridge: Harvard University Press.

Latour, Bruno (2005): Reassembling the social. An introduction to actor-network-theory, Oxford: Oxford University Press.
Latour, Bruno (2013): An Inquiry into Modes of Existence. An Anthropology of the Moderns, Cambridge and London: Harvard University Press.
Latour, Bruno (2014): Making of Law. An Ethnography of the Conseil d'Etat, Cambridge: Polity Press.
Laube, Lena (2013): Grenzkontrollen jenseits nationaler Territorien. Die Praktiken liberaler Staaten zur Steuerung globaler Mobilität, Frankfurt am Main: Campus.
Leander, Anna (2005): "The Market for Force and Public Security: The Destabilizing Consequences of Private Military Companies," in: Journal of Peace Research 42, pp. 605-622. https://doi.org/10.1177/0022343305056237
Legomsky, Stephen H. (2005): "Secondary Refugee Movements and the return of Asylum Seekers to Third Countries: The Meaning of Effective Protection," in: International Journal of Refugee Law 15, pp. 567-677. https://doi.org/10.1093/ijrl/15.4.567
Lemberg-Pedersen, Martin (2013): "Private Security Companies and the European Borderscapes," in: Thomas Gammeltoft-Hansen/Ninna Nyberg Sorensen (eds.), The Migration Industry and the Commercialization of International Migration, Hoboken: Taylor and Francis, pp. 157-178.
Lemberg-Pedersen, Martin (2016): "Forcing Flows of Migrants: European Externalization and Border-induced Displacement," in: Martin Klatt/Marie Sandberg/Dorte J. Andersen (eds.), The Border Multiple. The Practicing of Borders between Public Policy and Everyday Life in a Re-scaling Europe, London: Taylor and Francis, pp. 35-54.
Leonard, Sarah (2009): "The Creation of FRONTEX and the Politics of Institutionalization in the EU External Borders Policy," in: Journal of Contemporary European Research 5, p. 371-388.
Luedemann, Susanne (2012): "'Zusammenhanglose Bevölkerungshaufen, aller inneren Gliederung bar.' Die Masse als das andere der Ordnung im Diskurs der Soziologie," in: Behemoth. A Journal on Civilization 7, pp. 103-117.
Lukács, Georg (1976 [1923]): History and Class Consciousness: Studies in Marxist dialectics, Cambridge: MIT Press.
Lutterbeck, Derek (2006): "Policing Migration in the Mediterranean," in: Mediterranean Politics 11, pp. 59-82. https://doi.org/10.1080/13629390500490411
Lutterbeck, Derek (2010): "Irregular Migration and Immigration Control in the Mediterranean," in: Ivan Ureta/Derek Lutterbeck (eds.), Migration, development, and diplomacy. Perspectives from the Southern Mediterranean, Trenton: Red Sea Press, pp. 127-145.

Makropoulos, Michael (1997): Modernität und Kontingenz, München: Wilhelm Fink.

Makropoulos, Michael (1998): "Modernität als Kontingenzkultur. Konturen eines Konzepts," in: Gerhart von Graevenitz/Odo Marquard/Matthias Christen (eds.), Kontingenz, München: Wilhelm Fink, pp. 55-79.

Mallia, Patricia (2010): Migrant smuggling by sea. Combating a current threat to maritime security through the creation of a cooperative framework, Leiden: Martinus Nijhoff Publishers.

Malpas, Jeff (2012): "Putting space in place: philosophical topography and relational geography," in: Environment and Planning D: Society and Space 30, pp. 226-242. https://doi.org/10.1068/d20810

Marchart, Oliver (2013): Das unmögliche Objekt. Eine postfundamentalistische Theorie der Gesellschaft, Berlin: Suhrkamp.

Marcus, George E./Saka, Erkan (2006): "Assemblage," in: Theory, Culture & Society 23, pp. 101-106. https://doi.org/10.1177/0263276406062573

Marx, Karl (1976 [1867]): Capital: A Critique of Political Economy (transl. Ben Fowkes), Harmondsworth: Penguin.

Mau, Steffen (2010): "Grenzen als Sortiermaschinen," in: Welttrends. Zeitschrift für Internationale Politik 18, pp. 57-66.

Mauss, Marcel (2016 [1925]): The Gift, Chicago: HAU Books.

McDougal, Myres S./Burke, William T. (1962): The Public Order of the Oceans: A contemporary international law of the sea, New Haven: New Haven Press.

McGee, Kyle (2014): Bruno Latour: The Normativity of Networks, Hoboken: Taylor and Francis.

Mehdi Lahlou, Insea (2006): "The Current State and Recent Trends in Migration between Maghreb States and the European Union," in: Nyberg Sørensen, Ninna (ed.) (2006): Mediterranean transit migration, Copenhagen: Danish Institute for International Studies, pp. 109-128.

Melvin, Don (2015): "EU asks U.N. to sanction military action against migrant boats in North Africa," at: CNN online, May 12, http://edition.cnn.com/2015/05/11/europe/eu-migrants-military-action/ (accessed September 29, 2015).

Messia, Hada/Wedemann, Ben/Schmith-Spark, Laura (2013): "Italy shipwreck: Scores dead after boat sinks off Lampedusa island," at: CNN online, October 3, http://edition.cnn.com/2013/10/03/world/europe/italy-migrants-sink/ (accessed September 29, 2015).

Meyer, Arne (2015): "Bundesregierung legt Opferzahlen vor: Der tödliche Weg nach Europa," at: tagesschau.de, August 25, http://www.tagesschau.de/inland/eu-aussengrenzen100.html (accessed October 1, 2015).

Meyers, Herman (1967): Nationality of Ships, Dordrecht: Springer. https://doi.org/10.1007/978-94-011-9510-2

Mghari, Mohamed (2005): "Maroc: dimension démographique des migrations," in: Philippe Fargues (ed.), Mediterranean Migration. 2005 Report, Florence: European University Institute, pp. 199-203.

Milà, Natalià Cantó. (2006): "Die Grenze als Relation. Spanische Grenzrealität und europäische Grenzpolitik," in: Monika Eigmüller/Georg Vobruba (eds.), Grenzsoziologie. Die politische Strukturierung des Raumes, Wiesbaden: VS Verlag für Sozialwissenschaften, pp. 185-197. https://doi.org/10.1007/978-3-531-90245-6_11

Miller, David L./Hashmi, Sohail H. (2001): "Introduction," in: idem (eds.), Boundaries and justice. Diverse ethical perspectives, Princeton: Princeton University Press, pp. 3-14.

Miltner, Barbara (2006): "Irregular maritime migration: Refugee protection issues in rescue and interception," in: Fordham International Law Journal 30, pp. 75-125.

Mittelstaedt, Juliane von/Popp, Maximilian (2014): "Aren't we human beings? One Year after the Lampedusa Refugee Tragedy," in: *Spiegel Online*, September 10, at: http://www.spiegel.de/international/europe/lampedusa-surviv ors-one-year-after-the-refugee-tragedy-a-994887.html (accessed June 27, 2015).

Monar, Jörg (2001): "The Dynamics of Justice and Home Affairs: Laboratories, Driving Factors and Costs," in: European Journal of Common Market Studies 39, pp. 747-764. https://doi.org/10.1111/1468-5965.00329

Monar, Jörg (2006): "The Project of a European Border Guard: Origins, Models and Prospects in the Context of the EU's Integrated External Border Management," in: Marina Caparini/Otwin Marenin (eds.), Borders and security governance: managing borders in a globalised word, Zürich: LIT, pp. 193-208.

Monroy, Matthias (2011): "Militarisierung des Mittelmeers [The Militarization of the Mediterranean]," in: *Telepolis*, April 8, at: http://www.heise.de/tp/ artikel/34/34515/1.html (accessed: October 19, 2019).

Moore, Gene M. (2000): "Newspaper Accounts of the 'Jeddah' Affair," in: The Conradian 25, pp. 104-139.

Moreno Fuentes, Francisco J. (2000): "Immigration Policies in Spain: Between External Constraints and Domestic Demand for Unskilled Labour," paper presented at the ECPR Workshop 'Beyond Fortress Europe? New Responses to Migration in Europe: Dual Nationality, Co-Development and the Effects of EU Enlargement,' Copenhagen, April 14-19, at: http://citeseerx.ist.psu.

edu/viewdoc/download?doi=10.1.1.531.9718&rep=rep1&type=pdf (accessed October 19, 2019).

Moreno-Lax, Violeta (2011): "Seeking Asylum in the Mediterranean: Against a Fragmentary Reading of EU Member States' Obligations Accruing at Sea," in: International Journal of Refugee Law 23, pp. 174-220. https://doi.org/10.1093/ijrl/eer005

Morgades-Gil, Sílvia (2015): "The Discretion of States in the Dublin III System for Determining Responsibility for Examining Applications for Asylum," in: International Journal of Refugee Law 27, pp. 433-456. https://doi.org/10.1093/ijrl/eev034

Mountz, Alison/Kempin, Ronja (2014): "The spatial logics of migration governance along the southern frontier of the European Union," in: Margaret Walton-Roberts/Jenna Hennebry (eds.), Territoriality and migration in the E.U. neighborhood. Spilling over the wall, Dordrecht: Springer, pp. 85-95. https://doi.org/10.1007/978-94-007-6745-4_6

Müller, Andreas (2013): "Territorial Borders as Institutions," in: European Societies 15, pp. 353-372. https://doi.org/10.1080/14616696.2012.717633

Mungianu, Roberta (2013): "Frontex: Towards a Common Policy on External Border Control," in: European Journal of Migration and Law 15, pp. 359-385. https://doi.org/10.1163/15718166-00002041

N.N. (1991): "Flüchtlinge: Gefährlicher Sommer," in: *Der Spiegel*, August 12, pp. 121-122.

N.N. (2000): "EU: Third-Country Migrants," in: Migration News 7, November, at: https://migration.ucdavis.edu/mn/more.php?id=2236 (accessed October 15, 2019).

N.N. (2013): "Italy calls for European help on refugees as scores drown in Lampedusa shipwreck," in: *The Telegraph*, October 3, at: http://www.telegraph.co.uk/news/worldnews/europe/italy/10353429/Italy-calls-for-European-help-on-refugees-as-scores-drown-in-Lampedusa-shipwreck.html (accessed September 29, 2015).

N.N. (2014): "Italy Takes Control of Migrant Ship on Collision Course," in: *Associated Press*, December 30, at: https://www.deseret.com/2014/12/30/20475118/italy-takes-control-of-migrant-ship-on-collision-course (accessed October 15, 2019).

N.N. (2015a): Two charts showing that 'deterring' migrant boats is failing," in: IRIN News, February 19, at: http://www.thenewhumanitarian.org/analysis/2015/02/19/two-charts-showing-deterring-migrant-boats-failing (accessed October 15, 2019).

N.N. (2015b): "Stop the boats. European Union ministers are turning their navies on the Mediterranean migrant traffickers," in: *The Economist*, May 19, at: http://www.economist.com/news/europe/21651693-european-union-ministers-are-turning-their-navies-mediterranean-migrant-traffickers-stop (accessed October 15, 2019).

Nagy, Boldizsár (2006): "The Frontier of the Sovereign," in: Anne F. Bayefsky/Joan Fitzpatrick/Arthur C. Helton (eds.), Human Rights and Refugees, Internally Displaced Persons, and Migrant Workers: Essays in memory of Joan Fitzpatrick and Arthur Helton, Leiden, Boston: Martinus Nijhoff Publishers, pp. 91-122. https://doi.org/10.1163/ej.9789004144835.i-0.35

Nassehi, Armin (1997): "Risikogesellschaft," in: Georg Kneer (ed.), Soziologische Gesellschaftsbegriffe. Konzepte moderner Zeitdiagnosen, München: Fink, pp. 252-279.

Neal, Andrew W. (2009): "Securitization and Risk at the EU Border: The Origins of FRONTEX," in: Journal of Common Market Studies 47, pp. 333-356. https://doi.org/10.1111/j.1468-5965.2009.00807.x

Nelson, Zed (2014): "Lampedusa boat tragedy. A survivor's story," in: *The Guardian*, March 22, at: https://www.theguardian.com/world/2014/mar/22/lampedusa-boat-tragedy-migrants-africa (accessed October 15, 2019).

Newman, David (2006a): "Borders and Bordering: Towards an Interdisciplinary Dialogue," in: European Journal of Social Theory 9, pp. 171-186. https://doi.org/10.1177/1368431006063331

Newman, David (2006b): "The lines that continue to separate us: borders in our 'borderless' world," in: Progress in Human Geography 30, pp. 143-161. https://doi.org/10.1191/0309132506ph599xx

Ohmae, Kenichi (1990): The Borderless World: Power and strategy in the interlinked economy, London: Collins.

Olsson, Gunnar (1991): Lines of Power/Limits of Language, Minneapolis: University of Minnesota Press.

Ong, Aihwa/Collier, Stephen J. (2005): "Global Assemblages, Anthropological Problems," in: *eid.* (eds.), Global assemblages. Technology, politics, and ethics as anthropological problems, Malden: Blackwell, pp. 3-21. https://doi.org/10.1002/9780470696569.ch1

Owens, Patricia (2009): "Reclaiming 'Bare Life'?: Against Agamben on Refugees," in: International Relations 23, pp. 567-582. https://doi.org/10.1177/0047117809350545

Paasi, Anssi (1996): Territories, Boundaries, and Consciousness: The changing geographies of the Finnish-Russian border, Chichester: J. Wiley & Sons.

Pagenstecher, Cord (2008a): "Das Boot ist voll. Schreckensvision des vereinten Deutschland," in: Gerhard Paul (ed.), Das Jahrhundert der Bilder. 1949 bis heute, Bonn: Bundeszentrale für Politische Bildung, pp. 606-613.

Pagenstecher, Cord (2008b): "'Das Boot ist voll' – Schreckensvisionen des vereinten Deutschlands," in: Gerhard Paul (ed.), Das Jahrhundert der Bilder. 1949 bis heute, Bonn: Bundeszentrale für Politische Bildung, pp. 606-613.

Painter, Joe (2010): "Rethinking Territory," in: Antipode 42, pp. 1090-1118. https://doi.org/10.1111/j.1467-8330.2010.00795.x

Papadopoulos, Dimitris/Stephenson, Niamh/Tsianos, Vassilis (eds.) (2008): Escape Routes: Control and subversion in the twenty-first century, London: Pluto Press.

Papastavridis, Efthymios (2009): "Interception of Human Beings on the High Sea," in: Syracuse Journal International Law and Commerce 36, pp. 146-227.

Papastavridis, Efthymios (2010): "'Fortress Europe' and FRONTEX: Within or Without International Law?," in: Nordic Journal of International Law 79, pp. 75-111. https://doi.org/10.1163/157181009X12581245929640

Papastavridis, Efthymios (2013): The Interception of Vessels on the High Seas: Contemporary challenges to the legal order of the oceans, Oxford: Hart Publishing.

Perkowski, Nina (2018): "Frontex and the convergence of humanitarianism, human rights and security," in: Security Dialogue 49, pp. 457-475. https://doi.org/10.1177/0967010618796670

Pickles, John (2004): A History of Spaces: Cartographic reason, mapping and the geo-coded world, London: Routledge.

Polovedo, Elisabetta/Cowell, Alan (2015): "Traffickers set freighter on a course for Italy and flee, leaving migrants aboard," in: The New York Times, January 2, at: http://www.nytimes.com/2015/01/03/world/europe/italy-migrants-rescue.html (accessed September 4, 2015).

Prescott, John R. V. (1987): Political frontiers and boundaries, London: Allen & Unwin.

Pries, Ludger (2008): Die Transnationalisierung der sozialen Welt. Sozialräume jenseits von Nationalgesellschaften, Frankfurt am Main: Suhrkamp.

Pugh, Michael (2000): "Europe's boat people: maritime cooperation in the Mediterranean," at: http://www.peacepalacelibrary.nl/ebooks/files/chai41e.pdf (accessed October 1, 2015).

Pugh, Michael (2004): "Drowning not Waving: Boat People and Humanitarianism at Sea," in: Journal of Refugee Studies 17, pp. 50-69. https://doi.org/10.1093/jrs/17.1.50

Pugliese, Joseph (2014): "Technologies of Extraterritorialisation Statist Visuality and Irregular Migrants and Refugees," in: Griffith Law Review 22, pp. 571-597. https://doi.org/10.1080/10383441.2013.10877013

Raffestin, Claude (1992): "Autour de la fonction sociale de la frontière," in: Espaces et sociétés, pp. 157-164.

Rajaram, Prem Kumar/Grundy-Warr, Carl (2004): "The Irregular Migrant as Homo Sacer:Migration and Detention in Australia,Malaysia, and Thailand," in: International Migration 42, pp. 33-64. https://doi.org/10.1111/j.0020-7985.2004.00273.x

Rah, Sicco (2009): Asylsuchende und Migranten auf See. Staatliche Rechte und Pflichten aus völkerrechtlicher Sicht, Berlin: Springer. https://doi.org/10.1007/978-3-540-92931-4

Ratfisch, Philipp/Scheel, Stephan (2010): "Migrationskontrolle durch Flüchtlingsschutz. Die Rolle des UNHCR im Kontext der Externalisierung des EU-Migrationsregimes," in: Sabine Hess/Bernd Kasparek (eds.), Grenzregime. Diskurse, Praktiken, Institutionen in Europa, Berlin: Assoziation A, pp. 89-110.

Rijpma, Jorrit/Vermeulen, Mathias (2015): "EUROSUR: saving lives or building borders?," in: European Security 24, pp. 454-472. https://doi.org/10.1080/09662839.2015.1028190

Robinson, Court (1998): Terms of Refuge: The Indochinese exodus & the international response, London: Zed Books.

Roe, Paul (2012): "Is securitization a 'negative' concept? Revisiting the normative debate over normal versus extraordinary politics," in: Security Dialogue 43, pp. 249-266. https://doi.org/10.1177/0967010612443723

Rosiere, Stéphane (2002): "L'Union Européenne, laboratoire d'une nouvelle hiérarchie des frontières," in: Mosella 27, pp. 47-52.

Ruggie, John G. (1993): "Territoriality and beyond: problematizing modernity in international relations," in: International Organization 47, p. 139. https://doi.org/10.1017/S0020818300004732

Rühle, Alex (2013): "Lampedusa nach dem Flüchtlingsdrama: Das Ende von Europa," in: *Süddeutsche Zeitung*, October 9, at: http://www.sueddeutsche.de/panorama/lampedusa-nach-dem-fluechtlingsdrama-am-ende-von-europa-1.1790273 (accessed October 1, 2015).

Rumford, Chris (2006): "Theorizing Borders," in: European Journal of Social Theory 9, pp. 155-169. https://doi.org/10.1177/1368431006063330

Rumford, Chris (2011): Cosmopolitan spaces. Europe, globalization, theory, London: Routledge.

Rumford, Chris/Geiger, Martin (2014): Cosmopolitan borders, New York: Palgrave Macmillan. https://doi.org/10.1057/9781137351401
Sahlins, Peter (1989): Boundaries: The making of France and Spain in the Pyrenees, Berkeley: University of California Press.
Salomon, Kim (1991): Refugees in the cold war. Toward a new international refugee regime in the early postwar era, Lund: Lund University Press.
Schindel, Estela (2017): "Migrants and Refugees on the Frontiers of Europe. The Legitimacy of Suffering, Bare Life, and Paradoxical Agency," in: Revista de Estudios Sociales, pp. 16-29. https://doi.org/10.7440/res59.2017.02
Schmitt, Carl (2003 [1950]): The *Nomos* of the Earth in the International Law of the *Jus Publicum Europaeum*, New York, Telos Press.
Schroer, Markus (2006): Räume, Orte, Grenzen. Auf dem Weg zu einer Soziologie des Raums, Frankfurt am Main: Suhrkamp.
Schubert, Inti (2008): Europol und der virtuelle Verdacht. Die Suspendierung des Rechts auf informationelle Selbstbestimmung, Frankfurt am Main: Lang.
Schulz-Schaeffer, Ingo (2008): "Technik in heterogener Assoziation. Vier Konzeptionen der gesellschaftlichen Wirksamkeit von Technik im Werk Latours," in: Georg Kneer/Markus Schroer/Erhard Schüttpelz (eds.), Bruno Latours Kollektive. Kontroversen zur Entgrenzung des Sozialen, Frankfurt am Main: Suhrkamp.
Schweitzer, Doris (2011): "Grenzziehungen und Raum in Manuel Castells's Theorien des Netzwerks und der Netzwerkgesellschaft," in: Christoph Kleinschmidt (ed.), Topographien der Grenze. Verortungen einer kulturellen, politischen und ästhetischen Kategorie, Würzburg: Königshausen u. Neumann, pp. 49-62.
Schwelien, Michael (2004): Das Boot ist voll. Europa zwischen Nächstenliebe und Selbstschutz, Hamburg: Marebuchverlag.
Schwengel, Hermann (1993): "Konkurrenz der Raumordnungen in Europa: Chancen und Risiken der regionalistischen Option," in: Heiner Meulemann/Agnes Elting-Camus (eds.), Lebensverhältnisse und soziale Konflikte im neuen Europa. 26. Deutscher Soziologentag Düsseldorf 1992. Berichte aus den Sektionen, Arbeitsgruppen und Ad hoc-Gruppen, Wiesbaden: Westdeutscher, pp. 322-325.
Scorzin, Pamela C. (2010): "Voice-Over Image," in: Christine Bischoff/Sylvia Kafehsy/Francesca Falk (eds.) (2010): Images of Illegalized Immigration: Towards a Critical Iconology of Politics, Bielefeld: transcript, pp. 101-110.
Scott, James W. (2011): "Borders, Border Studies and EU Enlargement," in: Doris Wastl-Walter (ed.), The Ashgate research companion to border studies, Farnham, UK: Ashgate, pp. 123-142.

Scott, James W./van Houtum, Henk (2009): "Reflections on EU territoriality and the 'bordering' of Europe," in: Political Geography 28, pp. 271-273. https://doi.org/10.1016/j.polgeo.2009.04.002

Şemşil, Sühal (2008): "Transformation of Migration Policies in Poland and Turkey in the EU Accession Process: Europeanized and /or Securitized?," in: CEU Political Science Journal 3, pp. 365-387.

Serres, Michel (2007): The Parasite, Minneapolis: University of Minnesota Press.

Siebold, Angela (2013): ZwischenGrenzen. Die Geschichte des Schengen-Raums aus deutschen, französischen und polnischen Perspektiven, Paderborn: Schöningh.

Siegfried, Detlef (2005): "Das Flugzeug," in: Alexa Geisthövel/Habbo Knoch (eds.), Orte der Moderne. Erfahrungswelten des 19. und 20. Jahrhunderts, Frankfurt am Main: Campus, pp. 47-56.

Simmel, Georg/Frisby, David/Featherstone, Mike (1997 [1908]): Simmel on Culture: Selected writings (Theory, culture & society), London: Sage Publications.

Simon, Julien (2006): "Irregular Transit Migration in the Mediterranean: Facts, Figures and Insights," in: Nyberg Sørensen, Ninna (ed.) (2006): Mediterranean transit migration, Copenhagen: Danish Institute for International Studies, pp. 25-66.

Spalinger, Andrea (2015): "Skrupellose neue Taktik: Vom 'Geisterschiff' gerettet," in: *Neue Züricher Zeitung*, January 2, at: http://www.nzz.ch/international/europa/italiens-kuestenwache-rettet-hunderte-von-migranten-auf-einem-geisterschiff-1.18453813 (accessed February 2, 2017).

Spijkerboer, Thomas (2007): "The Human Costs of Border Control," in: European Journal of Migration and Law 9, pp. 127-139. https://doi.org/10.1163/138836407X179337

Stabenow, Michael (1995): "Am Sonntag fallen die Grenzkontrollen zwischen sieben europäischen Ländern," in: *Frankfurter Allgemeine Zeitung*, March 25, p. 1.

Star, Susan L./Griesemer, James R. (1989): "Institutional Ecology, 'Translations' and Boundary Objects. Amateurs and Professionals in Berkeley's Museum of Vertebrate Zoology, 1907-39," in: Social Studies of Science 19, pp. 387-420. https://doi.org/10.1177/030631289019003001

Stobbe, Erhard (D. j.) (1989): Das Schengener Übereinkommen. - Inhalt, Wirksamkeit, Bedeutung - (Vorträge, Reden und Berichte aus dem Europa-Institut), Saarbrücken.

Tazzioli, Martina (2018): "Spy, track and archive: The temporality of visibility in Eurosur and Jora," in: Security Dialogue 49, pp. 272-288. https://doi.org/10.1177/0967010618769812

Tazzioli, Martina/Walters, William (2016): "The Sight of Migration. Governmentality, Visibility and Europe's Contested Borders," in: Global Society 30, pp. 445-464. https://doi.org/10.1080/13600826.2016.1173018

Teasdale, Anthony (2012): Adonnino Committee. The Penguin Companion to European Union, at: http://penguincompaniontoeu.com/additional_entries/adonnino-committee/ (accessed September 26, 2016).

Thompson, Larry C. (2010): Refugee Workers in the Indochina Exodus, 1975-1982, Jefferson: McFarland & Co.

Tondini, Matteo (2012): "The legality of intercepting boat people under search and rescue and border control operations with reference to recent Italian interventions in the Mediterranean Sea and the ECtHR decision in the Hirsi case," in: The Journal of International Maritime Law 18, pp. 59-74.

Töpfer, Eric (2008): "Mobile Daten: Auf dem Weg zum europäischen Informationsverbund," in: CILIP - Bürgerrechte & Polizei 91, pp. 19-32.

Torpey, John (1998): "Coming and Going: On the State Monopolization of the Legitimate 'Means of Movement,'" in: Sociological Theory 16, pp. 239-259. https://doi.org/10.1111/0735-2751.00055

Torpey, John (2000): The invention of the Passport: Surveillance, citizenship, and the state, Cambridge: Cambridge University Press. https://doi.org/10.1017/CBO9780511520990

Trevisanut, Seline (2010): "Search and Rescue Operations in the Mediterranean: Factor of Cooperation or Conflict?," in: The International Journal of Marine and Coastal Law 25, pp. 523-542. https://doi.org/10.1163/157180810X526754

Tsamenyi, B. M. (1983): "The "Boat People": Are They Refugees?," in: Human Rights Quarterly 5, pp. 348-373. https://doi.org/10.2307/762028

Tsianos, Vassilis (2009): "Notes on the high-tech industry of European Border Control: migration control and the arms industry in EU security research policy," in: Statewatch Bulletin 19.

Turner, Simon/Munive Rincon, Jairo/Nyberg Sørensen, Ninna (2006): "European Attitudes and Policies towards the Migration/Development Issue," in: Nyberg Sørensen, Ninna (ed.) (2006): Mediterranean transit migration, Copenhagen: Danish Institute for International Studies, pp. 67-100.

van Houtum, Henk (2005): "The Geopolitics of Borders and Boundaries," in: Geopolitics 10, pp. 672-679. https://doi.org/10.1080/14650040500318522

van Houtum, Henk (2010): "Human blacklisting: the global apartheid of the EU's external border regime," in: Environment and Planning D: Society and Space 28, pp. 957-976. https://doi.org/10.1068/d1909

van Houtum, Henk/van Naerssen, Ton (2002): "Bordering, Ordering and Othering," in: Tijdschrift voor Economische en Sociale Geographie 93, pp. 125-136. https://doi.org/10.1111/1467-9663.00189

Vasilache, Andreas (2007): Der Staat und seine Grenzen. Zur Logik politischer Ordnung, Frankfurt am Main: Campus.

Vaughan-Williams, Nick (2009): Border Politics. The limits of Sovereign Power, Edinburgh: Edinburgh University Press. https://doi.org/10.3366/edinburgh/9780748637324.001.0001

Vo, Nghia M. (2006): The Vietnamese Boat People, 1954 and 1975-1992, Jefferson: McFarland & Company.

Vobruba, Georg (2008): "Die Entwicklung der Europasoziologie aus der Differenz national/europäisch," in: BJS - Berliner Journal für Soziologie 18, pp. 32-51. https://doi.org/10.1007/s11609-008-0003-x

Vobruba, Georg (2010): "Die postnationale Grenzkonstellation," in: Zeitschrift für Politik 57, pp. 434-452. https://doi.org/10.5771/0044-3360-2010-4-434

Vobruba, Georg (2012): Der postnationale Raum. Transformation von Souveränität und Grenzen in Europa, Weinheim: Juventa.

Voermans, Wim (2009): "Is the European Legislator after Lisbon a *real* Legislator?," in: Legislação Cadernos de Ciência de Legislação, pp. 391-413.

Wain, Barry (1981): The Refused: The agony of the Indochina refugees, New York: Simon and Schuster.

Waitz, Thomas (2014): Bilder des Verkehrs.Repräsentationspolitiken der Gegenwart, Bielefeld: transcript. https://doi.org/10.14361/transcript.9783839425992

Walters, William (2002): "Mapping Schengenland: denaturalizing the border," in: Environment and Planning D: Society and Space 20, pp. 561-580. https://doi.org/10.1068/d274t

Walters, William (2004): "The Frontiers of the European Union: A Geo-strategic Perspective," in: Geopolitics 9, pp. 674-698. https://doi.org/10.1080/14650040490478738

Walters, William (2006): "Rethinking Borders Beyond the State," in: Comparative European Politics 4, pp. 141-159. https://doi.org/10.1057/palgrave.cep.6110076

Walters, William (2011): "Where are the Missing Vehicles: Critical Reflections on Viapolitics," lecture during the Summer School 'Border Crossing Selves,' at the Research Institute of Comparative History and Culture Hanyang University Seoul, June 25-29. https://doi.org/10.1177/1368431014554859

Walters, William (2014): "Migration, vehicles, and politics: three theses on viapolitics," in: European Journal of Social Theory 18, pp. 1-20.

Walters, William (2015): "On the road with Michel Foucault: Migration, Deportation, and Viapolitics," in: Sophie Fuggle (ed.), Foucault and the history of our present, New York: Palgrave Macmillan, pp. 94-110. https://doi.org/10.1057/9781137385925_7

Weber, Max (1972): Wirtschaft und Gesellschaft. Grundriß der verstehenden Soziologie, Tübingen: Mohr.

Weizman, Eyal. 2012. Hollow Land: The Architecture of Israel's Occupation, London; New York: Verso.

Whitley, L. (2017): "The disappearance of race: a critique of the use of Agamben in border and migration scholarship," in: borderlands 16, pp. 1-23.

Wimmer, Andreas/Glick Schiller, Nina (2002): "Methodological nationalism and beyond: nation-state building, migration and the social sciences," in: Global Networks 2, pp. 301-334. https://doi.org/10.1111/1471-0374.00043

Wouters, K./Den Heijer, M. (2010): "The Marine I Case: a Comment," in: International Journal of Refugee Law 22, pp. 1-19. https://doi.org/10.1093/ijrl/eep031

Yardly, Jim/Povoledo, Elisabetta (2013): "Migrants Die as Burning Boat Capsizes Off Italy," in: *The New York Times*, October 3, at: http://www.nytimes.com/2013/10/04/world/europe/scores-die-in-shipwreck-off-sicily.html (accessed June 4, 2015).

Zaiotti, Ruben (2011): Cultures of Border Control: Schengen and the evolution of European frontiers, Chicago: University of Chicago Press. https://doi.org/10.7208/chicago/9780226977881.001.0001

ZDF (2014) "Europa's Flüchtlingsdrama," in: Heute Journal, April 14.

Zielonka, Jan (2006): Europe as Empire: The nature of the enlarged European Union, Oxford: Oxford University Press.

Zielonka, Jan (2008): "Europe as a global actor: empire by example?," in: International Affairs 84, pp. 471-484. https://doi.org/10.1111/j.1468-2346.2008.00718.x

Zielonka, Jan (2013a): "Europe's new civilizing missions: the EU's normative power discourse," in: Journal of Political Ideologies 18, pp. 35-55. https://doi.org/10.1080/13569317.2013.750172

Zielonka, Jan (2013b): "The International System in Europe: Westphalian Anarchy or Medieval Chaos?," in: Journal of European Integration 35, pp. 1-18. https://doi.org/10.1080/07036337.2011.652626

Social and Cultural Studies

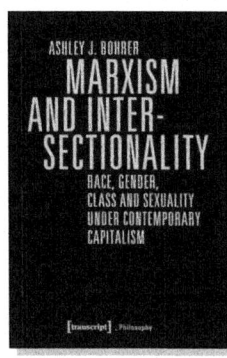

Ashley J. Bohrer
Marxism and Intersectionality
Race, Gender, Class and Sexuality
under Contemporary Capitalism

2019, 280 p., pb.
29,99 € (DE), 978-3-8376-4160-8
E-Book: 26,99 € (DE), ISBN 978-3-8394-4160-2

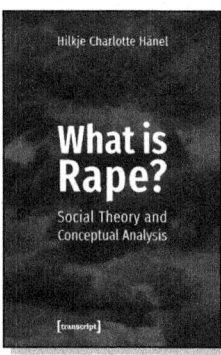

Hilkje Charlotte Hänel
What is Rape?
Social Theory and Conceptual Analysis

2018, 282 p., hardcover
99,99 € (DE), 978-3-8376-4434-0
E-Book: 99,99 € (DE), ISBN 978-3-8394-4434-4

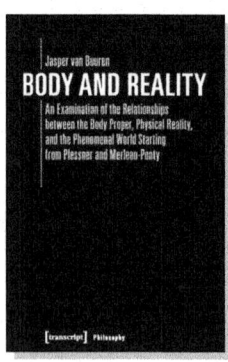

Jasper van Buuren
Body and Reality
An Examination of the Relationships
between the Body Proper, Physical Reality,
and the Phenomenal World Starting from Plessner
and Merleau-Ponty

2018, 312 p., pb., ill.
39,99 € (DE), 978-3-8376-4163-9
E-Book: 39,99 € (DE), ISBN 978-3-8394-4163-3

**All print, e-book and open access versions of the titles in our list
are available in our online shop www.transcript-verlag.de/en!**

Social and Cultural Studies

Sabine Klotz, Heiner Bielefeldt,
Martina Schmidhuber, Andreas Frewer (eds.)
Healthcare as a Human Rights Issue
Normative Profile, Conflicts and Implementation

2017, 426 p., pb., ill.
39,99 € (DE), 978-3-8376-4054-0
E-Book: available as free open access publication
E-Book: ISBN 978-3-8394-4054-4

Michael Bray
Powers of the Mind
Mental and Manual Labor
in the Contemporary Political Crisis

2019, 208 p., hardcover
99,99 € (DE), 978-3-8376-4147-9
E-Book: 99,99 € (DE), ISBN 978-3-8394-4147-3

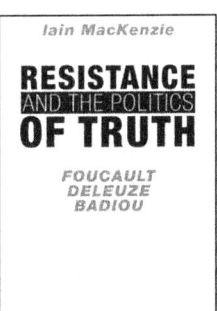

Iain MacKenzie
Resistance and the Politics of Truth
Foucault, Deleuze, Badiou

2018, 148 p., pb.
29,99 € (DE), 978-3-8376-3907-0
E-Book: 26,99 € (DE), ISBN 978-3-8394-3907-4
EPUB: 26,99 € (DE), ISBN 978-3-7328-3907-0

**All print, e-book and open access versions of the titles in our list
are available in our online shop www.transcript-verlag.de/en!**